Oxford Historical Society
NEW SERIES, VOL. XXX

CANTERBURY COLLEGE OXFORD

By
W. A. PANTIN
*Late Fellow of Oriel College
and Keeper of the University Archives*

Volume IV

OXFORD
At the CLARENDON PRESS *for the*
OXFORD HISTORICAL SOCIETY
MCMLXXXV (*for* MCMLXXXIV–MCMLXXXV)

The whole cost of publication of this volume has been borne by the Pantin Trust. The Oxford Historical Society records its gratitude for the generosity of the Trust, founded by its former editor.

Printed in Great Britain
at the University Press, Oxford
by David Stanford
Printer to the University

CONTENTS

Preface		v
Abbreviations		xi
Chapter 1	Prehistory	1
2	History	9
3	The Monk-Fellows	51
4	*Pueri Collegii*, Servants, Sojourners, Benefactors	85
5	The Economy, Internal and External	105
6	The Site and the Buildings	131
7	The Library	155
8	Extracts from Accounts	167
9	Documents Concerning Monastic Students Before the Foundation of Canterbury College	207
10	Biographical Data	213
11	List of Wardens	227
Index of Names		231
Index of Subjects		253
Index of Books and Authors		269

PREFACE

It may be wondered why a work that appeared between 1947 and 1950 should have had to wait so long for completion. There were doubtless several reasons while the author was still alive, such as that he never found time to finish the last volume to his own satisfaction and that other men's writings had prior claims to publication; but if the manuscript remained undetected for so long after his death, the cause was incontestably the colossal muddle which he never failed to create in his surroundings.

Mortimer Wheeler declared in 1954 that the sight of the 'famous Pantin study' had filled a gap in his experience and that it set the standard for all time. Joyce Grenfell found it 'frightening' and the BBC omitted to show it on television— for technical reasons according to its owner, but actually (so it was thought) because the confusion was so excessive that it would have looked inauthentic. It was more noticeable still in later years, after the move to smaller premises. John Betjeman, suddenly confronted with it one day at tea-time, was highly amused, especially as the first distinct object that met his eyes proved to be J. W. Clark's *On The Care of Books*. He could do no more than say: 'Oh Billy!'

It was not just that there was so much of everything, but that the storage was so disorderly, the rows of cardboard boxes notwithstanding. One of these boxes, taken pretty much at random, contained a number of folders, the topmost of which was marked 'Old Houses — General'. Its actual contents were: a sheet of notes, apparently relating to old houses; eleven sheets of blank paper, crumpled and of various sizes; a lecture list; agenda for a meeting of the Bodleian curators; a circular about motoring and camping in Germany; one of the bulletins of the British Archaeological Association; a circular from the Council for British Archaeology; a cyclostyled analysis (by himself) of Stubb's *Charters*; an order-form for 'Hoboken, Haydn Catalogue'; a business-reply card for information about the National Trust; a salary-advice sheet; two used envelopes; two letters from the Oxfordshire County Archivist; a copy of a letter to W. H. Godfrey about petrol to be used in visiting old houses; some drawings labelled 'Fox — Lower Petergate'; a stamped addressed envelope meant for the County Archivist; an application for petrol; a request from the Warden of St Anthony's for a reference; the candidate's own letter; a final demand for the payment of income tax; a letter from Christopher Hohler; a letter from M. N. Todd; a request from the Pelican Society at Corpus for a lecture; an advertisement for a French book; a query about the stone used in the building of the examination schools; some pencil jottings; an invitation to a sherry party for the new proctors. At this point another folder (in tatters) had been inserted and this *was* entirely devoted to old houses.

As the principle illustrated here was applied in innumerable instances, there will be no difficulty in seeing how it affected the fate of the present volume. The *disiecta membra* of the manuscript, mingled with blank papers, successive drafts and early transcripts and notes, appeared in the main to be raw material for essays dating from the author's undergraduate and early graduate days. At most, it seemed when the papers were first sorted, there might be material for an article. Recent examination, however, revealed the true nature of the case. From one point of view, the delay is only an extension of the genuine Pantinian tradition: for it could take him seven weeks (with prodding) to decide about publishing work offered; and once after acceptance an editor was kept waiting for ten years—which left ample time for a nervous breakdown with the direst of consequences.

The appearance of this volume crowns a lifelong association with Canterbury and an interest in Canterbury College which went back to the twenties. Even in childhood there were visits to the cathedral and precocious reading of books like Dean Stanley's *Historical Memorials*, M. R. James's *Ancient Libraries* and the *Inventories* of Wickham Legg and St John Hope, improbable though it may seem. The vocation was an early one and its fruits were revealed in conducted tours given with perfect assurance at the age of twelve or so.

During school-days, Westminster may have replaced Canterbury as the object of predilection, but from 1920 residence in Canterbury Quad at Christ Church (in typically cluttered surroundings even then — five tables, for instance, jamming the sitting-room and a sofa and bookshelves reducing the size of the bedroom) brought back the old interest. It was at this time, too, that a fellow Westminster man, the future Dom Gregory Dix of Nashdom, bestowed on him the name of the Canterbury Lamb.

From 1920 also dates what for years was to be an annual practice: a pilgrimage to Canterbury on foot with a friend, starting from his home at Blackheath or somewhere nearby. These affairs were a characteristic mixture of religion, antiquarianism and pleasure, as his description of the event in 1921 makes clear. 'We started from sevenoaks on the Thursday,' he said, 'and went through Otford Kemt'n and wrotham and spent the night at W. Malling next day

PREFACE

through Aylesford where I rubbed a brass so that we discover'd after lunch that we had only walked about ⅛th of the way we ought to do that day, in the morning — we pushed on — and arrived at nine that night at Charing where there is a charming inn and the ruins of an Archiepiscopal palace. Next day we went on through Godmersham and a place rejoicing in the delightful name of Boughton Aluph To chilham. Then finally at about half-past eight on Saturday night we just sighted the Angel Tower of the Cathedral, from a wooded hill — and burst into a "Te Deum". I spent about ten days at Canterbury — rubbing brasses hard for miles round.'

The 1922 pilgrimage, made with the man who was to become Dom William Price of Ampleforth, was equally typical. 'It was quite enjoyable Tho' it rained a lot — and my oilskin Coat came literally to pieces, because I had to ride in it about three miles on a hired bicycle, to rescue my pretious walking stick, "Thomas" (which has a vegetable relick of St. Thomas of Canterbury — of a fig tree supposed to have been planted by him) — which walking stick I had left at a village a mile or so back in an inn with a drunken innkeeper, where we had tea — all this ride was in the Rain! O quanta pietas! Quantus O labor! (note the elegant inversion as used by writers of the "Latten" Age!).'

In 1921 a major influence came into play through Anthony Milton, curate of the Catholic church at Canterbury. A former novice of Downside, he had retained a great love of Benedictinism, was fascinated by local history and greatly admired Edmund Bishop, an enthusiast (among other things) for the Canterbury saints. It was owing to him that the undergraduate turned his attention to Canterbury College, on the site of which he was living, and initiated himself into research by consulting the Corpus Christi MS. 256 and spending a few days at Canterbury looking at inventories and accounts in the cathedral library. After schools in 1923, formal research into Canterbury College began under the direction of H. E. Salter, the chief authority on the history of Oxford. The supervision was confined, apparently, to occasional tea-parties and conversations in the Selden end of the Bodleian (where, it was held by a blandly impudent fiction, nobody would be disturbed), so that its negative qualities perhaps came through as clearly as the positive ones. Salter's solid erudition was accompanied by the unreasoned assumption that his documents were largely self-explanatory, by a certain timidity in amending texts and by pursuit of matter to the detriment of form. These characteristics, doubtless present already in the pupil, must have been strengthened by the example of the master.

They were, however, offset by two blissful terms in the cathedral library at Canterbury and in September 1924 there was a further visit for the seventh centenary of the arrival of the Franciscans. The titular prior of Canterbury, Dom Wilfrid Corney of Downside, being also present, Father Milton took the opportunity of showing him round and afterwards a document was drawn up in mock-medieval Latin, purporting to record his installation in the chapterhouse. The priest was described as his chaplain and Willelmus A. Pantin was his *seneschallus*. It was the sort of rather childishly exuberant play that delighted them both — like the 'seneschal's' pretence some years later, when waiting with another devotee of Canterbury, R.A.L. Smith, for a train to pass at a level crossing, of intoning the verse, *Attolite portas, principes, vestras* and inclining profoundly at the *Gloria Patri*.

However, out of all this effervescence there came in 1923 papers on Canterbury College for the Oxford University and Canterbury Archaeological Societies and in 1924 another for the *Ampleforth Journal*. All these outlined the points developed by the present four volumes, as did also a paper for the Friends of Canterbury Cathedral in 1942.

Election to the newly-founded Bryce Scholarship in 1924 meant the end of work on Canterbury College for the time being but the new subject, the medieval chapters of the English Benedictines, was cognate with the old, for much of the capitular legislation was concerned with providing for monks at the universities, albeit not at the same house. Interest never flagged, much material had been transcribed and some, at any rate, of the text seems to have been written before the publication of the first volume of the *Chapters* in 1931. It received repeated revision until the author's death.

Enthusiasm for Canterbury was not limited to the present work. Articles appeared on the see in the *Dictionnaire d'Histoire et de géographie ecclésiastiques*, on the saints in *For Hilaire Belloc* and on John Mason, monk of St Augustine's, in the Bertie Wilkinson *Festschrift*. There was a youthful attempt, marred by ignorance of canon law, to restore the cultus of the local saints and a good deal of activity during the war and later over the damage done by enemy action and the even greater damage likely to be done by the rebuilding. There were visits to the library, where much-appreciated services were rendered by W. P. Blore and his assistant, William Urry. Death itself respected the association, for the end came a few yards away from Canterbury Quad on the feast of St Justus, companion and successor of St Augustine.

Though never definitively revised and therefore rather rough in some respects, the book is in the main what the author intended it to be. Certain passages, such as the section on Vine Hall in chapter 6, were marked for rewriting; but judging from the pieces that actually received that treatment, the alterations would have affected the form only and not the substance. Chapter 6 suffers from the lack of the plan that was meant to accompany it and, if the author had lived, would have included a detailed analysis of the accommodation assigned to the sojourners, while the section on the chapel might have had something to say about the vestments. It seems that the entire chapter would have been amplified and clarified, though it is doubtful if any radical improvement could have been made, for the topography of this part of Oxford is far from certain. The existing presentation must therefore remain somewhat conjectural — as was often the case, for that matter, with Dr Pantin's attempts at this sort of reconstruction, which at times were so hypothetical as to border on caricature. Perhaps it is as well that no more ambitious speculations have survived.

Chapter 10, on the other hand, was written with unnecessary fulness, after the plan followed in the biographical section in volume iii of the *Chapters of the English Black Monks*. As the particulars given would to a large extent have duplicated the index and had in any case been mostly superseded by Emden's *Biographical Register*, they have been reduced to such scraps of information as are not contained in that work, except that where Emden confuses two persons, the full details are given for greater ease of identification. 'I do implore you, Billy', said Dr Emden once when the author was proudly explaining his intentions, 'not to put in anything that's in BRUO.' A crestfallen silence followed. Nevertheless, the iconoclast was right.

The projected description of sources was never finalised, but as the sources are repeatedly stated in the course of the work, that need cause no great inconvenience. The summary list in iii. xi will help to bring the details together.

It has not been practicable to indicate editorial interventions, for in such an unfinished work they necessarily occur at every turn. Judgement has had to be used in deciding between alternative drafts, arranging and heading the various sections, and occasionally making slight verbal changes in a hastily-written text. Endless trouble has been caused by the punctuation, a weak point with the author throughout his life. The quotations above give some idea of what it was like in his youth. In 1939 the priest who had received him into the Church ventured to say to him: 'I think a full stop and a fresh sentence better than so many semi-colons. These latter are said to give a "weak" appearance to a sentence! But I may "speak as one less wise".' Professor Powicke, who perhaps had fewer doubts about his own wisdom, roundly declared that the punctuation was deplorable.

'Can't you strike out a lot of the semicolons and put in full stops?' he asked, but to little effect. Even as late as 1972 another distinguished (though gentler) friend was driven to remark that the punctuation was a bit erratic, 'nicely so at times in giving a vivid impromptu impression, but at times puzzling'. In the original version of the present text the disconcerting stop was the colon, which was accompanied by showers of commas, occurring like expletives at intervals of every few words. If the effort to normalise all this has not always succeeded, the reader will understand why. Similarly, in a work which has been on the stocks as long as this one, inconsistencies are likely to appear. Such difficulties cannot always be resolved with absolute certitude: here and there a contradiction may appear.

Since the text was written, many of the manuscripts referred to in the notes have appeared in print. The appropriate references have accordingly been given and more recent works have sometimes been added to those cited, but no systematic attempt has been made to bring the whole bibliography up to date. The books mentioned are still serviceable.

W.T.M.

ABBREVIATIONS

Arch. Cant.	*Archaeologia Cantiana*
BRUO	A.B. Emden, *A Biographical Register of the University of Oxford to A.D. 1500*, 1957–9.
BRUO 2	A.B. Emden, *A Biographical Register of the University of Oxford A.D. 1501 to 1540*, 1974.
Cart. St. Frid.	*The Cartulary of the Monastery of St Frideswide at Oxford* ed. S.R. Wigram, 1894, 1896.
CCR	*Calendar of Close Rolls*, 1914–.
Chapters	*Documents illustrating the activities of the General and Provincial Chapters of the English Black Monks, 1215–1540*, ed. W.A. Pantin, 1931–7.
Christ Church Letters	*Christ Church Letters*, ed. J.B. Sheppard, Camden Society 1877.
Collectanea III	*Collectanea*, third series, ed. M. Burrows, Oxford Historical Society 1896.
CPR	*Calendar of Papal Registers*, 1894–.
DNB	*Dictionary of National Biography*.
Dugdale, *Monasticon*	W. Dugdale, *Monasticon Anglicanum*, ed. J. Caley etc. 1817–30.
EHR	*English Historical Review*.
James	M.R. James, *The Ancient Libraries of Canterbury and Dover*, 1903.
Lit. Cant.	*Literae Cantuarienses*, ed. J.B. Sheppard, Rolls Series 85, 1887–9.
Mallet	C.E. Mallet, *A History of the University of Oxford*, 1924–7.
Mun. Acad.	*Munimenta Academica*, ed. H. Anstey, Rolls Series, 1868.
Pearce	E.H. Pearce, *The Monks of Westminster*, 1916.
Poole Essays	*Essays in History presented to R.L. Poole*, ed. H.W.C. Davis, 1927.
SA	*Statuta Antiqua Universitatis Oxoniensis*, ed. S. Gibson, 1931.
Salter, *Survey*	H.E. Salter, *Survey of Oxford*, 1960, 1969.
Searle	*Christ Church, Canterbury: Chronicle of John Stone*, ed. W.G. Searle, Cambridge Antiquarian Society octavo series 34, 1902.
Tanner	T. Tanner, *Bibliotheca Britanno-Hibernica*, 1748.
TRHS	*Transactions of the Royal Historical Society*.
VCH	*Victoria County Histories*.
Wharton	H. Wharton, *Anglia Sacra*, 1691.
Wilkins, *Concilia*	D. Wilkins, *Concilia Magnae Britanniae et Hiberniae*, 1737.

I
PREHISTORY

CANTERBURY College Oxford was a small community of student monks from the cathedral priory of Christ Church Canterbury. It received its formal foundation from Archbishop Islip between the years 1361 and 1363 and came to an end with the dissolution of its parent monastery in 1540. Its history, to be rightly understood, must in the first place be considered in relation to the general history of the black monks in Oxford.

Unlike the mendicants, the English black monks had no connexion with the early development of the universities, but by the middle or later part of the thirteenth century they became conscious of the need of getting in touch with the universities and scholastic theology if they were to keep up their past traditions of learning, *ut nostra religione refloreat studium*; and this was to be done partly by the introduction of theological lectures into the monasteries, partly by sending monks to study at the university.[1] The new policy or study movement was especially the work of the general chapters of the black monks. It was put forward first, apparently, about 1247 and more definitely and completely in the chapter of 1277. By the end of the thirteenth century, after some difficulties, Gloucester College had been established as the *locus communis* or joint house of studies of the black monks in Oxford, where each monastery could have its own set of rooms for its students; and in 1298 the first black monk incepted in theology. When Pope Benedict XII in 1336 issued his reforming Constitutions for the black monks, the sending of monk-students, one out of every twenty in the monastery, to the university became a legal obligation. Henceforward a *prior studentium* was in charge of the black monks in Oxford, who were as far as possible not to live dispersed, but in groups of not less than ten; and the ideal clearly was that all monk-students should be sent to Gloucester College, to be immediately under the *prior studentium* and the monastic regent doctor in theology. In fact, however, there were always exceptions. The monks of Durham cathedral priory had their own college,

---

When citations are given without a title, the reference is to the present work.

[1] For the study movement and Gloucester College, see TRHS (1927) 210 ff.; *Chapters* i. 27 f., 60 ff. and passim (cf. Index s. v. 'Oxford' and 'University'; *Snappe's Formulary*, ed. H.E. Salter (1924) 337 ff.; *V.C.H. Oxford* ii 70.

Durham College, which was as old as Gloucester College itself and was in some ways analogous to Canterbury College;[1] and even as late as the fifteenth century there were monks living in Burnell's Inn.[2]

What part would the monks of Christ Church Canterbury play in this movement? Would they throw in their lot with Gloucester College, or would they set up an independent college like Durham? To answer this question, we must examine first the relations between Christ Church and the general and provincial chapters of the black monks (who were organising the study movement and Gloucester College) and secondly the actual steps taken by Christ Church to promote study.

As regards the relations with the general chapter Christ Church, standing on its metropolitan dignity, as a rule refused to submit to the general chapter and is not known to have attended any of its meetings, except once under great external pressure. It is easy to see that the prior of Canterbury would object to yielding precedence to the smallest of abbots, like Athelney or Walden. We do not know when the open controversy began. In 1329 Christ Church registered a summons to the general chapter, but without indicating whether it was obeyed or not.[3] Two years later some of the monks were quoting a past statute of the general chapter on a liturgical problem, but it was not accepted as final, though the prior and one of the Oxford students supported it.[4] At that time the general chapter was in a weak condition, but when it was given new life and powers by the Constitutions of Benedict XII it openly declared war on Christ Church as a rebel and for that end planned to send proctors to Rome in 1340 and 1343.[5] This phase of the quarrel, as we shall see, coincides roughly with the period of the hired hall by St Peter's in the East (1331–42). There may have followed a lull, but from 1360 the quarrel broke out with greater violence, quite literally, for the Canterbury monks beat and imprisoned the messenger sent to summon them to the chapter. It was (most conveniently) just at this time that the monks found in Islip's foundation a foothold in Oxford which would make them independent of Gloucester College: for it would be extremely awkward to make use of that college while quarrelling violently with the general

---

[1] *Collectanea III* (1896) 1 ff. It was, however, more natural for Durham to keep aloof, since before 1336 it belonged to the northern province, while Gloucester College was then confined to the southern province.

[2] *Chapters* iii. 162 (c. 1411–14); H.E. Salter, *Registrum Cancellarii* i (1932) 267 ff.

[3] Canterbury Register I, fo. 429ᵛ. Cf. also a letter concerning a subsidy for Gloucester College, mentioned as among the muniments: *Chapters* i. 131 n.

[4] *Lit. Cant.* i. 370; cf. *Chapters* i. 71 (statute of 1277).

[5] *Lit. Cant.* ii. 224; *Chapters* ii. 23.

chapter which controlled it. Then the expulsion of the monks and the secularisation of Canterbury College, from December 1365, was followed by another defeat for the monks in September 1366, when they were forced by Edward the Black Prince, their powerful friend, to submit to the general chapter.[1] It would then be feasible for them to occupy rooms in Gloucester College, though there is no precise evidence on this point. By 1371 the monks were restored to Canterbury College; in 1375 and 1378 they were again defying the general chapter, with the support of the archbishop;[2] and finally in 1379 they obtained from the pope exemption from the jurisdiction of the chapter.[3] In this way it seems that the movements of the Christ Church monks at Oxford in some way correspond to their attitude to the general chapter and that their separate college was a symbol of exemption claimed and won. It is important to bear in mind this background of struggle with the chapter in considering the history that follows.

As regards practical steps to promote study: in the matter of providing claustral lectures, Christ Church was clearly active and probably one of the pioneers. Between 1275 and 1314, Franciscans were brought into the monastery to lecture in theology and were only dispensed with when the monks were considered capable of continuing the lectures themselves. As regards the other side of the programme, the sending of monk-students to the university, the policy of Christ Church seems less steady and continuous, or at any rate less clearly traceable, than one might have expected. There seem to have been, in effect, a series of changes and experiments down to the foundation of Canterbury College in 1363. In the first place, the great Prior Henry of Eastry seems to have preferred sending monk-students to Paris instead of to Oxford, for we find some Christ Church monk-students at Paris in 1288, 1304–6 and perhaps 1307–9: the evidence is surprisingly scanty for such a long and active priorate. It was about this time that Worcester cathedral priory was sending one of its monk-students to Paris[4] and Henry of Eastry is known to have maintained or assisted secular scholars at Paris, Orleans and Bologna as well as Oxford.[5]

We cannot be certain when the monk-students from Christ Church

[1] TRHS (1927) 223; *Chapters* ii. 4 n., 56–60.
[2] *Chapters* iii. 73, 78.
[3] Wilkins, *Concilia* iii. 126; cf. *Lit. Cant.* ii. 511 (c. 1374).
[4] *Worcester Liber Albus*, ed. J.M. Wilson (1919), nos. 397–400, 542, 659; A.G. Little and F. Pelster, *Oxford Theology and Theologians* (1934) 244 (John of St Germans).
[5] *Arch. Cant.* xxxix. 10 ff.

first came to Oxford: there is no clear evidence of it until 1331. When they came, they sometimes apparently made use of Gloucester College and sometimes used a hired hall of their own. Thus on the one hand the monks of St Augustine's granted them the temporary use of their chamber in Gloucester College at some period presumably before or after the period of the hired hall (1331–42); and towards the end of the experimental period (perhaps c. 1355) Christ Church acquired a chamber of its own in Gloucester College, which it sold to Westminster in 1371, when its possession of Canterbury College had become assured.[1] These sojourns in Gloucester College were probably rather short and uneasy, in view of the relations with the general chapter, as has been pointed out.

On the other hand, with regard to the period when the monks occupied a hall of their own, from 1331 to 1342, there is a good deal of evidence in a series of interesting letters and entries in the monastic accounts, which admirably supplement each other.

In September 1331, a certain William de Mondham (not a monk) hired a hall near the church of St Peter in the East for the three students who were coming up.[2] It was the hall where the Archbishop of Canterbury used to lodge and so was probably of some size. The rent was six marks, a high one,[3] and it contained a hall, *camerae* and a *deportum*—apparently a common room.[4] It may perhaps be identified with the hall with a large gateway which is known to have stood opposite the west end of St Peter's church and was afterwards acquired for Queen's College.[5] On 22 March 1332, the Bishop of Lincoln licensed the monks to say mass in an oratory in their hall.[6] The monks apparently had studies, which had to be repaired.[7] Either this hall or another was bought by the monks in 1334 and finally sold by about 1342–3.[8]

---

[1] iii. 21; cf. iii. 50.

[2] *Lit. Cant.* i. 392.

[3] A.B. Emden in *An Oxford Hall in Medieval Times* (1927) 50, taking a group of academic halls at this period, reckons that only 3 per cent were let at rents over £3. Cf. Mallet i. 304, n. 2.

[4] The meaning of this word is discussed by R. Willis in *Arch. Cant.* vii. 59–60.

[5] Emden, *An Oxford Hall* 112, n. 2; J.R. Magrath, *The Queen's College* i (1921) 327 (with plan).

[6] *Lit. Cant.* i. 358. The same house may have been licensed to have an oratory in 1300: Magrath, *loc. cit.*

[7] *Lit. Cant.* i. 414.

[8] One might expect the monks to have bought up the hall where they were living; but the hall with the large gateway seems to have belonged throughout this period to Thomas de Wynnesbury and Margaret his wife, from whom it was acquired in November 1341 by William de Muskham, who gave it in January 1353 to Queen's College: Magrath i. 326 f.

On 28 October 1331 the three monks, Hugh of St Ives, Roger de Godmersham and James de Oxney, came up to the hall. Out of the 50s. given to them they had to spend 37s. on the journey. Hugh was evidently the senior, in charge of the rest. He had been acting as lector at Canterbury since 1327 and it seems likely that he had already spent some time at Oxford, since he was ready to 'enter upon the reading of the Sentences', i. e. to take the degree of B.D., in Lent 1332. In the next year, with surprising haste the university invited him to incept but the prior declined the offer, perhaps for financial reasons, and Hugh seems to have returned to Canterbury for good in 1333. Another of the monks, Godmersham, died soon after their arrival, before 27 December 1331. The books, clothes and plate which he had been allowed to take to Oxford were to be carefully kept.[1]

The prior in his letters to the monks at Oxford dwells specially on two points: the need for charity and mutual forbearance, and the opportunity they had at Oxford for getting hold of *scolares ydonei*, suitable recruits for the monastery. The black monks were always glad to receive scholars, and this was no doubt an important motive in their settlement at the university. By November 1336, one of the students had found two canons of St Frideswide's who were anxious to become monks of Christ Church.

The number of students at this time varied from two to three. They were at Oxford for three quarters of the year, usually going up at about Michaelmas and going down at the end of June, in time for the feast of the Translation of St Thomas (7 July) at Canterbury though a student might, apparently, be allowed to stay up during the vacation.[2] On one occasion the students seem to have been on 30 December at the manor of Newington, an Oxfordshire property of Christ Church.

As regards their maintenance, besides various minor expenses (for journeys, *cappae* etc.) the monastic accounts mention large sums to cover their stay at Oxford, averaging about £7 a head per annum. The 'sergeant' of the manor of Newington had to supply the students with money and perhaps also in kind, borrowing for the purpose if necessary. He would be repaid or have the amount 'allowed' to him in his account.[3] It is not clear whether the payments by the sergeant were in addition to, or part of, the large sums in the monastic accounts already mentioned. When Hugh of St Ives took the degree of B.D., the inevitable feast was supplied partly by the sergeant and partly, it

[1] For letters concerning the monk-students at Oxford, see *Lit. Cant.*, index, s.v. 'Oxford'.

[2] *Lit. Cant.* ii. 222.

[3] *Lit. Cant.* i. 416 (1331), 468 (1332). I take the 'reasonable allowance' to correspond to the 'allocatio' that one finds, for instance, in the later college accounts.

seems, by the prior, who sent two swans and thirty hens, and pocket money coming from offerings at the 'corona' and the Martyrdom of St Thomas in Canterbury cathedral.¹ The affairs of the students were a matter for careful discussion by the whole chapter of Christ Church and their chief concern was naturally economy: *fratres nostri libenter aures suas inclinant ut audiant nova de vobis quoad expensas moderatas*.²

In June 1340 there were several monks at Oxford: J. de Oxene, J. de Frome, T. de B. (perhaps Thomas de Bockynge) and another monk unnamed. In 1343 J. de Oxene was at Oxford and was asked by the prior to act as tutor to the son of a friend, Hugh Chaumpeneys.³ The monastic accounts between 1343 and 1350 are unfortunately missing. When they begin again in 1350, they show no reference to the students and in February 1355 the archbishop had to write, complaining that there were no monk-students from Christ Church at the university. The glory of the monastery was its learned monks. These would die out unless renewed by a succession of younger students and besides, Christ Church would cut a poor figure at the university in comparison with smaller but keener houses.⁴ It may be noted that the archbishop does not refer to the Constitutions of Benedict XII, which very definitely obliged monasteries to send up their students. The monks appear to have taken the hint: the accounts for 1355–6 refer to J. de Oxene and his companions at Oxford. At a visitation of Christ Church in September 1357 three monks—John de Frome, William de Cantuaria and Michael de Cornubia—were excused as being in remote parts. Some of them, the first and the last especially, may have been at Oxford.⁵ On 20 December 1357 at Oxford a certain religious, perhaps a mendicant, had to make a public apology to a certain monk of Christ Church called Master John Bodi (presumably a D.D.). This name does not appear in the list of Canterbury monks, but may be an alias or family name—of John de Frome, for instance.⁶ On the other hand, in November 1359 the archbishop had to write again, this time on behalf of Michael de Cornubia, who had been withdrawn from the university and was pining to get back to his studies.⁷

As regards housing: as we have seen, Christ Church wavered between a chamber in Gloucester College and the use of a private hall. It is not clear whether this lack of a settled habitation was a cause or a result of the irregularity in maintaining students. The irregularity

---

¹ *Lit. Cant.* i. 417–9.
³ *Lit. Cant.* ii. 222, 266.
⁵ *Lit. Cant.* ii. 361.
⁷ *Lit. Cant.* ii. 386–9.

² *Lit. Cant.* i. 414, 417.
⁴ *Lit. Cant.* ii. 332.
⁶ *Mun. Acad.* i. 203.

PREHISTORY

may have been due partly to financial reasons. The existing system of monastic finances was complicated and inelastic; revenues were largely earmarked for the departments of particular obedientiaries and the raising of a fund to meet a new and regular expense like the maintenance of students was at least awkward. In some monasteries it was done by making various obedientiaries pay a kind of income tax or 'contribution' on the revenues of their office to provide the pensions of the scholars: there is evidence of this at St Albans,[1] Ely,[2] Norwich,[3] Winchester[4] and (for a time) Westminster;[5] and some such income tax seems to be recommended in the Constitutions of Benedict XII, at least as a temporary measure. Christ Church Canterbury did not, presumably, need such a device, for its finances were comparatively centralised. There were two treasurers, through whose hands most (but apparently not all) of the revenues passed;[6] and in fact the payments for the Oxford students appear partly in the treasurers' accounts, partly in the priors' accounts.

But whatever system prevailed, it was obviously most desirable to obtain some permanent specific endowment to provide the expenses of the students. Benedict XII had recommended the appropriation of 'priories, or benefices without cure, accustomed to be assigned to monks'.[7] The commodities he envisaged can hardly be said to have existed in England. Here, as one might expect, the obvious solution seemed to be the appropriation of churches. The general chapter of 1343 agreed to send representatives to the court of Rome to obtain such appropriations for the support of students[8] and a number of individual monasteries petitioned for appropriations for that purpose. St Augustine's Canterbury asked for the churches of Willesborough, Stone in Oxney and Burmarsh for four monk-students (1327, 1330, 1334 postponed to c. 1349).[9] Worcester, where the bishop had already been licensed to support two monk-students out of the episcopal income (1342), asked for the church of Overbury for two

[1] J. Amundesham, *Annales* (Rolls Series) ii. 307–10. For contributions for other purposes, cf. *Gesta Abbatum* (Rolls Series) iii. 456, 496.
[2] Information supplied by the Rev. Seiriol Evans.
[3] H.W. Saunders, *An Introduction to the Rolls of Norwich Cathedral Priory* (1930) 184–5.
[4] G.W. Kitchin, *Computus Rolls of St Swithin's Winchester* (1892) 48, 54, 56, 70.
[5] E.H. Pearce, *Monks of Westminster* (1916) 26, 81 (1339–40). Later (from about 1359–60) the whole pension was paid by the treasurers (*ibid.* 26–7).
[6] R.H. Snape, *English Monastic Finances* (1926) 39, 51; *Lit. Cant.* ii. xliv ff.
[7] Wilkins, *Concilia* ii. 597.
[8] *Chapters* ii. 22–3.
[9] CPR *Letters* ii. 278, 315, 401. Cf. Thorne in Twysden, *Decem Scriptores* 2039 ff.; Bodleian MS. Rawlinson C. 7, fo. 35–6.

monk-students (1346).¹ St Albans asked for the church of Appelton for five monk-students at £10 a year each (1349)² and subsequently appropriated the cell of Beaulieu (1435).³ Norwich sought to appropriate a church for two monk-students (c. 1336–7).⁴ Gloucester asked for the church of Chipping Norton for three or four monk-students at £10 a year (1391, 1403).⁵ St Mary's York apparently asked for a pension from the church of Hornsea for one monk-student and one secular (?c. 1441–25).⁶ Durham College also was endowed with the churches of Frampton, Fishlake, Bossall and Ruddington.⁷ It must be remembered too that some of the secular colleges, like Oriel and Exeter, at first relied considerably for their revenues on appropriated churches. This widespread use of appropriated churches for the endowment of students is important, for it helps to explain the early history of Canterbury College. By consenting to the appropriation of Pagham and by claiming a main share in Islip's college, the monks were in effect following the fashion.

¹ CPR *Letters* iii. 70; *Petitions* i. 121.
² CPR *Petitions* i. 171; *Letters* iii. 332.
³ Amundesham ii. 107 ff.
⁴ Bodleian MS. Tanner 342, fo. 109.
⁵ CPR *Letters* iv. 406.
⁶ CPR *Letters* v. 2, 192; vii. 374, 410; *Valor Ecclesiasticus* v. 6.
⁷ *Collectanea III*. 13.

2
HISTORY

In 1361, the monks found the opportunity of obtaining what they needed by claiming a share in the college which Archbishop Simon Islip had decided to found at Oxford. In this way Canterbury College came into existence—a stormy and uncertain one for the first twenty years.

Before the archbishop's projected college could be actually founded, and even before it was clearly planned out, it was necessary in the first place to obtain the king's licence for the foundation and the alienation of property in mortmain. This document was dated 20 October 1361.[1] It must not be considered as a charter of incorporation, or as corresponding to the act of parliament now necessary for the foundation of a college. The king is not really interested in the existence of a community of students as such, though incidentally he may patronise it and strike a spiritual bargain for its prayers. He is content to leave to the archbishop's discretion the exact form of the institution, except that it is understood to be a mixed body of monks and seculars. On the other hand the licence is, in a very real way, the college's legal title to existence. It is a dispensation from the effects of the Statute of Mortmain and so it is mainly concerned with the property to be held by the college. It is precisely this point which gives the king his interest in and control over the future college. The successive archbishops and the monks may discuss and determine and litigate over the constitution and statutes of the college without reference to the king; but once the very wide terms contained in this licence are overstepped, so that the college has been made into something essentially different from the institution originally licensed to hold property, then there will be great danger of the king treating the licence as void and proceeding to present to the church of Pagham, the main possession of the college, and even the Oxford property will be in danger.

The licence is based upon a plea of expediency and public utility: the archbishop's design was to help in repairing the defects which the clergy of the realm had suffered from the recent pestilence. *Clerus* can hardly be taken in this context to mean a supply of parish priests: Islip was not founding a seminary. It was rather, in a more general sense,

[1] iii. 1.

true religion and sound learning, the 'republic of letters', that he meant to benefit, and the idea was further expressed in the deed appropriating Pagham rectory,[1] where the *clerus* was personified in the suffering university of Oxford. The archbishop is authorised to found a hall or house, to be commonly called Canterbury Hall, in Oxford, for a certain number of scholars both monks and seculars, who are to study and pray for the king and the realm according to the form of an ordinance to be made by the archbishop, and further to endow this hall when founded with the advowson and appropriation of the church of Pagham.

Of the two points raised in the licence—the constitution and the endowment of the hall or college—it will be convenient to examine the latter first, as it helps to explain the former. The archbishop is described as founding the college out of his own means (*suis sumptibus erigere*) and this seems to have been literally true as regards the provision of the actual site;[2] but the real source of support for the students was to come from the advowson and appropriation of the valuable rectory of Pagham in Sussex, which was already of the archbishop's immediate jurisdiction and advowson ex officio and was now promised to the college.

The practice of appropriating the fruits of rectories as a source of income and endowment is, of course, a well-known and interesting feature of the later middle ages.[3] The appropriated church might be a new one, acquired outright, or one of which the advowson was already possessed by the appropriator. The latter was obviously the easiest and most tempting method of endowment for churchmen with great public projects and little private means. Apart from the necessary ecclesiastical and temporal sanctions to be obtained, it was a simple step from advowson to appropriation: it practically meant that the patron presented to the vacant benefice the institution which he wished to endow as a kind of perpetual rector.

In appropriating the church of Pagham, the property of his see, to his new foundation the archbishop could not act alone, without his chapter. Although the possessions of the archbishop were in practice distinct and separate from those of the cathedral chapter, in a certain sense they were all regarded as the common property of the church of Canterbury, under common control. To alienate any of this property permanently by such an act as the appropriation of a church, it was necessary for the archbishop to consult his chapter and obtain their

---

[1] iii. 5.
[2] Cf. the *octo hospicia conducticia* in the *tenor fundacionis*, iii. 4.
[3] R.H. Snape, *English Monastic Finances* (1926) 74–91.

consent. This was a very important legal point, on which the Decretals contained a whole title: *De iis quae fiunt a praelatis sine consensu capituli*.[1] Archbishop Islip is represented by Stephen of Birchington, the historian and monk of Christ Church, as being too free with the archiepiscopal property in such matters as the felling of trees or the selling of a perpetual annual income for ready money;[2] but in the present case he could hardly ignore the law.

There are plenty of examples of alienations, exchanges and other important acts made by the archbishops and confirmed by the chapter about this time and later. The usual course was either for the archbishop to send the letters containing his proposed grant or ordinance or confirmation to the prior and chapter to be discussed, confirmed and sealed, and then for the latter to issue an *Inspeximus* of these letters, the right of the chapter being plainly laid down: '... quia tamen unionem, annexationem, appropriationem ipsas absque consensu vestro finaliter non intendimus, sicut nec de iure expedire debemus...'[3]; or else for the archbishop to come in person to discuss the matter with the chapter, when the document in question would be confirmed and sealed by both parties on the spot, the chapter's rights being expressed here also: '... demum super hiis cum religiosis viris filiis nostris priore et capitulo nostre Cantuariensis ecclesie in ipsius capitulo tractatum diligentem habuimus et solempnem, prout requiritur in concessionibus huiusmodi perpetuis et alienacionibus ecclesiarum.'[4] It was by this second, rarer and more solemn form of agreement that the appropriation of the church of Pagham was made.[5]

This constitutional point is of the utmost importance, as it gave the prior and chapter from the first an interest in and control over the college as great as the king's, and for the same reason: i.e. on account of the endowment. If the archbishop made the college into something essentially different from the institution which they, the prior and chapter of Canterbury, had concurred in endowing, they like the king could treat the endowment as void, at least on the death of the existing archbishop, and with the help of a friendly successor they, like the

---

[1] X 3. 10.
[2] Wharton, *Anglia Sacra* i. 45–6. In the latter case, the commutation of the annual payment of venison from the Earl of Arundel which Birchington resented so much, it must be noted in justice to the archbishop that if he omitted the full legal formalities, he did eventually contrive to get his act ratified by the chapter: *Lit. Cant.* ii. 432–6.
[3] *Lit. Cant.* iii. 296. Other cases *ibid.* ii. 219–20, 267, 285, 326, 337–42, 432–6, 436–42; iii. 58, 63, 294–8, 306–9.
[4] *Lit. Cant.* ii. 253; iii. 201–2. Cf. the college statutes of 1384, triply attested by the archbishop, the chapter and, subsequently, the college: iii. 183.
[5] *Lit. Cant.* ii. 445–7.

king again, could take active measures and have the revenues of Pagham sequestrated.

Although the actual appropriation did not take place until eighteen months after the mortmain licence, it must have been obvious to the archbishop from the first that he would sooner or later have to come to terms with the prior and chapter, to obtain their consent; and it is difficult not to regard this situation as helping to determine the remarkable character of the *constitution* of the college, which was to consist of students *tam religiosorum quam secularium*. This was a bold and almost unprecedented experiment,[1] for though Durham College already existed, it did not assume its similar mixed composition until 1380.[2] It would be unjust to both parties to suppose that the archbishop was forced entirely against his will into admitting monks into his college.[3] Whatever his faults in the eyes of the monks, Islip was a conscientious man, who among other things had entered into the spirit of the legislation of Benedict XII by urging the prior to maintain monk-students at the university, as we have seen. He now had the opportunity to prove his interest and zeal by material help. It goes without saying that he was at the same time keenly interested in the wellbeing of the secular clergy—rather too keenly for the comfort of the clerical underworld. On the other hand, his relations with the chapter were sufficiently formal, even strained, to make the latter willing to exact a consideration for their concurrence. The result was a college designed to satisfy both parties: the archbishop by providing for the secular *clerus*, the monks by providing places for their students.

The king's licence speaks of an *ordinacio*, to be made by the archbishop for his college and students. The date, manner of execution and exact scope of these original statutes are not known, but two things seem certain: firstly that the 'secular' statutes that Wilkins printed[4] and arbitrarily dated at 1362–3 are not the original statutes, but represent a later draft; and secondly that by the time of the appointment of the first warden, early in 1363, some sort of ordinance, at least on that subject, had been made by the archbishop. On 13 March 1363, the prior and chapter nominated to the archbishop three monks—Henry Wodehull S.T.P., John de Redyngate and William Rychemond—for the office of warden,[5] and out of these the

[1] H.B. Workman (*John Wyclif* i. 174 and n. 7) speaks of this as a 'favourite dream of the times', but only on the strength of three such projects in 1280, 1381 and 1481. The first of these, made by Bishop Balsham at Cambridge, was a failure.
[2] *Collectanea III*. 12. Even there, the seculars were strictly subordinate.
[3] As Mallet rightly points out, we must not overstate the power of the chapter to dictate terms to the archbishop: *Hist. Univ. Oxford* i. 305.
[4] Wilkins, *Concilia* iii. 52. Cf. TRHS (1914) 60.　　　　　　　　　　[5] iii. 2.

archbishop chose as warden Henry Wodehull in a letter dated 19 March 1363.[1] J.B. Sheppard, the editor of *Literae Cantuarienses*, speaks of this nomination as 'probably by the founder's special permission, given *pro hac vice*';[2] but there is no warrant for regarding it as exceptional. Sheppard was probably misled by a misunderstanding of the phrase *in hac parte*, and still more by a desire to reconcile this proceeding with the 'secular' statutes printed by Wilkins, which he took to be the original statutes. In reality, it is quite clear from the wording of the two letters that the whole proceeding was in obedience to a formal statute or ordinance made by the archbishop, and in fact we have what professes to be an extract from this ordinance entered into the Christ Church register together with the letter of nomination: *verba ordinacionis quoad custodem huiusmodi*.[3] The extract, with a few verbal differences, is practically identical with the corresponding section in the statutes of 1384, where Archbishop Courtenay professed to be quoting from Islip's original statutes.[4] There is nothing to show that it is a forgery. It appears to be the only surviving fragment of Islip's original statutes, and indeed of any statutes of certain date and authentic execution, before 1384. There is no evidence yet about the other members of the college.

After obtaining the king's licence, nothing had been done about the college during the year 1362, but in the following year the appointment of the first warden was followed by a number of important acts and the college apparently became a working reality. This renewed activity is curious, for the archbishop was suffering from a paralytic stroke, received at the end of January 1363, and he did not fully recover until July.[5] Soon after the nomination of the warden, the archbishop issued at Mayfield, 13 April 1363, the *tenor fundacionis*, the official and direct instrument of foundation[6] (the licence of 1361 had been indirect and tentative). This document, though not very explicit, contains some interesting developments, both in its additions and in its omissions.

In the opening clause the archbishop explains his motives, with more unction than would have been possible in the king's licence.

For the first time, the number of students on the foundation is fixed—at twelve: an ambitious scale which, as events proved, could

---

[1] iii. 3.
[2] *Lit. Cant.* ii. xxv.
[3] Reg. L, fo. 93 (iii. 3). The second nomination of Wodehull (in 1367) was added in the same place later. See Cronin, TRHS (1914) 58.
[4] iii. 3, 173.
[5] Wharton, *Anglia Sacra* i. 46 (Stephen of Birchington).
[6] iii. 4.

not be kept up on the endowments provided. The church of Pagham was valued on paper at £110 per annum,[1] but in practice gave a net income which, so far as records show, never reached £80 and in the fifteenth century sank to about £50. While the college was on its own resources, it usually supported four monks and five secular scholars at a much cheaper rate.

The archbishop provides *suis sumptibus* the actual 'place', the site and housing for the students, together with eight neighbouring tenements, *hospicia conducticia*, the latter apparently as a source of revenue (*in partem ... dotis et sustentacionis*) rather than for accomodation. Probably they were to be let out for the time being, but would provide an enlarged site when the college came to have buildings of its own.

In addition, the founder has procured for the college the manor of Wodeford, Northants., in the diocese of Lincoln, belonging to his nephew, William de Islip.

A most striking feature of this document is the entire omission of the two very important and closely related points raised in the licence of 1361: the mixed composition of monks and seculars and the appropriation of Pagham. In view of later developments, one is tempted to detect here a certain secular tone, an attempt to do without the Christ Church monks, their concurrence and their claims. If so, the new secular policy was as yet uncertain and not fully revealed, for this document of 13 April 1363 closely follows on the appointment of the first monk-warden in March and a month later, on 11 May 1363, ostensibly from Canterbury, the archbishop issued the document appropriating the church of Pagham to the college with the concurrence of his chapter.[2]

Here a fresh problem is raised. According to Stephen of Birchington, the archbishop seems to have been at Mayfield suffering from the effects of his paralytic stroke from January until the beginning of July 1363, when he was carried gently in a litter towards his palace at Charing; yet Islip dates the deed of appropriation in May from the chapter at Canterbury, after 'solemn and diligent treaty' with the prior and chapter. Either Stephen of Birchington was mistaken, or the archbishop's dating was a legal fiction and the negotiations with the monks had taken place on another occasion.[3]

---

[1] *Taxatio ecclesiastica P. Nicholai* (1291) 138 b.
[2] iii. 5.
[3] Islip's register at Lambeth seems to support Stephen of Birchington: from January 1363 (fo. 190ᵛ) to 26 June 1363 (fo. 195) his letters are dated at Mayfield and from 5 July 1363 (fo. 195) at Charing. On 7 August 1363 (fo. 196) he was at Canterbury.

The appropriation of Pagham was now arranged: the college could enter into actual possession as soon as the existing incumbent was out of the way.¹

The document throws no fresh light on the constitution of the college but it gives a peculiar account of the endowment, according to which the archbishop has endowed his 'collegiate hall' with certain temporal possessions—evidently an allusion to the eight *hospicia conducticia* and the manor of Woodford—but the scholars, finding these not enough to live on, have asked the archbishop to give them in addition the church of Pagham. This presentation of the facts, which seems to represent Pagham as an afterthought, is at variance with that given in the king's licence in 1361, where appropriation of Pagham was contemplated from the first, before the students existed. If anything is an afterthought, it is rather the temporal possessions: the manor of Woodford (not mentioned until the *tenor fundacionis* in April 1363) and perhaps also the eight *hospicia*. This new and rather perverse statement of the case is a comparatively small point, but it may have been intended to emphasise the secular and private part of the endowment, even while actually dealing with Pagham, the part in which the monastic chapter was concerned.²

Islip obtained letters patent dated 1 June 1363, authorising the conveyance of various tenements in Oxford to the college, the Statute of Mortmain notwithstanding.³ As this is the earliest record of such a conveyance, it must include the eight *hospicia conducticia* already referred to. They may be perhaps be identified with the tenements of St Frideswide's priory included in this licence and actually handed over to the college in July 1364.⁴

William de Islip granted his manor of Woodford, Northants., in a charter dated at Mayfield 4 June 1363, which for greater security was attested by a public notary.⁵ The tone of this document is even more secular than the previous ones, the grant being made to the warden and *clerici* of the hall. Although a good deal was made of this endowment at the time, it is a curious fact that the manor of Woodford never appears again in the history of the college. It certainly never

---

¹ iii. 6. William in the Hieyne, the incumbent of Pagham, resigned the rectory at Mayfield 24 May 1363: Foxe, *Acts and Monuments* (ed. Pratt) ii, Addenda, p. 924, from Reg. Islip, fo. 301.
² This point of view is again expressed by the seculars in the lawsuit at Rome, iii. 184; also by Workman, *John Wyclif* i. 174–5.
³ iii. 7.
⁴ iii. 10.
⁵ For Woodford, see *VCH Northants*. iii. 255 ff. Land was held by the Islip family in the adjoining parish of Islip (*ibid*. 215 ff.). It was perhaps from this Islip and not from the Islip near Oxford that the archbishop took his name.

contributed to the college revenues as answered for in the *computi* of the monastic period of the college, after 1370, nor does it appear at the dissolution; and even while the college was in the hands of the seculars, before 1370, they cannot have found it lucrative, for their representative in the lawsuit at Rome admitted that Pagham constituted almost their entire means of subsistence, so that the sequestration of the church would reduce them literally to beggary, *in opprobrium cleri*.[1] Perhaps the gift of Woodford was never actually executed, or was withdrawn in the unsettled times that followed Islip's death;[2] or again, it may have been sold by the seculars (as some of the Oxford property was) and not considered worth recovering by Christ Church.

A few months later (21 September 1363) the archbishop applied to Rome for papal confirmation of his new foundation, asking for the following privileges:

(1) papal confirmation of the foundation of the hall or college and of the appropriation of Pagham. Here the archbishop's petition closely follows the wording of the deed of appropriation (11 May 1363), notably omitting reference to the mixed constitution of regulars and seculars and representing Pagham as an afterthought.

(2) the college to have a chapel, to be dedicated to the Blessed Virgin and St Thomas the Martyr.

(3) the 'ordinations' or statutes for the rule of the college, which have yet to be drawn up *provida deliberacione*, to have the force of papal authority. Evidently, apart from the particular *ordinacio* concerning the appointment of the warden, the full constitution of the college had not been drawn up.

(4) the college to be immediately subject to the archbishop's jurisdiction, saving the authority of the university.

The pope gave his consent to all these points except the appropriation of Pagham. His refusal, however, did not prevent the appropriation taking place and eventually, in 1379, the papal confirmation of it was obtained.

To sum up: our first-hand knowledge of the constitution of the college in this first period, 1363–5, is not precise or extensive.[3] It is certain that the first warden was a monk of Christ Church and this was apparently meant to be the regular practice. According to the terms of the king's licence, it was to be a mixed body of monks and secular

---

[1] iii. 185.

[2] The manor of Woodford was conveyed by Roger de Boys to John Pyel in February 1369: *Cal. Close Rolls* 1369–74, p. 68.

[3] Archbishop Courtenay in 1384 claimed to be quoting Islip's original statutes to a large extent. There seems no valid reason for doubting his word, but at the same time his version cannot be taken as first-hand evidence.

students, and we also know that twelve was the number contemplated. Whether the full number was actually reached and what was the proportion of monks to seculars is not so certain. Cardinal Langham in the lawsuit at Rome afterwards stated that there were to have been four monks, including the warden, to eight seculars.[1] One would expect some such proportion, to justify the description of the college as a mixed body; and moreover, the association of three secular fellows with the secular warden in the great lawsuit with which we shall soon have to deal suggests that these three fellows replaced precisely three monk-fellows, companions of the evicted monk-warden. As regards the appointment of the monk-fellows Cardinal Langham said, rather vaguely, that having been duly nominated or elected they were admitted by the archbishop. It is not clear whether their choice ultimately lay with the archbishop or the chapter of Christ Church and it was this very point which came into dispute later, when the monks had been restored and just before the constitution was finally determined in 1384.[2] Under the earliest régime, then, the monks formed at least a strong minority.[3]

At the end of 1365, a change was made and the college was secularised. In place of the monk, Henry Wodehull, Islip appointed Master John Wyclyve or Wyclyf as warden (the vexed question of his identity does not directly affect the sequence of events).[4] Cardinal Langham said that this coup d'état was carried out in the lawful absence of the monk-warden and monk-fellows. What exactly happened with regard to these monk-fellows as distinct from the monk-warden is not clear, since the subsequent lawsuit concentrated on the disputed wardenship; but the royal pardon given to the monks in 1372 certainly speaks of all the monks having been ejected and, as has been suggested above, it seems likely that the three monk-fellows were replaced by the three secular fellows William Middelworth, Richard Benger and William Selby, the associates of Wyclif.

There are the archbishop's motives for this change to be considered. Cardinal Langham seemed to insinuate that Wyclif secured his appointment by craft and undue influence over the archbishop, who was then suffering from a grave infirmity and, the suggestion seems to be, not fully responsible for what he did.[5] But of such

---
[1] iii. 186.
[2] iii. 42 ff.
[3] Mallet seems to doubt whether Islip originally intended the monks to have a governing voice in the college: *Hist. Univ. Oxford* i. 305. But it is difficult to see what else the appointment of a monk-warden could have meant.
[4] The name is spelt Wyclyve in the archbishop's appointment, Wyclyf and Wiclyf in the account of the Roman lawsuit in the Canterbury cathedral register B.
[5] iii. 186.

matters one could hardly expect to find documentary proof. It is true that the archbishop seems greatly impressed with Wyclif's qualities in his letter of appointment, but one cannot be sure that his words are not common form. On the other hand, a modern writer has suggested that it was Wodehull's 'troublesome, self-willed' character that made the mixed constitution a failure.[1] Workman ingeniously argues, on the contrary, that Wodehull's character would commend him to Islip.[2] If Wodehull proved unacceptable to the archbishop, he could surely have been replaced by another, more tractable monk. No personal explanation by itself seems sufficient. The idea of catering for the secular *clerus* had always been an important, if not a predominant part of Islip's scheme for the college. Perhaps the suggestions made above as to a growing secular tone in the documents as early as 1363 are not entirely fanciful. One possible explanation is that the endowments seemed inadequate for the support of a double community and that Islip naturally preferred to sacrifice the monastic side to the secular. Workman suggests that Islip was influenced by a scruple that the mixed constitution brought the college under the censure of the Constitutions of Benedict XII for the black monks; but the pope had aimed at excluding seculars from the monastic claustral schools and does not seem to have had in view in his prohibition such an institution as Canterbury College.[3]

If Simon Langham was unpopular,[4] there was at least one body of men in Kent who welcomed his translation to the see of Canterbury: namely, the monks of Christ Church, now disinherited from their college in Oxford. A black monk himself,[5] Langham was certainly not likely to share the secular policy of Islip's later years. He was provided to Canterbury on 24 July 1366, he received the pall on 4 November of that year and on the following Lady Day, 25 March 1367, he was enthroned. He lost no time in taking active measures with regard to the college and the developments that followed can be traced partly from actual documents, partly from the rival statements or 'expositions' made by the parties in the lawsuit at Rome.

---

[1] H.C. Maxwell Lyte, *Hist. Univ. Oxford* (1886) 177. But see Cronin, TRHS (1914) 63, n. 1.
[2] Workman, *John Wyclif* i. 175–6.
[3] *Ibid.* i. 178.
[4] Wharton, *Anglia Sacra* i. 47: 'Exultent celi quia Simon transit ab Ely, / Ad cuius adventum flent in Kent milia centum.'
[5] Abbot of Westminster 1349–62. He was apparently one of the few prominent monks who never had a university career: E.H. Pearce, *Monks of Westminster* (1916) 92–4; DNB; D. Knowles, *Religious Orders* ii (1955) 54.

HISTORY

Langham regarded Wyclif's appointment as unconstitutional and void from the beginning[1] and in any case Islip's original statutes, if quoted correctly by Archbishop Courtenay in 1384, must have given the archbishop power to remove the warden at will, *absque iudiciali strepitu*.[2] On 31 March 1367 he proceeded to appoint a monk of Canterbury, John de Redyngate, as warden, at the same time issuing a mandate to the scholars of the college to obey the new warden.[3] The letter which must have preceded from the chapter, nominating candidates for the archbishop's choice, has not survived. In the letter of appointment, which became the traditional model in these matters, stress is laid on the fact that the hall was founded 'out of the goods of the said church of Canterbury' and on the previous nomination by the prior and chapter 'according to the form of the foundation of the said hall'.

Redyngate was only warden for about three weeks and could have had no time to make his wardenship a reality. On 20 April the prior and chapter were sending in nominations for a new warden and on 22 April 1367 the archbishop reappointed Henry Wodehull.[4] The most probable explanation of this sudden change of plan is that Langham realised that his legal, or at least his moral position would be much stronger if instead of making an innovation by appointing a fresh warden, he simply reinstated Wodehull, the original choice of the founder himself. The appointment of Redyngate was apparently a 'false start' and was ignored by both parties in the subsequent lawsuit.

Langham aimed at the restoration of the original constitution, giving the monks their place in the college, *ne fructus scolastice discipline inter monachos ut premittitur inchoatus in aliquo deperiret*.[5] There spoke a great Benedictine statesman, in the tradition of Benedict XII and of the general chapters that had established the monks at Oxford before him; and it was a sentiment which Islip himself could not have helped echoing. What Langham tried to do was to secure the wardenship, and with it the obedience of all the fellows, to a monk of Christ Church. He does not appear to have gone further than this: perhaps he meant to introduce the other three monk-fellows gradually. Even his opponents did not accuse him of

---

[1] iii. 186.
[2] iii. 173. What Langham and the monks contested was not the power of the archbishop, e. g. Islip, to remove a particular person, e. g. Wodehull, but the power to alter the fundamental constitution by appointing a secular.
[3] iii. 14. John de Redyngate had entered Christ Church in 1339 (Searle 180) and so was a man of considerable seniority. He had been one of the three nominated in 1363, when Wodehull was appointed.
[4] iii. 15.
[5] iii. 157.

expelling any of the secular fellows, not even the three companions of Wyclif, who were probably 'intruded' in place of the monks. It was only when the case went to Rome that the pope laid down the complete exclusion of one party or the other as the solution.[1] It is most important to realise that the dispute between Langham and the monks on the one side and the seculars on the other concentrated on the wardenship. It seems that the three secular fellows Benger, Selby and Middelworth, were involved not as intruders themselves, but as accomplices in the intrusion of Wyclif, the warden.

The secular warden and fellows refused to admit Wodehull, according to their own statement, on the grounds that to do so would have been contrary to the oaths they took at their reception into the college.[2] Thus they persisted in upholding the secularisation of the college. Langham's line of action was to oppose this secularisation as unconstitutional. He therefore cited them to produce their titles, the documents concerning the foundation, the ordinances of the college and the appropriation of Pagham. These, according to his account, they failed to produce;[3] according to theirs, he gave them no proper opportunity to do so.[4] In any case, the documents were not produced.

The archbishop then, regarding the seculars as contumacious, proceeded to sequestrate the revenues of the church of Pagham, on which the college mainly depended, and according to the seculars' statement detained the books and other legacies left by Islip to the college.[5] The sequestration, executed sometime in the late summer or autumn of 1367, made Langham master of the situation and forced the hand of the seculars. If they were in possession of the college, he was in possession of Pagham and this threw the burden of the action upon them, for he could afford to wait and to hold out and they could not. On 29 November 1367, therefore, John Upton, the substitute of Richard Benger, who was one of the 'pretensed' fellows and acted as their proctor throughout the process, came before the archbishop's commissaries at Otford and, stating his grievance, made a formal appeal to the Holy See and a formal demand for his *apostoli*, the letters addressed by the inferior judge to the superior judge (in this case the pope) to whom the appeal was being made. These letters testified that the appeal had been made and without them the appeal could not proceed in the superior court. The grievance was of course the sequestration, which the archbishop had imposed on account of the contumacy of the seculars in refusing to appear and produce their titles when properly cited. The seculars denied the contumacy and said that the sequestration was unjust. In ordinary cases the inferior

---

[1] Cronin rightly points this out in TRHS (1914) 66.   [2] iii. 185.
[3] iii. 187.   [4] iii. 17.   [5] iii. 185.

judge was bound to defer to an appeal, i.e. to stay the execution of the sentence during the appeal, but contumacy was one of the exceptional cases where the judge was not bound to defer, but was allowed to proceed with the sentence during the appeal. This course was all the more welcome to the archbishop in the present case as the sentence was the sequestration of Pagham, apparently carried out already, and to suspend it would have been to put the seculars back in complete possession. Although the archbishop, as bound by canon law, 'refuted' the appeal of these contumacious persons as 'false and frivolous' and refused to defer to it, he was not allowed to suppress it altogether, but had to pass it on to the Holy See by granting the appellants that kind of *apostoli* proper to such cases, the *apostoli refutatorii*.[1]

The result of the seculars' appeal was a lawsuit in the court of Rome, which finally determined the future of the college. We have a long account of the proceedings.[2] It relates a wealth of legal formalities, but is not always very explicit — as regards the chronology of the lawsuit, for instance. We do not know when the suit began: it may have done so at any time during the year 1368 or early in 1369. The sentence was passed in July 1369, though it was not finally promulgated until May 1370. Langham had been created cardinal on 27 September 1368, but did not leave England for the court of Rome until the end of February 1369.[3] By the time of his arrival, the suit had probably been going on for some time: it seems possible to mark the point at which he first intervened, much to the improvement of his and the monks' situation. He is styled cardinal throughout, but that throws no light on the beginning of the suit for the account would, of course, be drawn up at the end.

The principal parties concerned were:

(1) On the side of the seculars John Wyclif, M.A., S.T.B., the 'pretensed' warden, and his associates Selby, Middelworth and Benger. It was the last who acted throughout as proctor for the rest. As Workman pointed out, the appointment was not too fortunate, for Benger was an offender against canon law.[4]

(2) On the side of the regulars, firstly Cardinal Langham. It must not be presumed that because he was a cardinal, he was necessarily

---

[1] iii. 16. The question of appeals of this kind and of the *apostoli refutatorii* is discussed by F.W. Maitland in his *Collected Papers* iii. (1911) 142–51. See also Ducange, *Glossarium*, s.v. *Apostoli*.
[2] iii. 184 ff.
[3] DNB xi. 540.
[4] In the matter of his benefice of Donnington: Workman, *John Wyclif* i. 181, n. 4.

persona grata in the court of Rome and so wielded an unfair influence: he had been implicated in the rejection of the pope's demand for tribute in 1366.[1] Secondly, the prior and chapter of Christ Church Canterbury were involved, as claiming a share in the college; and thirdly, there appeared Henry Wodehull, the dispossessed warden. The proctor on this side was Master Roger de Freton, dean of Chichester.[2] He was a busy man and had to have two substitutes, to be used on occasion: Master Albertolus of Milan and Master John Cheyne. Both Langham and Wodehull were present in the curia.

The case seems to have followed a normal procedure. In the first place it came before the pope and the cardinals in consistory[3] and it was then committed by the pope to the tribunal of a cardinal.[4] The pope did not wash his hands of the case after committing it to the cardinal, but had it brought up again before him and recommitted it. This process was repeated several times during the suit, which consisted of four such stages, leading up to a final stage, which would constitute the actual trial according to modern ideas. It was then that witnesses and muniments were produced and learned opinion consulted, and the final sentence followed. Though the case seems dilatory and formal enough to a layman, it technically followed a 'summary procedure',[5] which dispensed with the formality of the *libellus* or written demand of the plaintiff and with the *litis contestatio* or formal contradiction by the defendant.[6]

The proceedings opened in the presence of Pope Urban V and some of the cardinals, in full consistory, with the hearing of the apparently oral 'expositions' or statements of the case put forward by both sides. These may be summarised as follows:

On behalf of John Wyclif and his associates, the statement that:

(1) Archbishop Islip founded Canterbury College in Oxford out of his personal property, as distinct from his archiepiscopal property, for a warden and eleven secular clerks.

(2) At length, he appropriated to it the church of Pagham.

(3) He appointed John Wyclif as warden and meant the office to be secular and perpetual. He left books etc. to Wyclif in his will.

(4) On Islip's death Archbishop Langham tried, without reason-

---

[1] Cronin, TRHS (1914) 67; Workman, *John Wyclif* i. 181.
[2] For his career see Workman, *John Wyclif* i. 182, n. 4.
[3] G. Mollat, *Les Papes d'Avignon* (1965) 483 ff.
[4] *Ibid.* 486 ff.
[5] iii. 188.
[6] Mollat, *Les Papes d'Avignon* 487; P. Fournier, *Les Officialités au moyen âge* (1880) 231–2.

able cause, to replace Wyclif by Henry Wodehull, monk of Christ Church Canterbury.

(5) On the resistance of the warden and fellows to this as contrary to their oaths, Langham sequestrated the revenues of Pagham, practically their whole income, so as to reduce them to beggary, and also unjustly detained some of Islip's legacies.

(6) Consequently, the secular warden and fellows appealed to the Holy See against this sequestration.

This was immediately followed by the statement on Langham's behalf that:

(1) Archbishop Islip, wishing to help students, and in particular to increase study among monks, founded Canterbury College out of the goods of the archiepiscopal see (i.e. Pagham).

(2) At the foundation he laid down that the college was to consist of twelve persons, of whom the warden and three fellows were to be monks of Christ Church Canterbury and the other eight scholars were to be seculars, under the governance of the warden.

(3) The warden was to be nominated by the prior and chapter of Canterbury and appointed by the archbishop according to the ordinances and statutes, which Langham asked the pope to take as read (*haberi pro expressis*).

(4) In accordance with this constitution, Islip appointed Henry Wodehull and three other monks as warden and fellows.

(5) Subsequently he appropriated the church of Pagham to the college.

(6) But in the lawful absence of the monks, John Wyclif caused himself to be made master (or warden) of the college, with the connivance of Islip, who was then ill.

(7) On the death of Islip Langham, seeing the college under the rule of a secular contrary to the original constitution, ordered Wyclif and his associates, accomplices in his 'incursion', to admit Henry Wodehull again.

(8) On the refusal of the seculars to do this, the archbishop determined on a thorough inquiry and ordered the seculars to produce their titles.

(9) They failed to do this and Langham threatened to sequestrate the revenues of Pagham (he speaks as though he did not actually carry out the sequestration): hence the present appeal.

Both statements are admittedly *ex parte*, but from the little that we do know definitely the seculars' statement seems weak and even, in places, disingenuous. With regard to the real cause of the dispute, the wardenship, anyone unacquainted with the facts would gather from the seculars' account that the college was entirely secular from the beginning[1] and that Wyclif was the first warden. That is quite untrue, as we have seen. Langham's account, though it goes further than the surviving evidence, does not seem to clash with it. Again Langham, in supporting the monastic claims, is able to appeal boldly to the original statutes, though he does not produce them at this stage. The seculars do not appeal to any definite statutes—evidently the secular statutes printed by Wilkins were of no legal value[2]—but seem to base their position on the personal will of the founder. Both sides seem a little embarassed by the truth about the endowments. The seculars boldly assert that the archbishop founded the college out of his own private property but, rather awkwardly, have to go on to mention the appropriation of Pagham. Langham asserts that the college was founded out of the goods of the church of Canterbury. This statement is untrue if it is meant to apply to the Oxford site and the manor of Woodford, but probably Langham was referring to the appropriation of Pagham, which he mentions later. Both statements, taken literally, are inaccurate, but on the whole it is nearer the truth to say that Islip used the goods of his church. For a college, especially a medieval college, a permanent source of income like an appropriated church was of more vital importance than the actual site and the manor of Woodford does not seem to have counted for anything.

The pope, after hearing both statements, committed the case to Cardinal Andruynus, Androin de la Roche, a monk and sometime abbot of Cluny,[3] to hear and decide. Judgement was to be given to the effect that the college be made entirely monastic or entirely secular. Although the seculars had made their appeal primarily against the sequestration, the pope clearly recognised from the first that the real issue was the possession of the college and, moreover, that on this point there could be no more compromise. A mixed constitution had been tried by Archbishop Islip and had failed, with the present lamentable consequences for the college, if not for the lawyers.

Cardinal Androin entered on his duties. At the instance of Richard Benger, the seculars' proctor, he cited de Freton, Langham's proctor, to appear within a certain term to make any exceptions he wished against the cardinal's commission, no doubt especially with regard to the cardinal's fitness as a judge. On the day named, Benger appeared and accused de Freton, who did not appear, of contumacy. De Freton was therefore cited again, under pain of excommunication and this

[1] The same view seems to be put forward by John Wyclif, though without mentioning names, in the *De Ecclesia* (ed. J. Loserth 1886) 371: *pure clerici scholares*.
[2] Cronin, TRHS (1914) 66.
[3] Workman, *John Wyclif* i. 181, n. 6.

time he did appear and showed his credentials as a proctor. Afterwards, Albertolus of Milan was recognised as a substitute. Both Albertolus and Benger were now cited to appear again within a certain term, to bring forward any possible exceptions against each other's proctorial powers. Benger appeared; Albertolus did not and was pronounced contumacious on this point. These preliminaries were evidently aimed at establishing the validity of the powers of the judge and the proctors.

The next stage opened in the presence of the pope in consistory with a further statement on behalf of the seculars. In this they repeated their claim that they were justified in resisting Langham's appointment of Wodehull because the wardenship, which Wyclif held, was a perpetual office and the sequestration was therefore unjust. The appeal had in the first place been made by the seculars and in appealing they had naturally chosen their own ground. In taking their manifestos, their statement made at the beginning of the case (to a certain extent)[1] and still more their original appeal made at Oxford,[2] their further statement now being made[3] and their petition which was to come afterwards,[4] and comparing these with the corresponding manifestos of the monastic party, their statement at the beginning[5] and the articles which they afterwards put forward,[6] one cannot help observing how they make the sequestration the central point of the case and how the more abstract question of the college's constitution, with its history in the past and its expediency in the future, is comparatively put in the background—though the seculars, of course, have given their account of Islip's foundation and in particular they stress the perpetuity of Wyclif's appointment. They wish to emphasise the fact (certainly a strong point in their legal position) that they were in peaceful possession of the college, and that by the founder's wish. How that came to be so they had not come to Rome to discuss, though they could hardly avoid that question sooner or later. Their grievance was that Langham, because they would not carry out some personal, unreasonable demand of his, had unlawfully cut off their revenue. In this way, the case must have appeared at first as a dispute more about a church in Sussex than a hall in Oxford.

There was no chicanery or dishonesty in this. It was the seculars' appeal and they had a right to make it as they chose. They took the wisest course in relying on the 'blessedness of seisin' and in making that their starting-point. The weakness of this treatment was that it was really superficial: they could not expect their judge, still less their opponents, to remain content with it.

[1] iii. 185.
[2] iii. 17.
[3] iii. 189.
[4] iii. 190.
[5] iii. 186.
[6] iii. 192.

The seculars could not admit that the ownership of the college was under dispute. With the regulars it was exactly the opposite. Their strongest claims were (1) that the college as originally constituted had been mixed and closely connected with the church of Canterbury; (2) that the founder could not change this constitution on his own authority; and (3) that the archbishop for the time being had a definite claim to the obedience of the members of the college and a right to enforce obedience by direct action. They therefore refused to take the present ownership of the college for granted and pursued the dispute further back, to the monks' share in and claims on the college and to the validity of its secularisation. Once these fundamentals had been discussed, the problem of the justice or injustice of the sequestration would be found to be already solved.

This divergence of opinion is important, for the success of either party will depend to a large extent upon how far they can get accepted not merely their claims, but their chosen ground of dispute. At first the pope seemed to favour the monastic party's interpretation by insisting on a final solution of the constitutional problem, but he now acts in a way favourable to the seculars by committing to Cardinal Androin the matter of the sequestration to be considered. At the instance of Benger, Albertolus was cited to bring forward any possible objection against the recommission of the case; and this was no mere formality, for Albertolus produced certain exceptions, in writing, against this new commission. Unfortunately the exceptions are not given, but they were perhaps like the later protest of Langham[1] against the separate treatment of the sequestration. Benger however, so far from withdrawing, persisted in pressing in a formal petition for the relaxation of the sequestration.

At this point, the pope intervened and again committed the case to Cardinal Androin. The object of this fresh commission was to enable the suit to proceed without delay during the vacations of the summer of 1369, apparently, as the sentence was given in July that year. As a result, Albertolus was again cited at the instance of Benger to consider and make exceptions to this new commission. He did not appear and was held contumacious. There is no apparent reason for this conduct except, perhaps, as an act of passive resistance, a development of the previous protest.

However, a much more definite and much more successful expression of the regulars' protest was at hand. Cardinal Langham had apparently arrived at the curia and interposed with the pope on behalf of his party, pointing out that the seculars, by insisting on a discussion

---

[1] iii. 191.

of the sequestration, were deliberately avoiding the main issue, the right to the college and its endowments, so that the controversy might be indefinitely prolonged. Langham put his finger on the right spot when he said that his opponents were avoiding what he considered to be the main issue, but he was wrong in supposing that they wanted delay, unless they were really hopeless: for the 'status quo' which would prevail during the trial, if it left them in corporal possession of the college, apparently also left them deprived of its revenues.

Langham's appeal against waste of time was a happy one, for it was ostensibly on the practical grounds of saving the time and money of the litigants that the pope assented to his demands and ordered that the whole case, *tam in petitorio quam in possessorio et pretenso sequestro*, be dealt with *simul et semel* by Cardinal Androin. In this way, it seems that Langham successfully diverted the suit from a special consideration of the sequestration and possibly a temporary suspension of it in favour of the seculars.

As a result of this fresh commission it was necessary to cite Benger, to give him an opportunity of making exceptions in the usual form against the commission. At the appointed time he did not appear, but the monastic party's representatives did: de Freton, who now replaced his substitute, and Henry Wodehull, the monk-warden. It was the latter's first appearance: possibly he had come over in the train of Cardinal Langham. De Freton produced certain 'positions' and articles.[1] Unfortunately, as usual the text of these is not given, but we have the concluding petition, calling upon the judge to declare in favour of the restoration of the monks to the college and of the archbishop's sequestration as being canonical. Benger was cited to answer these articles but when the time came, de Freton and Wodehull appeared but not Benger, who was therefore held contumacious.

After this began the final stage in the suit, a continuation of the last, for there was no fresh 'commission' from the pope. The monastic party had put forward their 'articles'; the next step was a thorough examination of the evidence in the form of witnesses and muniments brought forward to support these articles. The result was reduced to writing but, as usual, no details are given. It is impossible to guess at the names of the witnesses; but the documents produced would most probably be the king's licence of 1361, the original statutes of Islip, which had been promised in the regulars' statement at the beginning,

---

[1] 'Positions' were interrogations put by the judge on behalf of one party to the other party in order to find out what were the confessed points; 'articles' formed the basis of the judge's interrogation of the witnesses: Fournier, *Les Officialités* (1880) 179–80.

the appointment of Wodehull and the joint act of the archbishop and chapter in appropriating Pagham. At the same time, it must be observed that a little more than a year later the Canterbury monks complained that they were unable to lay hands on any of the college's title deeds.

It was naturally intended that there should be a similar display and examination of evidence on the other side and to this end Benger, together with any of his principals who might be available, was cited. There seems to have been some difficulty in serving this citation on Benger: (1) because he was not to be found in his lodgings, but was notoriously known to be making himself scarce (*latitantem*). This is in contrast to the other cases of contumacious absence where, perhaps, the absentee was satisfactorily accounted for. (2) because owing to the vacations, the citation could not be made *in audiencia publica literarum contradictarum*[1] in the usual manner, but had to be made by putting up public notices on the doors of the cathedrals of Viterbo and Montefiascone, at which places the papal court was then *divisim* in residence.

At the appointed time de Freton and Wodehull appeared but not Benger, who was held contumacious. He was then cited again, in order to answer the evidence put forward by his opponents and to assist in or, if necessary, protest against the conclusion of the case. This time another substitute of de Freton, Master John Chopernus, and Wodehull appeared and again Benger failed to appear. Then for the third and last time the cardinal commissary, Androin, at the instance of Roger de Freton, who had reappeared for this important occasion, and Wodehull cited Benger, together with John Wyclif, the 'pretensed' warden, and his adherents, with the same difficulties attending the citation as before, Benger being 'maliciously' in hiding. Again de Freton and Wodehull appeared, again Benger was absent and therefore reputed contumacious. Then Cardinal Androin, after reviewing the evidence and consulting learned opinion, proceeded to pronounce the sentence. The monks of Christ Church Canterbury were henceforward to have sole possession of the college, the seculars being excluded, the former exclusion of the monks by Wyclif and his associates being unjust and invalid. The sequestration was of course to be relaxed in favour of the monks. Silence was imposed upon Wyclif and his associates, but they were apparently spared paying the costs,[2] which must therefore have come out of the college property. The sentence was dated Montefiascone, 23 July 1369. Afterwards,

[1] For this tribunal see Mollat, *Les Papes d'Avignon* (1965) 492.
[2] iii. 196: *condempnacionem expensarum omittentes*. In their petitions, each side had demanded costs from the other.

before the sentence was put into 'public form' and sealed, Cardinal Androin died (29 October 1369),[1] as did also the attendant notary. The pope therefore committed the completion of the formalities to Cardinal Bernard de Bosqueto, who concluded the document at Montefiascone, 15 May 1370.

A few days before this publication of the process, Pope Urban V issued a bull, dated 11 May 1370,[2] giving a summary of the legal proceedings described above and confirming the sentence. It was directed to the bishop of London (Simon of Sudbury), the abbot of St Albans (Thomas de la Mare) and the archdeacon of Oxford (Thomas Southam), who were to cause the bull to be published solemnly and put into execution. Sudbury had been formerly employed in the papal court and was, of course, to become Archbishop of Canterbury a few years later, when he came into not entirely amicable relations with Canterbury College.[3] De la Mare was probably chosen as an obvious champion of any Benedictine interests, the 'patriarcha monachorum Angliae', as the pope and the cardinals called him.[4] It was not altogether a tactful choice, for de la Mare was probably still president of the provincial chapter of the English black monks and in that capacity he had been very active against the monks of Christ Church Canterbury.[5] Southam was now present at the papal court, perhaps in attendance on Langham: he was certainly sometime auditor to Langham and eventually the executor of his will.[6] His services were appreciated by the monks of Christ Church, for they employed him as their proctor in the court of Rome in 1375.[7]

The next proceedings are explained in a public instrument dated at the Augustinian friary outside Montefiascone, 27 May 1370, and addressed to Wyclif and his three companions by Thomas Southam, archdeacon of Oxford and one of the executors named in the papal bull. Of the three executors, Southam was obviously the nearest at hand and it was therefore to him that de Freton went and presented the papal bull, together with the public instrument describing the process, sealed by Cardinal Bernard, which is evidently the account described above. Southam, being required by de Freton to put the papal mandate into execution, by the present instrument formally notified Wyclif and his companions under pain of excommunication that within six days of hearing the sentence they must give effect to it

[1] Workman, *John Wyclif* i. 182.
[2] iii. 198.
[3] iii. 36.
[4] John Amundesham, *Annales Mon. S. Albani* (Rolls Series) ii. 304.
[5] *Chapters* ii. 63; iii. 56.
[6] R. Widmore, *Hist. of the Church of St Peter Westminster* (1751) 184–91.
[7] Canterbury Cathedral Register B, fo. 381^v.

by handing over the college to Wodehull and the monks. He pronounced Wyclif and his companions removed from the possession of the college and the monks restored to the occupation of the college and its revenues. In token of this, he then and there gave the monks in the presence of their proctor 'seisin' of the college, as an English lawyer would say, by a curious symbolic act, handing over his doctor's cap to de Freton: *per biretti nostri* tradicionem.[1] The seculars are warned not to molest the monks, but to allow them peaceful possession of the college and to answer to them for the revenues.[2] Excommunication was threatened against all who disobeyed or hindered this mandate.

For the very reason that Southam was the most accessible of the executors, he was the least able to carry out the mandate in person, being occupied with business in the court of Rome. He therefore appointed as his deputies the prior of Lewes in the diocese of Chichester, the *prior studentium* of the black monks at Oxford (at Gloucester College),[3] the chancellor of Salisbury,[4] the dean of Chichester (de Freton himself) and Master Walter Baketon, doctor of decrees and canon of Chichester. Presumably de Freton's interest and the situation of Pagham accounted for the Chichester element in this list. These deputies (or some of them) were to go in person to Canterbury College and to John Wyclif's dwelling and other necessary places in Oxford to make known to the seculars the papal bull, the account of the lawsuit and the present document, to put the monks in corporal possession of the college and finally to publish the necessary excommunications. Evidently this document, though formally addressed to the seculars, was to be handed over first of all to the deputies. The documents mentioned were ultimately to remain with the master of the college and the other monks, but the seculars might have a copy made at their own expense.

As Southam had at present no seal of his own, he borrowed Langham's seal. The notary who attested the instrument was Richard de Croxton, another *familiaris* of Langham: he appears in Langham's

---

[1] Such symbolic acts were usual in such cases. For a similar instance see Mollat, *Les Papes d'Avignon*, p. 330.
[2] As a matter of fact, the seculars had 'wasted' the Oxford property.
[3] The *prior studentium* in 1370 is not known. The post had been filled by Adam Easton in 1366 (MS. Arundel 2, fo. 84ᵛ), but he was at Rome by this time (see below). Workman (*John Wyclif* i. 183, n. 2) suggests Ughtred Boldon; but he, being at Durham College, was probably the one prominent Benedictine scholar of the time who could not have filled the post which, so far as evidence goes, was always held by the head of Gloucester College.
[4] John Norton, 1361–1402: Le Neve, *Fasti Eccl. Angl.* iii (ed. J.M. Horn, 1962) 17.

will as his chamberlain.¹ Among the witnesses may be noticed Adam de Eston, S.T.P., the famous Benedictine scholar from Norwich, afterwards cardinal.²

It might be thought that once the monks had received the bull giving the sentence in their favour and the mandate to put it into execution, all their difficulties would be over, except that it was they, apparently, who had to pay the costs of the suit. As a matter of fact, their troubles were only beginning: what had sounded so well at Montefiascone was a very different matter when it had to be put into practice in England. The monks' troubles are set forth in a pitiful letter which they wrote to Cardinal Langham, 6 October 1370.³

(1) The letter begins, in great agitation, with excuses for the delay in writing to the cardinal. The papal bull had been issued in May and not to reply until October must have seemed ungrateful.

(2) But they have many troubles to put forward as an excuse. In the first place there was the long illness of their prior, Robert Hathbrand, followed by his death on 17 July 1370⁴ and the election of his successor, Richard Gillyngham. Hathbrand had been made prior in 1338, when only in the tenth year of his monastic profession. He was not such an outstanding figure as Henry of Eastry, but he was a man of prudence and spirituality;⁵ and it needed some moral courage to write, as he did, to Edward the Black Prince, elated with the victory of Poitiers, 'Treshonuree Seignur et treshumble', urging him to keep his humility: for the humility of Our Lady was more pleasing to God than her virginity.⁶ Ten years later the prince in his turn was able to give the monks a practical lesson in humility when he made them submit to the general chapter. It is important to bear in mind that Christ Church, during the struggle with the general chapters, 1340–3, 1360–3, and during the negotiations and struggles which had so far made up the history of Canterbury College, was governed by a man of Hathbrand's character. His death was a great blow to the monastery, morally and materially.

¹ Widmore, *loc. cit*. Mr Roger Croxton, Langham's registrar, is mentioned in the Canterbury treasurer's accounts 1373–4: extract 4 below.
² DNB; Tanner, *Bibliotheca*, p. 266; W. A. Pantin, *The English Church in the Fourteenth Century* (1955) 175; D. Knowles, *Religious Orders* ii (1955) 56.
³ iii. 18.
⁴ Searle, p. 161.
⁵ See his character and benefactions in Wharton, *Anglia Sacra* i. 142 (obituary): 'Qui mox post habitum susceptum virtutibus et bonis moribus florere cepit et continuavit in eisdem. Prior autem effectus modestum, benignum et affabilem cunctis se exhibuit. In divinis quoque officiis multum simplex (a fine epithet) erat et devotus. In ministerio altaris a fletibus et lacrimis perraro se continuit.' The Canterbury obituary is not usually so communicative on these interior matters.
⁶ *Lit. Cant*. ii. 346.

(3) As to the college: the cardinal has brought the suit 'lately despaired of' to a happy conclusion, the bulls in their favour have been received and for all this they are unspeakably grateful.

(4) But at the same time, they have to break to the cardinal the disastrous effects that his good offices have had. He must know that since the sending of the bulls has become known the king, according to report, has taken up the following attitude: that the original licence (of 1361) to appropriate Pagham was granted *tam religiosis scolaribus quam secularibus*; that this licence, according to legal opinion, is now null and void through the exclusion of the seculars in accordance with the papal sentence; that therefore the church of Pagham is to be treated as vacant from the death of Islip; and the king is only waiting for the monks to put their bulls into execution to present to the church of Pagham.

(5) Moreover, the same legal flaw involved not only Pagham, but even the 'many halls at Oxford lately acquired for the college': no doubt the eight *hospicia* of which Islip spoke and the various tenements conveyed according to the licence granted in 1363.[1] All these, with one exception, have been sold by the seculars and their feoffors (the abbot of Abingdon, the prior of St Frideswide's etc.) on the grounds that the exclusion of the seculars makes void the conditions of the feoffment, which had been made to both religious and seculars. It is difficult to see what logical justification the seculars had for their share in this profitable transaction, for if the enfeoffment was invalid, then the feoffs ought simply to have reverted to the feoffors or perhaps to the Crown. But to the seculars, hard pressed by the sequestration of Pagham, the legal confusion caused by the papal sentence and the present powerlessness of the monks must have presented a tempting opportunity of turning into ready money property which they could not hope to keep for long. That the tenements were actually alienated, as the monks said, seems to be borne out by the series of conveyances which were necessary later, from 1372 onwards. It is probable that the two indentures in March 1367[2] connected with Abingdon, John Reynham and Thomas de Wolton, the sale of Vine Hall by Master William Mydelworth, clerk, to Sir Geoffrey de Lucy in 1377[3] and the sale of a piece of land called Wyclyvislond by Master William Midilworth to the monks of the college in 1382–3[4] are further traces of alienations or appropriations by the seculars who, it will be remem-

---

[1] iii. 4, 6, 7, 10, 30.
[2] iii. 12, 13.
[3] iii. 33.
[4] ii. 130.

bered, included a Wyclif or Wyclyve and a William Middelworth.¹ Such action was perhaps only human, but was not a very creditable stewardship of the college which Islip had entrusted to them. It may be noted that it was nothing new for clerics to speculate in Oxford in house property: there are examples in the previous century.²

(6) To make the monks' position more hopeless still, they are unable to lay hands on any title deeds concerning the college: neither the royal licences for (a) the appropriation of Pagham and (b) for the halls in Oxford, nor (c) the deed of Islip appropriating Pagham. This lack of documentary support makes one wonder how the monks were able to produce 'muniments' in the course of the suit at Rome. It also in a most interesting way explains the series of confirmations which followed when the monks had made their peace with the authorities.³

(7) They dare not, therefore, put their bulls into execution. They have consulted legal experts who, especially the common lawyers, take a very hopeless view of the situation. The pope, they say, has no power to pass a sentence to the prejudice either of the king's acts, at least in temporal matters, or of the seculars' possession of the college and its temporal goods while the king, even if he were so disposed, could not carry out such a sentence without a proper trial: i.e. according to the law of the land. One of the difficulties of the case was that the state claimed that an advowson (which was the basis of appropriation) such as that of the church of Pagham was a temporal matter, belonging to the temporal courts.⁴

(8) Finally, the monks have to encounter the hostility of Langham's successor, the ruling archbishop, William Wittlesey, and his party, quaintly described as 'satraps', who were strongly in favour of the seculars and apparently echoed the warnings of the lawyers.⁵ We learn, incidentally, the very interesting fact that none of the seculars admitted under the original constitution (1363–5) were now left. As we have seen, it is probable that the college was first planned for twelve members—four monks and eight seculars—and that the four monks had been replaced by four seculars, including the warden. It was these four 'intruders' who monopolised the attention of Langham and the court of Rome. In the meantime, the other original eight seculars (if there ever were as many in fact), the only seculars

---

¹ Probably to be identified with the William Middelworth of Queen's College who does not seem to have had much respect for property and at one time was outlawed: Workman, *John Wyclif* i. 199–200, where also the careers of William Selby and Richard Benger are traced.
² A.B. Emden, *An Oxford Hall in Medieval Times* (1927) 56–7.
³ iii. 23 ff.   ⁴ Pollock and Maitland, *Hist. of Eng. Law*. i. 125–6.
⁵ The phrase *negocium in periculo positum* etc. is obscure.

with an indisputable right in the college, were ignored and it was they who suffered: in theory through the papal sentence, which excluded all seculars, and in fact because, according to this letter, they had already dwindled away, no doubt owing to the sequestration of Pagham. This information is inserted as a qualifying parenthesis (*quorum tamen nullus*): possibly the monks meant to point out that the exclusion of *all* the seculars, which was arousing so much criticism, was taking place only in theory and that in practice it was only the controverted four 'intruders' who were being evicted, the others having already left.

The letter ends with a renewed appeal for help, in particular to save the church of Pagham, and as the cardinal's return to England was shortly expected, with an invitation to take up residence in 'his monastery'. As a black monk himself and an ex-archbishop, he would receive a more hearty welcome than was always given to the ruling archbishop.[1]

For some reason, this letter in the Canterbury cathedral register H has been struck through and the address erased. Possibly it was not sent. There is no evidence as to any direct reply.

It was not, apparently, until a whole year had elapsed after the giving of the sentence that the monks summoned the courage to take definite action. Since October they had been waiting and hoping, perhaps, for some help from Langham and, as will appear, they succeeded in time in pacifying Archbishop Wittelsey; but even when they did take action, they still ran no less legal risk than at first, as the sequel shows. On 30 June 1371, the prior and chapter of Christ Church Canterbury issued a document[2] by which they appointed two of their number, Stephen Monyngham and John Aleyn, as their proctors, with power to present the papal bull and other documents (notably the mandate of Thomas Southam) to the executors named in the bull and the sub-executors (those appointed by Southam), to demand the exclusion of the seculars and to take actual possession of the college. There is no record of the actual proceedings at Oxford, but the monks must have taken possession sometime in July or early August 1371:[3] for on 10 August 1371, an indenture was drawn up by

[1] Contrast the prior's attitude to Islip in 1353: *Lit. Cant.* ii. 314.
[2] *Lit. Cant.* ii. 504.
[3] There is certainly no ground for Workman's suggestion (*John Wyclif* i. 198) that the regulars drove out the seculars soon after the giving of the decision at the court of Rome in July 1369, for the monks' letter of 1370 (which he strangely quotes to support his view) definitely states that they had not yet dared to execute the bull. Further, their *procuratorium* of 30 June 1371 speaks of the exclusion of the seculars as of something in the future. If Wyclif stayed at the college until forced to quit, he cannot have left, it seems, before July 1371.

HISTORY

which the prior and convent of Christ Church handed over the 'mansio' or set of rooms which they had built and owned in Gloucester College to the abbot and convent of Westminster.[1] The peculiar position of the Christ Church monks is shown in this document and 'dates' it admirably. On the one hand, they were already by this time in actual possession, 'inhabiting' Canterbury College, and so thrift demanded the giving up of the old 'mansio'. On the other hand, they evidently feared legal proceedings and eviction from the seculars' party or from the king himself and so they had to retain the right of re-entry into their old 'mansio' in such a case.

On 29 July 1371 Archbishop Wittelsey appointed a monk, John Bidyngden, warden of the college.[2] The previous nomination by the chapter has not survived. This act shows a great improvement in the monks' position: the archbishop was no longer hostile, but had completely fallen in with the monastic control of the college. Further, we must notice the remarkable and generally inexplicable rapidity with which one warden replaced another in this early period. In 1367 John Redyngate had been replaced after a few weeks by Henry Wodehull, who was useful as a legal figurehead in the Roman lawsuit; but now that the monks were actually returning to the college, he was replaced by John Bidyngden. The latter, however, did not rule for many weeks, for on 14 September 1371 he was replaced by William Richemond,[3] who in turn by the year 1372-3 had given place to Stephen Monyngham as warden.[4]

The monks had come to terms with the archbishop, but they still had to face the king and four days after the appointment of Bidyngden their fears were fulfilled, not indeed by actual eviction, but by the carrying out of the king's threat with regard to Pagham. The king had only been waiting for the monks to put the papal sentence into execution and on 14 August 1371 he presented John de Donton, clerk, to the 'vacant' church of Pagham.[5] The letters of presentation were sent to the archbishop, since the church was under his jurisdiction and he would therefore have to institute the presentee. He must have received the letters with mixed feelings, for the right of presentation had originally belonged to the archiepiscopal see, but it was now considered to have lapsed to the Crown, apparently through the archbishop's connivance at the irregular seizure of the college by the monks and his consequent failure to present a new rector to Pagham himself. The king's action in filling up the church of Pagham corresponds to the sequestration by Langham: both were effective methods of reducing a stubborn corporation by withdrawing their revenues.

[1] iii. 21. [2] iii. 20. [3] iii. 22.
[4] Extract 3 below. [5] iii. 22.

But while Langham genuinely aimed at restoring the monks the king, as events showed, was not really concerned with the restoration of the seculars, of whose exclusion so much was made. What he aimed at was evidently a profitable compromise: namely, that he should confirm the existing monopoly of the college by the monks and the exclusion of the seculars at a large price. In about six months the king succeeded in bringing the monks to these terms, which were after all the most satisfactory that they could hope to find. Cardinal Langham's expected visit to England took place between about the end of September 1371 and the beginning of February 1372,[1] and about the same time two monks of Westminster rode to Canterbury *cum una littera domini cardinalis pro domo scolarium Oxon*.[2] Possibly the cardinal helped to negotiate the reconciliation with the king.

On 8 April 1372, the king issued his letter of pardon to the monks. This is one of the most important documents in the history of the college, for it gives an official summing-up of the last ten years' happenings. Though it has a partiality of its own, an interest in proving both sides in the wrong and therefore financially at the mercy of the king, it is on the whole the clearest and most impartial account to be found in any one contemporary document. In effect, it is a confirmation of the licence of 1361. It recounts (1) Islip's original foundation and constitution of a mixed college and (2) the deviation from this licensed form, first by the secularising in 1365, then by the 'regularising' of the college as a result of the papal sentence. The king, out of his devotion to the church of Canterbury, for the security of the prior and chapter and of those monks placed in the college, and on payment of 200 marks into his hanaper, pardons the monks' deviation and transgression and any forfeiture which may have arisen out of it, approves and ratifies the papal sentence and confirms the monks in the possession of the college and its property. The lawyers' scruples as to the king's inability to carry out the papal sentence without a fresh trial seem to have vanished: but then, 200 marks is a handsome sum. This transaction with the king appears in the Christ Church treasurer's accounts for 1372–3,[3] where the total cost of the pardon, including fees and payment for 'help and friendship', amounts to £167, perhaps about £3,000 of modern money.[4] In the same account there also

---

[1] *The Anonimalle Chronicle* (ed. V.H. Galbraith, 1927) 69–70, Cf. Pearce, *Monks of Westminster*, p. 93.

[2] Pearce, *op. cit*., p. 95. Since the letter comes from the cardinal (Langham) the *domus scolarium* is more likely to have been Canterbury College than the *mansio* in Gloucester College recently granted to Westminster.

[3] Extract 3 below.

[4] This was written long before inflation set in.

appears a payment of £94. 13. 4 made to Edward the Black Prince on his first pilgrimage to St Thomas after his return from Aquitaine.[1] This also was perhaps a douceur to help on the pardon, though it is only fair to the prince to remember that he was already a good friend to the monks and did not need much inducement to help their cause. It will be seen that pilgrimages did not always tend so entirely to monkish profit as has sometimes been imagined.

A week after the king's pardon, on 15 April 1372, Archbishop Wittelsey confirmed the appropriation of Pagham.[2] This was a pressing legal necessity for, according to their letter in October 1370, the monks had lost their original deed of appropriation made by Islip in 1363 and they apparently never recovered it. For while the original deed was copied into the Canterbury cathedral register H, fo. 101^v, probably soon after its issue,[3] it does not appear in the numbered series of the muniments concerning the college and Pagham[4] entered into the Register B at the beginning of the fifteenth century.[5] Moreover, Wittelsey's confirmation expressly quotes the deed of appropriation not from the original, but from the copy in Islip's register.[6]

Of the college property that had been in danger, there now only remained the Oxford tenements to be confirmed. This was a serious task, for most of the tenements had been sold by the seculars and their feoffors and would have to be redeemed. In October 1372 the college got back a number of tenements from St Frideswide's, but had to give power of distraint, if necessary, for rent[7] and the same arrangement was made early in 1373 in obtaining property from Godstow.[8] The tenements of Abingdon and Balliol, perhaps formerly granted and lost, perhaps only promised, were not acquired for some years.[9] To crown the reconquests, on 24 September 1373 the college obtained

[1] He landed at Southampton in January 1371 and left England again in August 1372: DNB vi. 518.
[2] iii. 26.
[3] Neighbouring documents, fo. 100^v, 101^v, are dated 3 November 1363 and 8 January 1364 (*Lit. Cant.* ii. 454–5). There is also a small paper copy of much later date, perhaps made at the time of the lawsuit with the vicar of Pagham in 1524, when a number of pertinent documents were copied from the archbishop's registers.
[4] Including even documents concerning a chantry at Pagham, of no immediate interest to the college.
[5] When the Registers A, B, C, D were re-arranged: see *Hist. MSS. Comm. Report: Various Collections* i. 208–9.
[6] It was a *copy* of the appropriation and not the *carta* (as is wrongly stated in *Lit. Cant.* ii. 511) that the monks sent to Langham 1373–4.
[7] iii. 27.
[8] iii. 28.
[9] iii. 37, 38. Apparently the tenements had only been promised.

the royal exemplification of the original licence of 1363 for the acquisition of the halls and tenements in Oxford. Like the deed of appropriation, the original licence of 1363 was apparently lost for good when the halls were alienated. It does not appear among the college muniments entered into Register B or among the originals, but is only preserved among the patent rolls and in the exemplification of 1373.

With the king's pardon gained and Pagham and the Oxford property confirmed, the first stage of the recovery of the college was accomplished.

Down to about the year 1373, the efforts of the prior and chapter had been directed towards re-establishing the college in security and prosperity. Now that that object had been fairly well accomplished, it was possible to proceed to a more progressive and ambitious policy: firstly the gaining of fresh privileges and secondly the codifying of its latest development. The first part meant a campaign in the court of Rome; the second part was the outcome of negotiations and struggles between the chapter and the archbishop.

The first part of this policy was sketched in a letter written by the prior and chapter (c. September 1373—June 1374), evidently addressed to Cardinal Langham, though there is no explicit mention of his name.[1] This letter bears an interesting resemblance to the previous letter to Langham in October 1370 in its expression of gratitude, its statement of the difficulties of the moment and great confidence in the cardinal's patronage. After expressing a longing for another, now overdue, visit from the cardinal, it reports on the state of Canterbury College, described as the 'work of your hands', for it was Langham who had rescued it for the monks: the college was secure and flourishing and consisted of a master and seven monks. Taken as a statement of fact, this is an exaggeration, for the treasurer's rolls of these years do not show anything like that number at Oxford; but it was probably meant as a constitutional ideal, the language of a prospectus, perhaps coloured by a natural desire to magnify the good effects of the cardinal's patronage, and it is true that a few years later, in 1375–6, we find as many as six monks at Oxford. Next, the monks explain their wants. There seem to have been three distinct matters that needed furthering in the court of Rome:

(1) The college lacks privileges and exemptions, which it ought to possess.

(2) Strangely enough the church of Pagham, which had recently been so safe at the curia and so precarious in England, was now threatened at Rome by certain of the monks' enemies, who were trying

[1] iii. 31.

to 'impetrate' the church as vacant: i.e., apparently, to obtain the rectory by papal provision. There is no clue as to the identity of these 'emuli'. Is it possible that they were the evicted seculars?[1] In that case, however, it is strange that they are not mentioned by name. Apart from the use of influence or money, it is difficult to see what arguments the adversary could bring forward to prove that the church of Pagham was vacant and its appropriation invalid; but there was one weakness in the monks' position which might be seized upon: namely, that the appropriation, made and confirmed by the archbishops of Canterbury, had never yet received papal confirmation. When Archbishop Islip in September 1363 had asked for papal confirmation for his new foundation, the appropriation of Pagham had been pointedly omitted from the confirmation which was granted.[2] In view of their danger, the monks send copies of their titles to the church of Pagham: i.e. the king's letter of pardon and what was probably Islip's deed of appropriation. They seem to convey a hint to the cardinal to obtain a papal confirmation for them.

(3) The third matter concerned the old feud between the monks of Christ Church and the general chapter. As we have seen, it probably had more connexion with the history of the college than appears at first sight, but no doubt it was inserted here simply as one of the monks' grievances. Here too they seem to have in mind the possibility of procuring a papal exemption.

Finally, while committing these matters to the cardinal's care, the monks undertake to pay the costs.

The three matters mentioned in this letter have a corresponding sequel of documents: the desired privileges, obtained by degrees. In the first place, about this time (1373–4) Langham's registrar, Master Roger Croxton, was rewarded for his labours in the curia on behalf of the college.[3] Unless the reference is to the old process of 1370, these labours were probably the immediate result of the monks' letter to Langham. Then the monks made more serious preparations: in an instrument dated 20 July 1375 in the prior's chapel at Canterbury, they appointed Master Thomas Southam, the archdeacon of Oxford, as their proctor for all manner of business and lawsuits that any of their adversaries might bring against them in the court of Rome. The result of this appointment seems to have been the obtaining of the first of the privileges, a papal bull dated at Avignon 2 December 1375, *de statu magistri sive custodis collegii Cantuar' Oxonie*.[4] The rubric thus given is rather misleading, for the bull really deals with studies

---

[1] It was just about this time that Wyclif obtained the renewal of his promised provision of a canonry at Lincoln, 26 December 1373: Workman i. 203.

[2] iii. 9.   [3] Extract 4 below.   [4] iii. 32.

and degrees of both 'masters' (or wardens) and fellows of the college.

The death of Cardinal Langham at Avignon on 22 July 1376 deprived the Canterbury monks of their great patron and their proctor, Thomas Southam, was now busy as one of the executors of his master's will. It was not, apparently, until two years afterwards that the monks took up again their former policy. By that time, they had produced from among their own number an able representative to be sent to the court of Rome: Thomas Chillynden, afterwards prior of Christ Church. He became famous as a great builder and improver, but it was as a canonist that he was trained and first rose to distinction. Appropriately enough, he was an alumnus of the new Canterbury College; in fact, his legal mission to Rome came in the middle of his Oxford career, between his baccalaureate and his doctorate. He must have been sent to Rome about the end of 1378, for on 25 March 1379 he obtained a bull exempting Christ Church from the general chapters of the English black monks and thus successfully dealt with a long and troublesome problem, the third point raised in the letter to Langham.[1] There remained the appropriation of Pagham to be confirmed and Chillynden procured this a few months later, in a bull dated Rome 9 August 1379.[2]

Since the death of Langham, the prior and chapter had been forced to rely on their own initiative and their action in the court of Rome had been successful. It was natural that attention should be turned towards the constitution of the college now that its external position had been strengthened. The next five years saw the development of the constitution and its final settlement in the form which it was to retain for the rest of the college's existence.

Unfortunately, the first constitutional experiments showed more initiative than tact or consideration. Once more, as in Islip's last years, it was forgotten that the college was the joint concern of the archbishop and his chapter, and this time the monks were the offenders. They apparently appointed a warden to the college on their own authority, without consulting the archbishop (Simon Sudbury), who was not slow to vindicate his rights. On 19 March 1380 he appeared at the cathedral priory at Canterbury, forced the monks to apologise, annulled their appointment and announced his intention of making a

[1] Wilkins, *Concilia* iii. 126: 'Ista bulla fuit impetrata et concessa a domino Urbano vi A.D. MCCCLXXVIII et tempore regis Ricardi secundi anno ij° expensis prioris et capituli ecclesie Christi Cant' tempore domini Simonis de Sudbury, archiepiscopi Cant' et legum doctoris, ac venerabilis fratris domini Iohannis Vynche de Wynchelse prioris dicte ecclesie, et fratris Thome Chillingdene, monachi dicte ecclesie et bacalarii in decretis, procuratoris dicte ecclesie Cant' in Romana curia tunc existentis.'

[2] iii. 34.

fresh ordinance concerning the appointment of the wardens.[1] A few days later, on 27 March 1380, the archbishop filled up the vacant wardenship by appointing William Dover[2] and by this time, we learn, he had already made a composition with the prior and chapter concerning the appointment of wardens. Unfortunately, the text of the ordinance or composition has not survived; but the whole episode is very interesting, especially as it seems from a later reference that Archbishop Sudbury made some kind of revision of the statutes, which was probably used as the basis of Archbishop Courtenay's final codification.[3]

A little later, on 20 May 1380, the prior and chapter issued a licence to the college to pledge the college and its goods in a particular case.[4] There are two points of constitutional interest here. Firstly, this seems another high-handed action, for though the monks admit that the archbishop's consent is by statute necessary for such a licence, they seem to dispense with it in this case. Secondly, they mention the statutes for the government of the college 'which we have recently made'. Either this means that the monks by themselves had made some statutes, or else it is the monks' way of referring to statutes made jointly by the archbishop and the chapter. In that case the archbishop must have already framed his revised statutes, covering not only the vexed question of the wardens' appointment, but also other matters of government, such as the pledging of college goods here treated.

In 1381 Archbishop Sudbury was succeeded by William Courtenay, who was able and willing to keep the chapter in its place. On 15 September 1382, he absolved from office the principal obedientiaries at Christ Church—the subprior, the cellarer, the chamberlain, the precentor and the two penitentiaries—and, as we learn from another reference, this action was but part of a wholesale dismissal of all the obedientiaries appointed by his predecessor, Sudbury, at Christ Church.[5] It was quite within the archbishop's rights and was probably nothing very extraordinary, but it seems to show a firm determination to overhaul and control the administration of the cathedral priory. The warden of the college, as being in effect one of the obedientiaries, was naturally included in the changes. In the latter part of September the archbishop dismissed the existing warden, John Aleyn, and evidently intended to make a fresh appointment in the normal way. However, he changed his mind and on 18 October 1382 took the unprecedented step of suspending the wardenship and placed the college under the care of William Dover as temporary *yconomus* or administrator, *donec de magistro eidem collegio sit*

[1] iii. 36. [2] *Ibid.* [3] iii. 45.
[4] iii. 37. [5] iii. 39.

provisum.[1] For practical purposes, no doubt William Dover occupied much the same position as when he had been warden a few years before. The important point is that Courtenay kept the wardenship (or 'mastership') technically vacant for about ten months.

What could have been his motive? He could not, in the literal sense of his own words, simply be waiting to find a suitable candidate: that would not have reflected much credit on the qualities of the Canterbury monks. In view of both previous and subsequent developments,[2] it seems most likely that Courtenay had decided to take up the work of revising the constitution of the college begun by Sudbury in his ordinance or composition. From the very beginning of the college, the appointment of the warden had loomed large in all constitutional schemes, and for this reason it may have seemed best to keep the office vacant pending negotiations. It was perhaps as a preliminary survey for some such important work that Courtenay on 26 November 1382 made a personal visitation of Canterbury College[3] and a few days later, 2 December, he wrote to the prior and chapter informing them that at the visitation he had handed over to William Dover the 'real' administration of the college goods and forbidding them to hinder him, under pain of excommunication. Such a threat suggests that he expected some opposition, for usually the archbishops were content to send a simple admonition to the fellows, not to the chapter, to admit and obey the new warden.

Certainly, there is evidence of some excitement and anxiety on the part of the prior and chapter. Some Christ Church accounts for the sixth year of Richard II (22 June 1382—22 June 1383) record the sending of messengers and interviews with the archbishop on the subject of the 'yconomus'. Once it was thought necessary for the prior himself to come, inevitably at great expense, to London, to speak with the archbishop, and on another occasion Lord Cobham was interviewed on this matter.[4]

Unfortunately, we do not know what passed between the archbishop and the chapter until July 1383, when a crisis was reached. Courtenay had conceived some 'rancour' against the monks for something that they had done[5] and about the middle of July he proceeded, 'as justice demanded', to order the sequestration of the income from the farmed-out rectory of Pagham, stipulating however that the *yconomus* was to be allowed £12 for the payment of a tenth and other charges and that he was to be free to make his own arrangements for

---
[1] iii. 40.
[2] The archbishop and chapter soon came to discuss the constitution: iii. 42 ff.
[3] ii. 131; iii. 45. There are very few records of such visitations of the college.
[4] Extract 15 below.   [5] iii. 43.

the farming of the church.¹ It seems likely that the archbishop meant to strike at the chapter rather than at the college, especially in view of his consideration for the *yconomus*. In that case, the sequestration was a clumsy method of attack, for Pagham was always, strictly speaking, the property of the college, not of the chapter, and naturally the college would be the first to suffer. The prior and chapter would not keep their monks up at Oxford at a loss, but would begin to withdraw them. This was, in fact, what happened. In the quarter beginning at midsummer 1383, according to the college accounts, the fellows' salaries cease altogether: some of them go down, those that remain are paid privately by the prior and chapter.² It is impossible not to connect this retrenchment with the sequestration.

At about the same time that Courtenay ordered the sequestration, the prior and chapter wrote to him (19 July 1383).³ In their letter they explain, in a humble enough manner, what they think ought to be the constitutional programme of the college, viz.:

(a) As to the office of warden, they suggest the traditional method, used from the beginning, by which they nominate three persons, one of whom is chosen by the archbishop.

(b) As to the other monks, scholars or fellows of the college: one is to be appointed in the same way as the warden and the other is to be appointed freely by the prior and chapter alone. For the present, the funds of the college will not support more than two fellows in addition to the warden. This estimate is very different from the establishment of a warden and seven fellows which the monks had sanguinely described to Langham ten years before: it perhaps erred as much by way of underestimation.

(c) As to the five secular 'poor scholars', who are not fellows but live on the charity of the college, three are to be chosen by the archbishop and two by the chapter. Of the archbishop's nominees, one is always to be a native of Pagham. This is our sole source of information concerning this 'close' scholarship.

The monks ask the archbishop to assent to this scheme and send two of their number, Thomas Chillynden and William Breggar, to discuss it with him if necessary. Evidently this document is a continuation of the interviews already mentioned.

However, the archbishop was not satisfied and at the same time the sequestration must have been put in force. Hence the monks had to reduce their claims very considerably in their next letter, 5 August 1383.⁴ For the peace of their house, they make the following concessions:

¹ iii. 41.
² ii. 130.
³ iii. 42.
⁴ iii. 43.

(a) The office of warden to remain as in the previous scheme, except that for this particular occasion the archbishop is to be allowed to put up one of the three nominees from whom the warden has to be chosen.

(b) Apparently the fellowships were the real cause of dispute: here the greatest concession is made. During the time of Courtenay himself *all* the fellowships, as many as the college can afford, are to be filled in the same way as the wardenship, the archbishop choosing one of the chapter's three nominees. After Courtenay has ceased to be archbishop, however, the prior and chapter intend to fill up the fellowships at their own discretion. Even in their humiliation the monks grimly hint that an archbishop is mortal, while a chapter is immortal and has the last word.

(c) The 'poor scholars' are to be chosen as described in the previous letter.

If this scheme does not please the archbishop, he must do what he thinks best with the college and its goods; but the monks entreat him in the most solemn manner to accept these articles and to bring to effect the statutes lately conceived by Archbishop Sudbury, with necessary additions. Here is a most important reference to Sudbury's revision of the statutes; and it was probably out of this suggestion and as the termination of these long and sometimes painful negotiations that Courtenay's final revision of the statutes arose.

It seems that the archbishop accepted these proposals in almost all particulars. In the first place, he proceeded to make appointments to the wardenship and the first and second fellowships, in each case selecting one of three nominees put forward by the chapter.[1] In some respects, he seems to have departed from the chapter's last proposals: apparently he allowed the chapter to put forward *all three* nominees for the wardenship instead of naming one himself, as had been arranged.[2] Moreover, he appointed to the first fellowship Thomas Everard, one of the candidates for the second fellowship, and to the second fellowship Thomas Dover, one of the candidates for the first fellowship; and a few days later he replaced Thomas Dover by another. Finally William Dover, in consideration for his work as *yconomus* and warden, was made 'perpetual master or warden' by the archbishop on 29 January 1384.[3] Perhaps this was literally intended to be an appointment for life, for there is provision for such a case in Courtenay's statutes,[4] but for some reason it was not strictly carried out: William Dover lived on until 1414, but had ceased to be warden by 1394.[5] By the time that this appointment was made, Archbishop Courtenay had carried out the final proposal so earnestly made in the

[1] iii. 45 ff.   [2] iii. 45.   [3] iii. 48.
[4] iii. 173.   [5] iii. 53.

monks' letter of 5 August 1383[1] by publishing the final revision of the college statutes, on the occasion of a visitation of Christ Church chapter on 16 January 1384. After solemn treaty and mature deliberation between the archbishop and the chapter, both parties set their seals to the document, which was then sent on to Oxford to be sealed by the warden and fellows.

Courtenay declared that he was basing his new statutes on the original statutes of Islip, of which he was preserving and republishing some parts and abolishing others, and that he was finally making some additions, as the monks had already suggested in their letter. The question arises, how much of these revised statutes represents the original ones? We may at once put on one side the concluding sections, which are explicitly described as Courtenay's additions.[2] The preceding, longer and more essential part claims to be a repetition of Islip's enactments.[3] This claim has been rejected by some writers: by Rashdall, who thought the monks had imposed upon Courtenay, and by Sheppard, who thought that Courtenay must be quoting some statutes made by *Simon* Langham in mistake for those of *Simon* Islip.[4] Both hypotheses are really groundless, as more recent writers have realised. It would surely have been against Langham's policy to make *new* statutes for the college, even if he had had time to do so, since in restoring the monks he simply claimed to be restoring the *status quo*. As to Courtenay's being imposed upon, the foregoing narrative will have shown that he was astute and firm enough in dealing with his chapter. This problem of the supposed deception of Courtenay is simply created by those statutes of Islip printed by Wilkins, which are so secular in tone. So long as historians believed that these were the original foundation statutes, it seemed impossible to take Courtenay at his word when he proceeded to quote a document of a monastic tone. Once we realise how little claim the secular statutes from Wilkins have to be taken as the foundation statutes, there remains nothing to disprove Courtenay's statement. One half of Islip's original statutes must have dealt with the monk-warden and monk-fellows, who certainly formed part of the original scheme; and it was presumably this half that Courtenay was quoting. On the other hand, it must be admitted that there is nothing by which to check the accuracy of Courtenay's quotations except the *verba ordinacionis*, which are apparently a fragment of the original statutes and certainly do tally with Courtenay's version.[5]

---

[1] iii. 45. And finally a formal request had been made for the revision by the warden and fellows, according to the preamble: iii. 173.
[2] iii. 179.
[3] iii. 173, 178.
[4] *Lit. Cant.* ii. xxxi.
[5] iii. 3. 173.

There is one point worth noting. Courtenay was not the first to try his hand at revising the statutes: the monks invited him to bring to effect the revision of the statutes in the form lately conceived by Sudbury. The need for revision had naturally been felt so long as the original statutes were still technically in force. All those parts dealing with the original secular fellowships had become obsolete since the papal sentence in 1370, and it was doubtless these that Courtenay rejected. The mutilated body that remained would need patching and smoothing off. In view of the successive revisions, while we may believe that Courtenay was substantially republishing the monastic parts of Islip's statutes, we need not believe that he was always quoting verbatim.

The publication of Courtenay's statutes in January 1384 closes the first, eventful and formative period of the college's history. What follows is simply the working of the constitution as then fixed and the succession of small careers. It is of no less interest, but demands a separate treatment: analysis, not narrative.

After the publication of Courtenay's statutes in 1384, the college settles down to a comparatively uneventful course. There were, however, a few outstanding landmarks. In or about the year 1393, when a solid block of land had been acquired, the energetic Prior Chillynden set about rebuilding the college in a permanent form. He seems to have completed the western, southern and eastern ranges, including the chapel, and to have left only the northern range and the library to be added in the course of the fifteenth century. Then came the brilliant career of Sellyng and the friendship of Chaundler of New College. The college was brought, very slightly and gently, into touch with the vanguard of the Renaissance in England and possibly sheltered Linacre and More. At the end of the century the college owed much to Cardinal Morton, who enriched the chapel, increased the number of monk-fellows and made the college the dispenser of his exhibitions for seculars.

The registers of the chancellor's court throw a certain amount of light upon the monks of the college in the sixteenth century. This court seems to have been held sometimes within the college itself, when the warden or a sojourner happened to be acting as commissary or vicechancellor.[1] The monks generally come before the court as suing to recover debts; in fact, they appear rather in the light of

---

[1] For the court see *Mun. Acad.* i. ci-civ; Mallet i. 171–4. On 1 November 1502 when Thomas Walker, maniciple of Durham College, was accused of clipping coin, a witness was examined at Canterbury College, apparently before Dr Atwater (*Registrum Cancellarii 1498–1506*, ed. W.T. Mitchell (1980) 279).

amateur pawnbrokers to their neighbours. This was not unnatural, for the warden especially would be handling large sums of money and could readily oblige a local tradesman or his wife. There is no evidence of usury, though such a thing was not unknown, even among ecclesiastics.¹ Still, such a practice seems obviously out of keeping with the monastic state and on one occasion gave rise to some malicious gossip spread by the manciple of Peckwater Inn about one of the monk-fellows, John Deryng, and the wife of the college cook. However, the woman's dealings with Deryng were proved to have been merely a matter of borrowing 7s. 6d.² On another occasion, the warden's claim on a baker was met with a counter-claim for an unpaid bill.³ When a scholar of Canterbury College, John Thatcher, was summoned by the commissary for an act of violence, the warden refused to give him up. 'My scholere schall not cum: Y am as able to rule my howse as he [the commissary] ys.'⁴ Another interesting sidelight upon the college life is given when a former manciple confessed that one John Bagwell, a member of the college (but happily not a fellow), had ordered him to falsify the buttery book.⁵

There is one case in which the monks appear not as creditors but as debtors, namely in their relations with the great college which grew up beside them. When in 1525 St Frideswide's gave place to Cardinal College, it seems that Canterbury College went on paying to the new college the rent of 40s. formerly due to St Frideswide's;⁶ but when Henry VIII refounded the college in 1532 as King's College, the Canterbury monks apparently tried to avoid payment. In 1534 the dean and canons of the King's College complained of this to Cromwell and in 1536 they produced in the vicechancellor's court a bond signed by the warden of Canterbury College for the payment of £9, which may represent four and a half years' arrears. When the warden did pay the rent, he complained that he was forced to pawn the college plate since his master, the prior of Canterbury, would make him no allowance for the purpose.⁷

At the beginning of the sixteenth century, there was no sign of decline in the prosperity of the college: it is only because we look backwards in the light of subsequent events that we seem to see something ominous in the appearance of Edward Bockyng, first as fellow in 1504, then as warden 1510–18. His fellow-sufferer, John Deryng, was many years his junior, having entered Christ Church in 1519 and appearing as a fellow in 1528. Bockyng appears to have been a normal, respectable product of the college. He studied and graduated in theology, preached to his brethren and was eventually

¹ Cf. Edmund Bishop, *Liturgica Historica* (1918) 425. ² iii. 267.
³ iii. 265. ⁴ iii. 271. ⁵ iii. 272. ⁶ ii. 261. ⁷ iii. 148, 155, 269, 270.

recalled to take office at home. But there is nothing in the college documents to throw any light on the personalities of the two monks.

The warden from 1524 to 1534 was the notorious Richard Thornden, 'Dick of Dover'. The state papers show how he joined in the scramble for the favour of the new power, Thomas Cromwell. He was apparently commissioned to collect evidence against Deryng in 1534,[1] though it was reported that 'the Warden of Canterbury College is an enemy to the King's cause, and harps against it in his sermons and conversation'.[2] This may have been merely jealous gossip, for he kept in with Cromwell all the same. His great anxiety was to be promoted from the wardenship of the college to the wardenship of the manors of Christ Church, which office he did obtain, thanks to his patron.[3] He next coveted the prior's office itself in 1538. Cranmer wrote to recommend him to Cromwell in most laudatory terms. We can at least believe that he was 'veray tractable, and as redy to sett forwarde his pryncis causes, as no man more of his coote'.[4] However, it was a false alarm, for the existing prior remained in office till the dissolution. Next year Thornden got the suffragan bishopric of Dover, which he held till his death in 1558. In 1553 he was vice-dean of Canterbury and re-introduced the Mass into the cathedral—which caused Cranmer to revise his former opinion of him and denounce him as a 'false, flattering, lying and dissembling monk'.[5]

Thornden was succeeded as warden by William Sandwych, who was a rival suitor for the prior's office in 1538 and in the previous year had been appointed by Cromwell to preach at St Paul's cross.[6] One other member of the college played a notable part: William Jerome, whom Thornden praised and recommended to Cromwell as a suitable successor in the wardenship in 1534.[7] He did not get the office. He was a follower of the new order of things. In 1537 he got a dispensation from his monastic vows in a curious document issued by Cranmer under the authority of crown and parliament.[8] He became vicar of Stepney and was burned as a heretic in 1540.[9]

Among the state papers is a curious list, made after 1538, of the monks of Christ Church Canterbury, with their offices, degrees and ages and comments as to their character or ability: 'a good man', 'witty', or 'simple'. It was presumably drawn up for Cromwell's use,

[1] iii. 147.   [2] *Letters and Papers, Henry VIII* vii. no. 101.
[3] Cf. iii. 146–8.   [4] iii. 154.
[5] J. Strype, *Memorials of Archbishop Cranmer* (1854) 456.
[6] iii. 151.   [7] iii. 148.
[8] Searle, p. 194; D. S. Chambers, *Faculty Office Registers 1534–1549* (1966) 98.
[9] Hennessey, *Novum Repertorium*, 411; Foxe, *Acts and Monuments* (ed. Pratt) v. 429 ff.

perhaps as a guide to the giving of places on the new foundation. It shows that the community were under close observation or espionage.[1]

Three monks of Canterbury College were implicated as supporters of Dame Elizabeth Barton, the Holy Maid of Kent, and her revelations: W. Hadley II, Edward Bockyng and John Deryng.

When it comes to the end, we find no such heroic resistance among the monks of Christ Church as, for instance, among those stricter contemplatives, the martyrs of the Charterhouse. The destruction of Bockyng and Deryng was well calculated to produce a submissive frame of mind, to 'give understanding', as the inquisitors would have said. The monks of Christ Church acknowledged the royal supremacy on 12 December 1534 and in the next year came Cromwell's visitation. Of the last years in the college there is not much documentary evidence: only one annual account has survived for the period after 1521. The inventory of 1534 is a poor sort of document: for the first time, the scribe has not taken the trouble to give the second folios of the books and two of the fellows, Jerome and Warham, have either lost or sold the chalices entrusted to them. It looks as though the monks were already growing listless in the face of the inevitable destruction and spoliation. Some of the monk-fellows and one 'parson Parker', perhaps a secular sojourner, were reputed to have eaten fleshmeat in Lent.[2] What wonder if the old discipline was breaking down when Cranmer himself was lecturing on Hebrews at Canterbury.

The surrender of Christ Church in 1540 was naturally accompanied by the surrender of the college, together with the church of Pagham, to the crown, on 10 April 1540.[3] That meant the end of the college as an institution. The buildings and site, and Pagham, were regranted to the dean and chapter of the new foundation on 16 May 1541.[4] By their foundation statutes, the dean and chapter were bound to maintain twenty-four students at Oxford and Cambridge, and possibly there was some scheme for using the college for this purpose. However, on 13 March 1545 they leased the college to a certain Richard Maisters for ten years.[5] A few months later, in November 1545, all this was changed. The king, intending to found two colleges at Oxford and Cambridge, was pleased to remit the obligation of the dean and chapter to maintain students, in return for which they

---

[1] iii. 151.
[2] *Letters and Papers, Henry VIII* xiv. pt. 1. no. 684.
[3] *Letters and Papers, Henry VIII* xv. no. 488; Rymer, *Foedera* xiv. 670; *Eighth Report of the Deputy Keeper*, app. II. 36.
[4] *Letters and Papers, Henry VIII* xvi. no. 878 (59).
[5] iii. 156.

granted him the college, among other properties.[1] A few years later the college with the surrounding tenements was granted to the King's College, now refounded as the Cathedral Church of Christ in place of Oseney. The buildings of the college went to form the original 'Canterbury Quad' of Christ Church and survived down to the building of the present quad at the end of the eighteenth century. They can be seen in the top left-hand corner of Loggan's view of Christ Church. The earliest accounts of Christ Church contain periodical references to the repair of the buildings. Perhaps the only portion surviving now is part of the eastern wall of the deanery garden.

[1] iii. 156.
[2] iii. 157.

3
THE MONK-FELLOWS

THE warden and fellows of Canterbury College were monks of Christ Church and their life at Oxford was only a phase, though a very important one, in their monastic career. It is this fact that they were temporarily borrowed, so to speak, from quite a different sphere of life that distinguishes them from the members of the secular colleges. In the first place, the prelude to their Oxford life was, of course, their entrance into the monastery of Christ Church Canterbury, their condition and training.

The practice of training boys to the monastic life from an early age—still contemplated, for instance, in the constitutions of Lanfranc—seems to have died out in the later centuries of the middle ages[1] and the age of entrance and profession was comparatively late. J.B. Sheppard, speaking of the 'vital statistics' of the Canterbury monks, calculated from thirty-three cases that the average age at profession was 16.5 years.[2] It is hard to see how he arrived at such a low estimate. The materials on which he relied (and more) were later published, in substance at least, by W.G. Searle[3] in a chronological list of the monks of Christ Church Canterbury, giving the two essential biographical points, the dates of admission and (down to 1507) of death. The names of the monks are ranged under successive years, but unfortunately it is not clear whether these years are the dates of (a) the 'shaving' and clothing of the novices, or (b) their profession. The two functions might often fall in different years: the saints' days on which they took place are given in the list, more explicitly towards the end of the period. As seniority went by profession rather than by natural years, the age at death is not often recorded. However, thirty cases where the ages are given between 1432 and 1502, taken in conjunction with the corresponding dates of admission and death, give an average age of nineteen years at 'admission', whether that may mean clothing or profession. This seems to agree with the stricter requirements of canon law, which placed the lowest age of admission at eighteen,[4] although sometimes a much

---

[1] D. Knowles, *Monastic Order* (1949) 421.
[2] *Hist. MSS. Commission Report* ix (1) 127.
[3] Searle xxi, 172–96.
[4] X 3. 31. 6; Lyndwood, *Provinciale* 3. 18 (ed. 1679, p. 202).

lower age was allowed.¹ It is important to notice that this average age at Canterbury did not remain level: from 1432 to about 1470 the average is high—about twenty years; but after 1470 the age at admission seems to sink to about 17.3 years. Even that is higher than Sheppard's average.

There was, then, no question of 'kidnapping' the young, such as was alleged against the friars: on the whole, discrimination rather than proselytism was needed and admission into Christ Church was hedged about by recommendations,² a waiting list³ and some kind of entrance examination. Candidates were examined under oath in certain articles, which still survive, concerning possible canonical impediments to admission, such as matrimony, debts, homicide, excommunication, unfree birth.⁴ Moreover, they were expected to have attained already a certain standard in grammar and song: on these grounds, the prior and convent in 1324 rejected a candidate in other respects personally acceptable, who was advised to go back and learn the 'grammatical terms' and the 'use and art of singing and reading' before presenting himself again. The candidates are usually described as clerks and must evidently have passed through some kind of grammar school. One novice had been a chorister of the archbishop's and a secular scholar at Canterbury College,⁵ and others came from the almonry school.⁶ Probably the actual standard of education required varied from time to time. Besides these young clerks men from other monasteries, like Henry Wodehull, or from other orders (canons regular, for instance) were admitted, but men coming from the world late in life seem to have been rare.⁷

The monks, as their names show, were recruited chiefly from the villages of Kent and especially from those in which Christ Church priory had property. This double bond of landowning and recruiting helps to explain the priory as a social force in the countryside. It was from their places of origin that the monks took their rudimentary surnames, in order to distinguish between the innumerable Johns and Williams and Roberts: the practice began at least as early as the return from exile in 1207 and the connecting and explanatory 'de' dropped out about the middle of the fourteenth century. Identity of surname must therefore not necessarily be taken to show kinship. In the sixteenth century, instead of place names, patronal names were

---

¹ Fourteen or fifteen: X 3. 31. 8, 11; VI 3. 14. 1.
² e.g. *Lit. Cant.* ii. 300, 362, 452.
³ *Lit. Cant.* ii. 246.   ⁴ *Lit. Cant.* i. 331–2; cf. ii. 137.
⁵ Searle 187 (A.D. 1424).   ⁶ Searle 106 (A.D. 1468).
⁷ An exception is Master John Kynton, 1408: Searle 185.

sometimes assumed as surnames: e.g. Thomas Bekett, Henry Audoen, William Jerome, Thomas Anselme. In much the same way, there was at Hyde Abbey a John Alfred;[1] and some monks of Westminster even took allegorical surnames such as Faith and Verity.[2] All this was no doubt the origin of the more modern practice of taking a new patronal Christian name in religion. The surnames, then, usually concealed any family names that the monk might have had,[3] as was shown at the dissolution when some monks produced an alias, a family name. It is therefore very difficult to determine the social status of the monks. They were obviously expected to be educated men, capable of ordination, and no doubt they were drawn from much the same class as the beneficed secular clergy.

Monks were bound by law to make their profession not later than a year after their clothing[4] and at Canterbury they seem to have done so even sooner.[5] The young monk, before and after his profession, had to go through a double training, religious and scholastic. In the first place, he had to learn the observance of the rule and the customs of the house. As a novice, he was under the charge of the novice-master, known at Canterbury as the *magister ordinum*.[6] Amongst other things, the monk had to learn by heart the psalter and other parts of the divine office;[7] and it seems that, chiefly for this purpose, each junior monk was placed in charge of a senior, in some cases for several years. This practice seems indicated in the following extracts:

1435	In crastino sancti Thome martiris I. Cros fuit examinatus in redditu et bene reddit.[8]
1440 (Feb.)	Iohannes Nutun proclamavit W. Chart pro redditu finaliter qui nono kal. Marcii respondit de vi historiis vii responsoriis.[9]
1440 (July)	Proclamatus est Alexander Stapyll pro redditu suo finaliter a magistro suo W. Glastingbury.[10]

[1] Dugdale, *Monasticon* ii. 448.
[2] E.H. Pearce, *Monks of Westminster* 188, 190.
[3] An earlier exception is John Finch or Vynch of Winchelsea, prior 1377–91.
[4] X 3. 31. 22.
[5] See the double dates of *rasi* and *professi* from 1469 onwards in Searle's list, 190 ff.
[6] See Searle's list passim. In 1524 (p. 195) Thomas Lee is called both *magister ordinum* and *magister noviciorum*.
[7] *Chapters* i. 38, 64, 73, 173; ii. 50; T. Wright and J. O. Halliwell, *Reliquiae Antiquae* i (1841) 291.
[8] Corpus Christi Coll. Oxon. MS. 256, fo. 117ᵛ.
[9] Ibid., fo. 119.
[10] Ibid., fo. 119ᵛ.

1457   Item hoc anno xiij° die mensis Augusti frater Ricardus Godmersham fuit examinatus de redditu suo a precentore Roberto Bynne post mortem supprioris I. Wodenysbergh.

1468   Item hoc anno penultimo die mensis Aprilis frater Robertus Deene erat examinatus de redditu suo a precentore Roberto Bynne et senioribus.[1]

Magistri regule beati patris Benedicti instituti per dominum priorem Goldstone[2] cuius anime propicietur Deus

D. I. Sarysbery	I. Holyngborne per duos annos
W. Molasche	habuit R. Fonten et perfecit
	habuit R. Bonyngton et non perfecit
A. Stapyll	habuit R. Boxle si perfecit ignoro
I. Langdon	habuit Wynchylse non perfecit et Lamberherste perfecit
I. Garrard	Wyngham perfecit ⎫ perfecerunt
	Eastry Chylynden ⎭
N. Herst non perfecit ⎫	per duos annos
T. Wylfryde non perfecit ⎭	
R. Godmersham Mylton sunt novelli	
I. Shepeye	habuit dominum W. Lychefelde et dominum I. Ascheforde—non per duos annos
T. Goldstone	habuit Nunam Holden Arundel Sarysbery
I. Elphe si perfecit ignoro	
I. Chartt si perfecit ignoratur	
I. Sudbery audivit Iohannem Chartt.	

The young monk, who had already begun his education before entering the monastery, continued it in the cloister school where, according to the Constitutions of Benedict XII,[3] he was to be instructed in the 'primitive sciences'—in grammar, logic and philosophy—by a monk or, if necessary, a hired secular master. Visitation documents show that the instruction was sometimes lacking. As the matter was a domestic one, with no legal or financial side, at least where a monk and not an outsider was employed, there is very little

[1] Searle 68, 82, 103. Cf. also the regulations for the novices at St Augustine's Canterbury in the *Customary*, ed. E. Maunde Thompson (1902) 204, 212.
[2] Prior Goldstone II, 1495–1517. The list is from Scrap Book B 186.
[3] Wilkins, *Concilia* ii. 594 (c. 8).

evidence. At Christ Church Canterbury among Prior Chillynden's works and improvements was a *nova schola monachorum*.[1] The claustral *lector*, who will be discussed later, may have given this instruction, but was probably concerned with more advanced teaching. In any case, Canterbury College must have supplied a sufficient number of monks competent to teach grammar and 'sophistry'. The university recognised the claustral instruction in the 'primitive sciences' as a substitute for the study of arts in the university[2] and as the age of admission to the monastery sank at the end of the fifteenth century, the grammar element must have become proportionately more important. For the monks who were at Canterbury College, at least, the claustral instruction does not seem to have gone further than grammar in its widest sense. Logic and philosophy were done at Oxford.

The monk destined for the university spent several years in this way before being sent to the college. Owing to the gaps in the college accounts, it is difficult in most cases to determine the exact amount of time between admission to Christ Church Canterbury and arrival at Canterbury College. It is evident that the period varied, without any hard and fast rule, so that monks entering Christ Church together often came up to Oxford in different years. On the whole the monk usually came up after three or four years, but sometimes it was after only two years or eighteen months[3] or, in other cases, after as many as six or eight years.[4] These previous years in the monastery were very important in forming the monk, as he was cut off from the monastery, except for brief visits, during the many years at Oxford and immediately afterwards he might be caught up in some strenuous 'outriding' work or even journeys abroad. A man like Chillynden or Sellynge, once he left Canterbury for Oxford, had little continuous rest. It is the story, as old as St Gregory and St Bernard, of a man entering the contemplative life and being loaded with affairs.

It was only a few picked monks that were sent to the university. The Constitutions of Benedict XII had fixed the proportion of university students at one monk in every twenty in the whole community.[5] With Canterbury College it was finance, quite as much as the size of the community at Canterbury, that determined the number of fellows; but it must be remembered that after 1454 the income was simply a grant from the prior, varying according to the number of fellows he wished to maintain. The college revenues could never have supported the ideal dozen contemplated by Islip: in the early days the number of

[1] *Lit. Cant.* iii. 116.
[2] iii. 63.
[3] e.g. Reginald Goldstone.
[4] e.g. Thomas Humfrey, James Hartey.
[5] Wilkins, *Concilia* ii. 595 (c. 8).

fellows fluctuated, no doubt reflecting the uncertain fortunes of the college. Thus, the treasurer's accounts show that when the college was recovering from the lawsuit and the royal pardon in 1372–3 there were only three fellows and in 1373–4, apparently, only two;[1] in 1374–5 there were four and in 1375–6 six fellows. In 1382–3 there were five fellows, but their income failed in the midsummer quarter and in July 1383 the chapter told the archbishop that the college could not afford more than two fellows besides the warden.[2] Between 1393 and 1395, however, there were as many as seven fellows, but kept very economically.

In the fifteenth century, so far as is shown by the accounts, which are lacking for the first thirty-five years, the usual number of fellows in addition to the warden was three, occasionally two. This was more than most other monasteries maintained, to judge by the monastic sojourners in the college, but it can hardly have fulfilled the requirements of Benedict XII, for at least in December 1448 there were eighty-nine monks at Christ Church Canterbury.[3]

Towards the end of the fifteenth century, there was a remarkable increase in the number of fellows: whereas the college accounts show only two fellows besides the warden in 1486–7 and only one in 1487–8, they show from 1498 until at least 1522 as many as five or six fellows in addition to the warden. As a matter of fact, this increase in numbers was probably more gradual and started earlier than the college accounts suggest and goes back to Prior Sellynge's reign (1472–94). Between 1476 and 1495, side by side with the two or three fellows who appear in the college accounts, there appear in the accounts of the warden of the manors one, two or three additional monks, receiving payments *per assignacionem domini prioris* and *pro cameraria sua*; and from their position in the accounts and from other circumstances, it seems clear that they are students at Oxford.[4] It looks as though Prior Sellynge, as one might expect of him, showed his zeal for learning by maintaining these extra fellows as a piece of personal policy, without charging them to the ordinary college accounts; and then after his death, from 1498 onwards, they are charged to the college accounts. The increased number of fellows must have actually

[1] These figures may not be exhaustive. They are difficult to reconcile with the statement that in 1373–4 there were seven monks with the warden: iii. 32.
[2] iii. 43.
[3] Canterbury Reg. Various Accounts iv, 27 Hen. VI: 'Expense Generales. Et solutum iiii^{xx}ix fratribus die regressionis sancti Thome ...'
[4] e.g. William Chartham, who first appears in this way in 1476, received a gift *pro capa sua* (i.e. *pro capa scolastica*). Richard Sellynge, who only appears in this way, is known to have been at Oxford from a letter: iii. 126.

exceeded the required proportion of one in twenty, for in 1511 there were less than ninety monks at Canterbury.

In addition to this revival in numbers came a further increase from the generous bequest of Cardinal Morton. In his will,[1] as part of his scheme of exhibitions at Oxford and Cambridge for twenty years after his death, he directs that

> 'of those who are to study at Oxford two shall be monks, my brethren of my church of Christ in Canterbury, *over and above the six other monks* of the said church who ought and are bound to study always in the said university of Oxford at the expense of the priory of the said church of Canterbury. And I will that each of the same two monks so studying there at my expense receive yearly of my goods during the term of the said twenty years £6. 13. 4.'

Morton's obituary notice further explains that he educated the two monks at Oxford *ad fidem ortodoxam augendam et verbum Dei predicandum* for seven years during his lifetime, as well as for the twenty years after his death.[2] He had also given to the college chapel some vestments, presumably during his lifetime, as they are not mentioned in his will. In return for his various benefactions, the Canterbury monks in 1499, the year before his death, granted among other things that during his lifetime

> 'Item fratres in universitate studentes, viventes eius exhibicione, qui sacerdos fuerit ter in ebdomada ad minus celebrabit, qui vero sacerdos non fuerit tociens vii psalmos cum letania,'

and after his death

> 'Item fratres studentes in universitate eius viventes exhibicione, qui sacerdos fuerit ter in ebdomada ad minus celebrabit, si vero sacerdos non fuerit totidem dicet exequias pro eadem reverendissima dominacione.'[3]

The two monastic exhibitions must have begun in 1493 and continued until 1520. While there survive several accounts for Morton's exhibitions for seculars, there is only one which mentions explicitly the monks who received the exhibitions: viz. William Gillyngham and John Langdon in 1505-6.[4] They do not appear in the college accounts

[1] *Sede Vacante Wills*, ed. C.E. Woodruff (Kent Archaeol. Soc. Records Branch, 1914) 89.
[2] British Library MS. Arundel 68, fo. 67ᵛ.
[3] Ibid., fo. 68.
[4] iii. 242. According to an undated document, Roger Otforde (after 1512) received £3. 6. 8, obviously a half-year's payment of the exhibition: ii. 273.

for that year, which only show four fellows—a smaller number than usual.

The method of appointing the fellows had been a matter of contention between the prior and chapter of Canterbury and Archbishop Courtenay in the summer of 1383.[1] The archbishop wished to appoint not only the warden but also the fellows, in the same way as he appointed the higher obedientiaries at Canterbury: viz. by choosing one out of three monks nominated by the chapter. The monks had tried to avoid this control at home[2] and were very unwilling to see it extended to the college. They tried to meet the archbishop halfway but at last, for the sake of quiet, gave in entirely for the time being, promising to have their way with his successors. This grim hint seems to have had its effect on Courtenay, although he proceeded to appoint the warden and two fellows, for when in the following January he drew up the final statutes, the prior and chapter were allowed to appoint the fellows freely.[3] It was only if they failed to fill a vacancy within a month that the archbishop intervened to make good the defect.

The career of the monk-fellow at Canterbury College can best be understood by first considering his studies.[4] By the statutes, the fellows were to study theology or, in a limited number of cases, canon law. In this they were like all the other regulars, whether monks or friars, who came to form a very large part of the students of theology, as the university registers show, so that the dissolution of the monasteries for a time seriously depopulated that faculty. The study of theology by the regulars, however, was a matter of great technical difficulty, over which a long controversy was waged between the regulars and the secular authorities of the university. On the one hand, by the middle of the thirteenth century the university had decided that noone could graduate in theology without having previously graduated in arts; on the other hand, the regulars were prevented from graduating in arts, the friars by their own rules, the Benedictines at least by custom. This impasse could only be avoided by a grace or dispensation from the chancellor and masters, severely subject to a kind of blackballing, which was only modified, but not abolished, by an award in 1314.[5] It was the friars, first the Franciscans and then the Dominicans, who bore the brunt of this struggle. The black monks did not begin to come to Oxford until the end of the

[1] iii. 42.
[2] *Lit. Cant.* i. 423; ii. xx, 106.
[3] iii. 174.
[4] For a summary of the theological studies at Oxford, see SA cix ff., especially cxiii ff.; also A.G. Little and F. Pelster, *Oxford Theology and Theologians* (1924) 25 ff.
[5] SA 117.

THE MONK-FELLOWS

thirteenth century[1] and they do not seem to have had any difficulty in obtaining graces, no doubt because they could pay well. Nevertheless, all regulars were still subject to a vexatious technical disability and as late as 1388 the king had to reprove the university for obstructing their degrees.[2]

The monks of Christ Church Canterbury were foremost among the black monks in improving their position. Soon after their re-establishment in the college they obtained, in December 1375, probably through the final good offices of Cardinal Langham, a papal bull[3] by virtue of which the wardens and fellows of Canterbury College were always to be allowed to proceed to theology and, after the proper courses and examination, to receive the doctorate or 'mastership' in that faculty in spite of their not having 'ruled' or graduated in arts, provided that they had been 'otherwise sufficiently instructed in the primitive sciences' (i.e. grammar, logic and philosophy), the statute and custom to the contrary notwithstanding.

It is uncertain how far the Canterbury monks were able to put this privilege into actual practice. A generation later, in 1408 or 1409, they were able to share in a general privilege granted to all the black monks, this time by the university itself at the request of Archbishop Arundel, who no doubt had his own college of Canterbury specially in mind. By the terms of this, if any black monk had fulfilled the 'form' or requirements in the 'primitive sciences' laid down by the Constitutions of Benedict XII and approved by the university, whether he had done so at the university *or anywhere else*, on taking a corporal oath to this effect he was not to be constrained by the university to fulfil any further 'form' in the same 'primitive sciences': provided that the monk, so long as he studied philosophy or canon law in the university as a scholar, had a master in his faculty, to whom he was to pay the usual *collecta* or fees.[4] As the primitive sciences, ideally at least, corresponded to the subjects of the arts faculty, this privilege apparently amounted to a final and complete exemption from graduating in arts. More than a century later, in 1522, Richard Kidderminster, the scholarly and enthusiastic abbot of Winchcomb, procured a further dispensation, concerning the status in the university of monks who had already been admitted to logic or philosophy, according to custom, at home in their monasteries. This seems to have pushed the monk's privilege a step further back. Not only was the monastic training in the primitive sciences to be taken generally, on faith, as an

---

[1] The first black monk to incept was William de Brok in 1298: BRUO i. 272.
[2] CCR 11 Ric. II, p. 378.
[3] iii. 32.
[4] iii. 62.

adequate preparation for theology: it was even, apparently, to give the monk a footing in the faculty of arts itself.[1]

These privileges, while exempting the monk from waste of time and expense in incepting and ruling in arts, at the same time rightly insisted on the substance of a philosophical training in preparation for theology. It is clear that the monk was allowed to make this preparation in his own monastery and so the solution of the academic problem was linked up with the scheme, long cherished and finally elaborated by Benedict XII, of making the monasteries once more centres of study. It seems from the dispensation of 1522 that the monks of some monasteries, at least, began their logical and philosophical studies at home, as also the friars did.[2] The monk-fellows of Canterbury College must have finished their grammar in the monastery, but apparently did their logic and philosophy at Oxford. The college statutes say that the young monk-fellows, being put to the dialectical art *in primitiis eorum*,[3] are to study logic and philosophy for eight years continuously. This regulation is borne out during the fifteenth century by the fellows' graces (in theology), which speak of seven or eight years spent in philosophy.[4] The sixteenth-century graces speak of time spent in logic and philosophy, but without distinguishing it from the time spent in theology.[5] From the total number of years in all three subjects (from eight to ten years), a much shorter time must have been given to logic and philosophy than in the previous century, in spite of the fact that the monks, being on an average younger, really needed a longer preparation. There is nothing in the graces to show that these years of study were not spent at the university; whereas in another case, where a monk's years of study (in canon law) spent in the cloister are included in the grace, there is an explicit statement to that effect.[6] Perhaps the plainest indication of all that the fellows did their logic and philosophy at the university lies in the composition of the college library, which always contained a good proportion of books on logic and philosophy and even some on grammar (in 1501 the latter were kept in the *armarium artis grammatice* and consisted chiefly of Priscian and Hugutio).[7] The books were perhaps partly for the benefit of the *pueri collegi*, but not wholly so: the college records do not show an extraordinary amount of altruism with regard to these dependents.

[1] iii. 145.
[2] A.G. Little, *The Grey Friars in Oxford* (1891) 44.
[3] iii. 174, probably meaning 'when they first came to Oxford', not 'in their first years in the monastery'. The same expression, *in primitiis suis*, is used of the *pueri collegii*, who were seculars: iii. 179.
[4] e.g. iii. 256, 259.
[5] e.g. iii. 246, 248, 250.
[6] iii. 249.
[7] i. 44; cf. i. 27.

According to the college statutes the fellow, having finished his philosophy, was to study theology until he had 'read' (lectured upon) the Sentences or at least was licensed to do so: i.e. until he was ready to take the degree of B.D.[1] This was to be the minimum: it was contemplated that some fellows would stay up to take the doctorate. The university in theory required a religious to study theology for six years before being admitted to 'oppose' in disputation and afterwards to 'respond'.[2] Then, at the period in which Canterbury College existed,[3] the religious was apparently admitted to read the Sentences (B.D.) after 'opposing' for a year. After a further three years, he might incept as D.D. From the graces granted to fellows during the fifteenth century,[4] it appears that the university would in practice allow a monk to 'oppose' after five or six years. In one case it is further specified that the monk shall oppose for a year and in another case that he shall respond *preter formam* once before and three times after his degree, i.e. his admission to read the Sentences. The monk would therefore reach the baccalaureate after about eight years of logic and philosophy and six or seven years of theology—in all, about fourteen or fifteen years after his first coming to Oxford. In the case of one fellow, William Thornden, the graces also concern the doctorate in theology, giving the exercises which the university was willing to accept, but without indicating the actual amount of time required.

In the sixteenth century, after 1505, the evidence from graces becomes more abundant. The monk-fellow was now allowed to oppose after about eight or occasionally nine or ten years altogether of logic, philosophy and theology: i.e. at about the time, or a little later, when he would have been beginning theology in the previous century. In the same way, the period required between opponency and admission as B.D., which had previously been a year, now dwindled from two months (in 1506) to a few weeks in the later graces. Consequently, a sixteenth-century doctorate might be obtained more easily than a fifteenth-century baccalaureate—sometimes after thirteen or fourteen years of logic, philosophy and theology and in one case after only nine years.[5] On the other hand, while earlier practice had apparently only demanded three years between the baccalaureate and the doctorate, in the sixteenth century a much longer period was sometimes supposed to intervene: six or even eight years.[6]

[1] iii. 174.   [2] SA 48.   [3] SA 157, 50.
[4] They have survived, owing to the fragmentary nature of the university registers, only in three cases—those of W. Thornden, W. Sellynge and A. Permystede: iii. 254, 255, 259.
[5] William Sellynge II, 1516, apparently supplicating for D.D.: iii. 257.
[6] R. Thornden: iii. 257, 258.

It is important to remember that a grace represents not a record of fact, but the conditions of an agreement. In using the graces as biographical data, we must be careful not to presume that any particular fellow had already fulfilled the conditions of his grace at the time when he supplicated. Indeed, the grace had necessarily to be obtained in advance of the actual degree-taking: in one case the candidate was told to wait for a year[1] and in other cases the candidates themselves put off taking their degrees, especially the doctorate, for years, no doubt on account of the expense.[2] Sometimes it seems that the degree supplicated for was never actually taken: thus William Thornden supplicated for the doctorate in 1456 and again in 1459, but in 1475 he was still bachelor of divinity.[3] However, when there is evidence of a degree having been taken, the graces show the amount of time that must have been previously spent.

The long academic career indicated in the graces may be checked by the evidence of actual residence in the college accounts, but only to a limited extent. It is difficult to arrive at the normal length of a fellow's stay in Oxford, partly owing to the gaps in the series of accounts, partly because, of those fellows about whom there is most information a few were cut short by death[4] and others—a considerable proportion, about a third—had their careers as fellows also cut short artificially by their appointment to the wardenship.

In the fifteenth century, as has been said before, theological degrees required longer residence than in the following century. Perhaps the longest fellowship on record was that of Robert Eastry, a period of sixteen years (1474–90); but at the end of it, Eastry was no more than a bachelor of divinity. William Thornden, after residing as a fellow for about twelve years, in 1450 applied for a grace for his baccalaureate. Another five years later on, as warden, he supplicated for the doctorate. Other men, however, whose graces have not survived, seem to have obtained easier conditions. Reginald Goldstone was able to become B.D. after ten years (1459–69), partly as fellow, partly as warden. Thomas Chaundler resided for about fourteen years as fellow and warden and by the end of the period at least, in 1501, was doctor of divinity. A fellowship and wardenship, when consecutive, usually seem to have made up a total of about twelve or thirteen years' residence. Mere fellows seem sometimes to have resided about ten or

---

[1] A. Permystede: iii. 254.
[2] e.g. R. Holyngbourne, R. Thornden: iii. 250, 257.
[3] *Lit. Cant.* iii. 291.
[4] e.g. W. Chartham: iii. 128.

eleven years and to have gone down from the university without taking the baccalaureate.[1]

By the sixteenth century, degrees were more easily obtained. Men like Thomas Goldwell, John Langdon II and William Peckham were able to go down as bachelors after residing for ten years. Edward Bockyng (fellow and warden) and William Sellynge II (fellow) took the degree of B.D. together in 1513 after nine years' actual residence, which was more than was required by Sellynge's grace at least. After another five years of wardenship, Bockyng became D.D., while Sellynge resided as fellow for about four years more and, though he supplicated for D.D., apparently did not actually incept. These statistics, however, are simply based on existing records. In the early sixteenth century, just when there is most complete and continuous information as to the fellows' residence, a fresh element of uncertainty comes in owing to Morton's exhibitions for the two monks. Any fellow may have been in residence as Morton's exhibitioner before he actually appears in the college acounts. On the other hand the fellows cited above, with the exception of William Peckham, appeared in the college accounts so soon after their admission at Canterbury (after about three or four years) that there was very little time for them to have held Morton's exhibition previously.

Canon law was a far less exacting study than theology. For the baccalaureate the surviving graces of the fifteenth century[2] require in the first place from one to three years spent in the faculty of arts and then two or three years in canon law. One of the fellows, however, Richard Gravene, added to this six years' study of the Decrees 'in his cloister'. The graces do not mention the preliminary study of civil law required by the university statutes,[3] but on the other hand the books in the college library seem to show that the fellows made some study of civil law. In any case, the period required for the baccalaureate in canon law was very much shorter than that required for the degree of B.D. Thomas Chartham, one of the canonists, cannot have come to the college before 1463 and by 1469 he had apparently gone down, but in 1470 he was described as bachelor of Decrees. There are no surviving graces and very few precise biographical details to throw light on those fellows who proceeded to the doctorate.

Canon law was essentially the line of study to be taken up by a busy, efficient man of affairs like Thomas Chillynden, who was sent to Rome to obtain bulls for the monastery between his baccalaureate and doctorate; and in the same way another canonist, John Wodnysbrowgh, was sent as a proctor to the Council of Pavia. On the other

[1] e.g. A. Permystede, W. Sellynge I.
[2] iii. 249, 254.
[3] SA 46.

hand Richard Godmersham, doctor of canon law, seems to have led a quiet and scholarly life: after being warden of the college, he was for some years lector in the claustral school at Canterbury. There were never many canonists among the fellows and at the end of the fifteenth century they seem to have died out. At that time Richard Sellynge, apparently one of the monk-fellows, wished to turn from arts (probably in preparation for theology) to law. Whether he was allowed to do so we do not know.[1] In the sixteenth century, there is no evidence of any of the fellows taking a degree in canon law. This decay of the study of canon law in the college is all the more curious as the library continued to be stocked with books on the subject.

Between 1363 and 1540 there are just over a hundred wardens and fellows who can be traced by name in the college accounts and other documents, but there were, of course, many others, especially in the early fifteenth century, whose names are now lost. Out of these hundred recorded fellows there are thirty-nine who appear to have taken degrees at Oxford. In theology there were twenty-one bachelors and eleven doctors and in canon law four bachelors and three doctors. One fellow, Henry Henfylde (ob. 1396), is once described as a bachelor of arts. This is a very unusual degree for a monk: possibly it is a mistake for bachelor of divinity, which Henfylde certainly was, or he may have taken the degree before becoming a monk.[2] Moreover, five of the fellows are known to have taken degrees abroad and another, Henry Wodehull, the first warden, had already graduated before migrating from Abingdon to Canterbury.

The fellows were not allowed to take any degree without the permission of the prior and chapter of Canterbury; the warden had only to obtain the permission of the archbishop. Such a rule was necessary on account of the heavy expenses of graduation, which ultimately fell upon the prior and chapter. The expenses of the baccalaureate were not so heavy: the graces involved payments ranging from 20s. to 40s. in the fifteenth century and about 6s. 8d. or less in the sixteenth century. In 1378–9 John Aleyn received 73s. 4d. on graduating B.D.[3] and in 1452 William Petham received 20s. on graduating, apparently, as bachelor of canon law.[4] The fellows in the sixteenth century sometimes took their bachelor's degree in pairs, as Edward Bockyng and William Sellynge did in 1513, Richard Thornden and Roger Otforde in 1522.

The cost of inception in either faculty was enormous.[5] The inceptor had to feast the regents and to give fees and presents, 'liveries',

[1] iii. 126.
[2] iii. 45.
[3] Extract 10 below.
[4] Extract 62 below.
[5] e.g. iii. 84.

THE MONK-FELLOWS

gloves, even plate[1] to the masters, bedells and servants. By the university statutes the 'possessioned' religious, except the actual heads of monasteries, were allowed to pay a composition fee of 20 marks in place of the feast to the regents.[2] In actual fact, a grace of the fifteenth century demanded £20 in place of the feast.[3] The composition fee was reduced in the sixteenth century to 10 marks and even to £2 in the case of Richard Thornden in 1531 on the grounds of the financial difficulties of his monastery.[4] It was sometimes found convenient and economic for monk-fellows to incept in pairs, a theologian and a canonist together. Thus, in 1383–4 over £30 was granted towards the expenses of John Aleyn (theology) and Thomas Chillynden (law).[5] There is a full account of the expenses of the inception of John Langdon (theology) and Richard Godmersham (law) in 1410:[6] the total expenses of feasting and presents and journeys come to over £118—which, however, included a 'livery' at a cost of £53. 15. 0. There is a similar account for the inception of John Sarysbury (theology) and John Wodnysbrowgh (canon law) about 1428.[7] In this case the joint feast was compounded for by a payment of £20, but none the less there was a private supper (at £2. 14. 4) and a private dinner (at £4. 10. 8½) for the chancellor and various doctors and other presents and fees, the total cost amounting to £92. 0. 8. In 1498–9 Richard Copton spent over £17 on his inception feast, which included a buck bought from a servant of the president of Magdalen.[8] The prior and chapter bore the bulk of the expenses, but at the inception of John Sarysbury and John Wodnysbrowgh there were also subscriptions of £10 from the archbishop of Canterbury and 5 marks from the bishop of Rochester, John Langdon, a monk who had incepted in 1410 and was now in a position to help his college. The statutes of the provincial chapter of the black monks in 1343[9] and again in 1444[10] allowed an incepting monk to claim a grant from the common funds of the province; but apparently the monks of Canterbury College never made such a claim, as they definitely cut themselves off from the provincial chapter and in any case the scale of the grants allowed—for an inception in theology £20, in canon law 20 marks—would have been inadequate. Christ Church Canterbury as a corporate landowner could bear comparison with an aristocratic inceptor like the famous George Neville[11] and was expected to spend money accordingly.

[1] iii. 85.
[2] SA 290.
[3] iii. 259.
[4] iii. 258.
[5] Extract 19 below.
[6] iii. 63.
[7] iii. 84.
[8] iii. 134.
[9] *Chapters* ii. 56.
[10] Ibid., ii. 211.
[11] Mallet i. 198.

The monk-fellows usually went up to the college, as might be expected, soon after Michaelmas, at about the time of the 'resumption of the masters', 10 October; but sometimes they did not arrive until later in October.[1] Horses had to be hired for the journey[2] from such people as John Hackneyman[3] and in the sixteenth century at least servants were taken from the offices at Canterbury to accompany the monks to Oxford.[4] When a monk-fellow went up to the college for the first time, or returned on being appointed warden after any considerable absence, the removal was a more serious matter, involving the carriage of his *panni* or 'stuff' and his books. These were sent to Faversham[5] and from there, apparently, went by sea up the estuary of the Thames to London and so on to Oxford: that at least was the method of carrying the goods on the return from Oxford to Canterbury.[6] To judge from the treasurers' and other accounts at Canterbury, the prior and chapter must have paid for most, if not all, the travelling expenses of the monks to and from Oxford. In the late fourteenth century, it was apparently usual for the prior to give the departing monk a gift of money *pro benedictione*, a kind of tip accompanying the blessing.[7] The college only paid for journeys made by the monks or others strictly upon college business,[8] as for instance when the revenues of Pagham had to be collected.

Once at the college, the monk was not allowed to absent himself for a night without the warden's permission, nor even to miss a meal unless he was invited to some inception feast. He was allowed to be absent for a month's vacation in the autumn (i.e. in the long vacation) with the permission of the prior, but he was liable to lose 6d. of his salary for every day that he stayed away beyond this statutory month. Besides this, any monk-fellow who was recalled to Canterbury by the prior in order to preach a sermon or for some other cause was allowed a fortnight or three weeks' leave of absence. The accounts at Canterbury show that a monk-fellow was usually called to Canterbury to preach in Lent or Holy Week, returning after Easter:[9] on one occasion, the prior wrote to the warden of the college as early as January, appointing him to preach on 'Scher' (Maundy) Thursday.[10] In this way, the student's theological training was turned to account at home even before it was completed.[11] In 1445–6 a monk of York preached at Canterbury in Lent: possibly he was a student from

---

[1] e.g. ii. 133, 154.
[2] Extracts 37 and 39 below.
[3] Extracts 121 and 127 below.
[4] Extracts 136–9 below.
[5] Extract 42 below.
[6] Extract 32 below. Cf. iii. 150.
[7] Extracts 20–2 below.
[8] iii. 176.
[9] e.g. extracts 44 and 130 below.
[10] iii. 118.
[11] The same use of students as Passiontide preachers prevailed at Westminster Abbey: Pearce 27–8.

Durham College brought home by one of the monks of Canterbury College.¹ Sometimes at least, the preacher was accompanied by another fellow and the accounts give the impression that there was as much travelling between Oxford and Canterbury at Easter as in the autumn, and perhaps even more, especially at the end of the fifteenth century.² But the college does not seem to have migrated *en masse* at either season, or on any occasion except for the election of the prior or the archbishop. At such times the subprior (on the death of the prior) or the prior (on the death of the archbishop) wrote to the warden and fellows, citing them to appear at the election in the chapter-house at Canterbury.³ Even then the fellows, though cited, did not necessarily all come in person: in the spring of 1495, for instance, at the election on the death of Prior Sellynge, the warden and senior fellow appeared in person with a letter of proxy on behalf of the six other fellows left at Oxford.⁴ The migration of such a large body would have been a heavy and, as it seemed, unnecessary expense. It may be noticed that the election of the prior took place in the presence of the archbishop, who on one occasion himself sent a summons to the Oxford monks.⁵

Another event which might interrupt a monk's residence at Oxford was his ordination to the priesthood. In 1375–6, for instance, John Bertram had to go from Oxford to Canterbury and on to London to receive ordination, no doubt from the archbishop,⁶ and on 26 September 1456 William Sellynge said his first mass at Canterbury,⁷ having been ordained on the previous Saturday, 18 September.

A monk-fellow's career was brought to an end by his being recalled to Canterbury or sent to study abroad, or by his death or his appointment to the wardenship of the college. According to the statutes of the college, no fellow was to be recalled until he had qualified for the baccalaureate, unless he was particularly needed for some genuine business of Christ Church Canterbury. On the other hand a monk-fellow was not supposed to stay up at Oxford after taking his doctorate, unless he was not needed to teach at Canterbury and at the same time was actually needed by the university, in the absence of any other regent in his faculty (of theology). In such a case, he was allowed to remain at Oxford until another regent could be found to take his place, provided that he was actively engaged in his duties as regent and that the expenses of his prolonged residence were paid by

¹ Extract 54 below.
² There is a detailed account of a journey from Oxford to Canterbury by two monk fellows and their two servants in March 1483 at a cost of £1. 13. 11½: iii. 127.
³ e.g. iii. 72, 82.   ⁴ Extract 119 below.   ⁵ iii. 83.
⁶ Extract 6 below. Sometimes the Canterbury monks were ordained by a suffragan, such as the Bishop of Ross: Searle 27–91.
⁷ Searle 66.

the university or the 'community of black monks'.[1] The last phrase is a reference, apparently, to the provincial chapter of the black monks, who were bound by their own statutes[2] continually to maintain a regent doctor of theology of their own order at Oxford—normally, of course, at their official house of studies, Gloucester College. There is no evidence that any fellow of Canterbury College was ever maintained in this way by the university or the provincial chapter. With a few exceptions,[3] it was only the wardens or vice-wardens of the college who had the opportunity of attaining to the doctorate in theology and they, of course, were in any case bound to remain at Oxford after taking their degree, by reason of their office.

In some instances, a monk's recall from Oxford was only temporary. Thus, Thomas Chillynden was allowed to return to Oxford after his mission to Rome, 1378–80, and Thomas Dover, student about the years 1381–3, was again a student at Oxford in 1393–5 after having acted as *magister ordinum* at Canterbury in the interval. Usually, however, once a monk had been definitely recalled from Oxford, he did not return, except in some cases as warden.

It was one of the principal objects of the college to supply a succession of properly trained monks to lecture to their brethren at Canterbury: in the words of the college statutes, *ut inter confratres suos proficere valeat in legendo*.[4] This office of claustral lecturer was much older than the college itself: it was established in the late thirteenth century, at a time when there was a definite movement among the black monks to revive studies, partly by getting in touch with the universities, partly by theological lectures of this kind. In 1275, the monks of Christ Church engaged a Franciscan lecturer, perhaps as one who could teach them the new scholastic theology:

'Circa festum sancti Michaelis conventus ecclesiae Christi Cantuariensis de voluntate ipsorum admiserunt quendam fratrem de ordine Minorum Willelmum nomine, cognomento de Everel, ad legendum theologiam: qui dictus frater incepit legere die sancti Nicasii martyris: et istud a retroactis temporibus inauditum: et quid per istam lectionem et scholam subsequetur in futuro patebit, quoniam novitates pariunt discordias.'[5]

We fortunately have a good deal of evidence about the lector from the surviving accounts of the period. The *lector* or *magister* had a companion friar, *socius* or *consors*: this was perhaps insisted on

[1] iii. 174.
[2] *Chapters* ii. 55, 211.
[3] In the early days of the college Thomas Everard and William Gyllyngham, though apparently merely fellows, became doctors in theology.
[4] iii. 174.
[5] Gervase of Canterbury (Rolls Series) ii. 281.

by the Franciscan authorities for reasons of discipline. The two were supplied with habits, mantles and coverlets for their beds; also parchment and a special supply of oil for the lector's chamber. We learn from a later letter of Archbishop Reynolds[1] that the lector was given a study in the infirmary—most incongruously, as it seemed to the archbishop; but no doubt the infirmary was the easiest place in which to find a private chamber that was secluded, yet accessible. It was there that the subprior, for instance, had his chamber.[2]

The two friars had a servant (*garcio, puer, valectus*) to look after them and run their errands: he seems to have got through a good deal of shoe-leather at times. He received an annual 'robe' or livery. In 1282–3 and 1284–5 there is mention of the lector's clerk as well as his servant, and in the accounts between 1285 and 1293 clerk and servant alternate. It is just possible that they were one and the same person: their robes are of about the same value. From 1293 on, the clerk alone is mentioned, though the *valectus doctoris* appears again in fifteenth-century livery accounts. In 1314–15 the clerk is called *scriptor*. He probably acted as a copyist for the lector: hence the supplies of parchment.

As regards the lectures themselves, our information is scanty. We do not know exactly where they were given: the terms *lector claustri, in schola claustrali* need not literally refer to the cloister. Nor do we know the precise hour of the lectures. The thirteenth-century instructions for the novices of Christ Church do not appear to mention the lectures, but assign several periods to study: in the morning between prime and terce and at intervals throughout the afternoon, between dinner and compline.[3] It seems most probable that the lectures were given between prime and terce. According to the injunctions of Archbishop Winchelsey in 1298, these theological lectures were to be attended daily by the bulk of the community:

> 'Item omnes iuniores qui servitium suum complete reddiderunt et etiam alii fratres qui in cura reipublicae[4] tunc temporis minime occupantur, nec alia causa legitima nota praesidenti rationabiliter excusanti, lectioni divinae paginae cum aliis fratribus in scholis diebus singulis intersint.'[5]

---

[1] *Lit. Cant.* i. 46.
[2] We even find the use of a chamber in the infirmary being granted to a secular benefactor: iii. 38.   [3] Corpus Christi College Cambridge MS. 441, pp. 380–3.
[4] i.e. obedientiaries.
[5] Wilkins, *Concilia* ii. 246 (c. 3). For the almonry chapel see MS. Cotton Galba E iv, fo. 89. Cf. also fo. 88ᵛ: 'Et sciendum quod die sabbati et die dominica et aliis singulis diebus quando magister scolarum ordinarie non legit in scolis . . .' But this may refer rather to the public schools in the city.

Evidently some outsiders were admitted, for the six chantry priests attached to the new almonry chapel (c. 1320) had to attend:

> 'Item omnes presbiteri dicte capelle singulis diebus quando ... lector conventus legit in scolis missas suas privatas dicant in mane et post solempnem missam capelle ad leccionem sacre pagine in scolis conventus accedant, nisi ex causa racionabili fuerint impediti.'

(This roughly indicates the time of the lectures: the time after the solemn mass in the almonry chapel may have coincided with the free time between the conventual prime and terce.) The priests attached to the Black Prince's chantry (1362) also had to attend 'cum doctor aut lector alius in claustro monachorum more solito legerit ibidem.'[1] Perhaps by admitting secular clerks to these lectures, Christ Church as a metropolitan church fulfilled its canonical obligation of providing public theological teaching.[2]

Probably the lectures were given during three out of the four terms of the year, beginning at Michaelmas and ending at Midsummer: the accounts of 1365–8 refer to the Christmas, Easter and Midsummer terms and the lector's salary at that period was paid in three instalments. Among the Dominicans the academic year lasted from Michaelmas to Midsummer[3] and the academic year at Oxford was similar, the 'resumption' being on 10 October.[4] It is significant that the Franciscan lecturer at Canterbury, as we have seen, first began his lectures on 11 October.

For nearly forty years a succession of Franciscans carried on the lecturing at Christ Church. The prior and chapter had to write regularly to the Franciscan provincial, asking for the continuance of the lector: some of the correspondence between about 1286 and 1298 has survived.[5] In 1314 a change took place: the Franciscan lector, Robert de Fulham, was dispensed with, the pilot was dropped:

> 'Plures nostre congregacionis fratres ipsius sedulos auditores ita sacre scripture aspersione intima fecundavit, quod ipsos ad lectoris officium in scolis nostris subeundum ydoneos reputamus: nos unum de fratribus et commonachis nostris predictis loco dicti fratris Roberti ad huiusmodi ministerium exequendum duximus subrogare.'[6]

---

[1] *Lit. Cant.* ii. 427–8. [2] X 5. 5.
[3] C. Douais, *Acta capitulorum provincialium* (1884) 76.
[4] SA lxxx, 11.
[5] Little, *Greyfriars* 66, n. 1; *Collectanea Franciscana II* (British Soc. of Franciscan Studies, vol. 10) 4–8; C. Cotton, *Grey Friars of Canterbury* (1924) 35–6. [6] Little, *Greyfriars* 66.

We know from the accounts that the monk who took over the lecturing was Stephen de Faversham, who had previously studied at Paris. Robert de Fulham was not forgotten, for as late as 1324 he was receiving money from the prior. Soon after the change, about 1318–19, eighteen new studies (*diversoria*) were built for the monk-students: they were perhaps carrells in the cloister. The archbishop in 1321 ordered that the lector should move from his place in the infirmary into one of these studies.[1]

From 1314 onwards, it seems that the lector was always a monk. Unfortunately, the accounts become less informative. Franciscan poverty evidently meant that the lector's needs, even quite trivial ones, had to be supplied for him as they arose; Benedictine poverty allowed the lector a round salary for himself and his clerk, though there were still extra payments for parchment. Not that the first monk-lector established his right to a salary without some difficulty. In 1322–3 the salary was several years in arrears; the next year's account says grudgingly *pro feodo suo, ut dicit*; and down to 1335 it was always noted that the salary was paid 'by ordinance of the chapter' or 'by the grace of the convent'. From 1313 to 1324 the lector was allowed £1 for himself and 10s. for his clerk, and after that £2 a year for himself and his clerk.

When, from 1331, the monk-students began to be sent to Oxford, it was naturally from them that the lectors were recruited. Hugh of St Ives seems to have reversed the usual process by being lector at Canterbury before going up to Oxford, and he continued to hold the office of claustral lector while he was at Oxford: a difficult feat, one would have thought. Henry Wodehull, D.D., the first warden of the college, may have been transferred from Abingdon to Christ Church specially in order to fill the office of lector. Very soon after his entry we find him as lector, in 1362–3, and again after he was turned out of the wardenship to make way for Wyclif, in 1365. In the troubled and busy years that followed, the office of lector was vacant at least once, in 1372–3, and perhaps more often.

When the college was founded, therefore, the lector was an established institution. So far as we know, the first alumnus of the college to become lector was William Gillyngham, D.D., lector from about 1382 to 1390 and perhaps till his death c. 1410. Dr Gillyngham was probably succeeded by Richard Godmersham, formerly fellow and warden of Canterbury College, who incepted in canon law c. 1410 and

---

[1] *Lit. Cant.* i. 46. At St Albans a little later, Abbot Michael (1335–49) built 'ad quietem et solatium suorum studentium' some studies near the dormitory, over the ambulatory which led from the regular parlour to the prior's chamber and chapel: *Gesta Abbatum* (Rolls Series) ii. 302.

for many years filled the post of *lector in scola claustrali*. At length in his 'laudable old age', for the last twelve years of his life (1430–42), he was almoner. Whether this involved giving up his lectureship at once is not clear. It is curious that this time the claustral lecturer was not a theologian but a canonist, though he may, of course, have lectured in theology, especially as the canon law and theology of the middle ages to a considerable extent covered common ground and were drawn from common sources. At the same time, canon law was certainly studied in the monasteries, as can be seen from the large number of books on the subject in monastic libraries;[1] and at St Augustine's Canterbury, for instance, in the fourteenth century Master Peter of Dene, the curious refugee and quasi-monk, had given public lectures on canon law to monks and seculars. The lectures must have been appreciated, to judge from the trouble that was taken to recapture Peter when he ran away.[2] Prior Chillynden himself is a good example of a monk-canonist[3] and may well have been responsible for Godmersham's taking up law. In the same way, it was probably Godmersham's influence or teaching that led two monks in the middle of the fifteenth century, Richard Gravene and William Petham, to study canon law at Oxford. It is certainly stated in Gravene's grace that he had studied for six years in the cloister *in decretis*, and this must have been either under Godmersham or his successor.

Monks who were doctors were allowed the privilege of having a room and a servant of their own.[4] Consequently, some surviving accounts of the distribution of livery at Christ Church Canterbury during the time of Dr Godmersham and afterwards contain the following entries:

 1412 Iohannes valectus doctoris
 1416 famulus doctoris
 1417 Item duo valecti, supprioris
       et doctoris
 1420 famulus doctoris
 1423 famulus doctoris
 1429 famulus doctoris Godmersham
 1431 famulus doctoris Godmersham
 1432 valecti ... ii pro suppriore et doctore
 1435 valectus doctoris

[1] Cf. the books left by Priors Henry of Eastry and Thomas Chillynden: James, *Ancient Libraries* 144, 150.
[2] *Chronicon W. Thorne* (1330) in R. Twysden, *Decem Scriptores* (1652) col. 2055. [3] But not, apparently, a retired secular, as Leland thought.
[4] *Chapters* ii. 36; cf. ii. 120, 123. Cf. also James de Oxeney, *Canterbury College* iii. 38. For the following references see Bodleian MS. Tanner 165, fo. 123–67. The entries are for Christmas each year.

1437 valectus doctoris senioris
     valectus doctoris iunioris
1439 valectus doctoris senioris
     valectus doctoris iunioris
1441 serviens doctoris senioris
1443 valectus doctoris
1445 valectus doctoris
1447 valectus doctoris.

There are no corresponding entries in the liveries for 1448–66.

It seems likely that Godmersham, referred to explicitly in 1429 and 1431, was the 'doctor' and 'senior doctor' of the whole period 1412–41 (the year before his death). As regards the 'junior doctor' of 1437–9 and the surviving doctor of 1443–7, the probability points to another doctor of canon law, John Wodnysbrowgh (1413–57), fellow and warden of Canterbury College, who left Oxford, presumably for Canterbury, about Michaelmas 1437, returned again as warden on Lady Day 1441, but was absent again from a date not later than Michaelmas 1443 until 26 March 1448, when he was made warden for a third time. His movements would fit in well with the appearance of the junior and surviving doctor in the entries given above: it is possible that during his absences from Oxford, he first assisted and then succeeded Godmersham in lecturing in the claustral school.

After the middle of the fifteenth century, the office and personality of the claustral lecturer disappear from view. When John Wodnysbrowgh died in 1457, the community contained bachelors of either faculty, but no doctors until William Sellynge and William Hadley took their degrees at Bologna. The office of lector may have been in abeyance. But when Sellynge himself was prior and again after his death, when the college increased its numbers and its library in such a remarkable way, it is difficult to believe that there was no teaching of theology in the cloister and that Canterbury was less enterprising than Winchcomb, where Abbot Kidderminster established daily lectures in theology.[1] Certainly at the time of the reformation the theological lecture again became prominent at Canterbury, as elsewhere: 'the yere of our Lorde 1538 the archbishop of Canterbury dyd read the epistell of S. Paull to the Hebrues halfe the lent in the chapter house of the monasterie of the Holy Trinitie.'[2]

Apart from those who acted as claustral lecturers, the fellows and

[1] See W.A. Pantin in the *Downside Review* (1929) 199 ff.
[2] J.G. Nichols, *Narratives of the Days of the Reformation* (1859) 286.

wardens of the college were recalled to Canterbury either to be simple 'cloisterers' or, as in many cases, to take up office as obedientiaries. Sometimes a monk was unwilling to return even for the latter purpose: Warden Thomas Humfrey wrote to the prior, begging not to be recalled and stipulating that, if he must return, he should at least have such 'stuff and apparel' as he had at Oxford and an 'honest chamber'.[1] After the comparative independence and privacy of Oxford, a return to community life must have been a hard wrench. Another monk, however, probably Nicholas Bennett, on returning to Canterbury at Lent or Passiontide c. 1535–8, wrote that he was 'determined and fixed'[2] to remain there as sub-cellarer, and the contemporary warden of the college, Dr Thornden, so far from showing any reluctance, used the influence of Thomas Cromwell to obtain his own appointment to the office of warden of the manors of Christ Church.[3]

No attempt has been made in this work to follow with completeness the subsequent careers of all the members of the college, as such an undertaking would have involved an examination of all the obedientary rolls at Canterbury. But from the more or less casual evidence used, it appears that the offices to which the alumni of Canterbury College were most often promoted were those of chancellor (in charge of the registers) and penitentiary of Christ Church. These were obviously appropriate to men of literary and theological training. The penitentiary in particular, being in effect the vicar of the bishop for the administration of the sacrament of penance, held an office of perhaps greater responsibility and less purely domestic importance than any other obedientiary. It seems that the convent usually employed two chancellors and two penitentiaries.

Among other offices occupied by past members of the college may be mentioned those of subprior and *magister ordinum* and the more mundane posts of treasurer, warden of manors, cellarer and chamberlain. But the most remarkable fact of all is that out of thirteen priors between 1376 and 1540, eight were men who had been at the college: Stephen Mongeham, Thomas Chillynden, William Molasshe, John Sarysbury, William Pettham, William Sellynge, Thomas Goldstone II, Thomas Goldwell. One of the most distinguished members of the college was John Langdon I, who in 1417 was sent to the Council of Constance, where his life was saved by a cardinal's physician. Then, being 'called out from his cloister by the king's command', he spent two or three years in the service of King Henry V abroad and, after

[1] iii. 119.
[2] iii. 150: not 'decyvyd and surprisyd', as Sheppard read.
[3] iii. 146–9.

SUBSEQUENT CAREERS

just failing to obtain the see of Lisieux, was promoted to Rochester in 1421 and died at the Council of Basel.

Several of the monks, both fellows and wardens, died at Oxford: John Wy (fellow) in 1418, Robert Lynton (warden) and William Richemonde (fellow) within a few hours of each other, 18–19 February 1448, Richard Quenygate (fellow) in 1458, William Chartham (fellow) in 1487, Robert Eastry (warden) in 1496, Christopher Eastry (fellow) and Simon Islep (fellow) in 1507. Sometimes the causes of death are known. Pestilences, of course, were frequent in the university and are mentioned in some of the letters. The two deaths in 1448, so close together, suggest this cause. William Chartham certainly died of a 'vehement pestilence', no doubt the 'strange and unheard-of sickness' which had first appeared in Oxford in 1485[1] and is perhaps to be identified with the sweating sickness, 'Le Swete', raging about that time and carrying off nine monks at Canterbury.[2] Christopher Eastry's death was also due to a 'vehement pestilence.' In 1519 again the plague was in Canterbury College, to the inconvenience of Guy Gurgayne, one of the secular sojourners.[3] In order to escape the pestilence, the fellows sometimes left the college in charge of the servants and *pueri collegii*, as for instance in 1486–7,[4] and fled to the country, to the neighbouring manors of Christ Church Canterbury at Newington (Oxon.)[5] and Risborough (Bucks.). It was to this latter place that Richard Holden, warden of the college, fled 'for fear of death' in 1413, but in vain, for he also died there of a 'vehement pestilence' and was buried in the parish church.

Another disease which carried off monks of the college was consumption. Simon Islep died of this at Oxford in 1507 and another young fellow of the college, Haymo Throwley, had gone home to Canterbury to die of consumption in 1505. There were other monks who apparently died at Canterbury while still members of the college, as John Dunstan (fellow) did in 1458. The two wardens, William Chichele and Robert Holyngbourne, who died in 1474 and about Easter 1508 respectively, may have died at Oxford. Others died at Canterbury soon after leaving Oxford: Arnold Permystede (fellow) in 1464, John Langdon (warden) in 1496, William Sellynge II (fellow) about 1518.

Flight was not the only precaution and care taken with sickness. According to the statutes, a sick fellow was to keep to his room and to be provided with proper food and medicine and cheered with the company of one or two fellow monks. Any fellow with a lasting and

---
[1] Mallet i. 410.　　　　　　　　　　　　　　　　　　　　[2] Searle 191.
[3] C.W. Boase, *Reg. Univ. Oxford* i (1885) 108.
[4] ii. 217; cf. ii. 258.　　　　　　　　　　　　　　　　　　[5] iii. 120.

apparently incurable disease, however, was to be sent home to the monastery, as poor Haymo Throwley was.[1] By 1473, a special fund had been instituted for the sick fellows of the college out of the Christ Church lands in Romney Marsh reclaimed through the benefaction of Dr Thomas Chaundler. Every year the sum of 26s. 8d. was to be paid by the prior and chapter to the warden, who was to furnish a statement of the amount left in hand in his yearly account.[2] The money was kept in the common chest and if a large amount accumulated in this way the warden and senior fellow, with the consent of the prior, might spend it for some necessary and useful purpose. About 1501, for instance, they purchased a silver gilt cup out of this money.[3] In practice, the statements as to the sick fund in the college accounts are intermittent. The expenses in 1510 included 'fumigations' to keep off the pestilence and sometimes as much as £13 or £16 was left in hand.[4]

The monks who died at Oxford were usually buried in the neighbouring church of St Frideswide and in some cases the particular place of burial is given. Robert Lynton and William Richemonde were buried in one grave in the choir in front of the high altar, a place of honour, and their funeral was evidently attended by representatives from other colleges, as Exeter College disbursed 7d. for oblations on the day of the burial of the warden of the College of Canterbury (Lent 1448).[5] Robert Eastry (1496) and Christopher Eastry (1507) were buried near to each other in the Lady chapel. Robert Holyngbourne was probably buried at Oxford.[6]

Even when an Oxford monk died at home, as in the case of Haymo Throwley, a servant was sent round the town (of Oxford) to ask for prayers for his soul; and, of course, the names of the monks were taken by the *brevigerulus* round a wider circle of monasteries. As soon as the news of a death at Oxford reached Christ Church Canterbury (it took several days to do so) the letter was read in chapter[7] and then, as soon as might be, the dead monk was given the services due to a member of the community: the sung office and mass of the dead, the prior or subprior acting as celebrant. There is one curious and pathetic exception to the usual practice of burial at Oxford. When in December 1418 John Wy died at Oxford Thomas Guston, a fellow student and *socius sue rasture*—they had been tonsured, 'clothed' and professed together eight years before—brought his body in a cart all the way back to Canterbury, where the strange *cortège* was met in

---

[1] iii. 175.
[2] *Lit. Cant.* iii. 268, 269.
[3] i. 36.
[4] ii. 228, 244, 255, 257, 259, 261.
[5] C.W. Boase, *Registrum Collegii Exon.* (1894) lxvii.
[6] ii. 251.
[7] In the case of R. Quenygate at least.

procession by the superior and convent at the outer or Christ Church gate and the body was carried into choir by six of the monks.[1]

The warden of Canterbury College was appointed to his office in the same way as the subprior, cellarer, sacrist and other greater obedientiaries at Christ Church Canterbury,[2] being himself really an obedientiary of that house. The prior and chapter chose three of the monks most suited for the office and submitted their names to the archbishop, who chose one of the three to be warden. The archbishop made the appointment known in a letter addressed either to the prior and chapter[3] or to the warden elect.[4] In some cases he added another letter to the fellows of the college, enjoining obedience to the new warden.[5]

The warden was required by the statutes to be not only sober, honest and circumspect, but also a man of maturity and experience. All the wardens, except the very early ones like Henry Wodehull, were monks who had spent some years as fellows of the college.[6] In the majority of cases, they passed straight from a fellowship to the wardenship. A certain number, however, were appointed to the wardenship after an interval of a few years spent away from Oxford, at Canterbury, usually in the exercise of some office such as penitentiary, chancellor or *magister ordinum*: W. Charte, for instance, R. Eastry, R. Gravene, W. Sandwyche, W. Thornden, T. Wyking and probably R. Godmersham, W. Gillyngham, R. Holden and W. Molasshe. In a few cases, the warden's tenure of office itself was broken into two periods by an interval of office-holding at home or by foreign travel, as with W. Dover, R. Goldstone, R. Holyngbourne and J. Langdon II. John Wodnysbrowgh even had three distinct periods of wardenship.[7] Leave of absence was apparently allowed to W. Thornden in his first year and to W. Hadley, the companion of Sellynge, in his last year of office.

By the statutes, the warden was to be removed from office as he had been appointed, by the archbishop alone, *absque iudiciali strepitu*, without any legal fuss.[8] No doubt in practice the wishes of the prior

[1] Searle 9.
[2] *Lit. Cant.* i. 117, 506; ii. 106, 318. But apparently lesser officials were appointed directly by the prior: ibid., i. 308.
[3] iii. 46, 60.   [4] iii. 46, no. 58.   [5] iii. 16, 21, 37.
[6] At first sight Richard Thornden (1524–34) seems another exception, but he may have previously been a Morton scholar, and in any case only two accounts have survived for this period between 1511 and 1528.
[7] He perhaps spent the interval as *lector in claustro*.
[8] iii. 173; cf. iii. 146.

had great weight, as may be gathered from Thomas Humfrey's letter of expostulation at his proposed recall, where there is no mention of the archbishop.[1] This 'absolution' from office[2] did not imply any disgrace or failure,[3] but was the normal termination of the wardenship. The archbishop had the power, with the consent of the chapter, to make a good man warden for life, but there is no formal evidence of such a life appointment.

The cases where a warden died in office are comparatively few and are probably due to the accident of an untimely death. The term of office, varying considerably, was not subject to any definite rule. On an average it lasted about five or six years, sometimes as long as eight or ten years,[4] while the longest wardenship on record was that of John Langdon II, from 1478 to 1495, with a break between 1482 and 1486. The headship of Canterbury College, then, like that of Durham College and the office of *prior studentium* at Gloucester College, was a temporary post, not a permanent resting-place, as was often the case in the secular colleges. It was simply a stage, like the other 'obediences', in the monastic career—to a studious monk, perhaps, quiet if isolated, to an ambitious monk like Richard Thornden certainly less attractive than the office of prior or warden of manors.

A possible sequel to a monk's stay at Canterbury College was to be sent to some university abroad. This practice went back at least to the time of Prior Henry of Eastry, long before the foundation of the college. About 1288 a Canterbury monk, Richard of Clyve (1286–1326)[5] was studying at Paris and at the same time reporting to the prior on the 'wine of St Thomas' from Poissy.[6] He was a student of canon law, to judge from the books he left to the Christ Church library,[7] and was at another time usefully employed by the chapter as a visitor *sede vacante*, in 1293.[8] In 1304 two other monks, Andrew Hardys (1294–1305)[9] and Stephen of Faversham (1295–?)[10] were sent to Paris.[11] Their books were mainly theological.[12] It was not only his own monks but also secular students that Prior Henry of Eastry helped and encouraged to study abroad.[13]

---

[1] iii. 118.   [2] e.g. iii. 59, 138.
[3] Thomas Asshe is a possible exception to this: iii. 97.
[4] e.g. E. Bockyng, W. Dover, R. Thornden.   [5] Searle 177.
[6] *Hist. MSS. Comm. Report: Various Collections* i. 277. Cf. *Christ Church Letters* xxiv.   [7] James, *Ancient Libraries* 140 (nos. 1756–72).
[8] *Arch. Cant.* (1917) 147, 161, 166.   [9] Searle 178.   [10] Ibid.
[11] C.E. Woodruff and W. Danks, *Memorials of Canterbury Cathedral* (1912) 251.   [12] James, *Ancient Libraries* 134 (nos. 1621–3), 139 (nos. 1738–48).
[13] *Hist. MSS. Comm. Report: Various Collections* i. 260, 278, 279.

STUDYING ABROAD

For the next hundred and fifty years there appears no evidence of monks studying abroad: no doubt they were satisfied with the college established at Oxford. Nevertheless, there was no lack of communication with the continent, particularly with Rome. Thus Thomas Chillynden was sent to Rome 1378–80, John Langdon was sent to the Council of Constance (1417), John Wodnysbrowgh was sent to the Council of Pavia (1424) and John Sarysbury to the Council of Basel (1433). All were Canterbury College men. Another 'special correspondent' at the general council, a pupil of John Sarysbury and so presumably a monk of Canterbury, writes from Rome about 1433–8.[1] In 1452 Thomas Esshford went to Rome, where he died soon after his arrival and was buried at Santa Balbina. There is no hint as to his business at Rome. He was perhaps of a literary bent, the composer of a metrical life of Our Lady, but he does not seem to have been a member of the college.[2]

It was possible to combine business and study abroad, as did Richard of Clyve, Chillynden and later, in 1492–3, Thomas Goldstone. The interesting point comes when monks were sent abroad once more purely for purposes of study, and no longer to Paris but to Italy, now after the pregnant half-century before the fall of Constantinople more important than ever as a centre of culture. The visit to Canterbury of the Emperor Manuel Paleologus in 1400 and perhaps also of the Greek scholar, Manuel Chrysoloras, may well have had an effect upon Christ Church, as Gasquet suggests. The early friendship of Christ Church with John Tiptoft, Earl of Worcester, a devotee of Italian culture, should also be remembered.[3]

William Sellynge was apparently the first, as well as the greatest, of the Christ Church monks sent to Italy purely for study. In 1464 he had been at Oxford for ten years and was probably ready for the baccalaureate in theology when, in Leland's words:

> 'Ecce subito illi prae oculis noctes atque dies observabatur Italia, post Graeciam, bonorum ingeniorum et parens et altrix. A praeside igitur suo impetravit facultatem commigrandi ad Italos, et viatico donatus satis amplo, iter aggressus est.'[4]

How this haunting vision of Italy had been raised in his mind, whether by reading or by some friend at Oxford, we do not know.[5] If, as Leland says, the initiative was on the side of Sellynge himself rather than his superiors, the whole enterprise shows great spirit and

---

[1] iii. 94.
[2] Searle 53, 196. Cf. extract 59 below.
[3] Cf. iii. 103, 104.
[4] Tanner, *Bibliotheca* 161.
[5] Perhaps from John Tiptoft, Earl of Worcester. Cf. his praising of Italians: EHR 35. 572.

originality in the former and also a broadminded and ready sympathy in the latter. In September 1464, the prior and chapter gave Sellynge letters licensing him to study in any university for three years.[1] Such credentials were necessary in order to show that he was not a vagrant or apostate monk, perhaps making for the court of Rome, and consequently similar letters were given to the other monks who studied abroad. It is curious that Sellynge and, in consequence, the monks that followed him chose to study theology at the university of Bologna, the great and ancient centre of legal studies, where the theological faculty was of comparatively recent origin. Leland indeed states that Sellynge studied 'both the laws' there and disputed on them with mature judgement to the delight, apparently, of his fellow monks;[2] but all contemporary records show that he was not another Dr Godmersham, but a student and graduate in theology both at Oxford and Bologna. It is often stated that Sellynge was accompanied by his fellow monk and fellow student at Oxford, William Hadley. The latter, however, did not receive his licence to travel until two years after, in September 1466, when Sellynge had already been at Bologna for some time. The names of Sellynge and Hadley appear in the register of the theological faculty of Bologna under the dates 22 March 1466 and 14 March 1467 respectively. It is not clear whether these entries signify incorporation or graduation. It seems strange that Hadley, who was not even a bachelor of theology, should have obtained the doctorate within six months of his departure from England. It is certain, however, that both monks did become doctors of theology at Bologna, and that at some date before August 1468, by which time they had returned to Canterbury.

About October 1469, Sellynge went out to Italy a second time, accompanied by the warden, Reginald Goldstone. This time the monks were bound for the court of Rome on the business of their house (the jubilee of St Thomas, 1470) and there is no evidence that Reginald Goldstone studied or graduated in any Italian university: in fact he was back at Oxford by Michaelmas 1470. But this journey, though not officially a *voyage littéraire*, was probably even more important than Sellynge's previous visit, for it must have been on this occasion that Sellynge met the 'Homeric youth', Politian, and collected his Greek and Latin manuscripts:

'Fervet opus. Graecissat ille quidem; et industriae et impensis nullum certe locum relinquens, Graeca exemplaria multa con-

[1] iii. 107.
[2] Tanner, *Bibliotheca* 161.

quisivit. Nec minori ulla cura in corradendis Latinis, sed antiquae notae, codicibus usus est: quos nec longo post tempore, tanquam thesauros plane incomparabileis secum deduxit, Durovernum repetens.'[1]

More than twenty years later, at the end of Sellynge's priorate, another fellow of Canterbury College and a licentiate in theology, Thomas Goldstone, was sent as a proctor to Rome, in 1492, and in April 1493 he was made a doctor of divinity by the university of Bologna.[2] Whether he actually studied there, or merely received this as a kind of honorary degree, it is difficult to say: he does not appear on the register of the theological faculty at Bologna. It may be noted that that register does include another English Benedictine, 'Tommaso Hamptun', under the date 9 April 1499.[3] This was probably the Thomas Hampton who became abbot of St Augustine's Canterbury in 1509.

The monks of Canterbury College did not confine themselves to Bologna: one of them had even penetrated to Cambridge, where in 1472–3, 'concessa est gracia monacho priori collegii Cantuarie Oxonie ut possit cum forma ibi habita opponere hic in sacra theologia'.[4] This 'prior' of Canterbury College was apparently Warden William Chichele, who graduated S.T.B. about this time. There is no evidence, however, that he ceased to continue as warden of Canterbury College until his death in 1474.

In the sixteenth century, the monks no longer went to study in Italy but in the universities of the north: Paris (once more after two centuries) and Louvain. In 1511 Thomas Goldwell, then B.D., and William Gillyngham, who had both been at Oxford for some years, studied at Paris but did not, apparently, graduate there. By Easter 1512, they had returned to Louvain and had already become doctors. At that time, the prior and chapter were anxious that they should return home, 'seing the world so jeobardus as it is nowe'.[5] Nevertheless, other monk-students were sent abroad right up to the end. According to a list drawn up about 1538, Thomas Wylfryde and John Waltham III were studying at Paris. The latter at least had been at Oxford. The two monks were then aged thirty-four and twenty-eight respectively.

---

[1] Leland: Tanner, *Bibliotheca* 161.
[2] iii. 130.
[3] S. Mazetti, *Memorie storiche sopra l'universita di Bologna* 314: 'Hamptun Tommaso, inglese monaco Benedettino.'
[4] Cambridge *Grace Book A*, ed. S.M. Leathes (1897) 97.
[5] iii. 141. For the reference to Wylfryde and Waltham at Paris see iii. 153.

Studying abroad was evidently a finishing process for a few monks chosen out of the fellows of Canterbury College, just as the latter had already been chosen out of the Canterbury community. Of this small, doubly distilled number, three—Sellynge, Thomas Goldstone and Goldwell—became in succession rulers of the cathedral priory, each within a few years of his return from the continent. The bachelor of theology or student of long standing was sent to get the doctor's degree which, to judge from these few examples, could be got abroad in a rather shorter time than at Oxford. This practice of snatching away the best monks would naturally be resented by the Oxford authorities. In July 1465, the university complained to the provincial chapter of the black monks that recently certain of the monk-students had removed themselves from 'this our university'.[1] Was this a reference to Sellynge's migration in the previous year, and was his action followed by others? On the other hand, how strongly monastic opinion was in favour of this finishing abroad can be seen from the grace of Richard Thornden (1531),[2] who frankly explained to the university of Oxford that it was an act of virtue and self-denial on his part to take his doctor's degree at Oxford instead of following the fashion by taking it abroad, like some other monks of his house, and that by this course he was losing money and the favour of friends. However, he soon found new friends, or appeased old ones, at court.

What was the value of this communication with the continent? With regard to the technical, academic purpose for which the monks were sent, there was probably at this period little to choose between the theological schools of Oxford, Bologna, Paris or Louvain. A pilgrimage to Paris no longer had the same meaning as in the twelfth or thirteenth centuries. What really counted was what went on 'out of school hours': the experience of the world, the personal contact with men of letters like Politian abroad, the friendship with the pioneers at home like Tiptoft and Thomas Chaundler, the befriending of the new generation like Linacre and perhaps William Latimer and More. It is a curious coincidence, if nothing more, that the Canterbury monks in moving northwards from Italy to Paris and Louvain followed the track of the revival, from the world of Politian to the world of Erasmus. In the same way St Augustine's Canterbury, which had sent Thomas Hampton to Bologna, later sent another monk, John Dygon (not the abbot), to sit under Vives at Louvain.[3]

The one outstanding figure, the one monk who made the fullest possible use of his opportunities of travel and study was, of course, William Sellynge, who came back to the priory with a knowledge

[1] H. Anstey, *Epistolae Academicae* ii (1896) 375.
[2] iii. 258.
[3] BRUO 2. 182.

STUDYING ABROAD

of Greek and a precious collection of manuscripts. Of his place in the revival of classical learning in England generally and of the credit which he did to the order and house that produced and supported him there can be no doubt; but the influence which he had on his own monastery in the matter of humane letters is much more difficult to estimate. We must avoid the 'department of imaginative fiction', as M.R. James reminds us. Certainly William Worcester testifies that Sellynge taught Greek grammar[1]—perhaps to the young scholars in whom he took an interest, like Linacre and Richard Tyll.[2] But Sellynge was too wise to attempt to force his own interests upon every one of his subjects. We must not imagine the *lector in claustro* (if he still existed) giving up the Sentences or the Decretals for Homer. Most of the monks were probably like Prior Thomas Goldstone II who, though he had been to Rome and was a doctor of Bologna, was content to be a good monk and a good Scotist: *vir pius iuxta et prudens, neque scoticae theologiae rudis*, as Erasmus described him.[3]

At Canterbury College also there was no room for the classics and humanism in the official curriculum of theology and canon law and little enough room in the official college library, even at its greatest, though there are a few exceptions. One book, described in 1501 as *copia litterarum apostolicarum de publicacione anni iubelei cum Plutarco in papiro inpress' de liberis educandis*,[4] sounds like a souvenir and most vivid epitome of Sellynge's journey to Rome in 1469–70, with its curious combination of classical lore and ecclesiastical business (the jubilee of St Thomas, it seems).[5] The slight traces of classical or humanist influence are shown in private, personal, unofficial ways. More significant, for instance, than the library catalogues, are the small lists of books in the possession of individual monks. Robert Eastry had the *epistolae familiares* of Cicero and a work of Laurentius Valla;[6] Thomas Goldwell more Cicero and some Virgil;[7] and Robert Holyngbourne's books included, besides much patristic and scholastic theology, Lactantius, the Commentaries of Caesar and Cicero *de officiis*, works by Picus de Mirandula, Philip Beroaldus, 'Phylelphus' and Petrus Crinitus.[8] The same mild cult of

---

[1] F.A. Gasquet, *Old English Bible* (1897) 313; MS. Cotton Julius F vii, fo. 118, *Notule de certis terminis grecorum in grammatica declaratis per doctorem Sellyng ecclesie Christi Cantuar*. Cf. the Greek alphabet and phonetic version of the diphthongs in Bodleian MS. Selden supra 65, fo. 146, a book from Canterbury College. See i. 112.
[2] iii. 122.
[3] In the *Peregrinatio Religionis Ergo*.
[4] Cf. Henry Cranebroke's notebook, MS. Royal 10 B ix, fo. 85ᵛ.
[5] i. 21, 102 (no. 133).
[6] i. 82.
[7] i. 81.
[8] i. 81, 85, 86.

classical elegance is also clearly shown in many of the letters of members of the college: even in 1452, Tiptoft had complimented Henry Cranebroke on his 'Tullian style'.[1] Most remarkable of all is the effect upon handwriting at an early date, not only in the case of Sellynge himself—a fine Italic hand appears in the Canterbury Register R in 1471, when he was chancellor, soon after his return from Italy—but also in the letters of other monks, who had never been to Italy and must have learned their hands from Sellynge. These hands are sometimes of a rounded Italian type, rather like the hand of Farley in the Oxford Register Aa, sometimes of a more pointed 'Italic' type. At least it can be said that Sellynge taught some of his monks to write like humanists.

[1] iii. 103: with more courtesy than accuracy, to judge from Cranebroke's letters.

4
PUERI COLLEGII, SERVANTS, SOJOURNERS, BENEFACTORS

IN the statutes of 1384, among Courtenay's additions there appear five secular scholarships for poor boys, free and of legitimate birth and probable candidates for holy orders or the religious life.[1] The prior and chapter were to appoint two and the archbishop three, of whom one was to be a native of Pagham.[2] This foundation can be traced in some form at an earlier date in connexion with the prior and chapter. Soon after the monks gained possession the Christ Church treasurer's accounts, in 1372–3 and 1373–4, show the maintenance of two secular scholars at the college.[3] In a humble way, they replaced the secular fellowships abolished by the papal award. From another point of view, they are interesting to compare with the poor scholars maintained in the almonry at Canterbury.[4] In the college accounts for 1382–3, there still appear no more than two secular scholars, who are already called by the name they generally bore afterwards, the *pueri collegii*;[5] but when the monks wrote to Courtenay, 19 July 1383, the complete foundation of five scholars was already planned.[6] The method of appointment given in this letter and the very words in which the scholars were then described, as not being fellows but living on the alms of the college, were incorporated into Courtenay's statutes.

Historically, it seems that these five scholarships were not a homogeneous foundation, the appointments to which were simply divided by a compromise between the archbishop and the chapter. It seems rather that in 1383 the archbishop added three scholarships to the two already started by the initiative of the prior and chapter. Possibly this increase of the secular scholarships was done in emulation of Durham College, which had adopted a similar institution a few years earlier, in 1380.[7] One cannot say whether the prior and chapter in 1372–4 were paying for the two scholars out of their own pocket, as at that time the college finances, both income and expenditure, only survive embedded in the chapter's accounts. From 1382 at least, all five scholars were paid for not by the chapter or by the archbishop, but out of college revenues.

[1] iii. 179. [2] Ibid. Cf. iii. 43, 44. [3] Extracts 3 and 4 below.
[4] *Lit. Cant.* i. 444; iii. 168; Searle 106, *Novicii*.
[5] ii. 129, 130. [6] iii. 43. [7] *Collectanea III* 15.

The statutes of 1384 fixed the maintenance of the five scholars as follows:

(1) The warden was to assign to them a room or rooms in college. From the college accounts it seems that they were given one room, on the ground floor in the north-east corner of the quadrangle. Considering their status and the standards of the time, this was probably not overcrowding.

(2) The college was to allow them 10d. a week each for board so long as they were actually in residence. Here Courtenay simply followed the practice already in existence: the accounts of 1382–3 show a quarterly allowance of £1. 1. 8 for the two scholars, i.e. 10d. a week each. The allowance was to be entrusted not to the scholars themselves but to the 'common servant', i.e. the manciple, who provided the food for the whole college. At the statutory rate the scholars, if resident all the year round, should have cost the college £10. 16. 8 a year; in actual practice very much less was spent on them. Some of the earliest accounts, it is true—those for 1382–3 and 1393–5—show the proper payment at the rate of 10d. a week, but the next surviving account (1435–6) shows only £7. 18. 5¼ spent on the scholars; and from this time on, the full amount of £10. 16. 8 was never reached in any of the existing accounts. On a few occasions it was nearly reached,[1] on others it sank to about £6 and once it was as low as £5. 6. 8, less than half the full amount.[2] The average sum was about £7 or £8.

No doubt this shortcoming is partly to be explained by the occasional absence of the scholars. According to the accounts for 1393–5, which alone give exact details of their residence, the boys seem to have resided on an average about eleven weeks out of thirteen in the two quarters (Michaelmas to Lady Day) given in 1393–4 and about twelve weeks out of thirteen in the same two quarters in 1394–5 (it should be noted that we are given no evidence as to the long vacation). The account for 1382–3 shows that the two scholars were paid for from Michaelmas to the beginning of the following August; but as that was a time of crisis, when the monk-fellows' salaries ceased altogether after midsummer, we cannot safely assume that the scholars were always absent for two months in the long vacation. We cannot explain the comparatively low expenditure, £7 or £8 instead of £10. 16. 8, entirely by the absence of the scholars without assuming that they were all habitually absent for three or four months out of the year—which does not seem likely.

---

[1] 1454–5 (ii. 174) £10. 0. 8, 1480–1 (ii. 208) £9. 19. 1, 1510–11 (ii. 253) £10. 2. 11, 1528–9 (ii. 260) £10. 4. 3.

[2] ii. 218.

The vacancies of scholarships would account for some money saved but not for much, unless they were improperly prolonged. On the whole, one is led to conclude that this comparatively low expenditure was due at least in part to an unlawful economy: that the college, being bound to maintain the scholars in kind, not in money, succumbed to the temptation of keeping them as cheaply as possible, irrespective of the statutory rate. In palliation, the college might plead that if the scholars received less than their legal allowance, so also for a long period did the monk-fellows, though the latter, of course, were far better able to afford the retrenchment. Also that 10d. a week was a high rate, compared with what other secular scholars managed to live on in the fifteenth century.[1]

There is no evidence that the college had to provide the scholars with any allowance for clothes or books. Presumably they had the use of the library. There survives an inventory of the clothes of John Style, *scolaris Oxon'*, 1451–2 (i. 80), who was probably one of the *pueri collegii*: he was not one of the monk-scholars.

In return for their keep, the scholars had certain duties towards the college: they were in fact servitors. In the first place, they had to assist at divine service in the chapel on feast days, when by the statutes mass and certain hours had to be sung.[2] At such times they were to be at the disposal of the warden or the monk-fellow who ruled the choir, to read lessons or sing, according to their capacity, *quilibet modo suo*, for they would be chosen chiefly for their academic qualities and were not mere choir-boys. Moreover, the scholars were to obey the warden and fellows *in licitis et honestis* and to wait upon them at table, but at the same time the monks were not to demand of them so much service as to interfere with their studies.

The scholarships were to last for seven years. During that time, the scholars were to begin by studying grammar. They were, of course, expected to have done some grammar beforehand: the archbishops' appointments speak of the candidate as 'already knowing his grammar competently'.[3] They were evidently junior to the monks, who were expected to have finished their grammar before coming up. After grammar, they were usually to proceed to 'sophistry' in preparation for the study of arts, but with the approval of the college one or two of the scholars might study civil law. There is the same reluctance to allow law as with the monk-fellows. Since the scholars were seculars, arts and civil law might serve as ends in themselves; nevertheless, the statutes regard them as possible stepping-stones to theology and canon law.

[1] H.E. Salter in *Poole Essays* 421 ff.
[2] iii. 179; cf. iii. 99.
[3] iii. 61, 101.

Of the individual scholars very little is known since, unlike the monk-fellows, their names are not given in the accounts. There is only one exception to this: the account of 1393–4, where all five scholars are given—W. Colvyle, John Newport, T. Prophete, Thomas Bron, John Wogoppe or Wohoppe.[1] When the archbishop made an appointment to one of the three scholarships in his gift, it seems that he sent a letter to the warden, directing him to admit the new scholar. A few of these letters survive in the archbishops' registers and give the following names:

>   Thomas Warde, appointed 2 September 1405[2]
>   Thomas Edyngham, 24 December 1405[3]
>   Walter Byseley, 18 October 1409[4]
>   William Mereden, 28 January 1416[5]
>   Thomas Astell, 28 January 1416[6]
>   William Bisshopp, 29 January 1444[7]
>   Thomas Bedynden, June 1445[8]
>   William Appylton, 15 October 1445.[9]

During a vacancy of the see, the prior and chapter apparently claimed the right to appoint to the archbishop's scholarships.[10] No example survives of an appointment to the chapter's two scholarships, but there is a letter in which the abbot of St Augustine's evidently asks for one of the scholarships for the son of a servant of his, the boy being one of the prior's subjects.[11]

On several occasions the warden and fellows had difficulty in keeping the *pueri collegii*, the secular scholars, in order. In 1436–7 the boys rebelled against the warden, who had to appear before the archbishop in his manor of Ford, in east Kent:[12] evidently there were two sides of the quarrel to be heard. In 1443, a more serious and complicated matter arose. The college account for Michaelmas 1443 to Michaelmas 1444 refers to a *sede vacante* visitation of the college before the period of account, while the wardenship was vacant.[13] This visitation must have been made during the vacancy of the see on the death of Archbishop Chichele, 12 April 1443. Now there survive in a very fragmentary state, lacking the date, some injunctions made at a visitation during the vacancy of the see by 'Thomas Abb...' and 'Stillington, LL.D.', the commissaries of the prior and chapter who exercised the archbishop's jurisdiction *sede vacante*.[14] The injunctions were confirmed by the succeeding archbishop, John Stafford, who succeeded in 1443. It seems almost certain that the document

---

[1] ii. 133, 135.   [2] iii. 61.   [3] Ibid.   [4] iii. 63.   [5] iii. 73.
[6] Ibid.   [7] iii. 100.   [8] iii. 101.   [9] Ibid.   [10] See under model form, iii. 136.
[11] iii. 82.   [12] ii. 153.   [13] ii. 165.   [14] iii. 99.

refers to the *sede vacante* visitation which we know to have taken place in 1443. Unfortunately, the document is very disjointed, one half of each line being missing. But apparently the scholars are enjoined to assist in their surplices at the divine office in the chapel; they are not to indulge in something—probably some kind of game—under pain of losing their commons; when the bell sounds for dinner or supper, they are to carry in the food from the kitchen to the warden and fellows (*comitiva*) in hall. There are some broken phrases which may possibly have meant that after meals, the scholars had to bring water to the warden and fellows for washing their hands (in the ewers and basins mentioned in the inventories); also to remove something, perhaps the tables or the dishes.[1] There are further duties which are undecipherable.

However, in spite of these injunctions the scholars neglected to attend the canonical hours in chapel and the lectures of their faculties: on 28 December 1443 the archbishop had to write admonishing them to obey the statutes on these points, or answer for their disobedience.[2] Further, the account for 1443–4 records several journeys and consultations and the drawing-up of documents in connexion with the 'reformation of the college'—evidently this affair of the scholars. Twice the warden had to go to Canterbury, one occasion being in Lent (?1444), and once he had to go to the archbishop when the scholars had appealed against the archbishop's injunctions—perhaps the monition of December 1443, perhaps the confirmation of the visitors' injunctions.[3] Again, in 1462–3 the scholars ran away from the college and the warden had to ride off to see the archbishop.[4]

It is difficult to judge the relations of the warden and fellows with the scholars, as we have not the complete case for either side. It does not seem that the scholars were always very contented, or very generously treated by the warden and fellows. The latter give the impression of trying to get as much work as possible out of the boys, while giving in return as little as they decently could in the way of board and lodging. On the whole, this does not seem the most pleasing side of the college history.

The two principal servants of the college were the *pincerna* and the cook. The *pincerna* was evidently the same as the 'manciple' referred

---

[1] These injunctions may be compared with similar ones for the secular scholars at Durham College, confirmed in 1432: *Hist. Dunelm. Scriptores Tres* (Surtees Soc. 1839) ccxxii.
[2] iii. 99.   [3] ii. 164.   [4] ii. 184.

to in college documents of the sixteenth century. He was an important and responsible official and his wages were double those of the cook. One *pincerna* was sufficiently well-to-do to present the college with a psalter.[1] The duties of the *pincerna* are not defined in the statutes but no doubt, like other manciples, he bought provisions for the college:[2] he certainly kept accounts, like the modern buttery book[3] which were kept in a chest in the promptuary.[4] It was perhaps in connexion with these financial dealings that the college was engaged in a lawsuit against a former *pincerna*, Humfrey Everard, in 1440–1.[5] A linen-chest was kept in the *pincerna*'s room.[6]

Besides the two principal and regular servants, there are occasionally evidences of a porter (*ianitor*), who had a room, and an under-cook (*subcocus*), both apparently employed in odd jobs like gardening and cleaning out rooms.[7] Once, in 1393–4, there appears a Bible-clerk.[8] It must be remembered also that the five secular scholars or *pueri collegii* were to act to some extent as servants, waiting on the fellows at table.[9] In addition, there were servants who accompanied the warden or fellows on their outridings to Pagham and elsewhere: these could hardly have been the permanent and indispensable members of the staff, such as the manciple and the cook. Sometimes, it seems, important visitors staying in the college brought their own servants.[10] Other persons employed, though probably not exclusively in the service of the college, were the barber and the washerwoman,[11] who apparently were normally paid by the monk-fellows out of their own salaries.[12]

The college accounts show no payment of regular wages before 1473. At that date Dr Thomas Chaundler of New College among other benefactions gave the college £50 to invest in property sufficient to bring in £3 per annum for the wages of the *pincerna* and the cook.[13] This property, like Pagham, was apparently kept in the hands of the prior and chapter, who included the £3 in the annuity which they paid to the college.[14] The *pincerna* received £2 and the cook £1. A letter of 1473 speaks of the *consueta salaria*: perhaps before Dr Chandler's endowment, these wages had been paid by the prior and chapter.

Throughout the fifteenth century the two servants received their

[1] i. 30. [2] SA 583. [3] iii. 150.
[4] i. 8. [5] ii. 161. [6] i. 38.
[7] ii. 153, 189. [8] ii. 133. [9] iii. 179.
[10] e.g. Dr Thomas Chaundler, ii. 201; the Abbot of Winchcomb, ii. 224.
[11] ii. 135. Cf. the washing of the chapel linen, passim.
[12] Thus William Chartham was in debt to his 'barbour' and 'lavender': iii. 128.
[13] iii. 114.
[14] This sum is put down separately among the receipts in the accounts of John Langdon, 1486–90: ii. 215, 218, 221.

livery, generally from the prior, who for these purposes usually classed them quite highly: among the *firmarii et bedelli* at first, but after 1441 among the *valecti*.[1] Occasionally the college had to pay for the livery,[2] at a cost of 16s., or at least for its carriage to Oxford.[3] In 1393–4 and 1394–5, the college supplied the servants with money for 'offerings' and throughout the accounts there are numerous gifts, rewards or 'tips', particularly when the servants were left in charge of the college in the absence of the warden and fellows. On one of these occasions, the *iocalia* of the college were deposited with the sacrist of St Frideswide's, who was given a pair of gloves for his pains.[4]

We have little personal knowledge of the servants. In 1475–6 the cook was John Mysden, perhaps from Missenden in Buckinghamshire,[5] and in 1524 a subsidy was paid by William Cooke (then apparently receiving 30s.)[6] and the manciple, Robert Wodman.[7] In 1436–7 a journey was made to Risborough, Bucks., to find a new porter—which suggests that the college servants were often recruited from the manors of the prior and chapter.[8] In 1473, the cook of Canterbury College appears among the debtors of Oriel College: 'Item cocus collegii Cantuar' pro uno termino pro quibus manucepit Iohannes pincerna de Oriell iiiis.'[9]

Since the warden, monk-fellows and secular scholars together usually numbered less than a dozen, it was necessary for the college to take in a certain number of outsiders in order to justify the larger scale in establishment and buildings that both dignity and economy demanded. A similar practice was found necessary at Durham College.[10] The outsiders lodging in the college are referred to in the accounts as *commorantes*. In English, they may be described as 'sojourners'.[11] According to the statutes,[12] they might be either regulars or seculars, but must be quiet and peaceful, students of arts, theology or canon law, like the members of the foundation. Graduates and noble persons might also be received if it was to the advantage of the college. The accounts from 1382–3 onwards show that the letting of rooms to these men brought in from £3 to £7 annually and between 1436 and 1449 as much as £8 or £9; but against this must be set the

[1] MS. Tanner 165, fo. 124ᵛ–176ᵛ.   [2] ii. 161, 169, 172, 223.
[3] ii. 148, 156.   [4] ii. 217, 258, 261.   [5] ii. 197.
[6] J.E. Thorold Rogers, *Oxford City Documents* (1891) 59.
[7] Ibid. 57.   [8] ii. 153.
[9] C.L. Shadwell and H.E. Salter, *Oriel College Records* (1926) 391.
[10] *Collectanea III* 19.   [11] Cf. iii. 121.   [12] iii. 177.

'allowances' made between 1443 and 1449,[1] apparently for money lost through rooms standing vacant, so that these high figures seem to have represented the ideal and not the actual profits. Probably the rebuilding of the north range in 1439–40 created a dislocation among the sojourners from which the college took some time to recover.

The rent paid by the sojourners varied according to the rooms taken. The best seem to have been those in the eastern range, from the rooms at the head of the chapel to the room over the *pueri collegii*; and for these the annual rent was usually about 20s. for an upper room and 10s. for a lower one. On the north side, near the kitchen and cellar, the upper rooms were cheaper: about 13s. 4d. a year. In the course of time, two of the best rooms went up in value; the other rooms that altered in value at all became cheaper. Sometimes reductions of rent were allowed—when, for instance, a sojourner had to share his room with one of the Canterbury monks;[2] or as a matter of favour when one of the long-established, if troublesome, succession of Peterborough monks was absent or by himself;[3] or again, when sojourners apparently paid for repairs in the room they occupied.[4] On one occasion there was a debt, probably for rent, owing from some former students from Evesham.[5]

The college accounts show no payment from the sojourners for board: no doubt they had their own accounts with the manciple. On two occasions[6] there are payments from the sojourners for 'dishes', which perhaps they were usually expected to provide for themselves. On the other hand, the college provided some furniture[7] and an astonishing number of locks and keys to protect both the chambers and the studies of the sojourners.[8] It is evident that the sojourners in priest's orders, not only the monks but also the seculars, had the use of the college chapel for saying mass, for the service books include a missal of the Sarum use given by Thomas Bourchier some years before he became Archbishop of Canterbury.[9] Perhaps he himself had at one time been a sojourner. There is no evidence that any non-foundationers, even the monastic sojourners, were strictly required to be present at the divine office in the chapel.

Comparatively little is known about the sojourners themselves until after 1454, the room-rents being hitherto given in a lump. After that date Christ Church Canterbury, taking over the college endowments, naturally demanded a stricter account from the warden and so the

---

[1] ii. 166, 170, 173. [2] ii. 200, 204. [3] ii. 218, 221.
[4] ii. 179. [5] ii. 181. [6] ii. 233, 250.
[7] e.g. a bed: ii. 161. [8] e.g. ii. 165.
[9] This missal appears in the earliest inventory, 1443, where Bourchier is described as Bishop of Ely: i. 4, no. 21.

college accounts regularly include a detailed statement of the rooms let and their occupiers, the seculars by name and the monks usually distinguished only by their monasteries (*monachi Roffenses*, etc.) but sometimes also by name.

The series of monastic sojourners at Canterbury College is of the greatest importance for the history of the black monks in Oxford. The accounts of Durham College are disappointingly jejune on the subject of outsiders;[1] and as regards the greatest of the Benedictine establishments, Gloucester College, while the permanent *camerae* of the monasteries can be traced,[2] the actual numbers and personalities of the monks remain to be worked out from the accounts of their particular houses. Some monasteries sent their monks so regularly to Canterbury College that by about 1475 they had given their names to the rooms they habitually occupied, such as 'Winchester chamber' or 'Rochester chamber',[3] though without acquiring any real proprietary right as with the *camerae* of Gloucester College. These monasteries were Winchester, Coventry, Bath, Peterborough, Evesham and Rochester. Monks were sent regularly, though without permanently appropriating any particular room, from Battle, Reading and, to a less extent, Muchelney; also from Sherborne after 1469 and the Cluniac priory of Lewes after 1486. There were also for various short periods monks from Hyde, Milton, Tavistock, Winchcomb, Worcester, Abbotsbury, Burton, Cerne and Chertsey.

The other monastic colleges also had their own regular associations, based partly upon geographical distribution, partly upon monastic politics. Durham College naturally received students from York and Whitby, houses that had formed the old northern chapter before 1336. Gloucester College, the official 'common place' of the black monks, was regularly patronised by the greater houses like Glastonbury and St Augustine's and especially those that dominated the provincial chapters in the later middle ages—St Albans, Westminster and Bury St Edmunds; also by groups of monasteries belonging roughly to the Thames and Severn valleys and East Anglia: Abingdon, Winchcomb, Malmesbury, Gloucester, Tewkesbury, Evesham, Worcester, Pershore, Norwich and Ramsey; also Hyde Abbey, Winchester. The connexions of these other monastic colleges seem to throw some light on Canterbury College: it too drew largely upon a geographical group of houses throughout the southern counties: Rochester, Battle, Lewes, Winchester, Sherborne, Muchelney, Tavistock.

[1] *Collectanea III* 19.
[2] *Snappe's Formulary*, ed. H.E. Salter (1924) 337–86.
[3] ii. 195, 200.

There still, of course, remain other houses whose connexion with the college has to be accounted for. Perhaps Reading and Peterborough, great and wealthy houses yet for some reason not playing a great part in the provincial chapters, on that very account preferred the privacy of Canterbury College. In any case these suggested divisions, geographical and political, cannot have been rigid, for monks sometimes migrated from one college to another. In this way, the unruly monks of Peterborough were sent away from Canterbury College to Gloucester College while William Chichele was warden, after 1471; and a few years later, in 1476, the next warden, Thomas Humfrey, readmitted them, though it was some years before they could regain their traditional room, which had been occupied by a monk of Battle. After 1490 the monks of Evesham disappeared, apparently under more respectable circumstances, to appear later at Gloucester College.[1] A list of the members of Gloucester College in 1538 includes some monks, apparently, from monasteries that had formerly patronised Canterbury College: Evesham, Hyde, Battle and perhaps Peterborough.[2] In this way, Canterbury College missed having the great John Feckenham, then a monk of Evesham.

After 1454, it is possible to arrive at the number of monastic sojourners in the college. In some cases monasteries sent a single monk, either to occupy a room by himself or, more rarely, to share it with a monk from another monastery or even a secular.[3] The larger monasteries like Peterborough and Winchester sent several monks, usually unspecified in number, to occupy their rooms. Probably a room would normally hold two monks, for there is definite evidence of this arrangement in certain cases,[4] while there is no definite evidence of a room being shared by more than two; and it is significant that when four monks were sent by Battle, between 1502 and 1504, they occupied two rooms.[5] Battle throughout shows an interesting development: it sent one monk until about 1490, then two and finally the unusually liberal contribution of four—which may perhaps be connected with the stay of the Abbot of Battle in 1500–1.[6] The accounts of Winchester show that that house usually sent two monks to Oxford, but sometimes only one and never, apparently, more than two.[7] On the other hand Peterborough at the time of the election of Abbot William Ramsey in 1471 had three scholars among its monks: whether

---

[1] C.H. Daniel and W.R. Barker, *Worcester College* (1900) 24, 85.
[2] Oxford University Archives, *Registrum Curiae Cancellarii* EEE, fo. 194ᵛ.
[3] ii. 207. [4] e.g. ii. 201, 207, 210.
[5] ii. 236, 239. [6] ii. 231.
[7] G.W. Kitchin, *Obedientiary Rolls of St Swithun's Winchester* (1892), index under 'Oxford, scholars at' and 'Scholars at Oxford'.

these were all sent to Oxford it is impossible to say.[1] Other houses, like Reading, were irregular in the number of students sent. If we take 'monks' to mean two, we arrive at a rough yearly average of about ten monastic sojourners in all down to about 1490. After that date, the average sinks to about five.

In view of later developments it is tempting, but rather dangerous, to generalise about this decline. In the first place, we know too little about migrations to Gloucester College, or again, the possibility of monks being sent abroad to Paris or Louvain, as was certainly done by Christ Church Canterbury, though only the wealthier monasteries would have been able to afford this luxury: we cannot be quite certain how far this decline at Canterbury College represents a real withdrawal of students. And there are some examples to the contrary: the accession from Lewes, the increase from Battle and Canterbury itself. On the other hand, there had always been slackness and apathy in some quarters ever since the black monks had begun to come to Oxford, as is shown in the general chapters by the 'defect of students'.

Perhaps this decline may best be considered from an economic point of view. In the original instance, the idea of renting rooms in Canterbury College must have seemed particularly attractive to those monasteries which felt that they could not spare the capital necessary for buying a plot and building a *camera* in Gloucester College. But the outlay involved in the latter course would in time have been abundantly justified, whereas the rent for rooms in Canterbury College was a continual drain upon the resources of any not very wealthy monastery, suffering perhaps from a decaying revenue or a rising standard of living, though the financial embarrassments must not be exaggerated.[2] An external enterprise like the maintenance of monk students would naturally be the first victim of retrenchment. It is certainly noticeable that of the regular patrons of Canterbury College those monasteries that disappeared by 1490—Bath, Coventry, Muchelney, Rochester and Sherborne—were of a second-rate income as Benedictine incomes went (about £500–£750 gross), while those monasteries that went on sending monks for some time, or even to the end[3]—Battle, Lewes, Peterborough, Reading and Winchester—all except Battle had a gross income of over £1000. Evesham, as we have seen, did not really drop out, but only migrated to Gloucester College.

In the matter of discipline and jurisdiction, Canterbury College

---

[1] Dugdale, *Monasticon* i. 363, note b.
[2] A. Savine in *Oxford Studies in Social and Legal History*, ed. P. Vinogradoff, i (1909) 210; R.H. Snape, *English Monastic Finances* (1926) 119.
[3] It must be remembered that the surviving accounts almost cease after 1511.

had no such quarrel with the *prior studentium* as Durham College had,[1] for soon after the foundation of the college the Canterbury monks, after a hard struggle,[2] had established their independence of the provincial chapter, in 1379.[3] It may be noted that in 1452 Christ Church Canterbury paid 13s. 4d. to the *prior studentium*, apparently as a voluntary contribution: Gloucester College was often appealing apparently for building funds.[4] However, while the warden and fellows were thus immune, the other black monks sojourning in the college were undoubtedly, in theory, subject to the *prior studentium* at Gloucester College. In 1426, the provincial chapter declared that these sojourners at Canterbury College must follow the practice enforced at Gloucester College as regards the eating of fleshmeat:[5] probably they had been trying to avail themselves of the papal indult on this subject recently granted to Canterbury College, 4 May 1423.[6] But the power of the *prior studentium*, at a distance, could not have been very real and the warden of the college was not, apparently, *in loco parentis*, but simply a landlord: the most he could do was to complain to the religious superiors of the sojourners and, if necessary, expel them.

In consequence of this lack of control, a bad set of sojourners could sometimes cause a good deal of trouble to the college. The monks of Peterborough in particular earned a bad reputation. An early instance may be found in a letter apparently written on 2 September 1438.[7] The writer, William Burghe of Peterborough, and his companion, Richard Assheton, left much to be desired in their conduct—e.g. in intercepting the letter, however 'cruel', sent to their prior from the warden, who made the familiar charges of tavern-haunting and dicing against them. Perhaps in regard to these charges it was the warden who was acting unjustly, for apparently just at this time, in August 1438, Warden Thomas Asshe, who was himself not above suspicion,[8] was superseded, after holding the wardenship for one year only, by John Waltham,[9] a friend of the Peterborough monks. One redeeming characteristic of the Peterborough monk is his sincere affection for his friend and namesake, to whom he addressed his letter: probably William Richemonde, who was at Canterbury College at this time. About fifty years later, the longstanding unruliness of the Peterborough monks was brought into evidence, this time from the warden's

[1] *Collectanea III* 25–35, 76 (A.D. 1422).
[2] *Gesta Abbatum Mon. S. Albani* (Rolls Series 28) ii. 403–4; *Chapters* iii. 56 ff.
[3] Wilkins, *Concilia* iii. 126–7.   [4] Extract 61 below.
[5] *Chapters* ii. 173.   [6] CPR *Letters* vii. 289.   [7] iii. 96.
[8] In 1443 he was excommunicated for holding property, contrary to the Rule: *Lit. Cant.* iii. 176–7.
[9] iii. 95; ii. 154.

point of view and with evident justice on his side. The temporary exile to Gloucester College had done them no good and now they were setting the other sojourners against authority.¹ One begins to wonder whether the disappearance of the monastic sojourners was not perhaps due to a definite policy of the college; only, the Peterborough monks were among those that stayed on for some years after 1490. In the case of one sojourner from Coventry it was not the Canterbury monks, but his own prior that was dissatisfied and removed him.² It would not be just to take these disorders as normal: even from the lowest point of view, the monks picked out to be sent to Oxford must generally have been too prudent to wish to ruin their university career, which was the greatest opportunity in a monk's life. And on one occasion when a sojourner from Evesham was unjustly accused and recalled by his monastery, the college joined in testifying to his good character.³

Besides Benedictines, the college occasionally lodged other religious, chiefly canons regular. Although St Mary's College had been founded in the middle of the century,⁴ there were Augustinian canons from Bristol⁵ and from Leeds (Kent);⁶ also a canon from 'Byleth', perhaps the Premonstratensian house of Beeleigh,⁷ and an unnamed canon in 1487–8, perhaps from Bristol.⁸ There were also in two cases religious of a rare type: a member of the house of Bonshommes at Ashridge in 1443–4⁹ and, in 1466–7, Servite friars,¹⁰ who may have been foreigners, as the Servites are not known to have had a house in England during the middle ages. At some time before 1496 the college lodged an 'Abbot of St Augustine's', perhaps from Canterbury but more likely from Bristol, as he used the room once occupied by the Bristol canons.¹¹

The secular sojourners were at first far fewer in numbers than the monastic sojourners: in some years there might be only one secular, or even none at all. But from the end of the fifteenth century, when the monks partially disappeared from the college, there was a corresponding increase in the number of seculars. Unlike the monk, the secular sojourner usually occupied a room by himself (though there were exceptions):¹² consequently the total number of sojourners decreased slightly as a result of this change. Again in contrast to the monks, the secular sojourners seem usually to have been men who were already

---

¹ iii. 121. ² iii. 116. ³ iii. 81.
⁴ H.E. Salter, *Chapters of the Augustinian Canons* (1920) xxxii, 83 and index s.v. 'Oxford'.
⁵ ii. 213. ⁶ ii. 221. ⁷ ii. 258.
⁸ ii. 218. ⁹ ii. 165. ¹⁰ ii. 185.
¹¹ ii. 224. ¹² ii. 258, 259.

graduates, being described as Master and Doctor, and they had in some cases already been fellows of other colleges.

Robert Rugge (or Rygge) was apparently a sojourner, one of the earliest recorded, c. 1379–80 or c. 1383–5. He had been fellow of Exeter and bursar of Merton and by 1380 was chancellor of the university; for a time (in 1382) he was a supporter of the Wycliffites.[1] The college lodged another chancellor, Thomas Chaundler of New College, and on other occasions the commissary or vice-chancellor. It was evidently appreciated as offering comfortable quarters for senior members of the university. Another type of sojourner, or perhaps the same type of academic at a later stage of his career, was the well-beneficed ecclesiastic. In 1439 there was 'unus venerabilis commorans in collegio, canonicus Herfordensis', who partly paid for the paling in the quadrangle between the hall and the chapel.[2] In 1466–7 the dean of Wells, Nicholas Carent, lodged in the upper room at the 'head' of the hall, probably the best room in the college;[3] and the same room, with the room under it, was occupied in 1469–71 by Master John Bourgcher, evidently a relation of the Archbishop of Canterbury, Cardinal Thomas Bourchier.[4] John left behind him the large debt of £13 owing to the warden, nearly all of which had to be paid by the archbishop.[5]

One of the sojourners between c. 1496 and 1504 was Dr William Atwater,[6] who had been a fellow of Magdalen and had become doctor of divinity in 1493. He was several times vice-chancellor during his stay in the college and once, in 1500, he acted as temporary chancellor. He gave up his room in Canterbury College about midsummer 1504,[7] being at that time appointed canon of Windsor and registrar of the order of the Garter. He crowned a successful career by becoming Bishop of Lincoln in 1514. Dr Foderbe, a sojourner at times in 1498–1500 and 1504–6, had been a fellow of Lincoln College and of Magdalen and eventually became precentor of Lincoln cathedral. He also served several times as vice-chancellor.[8] Mr Lotomer, Lathemar or Lottemerus, who appears as a sojourner in the accounts of 1516–17, 1521–2 and 1528–9, was evidently the distinguished humanist and

---

[1] ii. 127. Cf. Workman, *John Wyclif* ii. 142, 274, 279–82; BRUO iii. 1616.
[2] ii. 157. [3] ii. 185.
[4] ii. 190, 193. [5] ii. 195; iii. 116.
[6] ii. 224, 226, 229, 231, 241; DNB ii. 241; BRUO i. 73. For his tenure of office in the university, see *Reg. Canc. 1498–1506*, ed. W.A. Pantin and W.T. Mitchell (1972) 3, 19 ff. [7] ii. 241.
[8] ii. 226, 229, 241, 244; BRUO ii. 702; *Reg. Canc.* u.s.

friend of Erasmus, William Latimer, fellow of All Souls,[1] who by 1513 had returned to Oxford after his visit to Italy.

Two great names have been traditionally associated with Canterbury College: Thomas Linacre and St Thomas More—the former as a pupil and protégé of Prior Sellynge, the latter as a protégé of Archbishop Morton. The early dates of Linacre's life are uncertain, but he was probably born about 1460, he certainly became a fellow of All Souls in 1484 and in 1487 he went to Italy with Sellynge. The years 1480–4, then, may be taken as roughly the time when he was most likely to have been at Canterbury College; but there is no trace of him among the sojourners in 1480–1, or in 1481–2, or in any of the other accounts.

More was born in 1478 and was apparently at Oxford about 1492–4 (it happens that there are no surviving accounts between 1490 and 1496). The tradition of his stay in the college goes back to a statement made by his descendant and biographer, Cresacre More, who after speaking of More's upbringing by Archbishop Morton, goes on to say:

> 'But when this most excellent Prelate sawe, that he could not profitt so much in his house, as he desired, where there were manie distractions of publick affairs, having great care of his bringing up, he sent him to the Universitie, and placed him in Canterbury Colledge at Oxford, now called Christs-Church:[2] where in two yeares space that he remained there, he profitted exceedingly in Rhetorick, Logick and Philosophie …
>
> There his whole mind was set on his booke; for in his allowance his father kept him verie short, suffering him scarcelie to have so much monie in his own custodie, as would pay for the mending of his apparell; even no more than necessitie required; and of his expences, he would exact of him a particular accounte, which course of his fathers he would often both speak of, and praise it, when he came to riper yeares.'[3]

There are several reasons for thinking that probably neither Linacre nor More were at the college in the capacity of sojourners. Firstly, with regard to Linacre, the evidence of the college accounts is against the supposition. Secondly, More was only a boy when he came up to Oxford. Now a young undergraduate, sent up to the university for a few years before following his father's profession of law, does not seem at all the normal type of the secular sojourner, who was by preference a man of some standing, a graduate or a well-beneficed

---

[1] BRUO ii. 1106.
[2] He refers to the absorption of the college buildings in Christ Church.
[3] Cresacre More, *Life of Sir Thomas More* (1726) 9.

ecclesiastic, as we have seen. Juniority might also be an objection to Linacre, only we know so little about his age. On the whole, it seems more likely that Linacre and More, if they entered the college at all, did so as secular scholars, *pueri collegii*. Both the prior and the archbishop had the right of appointing to these scholarships, which thus offerred just the sort of provision which Prior Sellynge in the one case and Archbishop Morton in the other would wish to make for their young protégés. If any importance can be attached to Cresacre More's precise words, the 'placing' of More in the college might seem an exact description of such an appointment. It is true that the more or less menial character of the scholarships might be an objection, at least with a youth of More's position; but even this might fit in with his father's Spartan and thrifty ideas and his own later references to the hard fare at Oxford.[1] Again, More's studies fit in well with those required of the *pueri collegii*. In that capacity, too, he would have been allowed to go on to the study of civil law if he had stayed long enough. It is possible that Linacre was neither a sojourner nor one of the *pueri collegii*, but was maintained specially by the prior, as was apparently another of Sellynge's protégés, Richard Tyll.[2]

From time to time, the college had its benefactors and friends. Courtenay's statutes name several for whom the fellows were bound to say mass and the scholars to pray: the founder, Islip; the re-shapers of the college—Langham, Sudbury and Courtenay himself, for his pains; also a contemporary layman, Sir Geoffrey Lucy.[3] A few years ealier, 16 October 1381, the prior and chapter had granted Lucy for the term of his life, in return for the 'immense benefits' received from him, the use of a room in the monks' infirmary at Canterbury and stabling there for his horse; also a room in the college at Oxford at the west end of the chapel,[4] together with stabling. It is not stated what his 'immense benefits' were, but it seems likely that he gave Vine Hall to the college some time between 1377 and about 1383 and was asked to contribute towards the rebuilding.[5] He was also entertained at the college.[6]

In the next century, friends were repaid by participation in spiritual, not material goods. Master John More, B.C.L., in 1468[7] and

---

[1] Wm. Roper, *The Lyfe of Sir Thomas Moore, knighte*, ed. E.V. Hitchcock (1935) 53.   [2] iii. 122. Cf. BRUO iii. 1922.   [3] iii. 181.
[4] iii. 38. This was apparently before the rebuilding of the college. If the topography was the same as later, the room would have been the one at the upper end of the hall (south).   [5] ii. 128-9.
[6] ii. 128, 131.   [7] Canterbury Register S, fo. 229; ii 189.

Thomas Stevenys, S.T.P., commissary at Oxford, in 1474[1] were given letters of confraternity by the monks of Christ Church Canterbury, the former evidently as a reward for services rendered in the lawsuit against Oriel in 1466–8.[2] Similarly in 1463, Master John Cokkys, bachelor of civil law and physic, canon of Lincoln and rector of Witney, was given a letter of confraternity on account of 'the sincere love which he is known to have shown hitherto and still to show freely every day towards our brethren studying at Oxford.'[3] Some of the friends gave books: a certain W. Durant, for instance, in 1467–8 (he was perhaps the same as the William Duraunt mentioned in a charter of Edward IV concerning Pamfield manor, 30 November 1472).[4] Master T. Graunt is more than once mentioned as a donor of books c. 1469–75[5] and in 1470 he was given a letter of confraternity.[6] The Italian journeys of Sellynge and Hadley produced quite a crop of letters of confraternity to those who had helped them: to Johannita Bely, the widow of a Venetian citizen (1468),[7] to Peter de Malinis, a Roman citizen (1469),[8] to the Bishop of Urbino (1471).[9]

The end of the fifteenth century brought a very notable benefactor, Archbishop Morton, whose generosity greatly revived the college. In the early sixteenth century, the college seems to have made friends with the scholarly and enterprising abbot of Winchcomb, Richard Kidderminster,[10] who in January 1507 presided at the inception of the warden, Robert Holyngbourne,[11] and in 1510–11 paid a visit to the college together with the Prior of Winchester.[12] Another visitor in that year was the Spanish ambassador, who was apparently being shown round the university.[13]

The greatest friend and most notable benefactor who was not bound to the college by natural ties, so to speak, as were the archbishops and priors, was Thomas Chaundler, S.T.P. Born c. 1417, he became a fellow of New College in 1437, Warden of Winchester in 1450, Warden of New College 1454–75. In addition, he held various prebends and dignities in the churches of Wells, York, St Paul's and St Stephen's Westminster and finally became Dean

[1] Reg. S, fo. 265.   [2] ii. 187, 189.   [3] iii. 107.
[4] ii. 189; *Lit. Cant.* iii. 258.   [5] i. 112; ii. 192, iii. 111.
[6] Reg. S, fo. 244ᵛ.
[7] *Christ Church Letters* xxxviii.
[8] Ibid. xxxix.
[9] Reg. S, fo. 245ᵛ. On the subject of monastic letters of confraternity see E. Bishop, *Liturgica Historica* (1918) 349 ff.
[10] BRUO ii. 1047.
[11] Oxford University Archives, Register of Congregation G, fo. 31ᵛ.
[12] ii. 253.
[13] ii. 254.

of Hereford in 1482. At Oxford he was chancellor 1457–61, vice-chancellor 1463–7 and again chancellor 1472–9. We do not know when or how he first came into touch with the Canterbury monks or the college, but by 1468 he had already earned a letter of confraternity.[1] During his second chancellorship, in November 1473, Chaundler received recognition from both the Canterbury chapter and the college for the benefits which he had conferred on them. He had paid for the consecration of Canterbury College chapel and the building of (stone) altars in it; he had given £50 towards finding the wages of the manciple and cook and 200 marks (£133. 6. 8) towards reclaiming land near Romney Marsh; he had defrayed the expenses of procuring a bull for a plenary indulgence for the monks of Christ Church. In return, the prior and chapter promise to keep his obit as solemnly as that of Prior Wibert (ob. 1167) and at the same time to distribute £4 every year out of the reclaimed marshland to the sick monks at home and £1. 6. 8 to the sick monks at Oxford.[2] Further, the college promises that Chaundler shall be prayed for by name in the daily mass for benefactors and in the grace after meals in hall. The cook and the manciple are also to be bound under oath to recite the Lord's prayer and the Hail Mary in the chapel daily for his soul.[3]

It seems that Chaundler soon afterwards received not only spiritual, but also material recompense, like Sir Geoffrey Lucy, by being lodged in the college, perhaps on ceasing to be Warden of New College in 1475. The college account for 1476–8, though it does not record him as an ordinary, rent-paying sojourner, refers incidentally to the 'chancellor's', chamber (he was at that time chancellor of the university) and to the accomodation of Dr Chaundler's servants.[4]

Next, there are two letters concerning Chaundler, which must be later than 1482, when he became Dean of Hereford, and are probably earlier than 1486, on account of their references to Thomas Goldstone, who had left Oxford by that year.[5] One of these letters, dated Canterbury 1 July, is addressed to Chaundler himself by Prior Sellynge, who had been hoping that Chaundler would pay a visit to Canterbury. He refers to the latter's past benefactions and to a new one which is being planned. The other letter (Oxford, 3 September) was written to Prior Sellynge by Thomas Goldstone, who had been entrusted with a message from the prior to Chaundler. Unfortunately, the latter, who had been visiting Oxford, had gone back with all his household to the deanery of Hereford.

[1] Reg. S, fo. 229.
[2] *Lit. Cant.* iii. 267.
[3] iii. 114.
[4] ii. 201–3.
[5] iii. 123, 125. Sheppard's conjectural date, 1473, is out of the question.

It seems evident from these letters, particularly from the first one, that Chaundler was not only a benefactor, but a personal friend of Sellynge. It may be that their friendship went back to the period c. 1454–64, when Sellynge first came up to Oxford and Chaundler was Warden of New College, and that it was Chaundler who suggested and supported the project of Sellynge's first visit to Italy. At any rate, this friendship seems to be the most certain connexion that Sellynge had with the rather older group of enthusiasts like Flemyng, Gray, Free, Gunthorpe and Chaundler himself, who first brought the classical revival into England in the middle of the fifteenth century.[1] Sellynge and Chaundler shared the same tastes and enthusiasm. The latter, though he himself had never visited Italy, gained a reputation for pure Latinity—which was perhaps reflected in the studied elegance of the letters of Sellynge and some of his fellow monks.[2] While Warden of New College, he played a part in the restoration of classical letters by inciting an Italian scholar, Cornelio Vitelli, to lecture in the college. It was perhaps thus that Grocyn as a young fellow of New College first learned Greek.

Another friend of Christ Church Canterbury, of similar tastes but of a very different character and career, was John Tiptoft, Earl of Worcester (c. 1427–1471), who was destined to die on the scaffold, hated for his cruelty. Though the friendship may in part have had a political motive,[3] it began when Tiptoft was quite a young man and it had a certain attractive, personal side. This can be seen in some letters (1452) between the young earl and one of the Canterbury monks, Henry Cranebroke, who was no distinguished scholar like Sellynge, but evidently shared Tiptoft's taste for classical elegance.[4] Tiptoft was present at the enthronements of Archbishop Kemp in 1452[5] and Archbishop Bourchier in 1455.[6] When he was at Padua during his visit to Italy (c. 1459–61), the Canterbury monks wrote to him, asking him to help them procure a papal bull concerning the jubilee of St Thomas.[7] It was from the same city that he wrote to the university of Oxford, probably in 1460, urging the reading of good books in

---

[1] Mallet i. 342–3; P.S. Allen, *Age of Erasmus* (1914) 121 ff.
[2] A good example is Sellynge's letter to Chaundler: iii. 123. For Chaundler see Tanner, *Bibliotheca* 171; Wharton, *Anglia Sacra* ii. xvii, 355; *Collectanea III* 338 ff.; BRUO i. 398.
[3] Christ Church does not seem to have been firmly attached to either party, though it was ready to make friends with the Yorkists: C.E. Woodruff and W. Danks, *Memorials of Canterbury Cathedral* (1912) 205–6.
[4] iii. 103 ff.   [5] Searle 55.
[6] Ibid. 62–3.
[7] *Lit. Cant.* iii. 215–17. The date conjectured there, 1454, is too early. Apparently it was on this same business that Sellynge was sent to Rome in 1469.

order to restore the 'dignity of the lost Latin tongue' and so produce orators worthy to be sent, if necessary, by the king to Italy.[1] Perhaps he was impressed by the profit and careers that scholarship had brought to men like Valla and Poggio, but his words are a curious anticipation of the rôle afterwards played by Sellynge as ambassador and orator at the papal court; and perhaps messages of this kind from Italy had a part in forming that young man's aspirations. Tiptoft was solemnly received by the monks at Canterbury on his return from the Holy Land in September 1461, the prior going out to meet him at St Martin's.[2] He came to Canterbury in the train of Edward IV in 1462[3] and again in 1470, not long before his death.[4] He was given letters of confraternity and his name was duly entered in the obituary of Christ Church.[5]

The friendship of Chaundler and Tiptoft helps to illustrate the place of the college in the life of the university and the nation. The college was not illustrious or influential in its official capacity or its official studies; it did not, so far as we know, produce a great schoolman and perhaps one could hardly expect it to have produced a chancellor, though monks had served in that capacity. What importance the college had was due to the personal characters and connexions of its members—and this seems particularly true as regards the classical revival, as we have suggested in another place. It was, after all, more or less characteristic of that revival in its earlier phase that it was something personal, almost amateur, thriving among groups of friends rather than officially organised in the existing institutions. If, apart from Sellynge, the college made little positive contribution to the Renaissance, its friendships may at least do it credit and its history shows no evidence of the hostility which humanists sometimes felt towards the monasteries nor, on the other hand, of any reactionary prejudice on the part of the monks. It must be admitted that when we come to the later, more developed humanists—Linacre, More, Latimer—their connexion with the college seems all too uncertain; but from its fostering of Sellynge and its friendship with Chaundler, the college is certainly and honourably connected with the van of the English Renaissance.

[1] EHR 35. 570.
[2] Searle 84.
[3] Ibid. 87.
[4] Ibid. 113.
[5] MS. Arundel 68, fo. 45ᵛ.

5
THE ECONOMY, INTERNAL AND EXTERNAL

THE care and administration of the college in spiritual and temporal matters was entrusted to the warden. He probably acted as the confessor as well as the religious superior of the fellows, though we have no such formal commissions to hear confessions as at Durham College.[1] The first duty of the warden was to keep peace and order. If he failed in this, or was found to be in any way violent or immoral, he was to be first admonished and then reported to the archbishop.[2] There is no evidence of such an extreme step being found necessary. Similarly, if a fellow was at fault, the warden after a triple admonition, or in cases of grave scandal apparently straightaway, was to report the culprit (for recall and punishment in the monastery) to the prior and chapter or, if they failed to act, to the archbishop.[3] There survives the particularly interesting story of one insubordinate fellow, William Chartham. Being corrected by the warden, apparently with rather excessive severity, for insolence and negligence, he answered back, charging the warden with acting from a personal grudge. The prior and subprior at Canterbury, getting to hear of this and perhaps suspecting that the fault was not entirely on one side, made discreet and unofficial enquiries into the facts of the case. Before the matter proceeded further, however, it was brought to an edifying conclusion by a public apology from Chartham.[4] On the whole there is little trace of insubordination among the fellows, who were, after all, directly bound to the warden by the ties of religious obedience and formed with him the ruling caste in the college, with a full interest in its welfare. The danger to discipline seems rather to have come from the other, less responsible elements, less cordially connected with the government of the college: the servants, the sojourners, the *pueri collegii*.

The temporal administration brings out very well the two distinct, almost contradictory, characteristics of the college: its self-contained, corporate existence as a college and its dependence upon the church of Canterbury as a monastic department, like a cell or an obedientiary's office, or at least as tied to a partner, as a chapter was to its bishop.

[1] *Collectanea III* 29.
[2] iii. 177.
[3] iii. 178.
[4] iii. 117.

By the statutes of 1384,[1] the warden and fellows were naturally to have a common seal, which was necessary in order to express corporate consent to any transaction. But a seal is a dangerous instrument if it gets into the wrong hands. Hence the use of the common seal was, as usual, carefully guarded: deeds were only to be sealed after common and 'solemn' deliberation and with the consent of at least the majority of the fellows.

But besides this, the common custom of collegiate bodies, there is the further control of Canterbury. No deed alienating or pledging the goods of the college could be made or sealed without the written consent both of the archbishop and of the prior and chapter. There has survived one such letter of consent, issued on the part of the prior and chapter on 20 May 1380 in view of a particular emergency, apparently the acquisition of Staple Hall and Chimer Hall.[2] It is issued confessedly in virtue of an existing statute, afterwards embodied in Courtenay's statutes of 1384. According to his own account, Courtenay was compelled by actual experience to go further: quite apart from any corporate action, no individual member was to sell, pawn or 'enchest'[3] any books or other valuables belonging to the church of Canterbury without the special permission of the prior and chapter, under pain of excommunication and permanent recall from the college.[4] Here the college goods are definitely, it seems, conceived of as the property of Christ Church; and this point of view does in fact represent fairly accurately the actual method of acquisition, especially in the case of books.

Out of the general wealth of documents relating to the college, the number of those which originally bore the college seal is remarkably small and there are only two, apparently, which still preserve the impression of the seal, both of them being among the Balliol deeds.[5] The seal consists of a circular medallion representing the martydom of St Thomas of Canterbury (the patron of the college) with the figures of the archbishop, the four knights and the cross-bearer. Round the edge of the circle is the inscription: *Sigillum collegii aule Cantuarie in Oxonia*.

The warden of the college, being in effect assimilated to the other obedientiaries of Christ Church, had like them to render a strict account to the prior and chapter for all the goods and revenues of his office, and this not simply for the sake of administrative efficiency but

---

[1] iii. 174. [2] iii. 37.
[3] *Incistare*: i.e. to pledge to one of the university chests. These were, of course, intended for secular students, not for well-supported monks. See Mallet i. 322 ff.; G. Pollard in *Reg. Congr. 1448–1463* 418.
[4] iii. 181.
[5] *The Oxford Deeds of Balliol College*, ed. H.E. Salter (1913) 161, 164.

THE ECONOMY, INTERNAL AND EXTERNAL 107

also as a kind of religious duty, since any fraud or even concealment might take on the character of 'propriety', the *vicium peculiare*, the sacrilegious offence of holding private property, against the Rule. The 'status' of the office was declared in two ways: by means of inventories and through yearly accounts.[1]

The first thing the warden had to do, within a month of his appointment, was to make an inventory of the college goods taken over by him,[2] just as the newly elected abbot or prior of a monastery had to do according to the Constitutions of Pope Benedict XII.[3] The inventory was to be renewed from time to time, if necessary every year, and two 'indented' copies were always to be made, one for the college, the other to be sent to the prior and chapter. Eight complete inventories of the college are in existence. The following will show the dates, the wardens who drew them up and the occasion:

A	1443	Robert Lynton	on entering office
B	1459	William Thornden	on leaving office
C	1501A	Thomas Chaundler	on leaving office
D	1501B	Robert Holyngbourne	on entering office
E	1510	Edward Bockyng	on entering office
F	1521	William Hadley	during office
G	1524	Richard Thornden	on entering office
H	1534	William Sandwyche	on entering office.

It will be seen that with only one exception (Hadley, 1521) all these inventories were made when the warden either entered or left office: there is certainly no evidence of any attempt at renewing the inventories annually, as the statutes had suggested. Further, it does not seem that the inventories were regularly kept up to date by means of correction,[4] as the alterations and interpolations made in the existing documents are comparatively few and unimportant. On the whole, it seems likely that the college contented itself with making an inventory at the beginning and at the end of each wardenship. The complete series would thus have consisted of pairs of inventories, like those of 1501, made whenever the wardenship changed hands. The inventory of the outgoing warden would show in what state he left the college goods—whether better or worse than when he succeeded—and the

[1] For examples of these from the cells of Durham, see Surtees Society vols. 6 (Finchale), 12 (Coldingham), 29 (Jarrow and Wearmouth). Cf. Durham College documents in *Collectanea III*.
[2] iii. 175.
[3] Wilkins, *Concilia* iii. 603 (c. 14). For an actual example of such an inventory, see *Hist. Dunelm. Scriptores Tres* (Surtees Soc. vol. 9) appendix, p. cclxxxv.
[4] Like, for instance, the very interesting 'growing' inventories of church goods in the *Vetus Liber Archidiaconi Eliensis*, ed. C.L. Feltoe and E.H. Minns, 1917.

inventory of the incoming warden would act as a check upon the other and would lay down precisely the extent of the responsibility of the new warden. That the making of two inventories in this way within a few weeks of each other was no unnecessary formality can be seen from a comparison of the two inventories of 1501 where, particularly as regards the books (the most valuable of the college goods), there is a remarkable discrepancy.[1] Possibly in this case, the change of wardens was made an opportunity for a clearance and overhauling of the library.

The precise ground to be covered by the inventory was not laid down in the statutes, but by custom it came to consist of the contents of the chapel, the hall, the promptuary, the kitchen, the warden's chamber and the library (books only, not fittings). The inventory dealt only with movable furniture, not fixtures. It might include, for instance, an alabaster 'table' or altar-piece, or a *wooden* altar,[2] but not a stone one or a 'study' or an oven: things which could not be removed easily or without notice. It does, however, include the 'speer' or hall screen, which would probably have been fixed.

The inventory only dealt with the official parts of the college, for which the warden was directly responsible. It did not include the chambers of the fellows, which would be furnished with their own personal 'stuff'; still less did it take account of the chambers of the sojourners, the secular scholars or the college servants, except in so far as these rooms might sometimes temporarily house some official property: e.g. books out of the library in the rooms of the fellows at the time,[3] 'books in the great chest in the room of Dom William Pecham',[4] 'a chest in the manciple's room, in which to keep linen.'[5] Again, these inventories do not deal, as most inventories of monastic cells and offices do, with the store of food or drink in the college. It was the *pincerna* rather than the warden who was responsible for that.

As regards the keeping of accounts: according to the statutes, the warden and senior fellow are responsible for the safe keeping in the common chest of all the money received from Pagham or elsewhere and a kind of indenture or receipt is always to be drawn up between those who deliver and those who receive this money.[6] As a matter of fact, there is only one example surviving of any such separate account of receipts: that for the year 1432–3; and this may have been occasioned by abnormal circumstances, for it includes a loan from the warden of the manors of Christ Church and the receipts cover half the coming year as well as the current year.[7]

[1] i. 18, 39. [2] i. 3. [3] i. 43, 45.
[4] i. 62. [5] i. 38.
[6] iii. 175. [7] ii. 262.

THE ECONOMY, INTERNAL AND EXTERNAL 109

The warden was bound to render an annual account of all receipts and expenditure. Here the system was much less elaborate than at Durham College, where the warden was assisted by two bursars and accounts were made up quarterly as well as annually.¹ The only approach to the Durham College system was in 1440–1, when the warden and the senior fellow for some reason were joint administrators. The warden of Canterbury College was to submit his account either to the prior and a committee of senior monks at Canterbury—in which case the chapter would defray the expenses of the journey—or else, by the chapter's permission, to his own fellows at Oxford. Two copies of the accounts were to be made: one for the college, the other to be sent home and kept in the treasury at Canterbury.² It is these latter duplicates which have survived: in only one case have both copies of the same account survived.³ The *compotus* normally covered the year from Michaelmas to Michaelmas and, so far as existing indications show, it was 'made', audited and settled in the following March, April or May.⁴ Sometimes, however, the accounts were allowed to get behindhand: thus the accounts for 1502–3 and 1503–4 were not dealt with until 25 and 27 May 1506.⁵ About Easter was naturally the most convenient time for auditing these accounts, as there was always sure to be someone going from the college to Canterbury then to preach. It was perhaps this arrangement which induced the warden to experiment for a few years (1504–7) by making his accounts run from Easter to Easter instead of from Michaelmas to Michaelmas.

Each year, unless the receipts and expenditure tallied exactly, which was almost impossible to happen, the accounts would present *arreragia* or *superplusagium*. It is important to notice that these words denoted the exact opposite to the modern ideas of arrears and surplus. *Arreragia* meant that the receipts had exceeded the expenditure and so the accounting warden was so much poorer: 'et sic debet computans'—which does not mean that he is in debt but, on the contrary, that he has money left over which he 'owes' to his superiors or to next year's receipts, or to the common chest of the college. The more common *superplusagium* meant that the expenditure had exceeded the receipts and that the warden was so much out of pocket: 'et sic debentur computanti'—it is up to someone to make good this deficit to him. In either case, the outstanding sum could be dealt with in one of two ways. The *arreragia* could either be 'allowed', i.e. made over, to the warden as a favour or a reward,⁶ or else put into the

---
¹ *Collectanea III* 15, 56–67. ² iii. 175.
³ ii. 206. ⁴ ii. 187, 194, 210, 225.
⁵ ii. 240. ⁶ ii. 162, 206.

common chest and reckoned among the receipts in next year's account.[1] The *superplusagium* was sometimes carried forward and reckoned among next year's expenditure, or else the deficit was paid to the warden then and there by the prior and chapter, so that the college could make a fresh start next year. In such cases, one finds the warden receiving this money from the prior's chaplain[2] or from the prior himself,[3] the transaction taking place on one occasion in the infirmary chapel at Christ Church.[4] At other times, presumably when the account was made at Oxford instead of at Canterbury, the deficit is paid to the warden of the college by the warden of the manors when he comes to Oxford in the course of his 'progress'.[5] In one case, the order for payment through the warden of manors is written at the bottom of the account (the copy, no doubt, sent to Canterbury) and signed, apparently, with the sign manual of the prior, Thomas Goldstone.[6]

Some light may be thrown on the method of accounting by the alterations or additions in the accounts. In the first place, in some of the accounts the sums or totals of the various subsections have been written in, apparently, in a different hand and in one such case the totals have also been written, very small and faint, in Arabic numerals in the right-hand margin, very much like the scribbled directions to the rubricator that are sometimes to be found in manuscripts.[7] These circumstances suggest that the original accountant in such cases for greater security left the items to be added up and the sums to be filled in by the auditor.[8] Again the accountant, even when he has added up the totals throughout the account, including the grand total of receipts and expenditure, sometimes leaves the final touch, the reckoning and writing-in of the deficit, to someone else, presumably the auditor.[9] In some cases, this added deficit is written in Arabic numerals and in one account it is coupled with the order for payment to the warden, signed by the prior, as referred to above. Sometimes an acknowledgement of the receipt of payment for the *superplusagium* is added at the bottom

---

[1] Acc. 1439–40: ii. 159; acc. 1443–4 and 1444–5: ii. 166, 167; acc. 1475–6 and 1476–7: ii. 197; acc. 1498–9 and 1499–1500: ii. 228, 229.
[2] ii. 210.   [3] ii. 187.   [4] ii. 194.
[5] ii. 252.   [6] ii. 247.
[7] ii. 221. For sums in another hand, see ii. 135, 137 ff., 217 f.
[8] For another case of the totals throughout an account being left blank to be filled in by the auditor, see T.F. Hobson, *Adderbury Rectoria* (1926) 57. This work, which prints and comments on the accounts for the rebuilding of the chancel of Adderbury church 1408–19, is most valuable for its analysis of contemporary methods of construction, labour and account-keeping. For the latter see especially pp. 49–59.
[9] This occurs at the end of all the accounts between 1496 and 1506, with the exception of 1501–2.

THE ECONOMY, INTERNAL AND EXTERNAL

of the account or if, on the contrary, there is money to spare, the 'allowance' of some of it to the warden may be duly noted in the same place.[1]

There are numerous corrections, great and small. In 1508–9, when the accounting warden by a slip puts down the payment of an obsolete rent, the correcting hand strikes this out, marks it with a cross and adds a memorandum that this rent is not to be paid, 'because we have a perpetual acquittance, which is kept in the common chest at Oxford.'[2] Again, in 1496 in connexion with the payment of rent, the warden's calculations are thrown out by the fact that he is accounting for a half-year instead of the usual whole year. The correcting hand adds in the margin that 'he ought to compute [this] in the next account, because it is not paid except once a year'.[3]

The college accounts, from the earliest survivor of certain date in 1382 to the last in 1528, with very few exceptions[4] show a more or less uniform, traditional structure, which was no doubt in the first instance simply that of the ordinary monastic obedientiary's account, adapted to the peculiar needs of the college. The account was divided as usual into two main sections, receipt and expenditure, and these were again divided into a number of subsections. Within the subsections, the items were generally written in 'narrative' form, running on immediately one after the other and forming a compact mass of writing, instead of each item occupying a separate line with the money in the column on the right-hand side. This narrative form was economical, for several short items could be got into one line and its inconvenience for the purpose of adding was not so obvious when Roman, not Arabic numerals were used. The structure of the account sometimes varies as to the order of the subsections and the phraseology of the marginal captions which usually accompany the letters, but the component parts remain substantially the same. They may be summarised as follows:

I. Receipts
(1) The *arreragia* or balance in hand from the previous year.
(2) The main bulk of the income, from the rectory of Pagham or (after 1455) in the form of a grant from the prior.
(3) The proceeds from the letting of rooms in the college and also (until about 1448) of the 'tenement outside the gate of the college'.
(4) Occasional receipts, such as loans[5] or payments of old debts.[6]

[1] ii. 190, 194; ii. 166, 170. [2] ii. 252; cf. ii. 243.
[3] ii. 225. [4] ii. 132, 136, 197–203. [5] e.g. ii. 150.
[6] ii. 195.

II. Expenses

First, the salaries or living expenses of
(1) the monks, the warden and fellows;
(2) the secular scholars, the *pueri collegii*;
(3) the college servants; together with
(4) the college gaudies on the feasts of St Thomas of Canterbury, 7 July (the translation) and 29 December (the martyrdom).

The upkeep of the college:
(5) Chapel expenses.
(6) Repairs to the fabric generally and renewal of furniture and utensils.
(7) Rent to the ground landlords of the college site.
(8) Various expenses, journeys, lawsuits, liveries etc.
(9) Before 1455, expenses incurred at the rectory of Pagham, such as repairs, fines, alms.
(10) The *superplusagium* or deficit, if any, from the previous year has to be counted among the expenses.

The peculiar excellence of the Canterbury College accounts lies in this, that while most other monastic accounts devote a large amount of space to extraneous matters—the receipts from and expenses of the estates or churches[1]—these accounts deal almost exclusively with the college itself, even when Pagham rectory was in the hands of the college, and still more so when the rectory was taken over by Christ Church priory.

The warden and fellows were monks, bound to a common life and to individual, though not corporate, poverty. It therefore seems very strange at first sight that instead of receiving their board in kind they were given, as the accounts show, separate salaries in money, out of which to find their own keep, just as if they were secular students. Indeed, a secular student under the charge of a tutor might have very much less economic independence.[2] To say that the college was small and cut off from Canterbury is not in itself sufficient explanation, for in other monastic cells,[3] quite as small as Canterbury College, the monks were apparently boarded, not paid, as is shown by the general kitchen expenses; though they, like all monks of the period, received

---

[1] Thus, Durham College accounts contain surprisingly few entries about Oxford and very many about the appropriated rectories, though the latter were let out to farm. See *Collectanea III* 56 ff. It is this serious drawback which prevents so many documents of this kind from being printed in full.

[2] See H.E. Salter in *Poole Essays* 421 ff.

[3] e.g. Finchale, Coldingham, Jarrow and Wearmouth, dependent upon Durham. See Surtees Society vols. 6, 12, 29.

THE ECONOMY, INTERNAL AND EXTERNAL   113

certain additional money allowances, known by such names as *oblaciones*.[1] In the same way, the boarding of the monk-fellows might have been left to the warden. The opposite practice of paying salaries, however, had a historic reason behind it. When the monks first came to stay in Oxford, whether in separate, hired lodgings (like the Canterbury settlement near St Peter's in the East) or even in *camerae* at Gloucester College, each monk was an isolated unit, necessarily dependent upon a money allowance from his monastery. The only possible modification of this isolation lay in the fact that when there were several monk-students from one house, they might be in charge of their senior member and also that the *prior studentium* exercised some supervision over the way in which the monk-students spent their allowances.[2]

It is easy to see how it came to be regarded as a general rule that monks studying at the university were to be paid salaries. The practice was definitely sanctioned by Pope Benedict XII, who in his Constitutions laid down precisely the scale of salaries according to degrees:[3] in English money, £15 per annum for a doctor and £10 for a bachelor or student in divinity, £12. 10 for a doctor and £8. 15 for a bachelor or student of canon law. Out of these salaries, in all cases £5 went towards daily expenses and £1. 10 towards clothing, boots etc.[4] and the balance, varying according to the degree, was chiefly for buying books.

The statutes of Canterbury College in 1384 laid down a similar but simpler scale of salaries: the monk-fellows were to receive yearly £10, paid quarterly, while the warden was to have the same amount together with an extra £3 for his pains. The fellows' salary seems at first sight equivalent to that which Pope Benedict would have allowed them as bachelors or students of divinity, which they usually were; but in fact it was more liberal, as they were to receive their *cameraria* or clothes-allowance in addition, instead of having to take it out of their salary. The accounts of the college show that in practice this scale was not always strictly followed. The wardens, it is true, always received their full allowance of £13 per annum and down to about 1454 the fellows were paid at the full rate of £10 per annum; but from that time until the end of the century the salary sank to about £8. 6. 8

[1] The Durham College rolls show that the monk fellows there received commons and *oblaciones*: *Collectanea III* 58, 63, 66.
[2] Constitutions of Benedict XII in Wilkins, *Concilia* ii. 598. Cf. the suggestions of the Abbot of Glastonbury in 1360 for the regulation of commons etc. by the *prior studentium* and a committee of six: *Chapters* iii. 30.
[3] Wilkins, *Concilia* ii. 596. The provincial chapter (probably in 1363) stated that one pound sterling was equivalent to four of the small livres tournois in which Pope Benedict reckoned: *Chapters* ii. 78.   [4] i.e. *cameraria*. See below.

or £8 and from about 1498 onwards it was only the senior fellow who got £8, the rest receiving £6. 10 or £5.

This gradual decrease of salaries is quite contrary to what might have been expected. It can perhaps be explained partly by the decline of the college revenues,[1] partly by the changing policy of those who managed the college property. So long as the latter was controlled directly by the warden and fellows, they naturally saw to it that they received their full statutory salaries, but when, after 1454, the prior and chapter of Canterbury took over this deteriorating property, allowing the college an annual grant in return, it seems as though the Canterbury authorities quite as naturally determined on retrenchment, cutting down the salaries of the fellows. Such a policy would account for the first fall in salaries.

The second fall is perhaps more apparent than real, being due to a change in account-keeping. For some years before 1498, while the college accounts mention two or three fellows receiving £8 each, the accounts of the warden of the manors seem to show *additional* monk-students receiving £5 *ex assignacione prioris*, with or without £1. 10. 0 *pro cameraria sua*. What evidently happened about 1498 was that these additional fellows were brought into the college accounts, receiving as before at the rate of £6. 10. 0 or £5 per annum.

It is interesting to note that at Westminster in the same way, the monks at the university were each paid £10 a year until about 1435, when their salary was cut down to 10 marks (i.e. £6. 13. 4).[2]

The accounts simply record the payment of the salaries, without any details of the way in which they were spent by the individual monk-fellows, who were apparently left to manage their own affairs. William Chartham was found after his death to have contracted debts great and small, including his barber's and laundry bills.[3] As has been pointed out already the fellows, so far as the accounts show, were not boarded, but must have paid for their meals out of their salary. Probably, like the sojourners, they kept an account with the manciple.

A very important exception to the general rule is made in the accounts for the years 1393–5, when the warden and fellows did not receive salaries, but simply had their bare expenses paid. This cannot be explained as primitive simplicity, degenerating afterwards into the salary system, for the payment of salaries appears in one of the first surviving accounts of all, that for 1382–3. Most probably the rebuilding of the college about the years 1394–6 necessitated a drastic cutting-down of all superfluous expenses, especially in the maintenance of the fellows, where there was most room for economy. One

---

[1] The rectory of Pagham, let out to farm, steadily fell in value.
[2] Pearce 26–7.
[3] iii. 128.

may compare the way in which the monks at Canterbury about the same time gave up their spice allowance (or pocket-money) for the rebuilding of the nave of the cathedral.[1] The great building prior, Thomas Chillynden, saw to it that the rest of the community shared his enthusiasm, or at least his costs.

For us at least the economy is welcome, for it means that the accounts for once give the details of the monk-fellows' expenses. In the first place we are given the main boarding expenses of the fellows, their commons week by week, reckoned apparently from Friday to Friday and varying usually from about 18d. to 22d. a week, but occasionally sinking to 16d. or even 14d., or rising above 2s. The fluctuations were due mainly, no doubt, to mere accident or to the current price of victuals, but in some cases the larger sums spent on commons seems to be determined by the festivals of the Christian year. Thus the highest commons, 2s. 8d. and 2s. 5d., were at Christmas in 1393 and 1394 respectively. Shrovetide, with some kind of *mardi gras* celebration, perhaps accounts for the rate of 2s. in 1394[2] and 2s. 5d. in 1395,[3] Easter for 2s. 4d. and 2s. 5d. in 1394,[4] Pentecost for 2s. in 1394[5] and possibly Michaelmas for 2s. in 1393.[6] Wine and meat to the value of 7s. 9d. were bought for the gaudy on St Thomas' day (29 December) in 1393 and more wine was bought for St Benedict's day (21 March) in 1394. In the later years, there are references to the customary provision of a boar at Christmas. Thomas Everard received a special 'pittance' when he preached in the Lenten quarter of 1394. If about 20d. a week may be taken as the average rate of commons, the standard of living among the monk-fellows was distinctly high, for the secular scholars of the college during these years received commons at the unvarying rate of 10d. a week and in the fifteenth century it was possible to live on 8d. or even $4\frac{3}{4}$d. a week.[7]

Besides the commons, there were the battels of the monk-fellows to be paid, apparently at the unvarying rate of 6d. a week per head. The accounts throw no further light on their exact nature.[8] As regards academic dues, the accounts of 1393–5 show payments which work out sometimes at a rate of 13s. 4d., sometimes at 6s. 8d. a quarter from

[1] Searle 18.
[2] In the tenth week after Christmas (1393), Ash Wednesday falling on 4 March.
[3] In the ninth week after Christmas (1394), Ash Wednesday falling on 24 February.
[4] In the third and fourth weeks after Lady day, Easter falling on 19 April. But it must be admitted that on this liturgical hypothesis the price of commons went up too soon: in Holy Week.
[5] In the eleventh week after Lady day, Pentecost falling on 7 June.
[6] In the second week after St Matthew's day. [7] See *Poole Essays* 427.
[8] For discussion of the derivation and original meaning of 'battels', see Mallet i. 147 n., 252 n.

each fellow for 'ordinary' lectures, 'special masters' (perhaps for the other lectures) and 'quarterage'. There were also payments to the bedel.[1] The fellows had to pay *contribuciones* at a rate varying from 2s. 7d. to 3s. a quarter per head. There may have been further academic dues, *cumulaciones*; or they may mean that the monk-fellows of Canterbury College contributed towards the salary of the *prior studentium* at Gloucester College, in accordance with the Constitutions of Benedict XII.[2] Such contributions were paid voluntarily even by the monks of Durham College, who vigorously claimed to be exempt from the jurisdiction of the *prior studentium*.[3] Canterbury certainly made a contribution to the latter in 1451–2.[4] These academic dues and 'contributions' would presumably be paid in normal years out of the monk-fellow's salary.

Besides living expenses, some provision had to be made for the clothing of the monk-student. Normally, i.e. in the monastery, the chamberlain was entirely responsible for this provision: all that the monk need do was to apply for new clothes and return the old ones. 'Accipientes nova, vetera semper reddant in praesenti, reponenda in vestiario propter pauperes.'[5] It was in this connexion that the vice of *proprietas* or private property was feared and denounced, particularly in the prevalent abuse whereby monks were given not their actual clothes but the equivalent in cash.[6] But, as has been pointed out already, the monk maintained at the university was usually so cut off from his monastery that the strictly regular system of provision in kind was practically out of the question. Consequently, Benedict XII thought it necessary to set aside a definite portion of the monk-student's salary, £1. 10. 0 a year (6 livres tournois), for clothing, shoes etc.

Some definite provision for *cameraria*—'chamberlain's stuff', clothing—was clearly contemplated in the Canterbury College statutes of 1384, though whether in money or kind is not stated.[7] Until the college revenues could be increased for the purpose, the *cameraria* was to be provided from Christ Church Canterbury. In actual fact, the revenues did not increase but sank and, to judge from the silence of the college accounts, the *cameraria* must have come either from Canterbury to the end or out of the salaries of the monk-fellows. In a few cases, however, the *cameraria* enters into the college accounts as a money payment. In the years 1466–8 Thomas Chartham received no

[1] *Poole Essays* 423.
[2] Wilkins, *Concilia* ii. 598.
[3] *Collectanea III* 33.
[4] Extract 61 below.
[5] Rule of St Benedict, c. 55.
[6] General chapter of 1215: *Chapters* i. 11.   [7] iii. 175.

THE ECONOMY, INTERNAL AND EXTERNAL 117

proper salary, but only £1. 10. 0 *pro camera sua*.[1] In 1502–3 £6. 10. 0 was spent 'in pensione fratris Thome Goldwel ... una cum camera sua'[2] and William Hadley has a similar entry in 1508–9.[3]

The word *camera*, if taken in its more obvious meaning of chamber or room, will hardly make sense in the context. Lodging would naturally be given to the monk-fellows as a matter of course and it is difficult to see how it could enter in any way into the college accounts. There is no reason to suppose that on these occasions the fellows had to hire rooms outside the college. It seems more likely that the word *camera* should be taken here to mean what the statutes called *cameraria*, the clothing etc. (or the equivalent in cash) which it was the duty of a monastic chamberlain to provide. This is borne out by an entry in 1487, when Richard Copton received in addition to £2. 10. 0 (probably his half-year's salary) another 15s. *pro cameraria*.[4] The entries would thus mean that the college paid the clothes-allowance of these particular fellows, apparently by way of exception.[5] There are also in the accounts of the wardens of the manors more frequent payments for *cameraria* to the 'extra' fellows who only received £5, and these the fellows who received £8 did not get. This seems to show that fellows drawing full salary had to pay *cameraria* out of their salary.

As to the quantity and quality of the clothing to be provided: in addition to the Rule and subsequent general legislation, the customaries of different monasteries usually lay down the precise duties of the chamberlain;[6] but unfortunately, nothing like a complete body of customs for Christ Church Canterbury has survived.[7] However, MS. 265 of Corpus Christi College, Oxford, a book of miscellaneous notes mainly concerning William Glastynbury, monk of Christ Church 1419–48,[8] contains a list of the latter's clothing and bedding made in 1415, a year after his entrance into the monastery. Although there is no evidence that he was ever at Canterbury College, the list may be taken as an example of the equipment which a monk-fellow of the

[1] ii. 185, 188. In this instance it seems right to take *cameraria* or *camera* as the provision for clothing received in kind or money from the *camerarius*. For an early use of *camera* to denote the chamberlain's office or department, see J.A. Robinson, *Gilbert Crispin* (1911) 41, 43–5. Cf. *cameria* in the chronicle of Jocelin of Brakelond, *Memorials of St Edmund's Abbey* (Rolls Series 96) i. 309. For the use of *camera* as an allowance or revenue, see also A.H. Thompson, *Visitations of Religious Houses in the Diocese of Lincoln* i (1940), 98, 222; iii (1947) 273.
[2] ii. 236. [3] ii. 250. [4] ii. 268.
[5] Cf. the occasional payment for the servants' livery by the college: ii. 153, 161.
[6] e.g. *Customary of St Augustine's Canterbury and St Peter's Westminster*, ed. Sir E.M. Thompson (1902) 196 ff., 400–1. Cf. *Durham Account Rolls* (Surtees Society vol. 103) xxxv ff.
[7] The nearest approach is in certain parts of MS. Galba E iv.
[8] C.E. Woodruff in *Arch. Cant.* (1925) 121–51.

college would be given *qua* monk:

> Recept" domini Iohannis Wodnysbrowgh pro exhibicione dompni Willelmi Glastyngbyry anno Domini millesimo CCCC° XV°

Expense	In primis pro j lecto de Wynchester	xxij s. viij d.
	Item in j lecto de say	x s. vj d.
	Item in ij paribus de strayl'	x. s.
	Item in j pari blankettis	viij s. iiij d.
	Item in uno materas	iiij s. ij s.
	Item in iij paribus vestium secretarum	vj s.
	Item in iiij velaminibus	iiij s. ij d.
	Item in j pulvinari	iiij s. iiij d.
	Item in j bolster	iij s.
	Item in j pilio albo	iiij d.
	Item in j pelvi	iij s. xj d.
	Item in ij paribus ocrearum	iiij s. viij d.
	Item in j pari ocrearum nocturnarum	v s.
	Item in viij paribus meteynys	xx s.
	Item in j sona cum bursa et cultello	xviij d.
	In iij amisicis	vij s. iij d.
	In j panno pro rastura	xij d.
	In j panno pedali	viij d.
	In velamine pro pressura	iiij s.
	In iij habitibus	xxviij s.
	In ij tunicis albis	v s. vj d.
	In j tunica nigra	vj s. viij d.
	In ij tunicis furratis	xxiiij s.
	In j nigro pilio	vj d.
	In j braccali cum punctis	vij d.
	In j canamas	ijs.
	In j pari pyncis	vj d.
	In j pari tabellarum cum pectine eburneo	
	In barbitons'	v d.
	In ij paribus caligarum	xviij d.
	Summa viij li. ix s. v d.[2]	

[1] Corpus Christi College Oxford MS. 265, fo. 180.
[2] Cf. the similar list from Ely printed in D.J. Stewart, *Architectural History of Ely Cathedral* (1868) 232.

THE ECONOMY, INTERNAL AND EXTERNAL 119

This is, so to speak, the monk's trousseau. At the other end of the career, we have more relevant documents: the inventories, apparently *post mortem*, of two wardens, Robert Eastry, S.T.B., (ob. 1496) and Robert Holyngbourne, S.T.P., (ob. c. 1508), and that of Antony Wootton, who was apparently a monk-fellow for a short time c. 1508.[1] The inventories show a more lavish and haphazard accumulation than the one given above. The garments consist mainly of 'stamins' (the woollen shirts required by monastic law); a variety of tunics and coats, some lined with fur, one sleeveless; a riding cope; cowls;[2] 'amysys' (probably almuces of fur, which monks were sometimes privileged to wear);[3] hoods, 'birete' and 'pylyons' (? academic caps); and the appropriate scholastic habits—in the case of Eastry, his 'doctors abett'.

It must be remembered that the monk-student had to compromise in the matter of dress between his two capacities, so as to comply with the requirements of both. On the one hand, there was apparently a prejudice against some forms of academic dress as unbecoming to a religious: Benedict XII demanded that monks should be excused from wearing the scarlet cappa when lecturing on the Decretum.[4] The university authorities, too, expected sober dress in the monks. An ordinance of the faculty of canon law at Paris in 1387 on the dress of students and bachelors of that faculty, after condemning frivolous fashions among the secular students, goes on to say:

'Habitus autem honestus et necessarius est pro monachis ordinis sancti Benedicti floccus cum cuculla, vel cappa clausa cum eadem cuculla vel cum scapulari; non certe mantellus seu rotondellus nisi forsan contingeret ipsos extra villam proficisci.'[5]

At the same time, the monk-students were proud to wear their academic habit and were required to do so by the statutes of the order even outside the university—at a solemn sermon, for instance.[6] *Cappa scolastica* or *cappa scolarum* appears as a regular item in the expenses of the monks going up to the college.

The inventories already referred to include a considerable amount

[1] i. 82, 84, 87.
[2] *Cuculle, colys*. It is not clear whether these terms here simply meant the hood or included the flowing, long-sleeved choir garment also known as *floccus* or *froccus*, which does not appear in these particular inventories under that name, but which the monk student must have possessed. William Chartham was buried in his 'cowyll', which must have been the larger garment: iii. 129.
[3] *Chapters* i. 70, 80, 269; ii. 67, 155, 225.
[4] Wilkins, *Concilia* ii. 599 (c. 9).
[5] H. Denifle and A. Chatelain, *Chartularium Univ. Paris*. iii. (1894) 442, no. 1535; cf. 642, no. 1697 § 10; also SA 297.   [6] *Chapters* ii. 213.

of personal effects in addition to clothes: bedding, linen, plate, books. All these effects were apparently included in the comprehensive term *panni* or 'stuff' and they varied according to the official activities and opportunities of the monk, as can be seen from the contrast between the inventory of Robert Holyngbourne, the warden, and that of Antony Wotton, the fellow. The strictest monk would inevitably accumulate some small personal belongings: even the Venerable Bede had his *munuscula*—pepper, napkins, incense—to distribute at his deathbed.[1] In the later middle ages there was a strong tendency towards separation and privacy, militating against the common life and showing itself in certain practices, continually legislated against but almost ineradicable: e.g. cash allowances for clothing (as mentioned above) the division of the common dormitory into cells, the practice of eating apart,[2] the dividing-up of the refectory plate among the monks.[3] The process sometimes went so far that the inventory of a smaller house in the sixteenth century almost gives the impression of an ordinary dwelling house.[4] Some of these concessions had become tolerated and regularised even in the large and well-regulated houses: one may note that eventually monastic reformers, even those of the seventeenth century, gave up struggling to retain the common dormitory, so that the 'cell' has come to be regarded as a monastic characteristic rather than a monastic luxury. It was therefore the more to be expected that the monk-student who, owing to his exceptional position, was allowed a salary, as we have seen, should also come up to Oxford provided with a certain amount of property for his personal use.

We have several small lists of books given by the prior to the monk-students for their private use. They must be clearly distinguished from the common library and they are of considerable importance as indicating the man's personal studies and interests, usually so difficult to reach.[5] Besides the books he brought with him, the monk-student could buy books at Oxford out of his salary. William Chartham bought most of his books from a particular bookseller there.[6] In the course of time, the monk-student's collection of books would expand and change its character, as can be seen by comparing the modest list of books entrusted to Robert Holyngbourne, probably when he first went up to Oxford c. 1495,[7] with the very much larger list probably made after his decease c. 1508.[8]

[1] *Baedae Opera Historica*, ed. C. Plummer, i (1896) clxiii.
[2] See 'Meals, places of' in index to *Chapters*.
[3] See the inventory of the *iocalia fratrum* at Canterbury (1460) in Reg. N, fo. 230 ff.   [4] e.g. the inventories printed in *Arch. Cant.* 1867.
[5] i. 80 ff.   [6] iii. 128.   [7] i. 81.   [8] i. 84.

THE ECONOMY, INTERNAL AND EXTERNAL

The accounts show the expenses of carrying the 'stuff' from the monastery up to Oxford and then, when the time came to go down for good, back to Canterbury. Detailed instructions for such a removal are given in a letter of the sixteenth century from a monk-fellow to a sojourner from Winchester.[1] The heavier belongings—the wooden framework of the bed, the chests and tables (i.e. the trestles and boards)—are to be left at Oxford and some of them sold if possible, others left for the next occupier. The clothes, books and other objects (including a 'table' or picture of St Dorothy) are to be wrapped up in the mattress into a 'trusse' or package. The package is to be labelled and entrusted to 'Buccke', apparently a carrier. Some part of the journey is to be done by ship, naturally the easiest method. Perhaps the stuff was sent by carrier to London, then by ship down the Thames estuary to Faversham 'and from thens to our monastery' by land again.

When the owner of the stuff died at Oxford, the procedure was different. It is described in a letter written by the warden, John Langdon, to the prior on the death of William Chartham (1487).[2] Apparently there was no great hurry, for Chartham died on 12 August and the letter was written on 15 November. The prior sent servants to the college and at his command the warden made an inventory of the dead man's effects, apparently with a valuation, and also a statement of his debts and expenses. These documents were given to the prior, but have not in this instance survived. Chartham's clothes were few and in poor condition and his books were to be sold to pay his debts. Perhaps in less exceptional cases the books were usually sent back to Canterbury, or divided among the other monk-students. Even in this case, the warden picks out two books: one a concordance, for which he offers to pay, the other a 'Lyr', i.e. the gloss of Nicholas de Lira, for one of the fellows, Richard Copton. In one of the inventories, it is suggested to the prior that the small books should be distributed among the young scholars (either the junior monk-fellows or the secular scholars).[3]

Reference has already been made to Wardens Eastry and Holyngbourne. The former certainly and the latter probably died at Oxford. In these cases, it is not the correspondence with the prior, but the inventory of effects which has survived.[4] Besides clothing, already mentioned, the inventories include bed-handings and bed linen, table linen, table napkins, handkerchiefs, cupboard cloths, carpets, cushions, leather bottles, candlesticks and some more precious things: 'pairs' of beads, plate, drinking vessels, spoons etc. and money. On the whole, these seem to represent the personal effects of

[1] iii. 150.   [2] iii. 128.   [3] i. 88.   [4] i. 82, 84.

the dead wardens, as distinct from the official college property—even the similar articles, such as plate, described among the *reperta in camera custodis* in the college inventories.[1] The sum of £5. 16. 0 probably represents Eastry's private savings, for the official balance in hand, kept in the common chest, would hardly find its way into such a document at this. On the other hand, there were some things which were obviously not for personal use, but were simply the accumulated stores of raw material intended for public use which happened to be in the warden's hands at his decease: the thirty yards of new linen, for instance, and other materials which figure in Eastry's inventory.

The principal endowment of Canterbury College consisted of the appropriated rectory of Pagham, in the county of Sussex and the diocese of Chichester. This church was in the immediate jurisdiction of the Archbishop of Canterbury and, together with the manor of Pagham, was one of the ancient properties of the see. It will be convenient to consider Pagham under the two heads of its spiritual and temporal administration.

The church of Pagham consisted of the following members:
(a) The parish church of Pagham, served by a vicar.
(b) The chapel of Bersted, or South Bersted, served by a vicar. At first a mere dependency of Pagham, this came to be classed as a parish church. The church was consecrated in 1405[2].
(c) The chapel of Bognor, apparently a chapel of ease to Bersted, served by a chaplain.

By the time that the appropriation of Pagham took place, in the late fourteenth century, the appropriation of churches to monasteries was hedged round with various canonical regulations, though these were not always sufficient to prevent serious abuses. As far back as 1179, the Lateran Council had laid down that churches could only be appropriated with the bishop's consent: vicars must be presented to the bishop and could not be removed without his consent.[3] The

---

[1] i. 7, 16, 31, 37, 53, 59, 71, 75.
[2] *Sussex Archaeological Collections* (1873) 121.
[3] Canon 9: X 5. 33. 3. 2. An even earlier regulation was made by the Council of Westminster in 1102. For the system of monastic appropriations see A. Savine in *English Monasteries on the Eve of the Dissolution*, ed. P. Vinogradoff (1909) 101 ff.; R.H. Snape, *English Monastic Finances* (1926) 75 ff. I cannot see how Snape interprets the council of 1179 as ordering fixed stipends for the vicars. 'Ipsis vero pro rebus temporalibus rationem exhibeant competentem' seems to mean that the vicars must give an account to the appropriators: at least that is the interpretation of the rubric in the Decretals. Note the exception of churches which the patrons possess *pleno iure*.

THE ECONOMY, INTERNAL AND EXTERNAL   123

Council of the Lateran in 1215 ordered a definite stipend to be assigned to the vicar, for *os bovis alligari non debet triturantis*.¹ The Council of Oxford in 1222 carried this further by explicitly demanding a minimum provision of five marks per annum, and from this time bishops were busy establishing vicarages with fixed revenues.

The two principal documents authorising the appropriation are Islip's letter of 11 May 1363 and the papal confirmation of 9 August 1379.² It should be remembered that the Holy See at first, in 1363, had refused to sanction the appropriation, which however proceeded. It was to be effected on the retirement of the existing rector, which took place on 24 May 1363.³

With regard to appointments, we know from the documents of the lawsuit in 1529 that the practice before the appropriation was for the rector of Pagham to be collated by the Archbishop of Canterbury (by right of his immediate jurisdiction) and for the vicar of Bersted and the chaplain of Bognor to be presented by the rector of Pagham to the archbishop. After the appropriation, by the terms of Islip's letter the vicars of Pagham and Bersted and the chaplain of Bognor were all three collated by the archbishop. Accordingly the college, unlike many appropriators, had nothing to do with the presenting or appointing of these clergymen.

Both Islip and the pope insisted that the vicars of Pagham and Bersted and the chaplain of Bognor must be allowed the 'congruous portions', or revenues already assigned to them.⁴ There was no need for a fresh 'ordination' of the vicarage: as the Taxation of Nicholas IV and the register of Pecham show, Pagham had been served by a vicar long before the appropriation, no doubt owing to the non-residence of the important and wealthy rectors. We learn from an indenture of 1524 that part of the vicars' revenues consisted of the tithes of hay or grass in two fields in Pagham and Bersted.⁵ The vicarage of Pagham is assessed at £16. 13. 4 in the Taxation of Nicholas IV (c. 1291) and at £9. 18. 8 in the *Valor Ecclesiaticus* (1535), the vicarage of Bersted at £6. 13. 4 in 1291 and at £7. 18. 8 in 1535.⁶ The apparent increase at

---

¹ Canon 32: X 3. 5. 30. Cf. X 3. 5. 12. For Council of Oxford see Wilkins, *Concilia* i. 587 (c. 16).
² iii. 5, 34.
³ Reg. Islip, fo. 301: Foxe's *Acts and Monuments* (ed. Pratt) ii. addenda 924.
⁴ iii. 6, 35.
⁵ iii. 212.
⁶ *Taxatio Ecclesiastica* (1802) 132 b; *Valor Ecclesiasticus* i (1810) 311. The *Inquisitiones Nonarum* (1807) 360 in 1341 give the same figures as in 1291. It is there stated that 2700 acres had been lost to the sea and that the vicarages of Pagham and Bersted 'non habent glebas neque garbas'.

Bersted may be due to the inclusion in 1535 of the annuity of 5 marks claimed from the priory of Christ Church Canterbury (see below): we know from the complaint of the vicar about 1465 that Bersted, like Pagham, had declined in value, especially owing to the encroachment of the sea.

The chapelry of Bognor is not mentioned in the assessments, but the chaplain received an annual pension of 4 marks (53s. 4d.), directly or indirectly from the appropriators of Pagham. This pension, or part of it, occurs regularly among the payments in the accounts of the college from 1435 to 1455, after which the responsibility was handed over to Christ Church Canterbury.[1]

About 1465 Thomas Walton, the vicar of Bersted, explained to the prior of Christ Church that formerly he had served both Bersted and Bognor. This combination of two exiguous benefices had given him a decent living, but it involved saying mass twice in one day, which was against his conscience. At present half the duty was taken over by the chantry priest of Pagham, which eased his conscience at the expense of his pocket. He therefore on account of his old age and weakness prayed the prior for some remedy. Unfortunately, this letter to the prior is undated.[2] On 29 November 1465, the prior and chapter gave Thomas Walton full power, so far as they were concerned, to apply to the archbishop to have the benefices of Bersted and Bognor united.[3]

The revenues of the rectory of Pagham from tithe, glebe land, oblations etc. had to be converted to the use of the appropriators resident at Oxford. This was best done by letting the rectory to farm to a resident 'farmer', lay or clerical, who exploited it to the best of his ability and in return contracted to pay a *firma* or fixed sum every year.

The practice of farming out appropriated benefices to laymen is remarkable. Bishops had tried to fight against it, but it could not be prevented.[4] As Savine points out, this putting of the tithes in the hands of laymen paved the way for lay impropriation after the dissolution[5] and it had the immediate, unpleasant result of introducing a middleman who, like the appropriators, had to extract a living out of the parish. Probably Pagham had been farmed out ever since the monks got it back from Langham's sequestration (about 1371). It was certainly farmed by 1382–3.

[1] Extract 84 below.
[2] iii. 207.
[3] iii. 208.
[4] Innocent III seems to allow it, episcopal prohibitions notwithstanding: X 3. 18. 2. According to Lyndwood, the decretal modifies the prohibition of Archbishop Stratford: *Provinciale* 3. 9. 3, *Licet*, verb. *Laicis quovismodo* (ed. 1679, p. 160). Cf. the constitution of Otho, *Cum laicis*, verb. *Ad firmam* (ibid., p. 20).
[5] Savine, *English Monasteries* 110.

THE ECONOMY, INTERNAL AND EXTERNAL

The following table shows the farmers, the amount which they paid to the college and the times of payment:

Year	Farmer	Amount	Payment dates
1382–3	D. Peter Beamunde (Bersted)	£86. 0. 0	25 Mar. & 24 June
1432		£35. 0. 0	25 Mar.
		£9. 13. 4	1 Aug.
1435–6	Thomas Smyth[1]	£66. 0. 0	
1436–7	Thomas Smyth	£38. 10. 0	Three quarters only
1439–40	Thomas Smyth	£67. 0. 0	1 May & 22 July
1440–1	Thomas Smyth	£73. 13. 4	
1443–4	Thomas Taupener, Roger Sawyer	£67. 6. 8	
1444–5		£67. 6. 8	22 July & 2 Feb.
1448–9	Will. Markwyk (Pagham)	£26. 0. 0	
	John Dylmoth (S. Bersted)	£33. 0. 0	25 Mar. & 29 Sept.
	John Cooper (S. Mundham)	£6. 13. 4	
1454–5	Will. Markwyk (Pagham)	£26. 0. 0	
	Godfrey Whatlyngton (S. Bersted)	£29. 0. 0	25 Mar. & 29 Sept.
	Philip Ledok (S. Mundham)	£5. 6. 8	

Note the division of the district to be farmed. South Mundham is also mentioned in the prior's account of 1472–3.[2] It is the northern portion of the parish of Pagham.

Presumably these farmers were laymen, except Peter Beamunde, who is given the title *dominus* and may have been the vicar, acting as farmer. Such an arrangement existed later on, at the beginning of the sixteenth century and the profits of farming must have been a welcome addition to the vicar's 'congruous portion'.

No indenture between the farmer and the college has survived for this earlier period, but it is possible to reconstruct some of the terms of the contract. To judge from the treasurers' and the college accounts, the college was evidently required to do the necessary repairs as regards (a) the fabric and ornaments of the chancels of Pagham,

---

[1] William Lynder is mentioned as lately farmer. He is also given livery, in 1423 apparently as *serviens de Pagham* and in 1441 as *firmarius de Rysborgh*: MS. Tanner 165, fo. 129, 159.

[2] Extract 84 below.

Bersted and Bognor—even the hosts for the Easter communion had to be found by the rector and therefore (rather under protest) by the appropriators: (b) the buildings—dwelling house, tithe barn etc.—belonging to the rectory; (c) walls, hedges, sea walls, weirs, ditches; to which must be added (d) amercements for neglect and Peter's pence.[1]

The farmers shared in the livery of cloth which Christ Church Canterbury gave to its various dependents according to their rank. In the liveries recorded in MS. Tanner 165 we find, under the heading *firmarii et bedelli*, the *servient' de Pagham* in 1423 (fo. 129), *serviens rectorie de Pageham* in 1429 and 1431 (fo. 134, 135^v), *firmarius de Pageham* in 1437 and 1439 (fo. 153^v, 156^v). In the last year, however, a note is added: *quia super collegium*; and there are other instances where the college paid for the livery in addition to or instead of the prior's supply.[2]

In this period, the farmer was not bound to bring the *firma* to the appropriators: the latter had to collect it. Twice, or may be three times in the year, the warden or a fellow, accompanied by servants, had to ride all the way from Oxford to Pagham and back, at the cost of much personal time and expense, with the hiring of horses and the tipping of servants. The following will show the times, length and cost of these journeys *ad querendum firmam*:

1382–3	twice	£2. 0. 0	
1435–6	unspecified	£1. 12. 8	
1436–7	twice or thrice	£2. 8. 0	
1439–40	once, 22 July	£1. 2. 11½	
1440–1	once, c. 25 Mar.	£1. 17. 1½	
1443–4	twice	£1. 17. 1	second journey 9 days
1448–9	25 Mar.	£1. 2. 4	8 days
	and again	£1. 16. 0	10 days
1454–5	unspecified	£1. 10. 0	

As an exception, in 1440–1 the farmer of Pagham seems to have made part of his payment at Canterbury and receives an allowance of this account.[3] In 1435–6, when the rectory had to be leased out afresh, the warden had to spend ten weeks over a visit to Pagham, which was apparently distinct from the ordinary visit to collect the farm and certainly cost an additional £2. 9. 8. This fresh leasing probably held up the revenues, for the college needed money that year and by means

---

[1] Extract 3 below; ii. 131, 149, 166.
[2] ii. 148, 153, 155.
[3] ii. 162.

THE ECONOMY, INTERNAL AND EXTERNAL

of presents to the farmer's wife managed to borrow £10 from her husband.[1]

The yearly value of Pagham had been assessed at £110 in the Taxation of Nicholas IV, but in the course of the college's tenure it gradually sank to about half that amount, while the expenses of management, such as the journeys and repairs described above, naturally remained as high as ever.

	Gross income from Pagham	Expenses	Net income
1382–3	£86. 0. 0	£8. 0. 2	£77. 19. 10
1435–6	66. 0. 0	5. 19. 6	60. 0. 6
1436–7	38. 0. 0	4. 3. 2	33. 16. 10
1439–40	67. 0. 0	8. 7. 3½	58. 12. 8½
1440–1	73. 13. 4	11. 6. 4	70. 7. 6½
1443–4	67. 6. 8	11. 6. 4	56. 0. 4.
1444–5	67. 6. 8	10. 16. 4	56. 10. 4
1448–9	65. 13. 4	11. 16. 3	53. 17. 1
1454–5	60. 6. 8	8. 15. 10	51. 10. 10

It was absurdly cumbersome and extravagant for a small endowment to be personally managed by a small college which was really part of a great and well-organised monastic community. About 1455, a much-needed change of management took place. In August 1454 the prior of Canterbury, Thomas Goldstone I, paid the college at Oxford a visit of some solemnity or duration, for he spent £9. 3. 0.[2] No doubt as a result of this visit, the college account for the year Michaelmas 1454 to Michaelmas 1455, unlike all others, was drawn up not by the warden, William Thornden, who was then entering on his first year of office, but by the prior himself as *supervisor status collegii*. The immediate reason for a rather dramatic intervention at this particular moment is not quite clear, but may be connected with the transfer of the wardenship from Richard Gravene to William Thornden and the debts amounting to £9. 3. 11 which Gravene left behind him. The effects of the prior's intervention were far-reaching, for the year 1454–5 was almost certainly the last time that the college was allowed to manage its own revenues. The account for 1455–6 is unfortunately defective at the beginning, where the receipts would be given, but the hitherto customary expenses connected with Pagham—repairs, journeys etc.—are omitted, though all the other expenses of the college are given. Moreover, the total receipts given at the end of the account amount to £42. 8. 9, of which £6. 9. 6 came from room-rents, leaving a sum too small, probably, to represent the *firma* of Pagham.

[1] ii. 150.   [2] Extract 64 below.

In any case, the church of Pagham completely disappears from all succeeding college accounts.

Henceforward, the prior and chapter of Christ Church took entire charge of the rectory of Pagham, which was consequently swallowed up in the mass of Christ Church property under the general care of the warden of the manors, who made a circuit twice a year.[1] In return, the prior granted the college every year a round sum sufficient to cover its expenses.[2] After 1475, the college usually received this sum from the hands of the warden of the manors. In the lawsuit of 1529, the prior pointed out that all this management was rendered necessary by the decay of Pagham and was more to the profit of the college than the priory.[3] Pagham had of course been appropriated to the college alone, but in the lawsuit and elsewhere the prior is spoken of as the parson or appropriator. This suggests an interesting problem: whether a group of subject monks, legally 'dead' and only to be represented by their religious superior (the prior), could be strictly considered as the proprietors of a church.

The rectory of Pagham continued to be farmed, as is shown by some surviving indentures of the early sixteenth century. In one case, the farmer was the vicar of Pagham.[4] The appropriators are still bound to do repairs, as before, but it is now the farmer who has to bring the money to the prior's lodging in Southwark. The annual payment has sunk to £48 for the whole farm, or £24 for Pagham alone without Bersted and Bognor.

Pagham, Bersted and Bognor afford a useful illustration of a system that was 'bad at the best and intolerable at the worst'.[5] The seamy side of appropriation, the exploitation and neglect, are obvious. It is true that Canterbury College, to judge from its recorded expenses, took its responsibilities for the upkeep of the churches more seriously than some appropriators;[6] and since, like King Canute, it could not stop the encroachments of the sea, it is not to be held entirely responsible for the poverty and decay of the place. Still Pagham, the treasured possession of the archbishops, must once have been a

[1] *Valor Ecclesiasticus* i. 16.
[2] Both the revenues of Pagham and the expenses of the college were reckoned in the general budget of the prior: see extract 84 below. The prior's grant was handed to the college in two instalments by the warden of the manors during his twice-yearly circuits: cf. ii. 262 ff.
[3] iii. 222.
[4] iii. 212.
[5] Snape, *English Monastic Finances* 89.
[6] Contrast the defects in the archdeaconry of Totnes in 1342: EHR 36. 108–24. Note that churches under rectors were not necessarily better kept in repair. Cf. Hereford 1397: EHR 44. 279 ff., 444 ff.

flourishing place and an expenditure of money and trouble might have done something to keep it so. Appropriation ignored the right of a parish to benefit from the wealth it produced and so a decaying place had most of its wealth drawn away by absentees. Fortunately, we can get a glimpse of the problem from the other side. The college simply stepped into the shoes of the rector and tried to live on his income, with very little success: the appropriators were certainly not bloated profiteers. When Pagham was taken over by Christ Church, it simply became a small cog in a very big machine. The fact is that both appropriators and parish were victims of a cheap but preposterous system of endowment, which presupposes a church with a very much bigger endowment than is necessary or good for it. The 'patrimony of the poor' is lost sight of. The vicar has his stipend and the powers above have their fees, and the rest, the superfluous margin, has to support a college, complete with warden, fellows, building and ground-rent.

6
THE SITE AND THE BUILDINGS

THE site which Archbishop Islip chose for his college was part of a rectangle of land bounded on the north by Bear Lane, on the south by St Frideswide's churchyard, on the east by Shidyard Street and on the west by St Edward's Street. It had at one time been bisected by Shitebarne Lane, running east and west, but this was now enclosed.

In 1363, King Edward III gave licence to certain persons to convey certain tenements to the new foundation.[1] The tenements are not named, but since we know what most of the grantors did actually come to give the college afterwards, it is possible to conjecture the proposed site of the college in 1363 as follows. St Frideswide's, together with Abingdon and Balliol, was to provide a large area to the east, on the Shidyard Street side, while on the west, on St Edward's Street, Godstow was to provide Ship Hall and perhaps Vine Hall to the north was to be the contribution of W. Durant and John de Bolton. The tenement of Thomas de Gloucester alone remains unidentifiable.

The licence was a mere preliminary: it remained to get possession of the land. St Frideswide's priory, the most considerable landlord concerned, began by conveying on 20 July 1364 a number of tenements which gave Canterbury College most of the southern half of the Shidyard Street frontage.[2] These were perhaps the eight *hospicia conducticia* that the archbishop claimed to have provided about that time.[3] The preliminary *inquisitio ad quod damnum* (21 May 1363) had said that the St Frideswide's tenements were of no value, being quite vacant, without any buildings.[4] This seems to fit in with Stephen of Birchington's statement that the archbishop bought up some halls that had been demolished by the excessive force of the wind[5]—which we may probably identify with the famous gale of St Maurus's day, 15 January 1362.[6] It is an ill wind that blows nobody any good. No doubt the archbishop, anxious to acquire land, found the canons of St Frideswide's particularly willing to part with their devastated property; but he cannot be said to have got it as a bargain, for they charged an annual rent of £2 for what the *inquisitio* had declared to be of no value. This would be a good precedent for the

[1] iii. 30. [2] iii. 10.
[3] iii. 4.   [4] iii. 6.
[5] Wharton, *Anglia Sacra* i. 46: *demolitas* seems the better reading.
[6] *Chronica Johannis de Reading*, ed. J. Tait (1914) 150, 293.

more famous case of exploitation five years later, when the citizens of Oxford made William of Wykeham pay so heavily for the site of New College.[1]

Apparently the other tenements named in the licence were not acquired at this time and very soon the struggle of monks and seculars followed, making further growth out of the question: indeed the monks said that the seculars lost all the tenements except one. The monks, reinstalled, set to work to reclaim and to add. They must have got back all the St Frideswide's tenements by 1372, when the original grant of 1364 was ratified, subject to a rent charge and a power of distraint.[2] On 11 April 1373, the college obtained Ship Hall from Godstow.[3] It was already possessed of some land to the south of this and a few years afterwards Vine Hall to the north was added.[4] Thus the college was collecting property on the western, St Edward's Street, side; but a more pressing need was to consolidate on the east, where Staple Hall (Abingdon) and Chimere Hall (Balliol) formed an awkward enclave in the college property. These two tenements were acquired in 1380.[5] In 1382–3 and 1392 more pieces of land were acquired and finally, before 1435, a tenement to the north of the college, in Shidyard Street, was obtained from Oriel.

The college never possessed the northern part of the block: Edward Hall, Glasen Hall and the houses in Bear Lane. On the eastern side, it had an unbroken stretch of property from the Oriel tenement down to the south-east corner by St Frideswide's churchyard.

The tenements on the Shidyard Street side were as follows:

(1) *Marre's tenement* (Oriel). This came to Oriel College in 1362.[6] It was immediately to the north of Canterbury College. The accounts of 1435 and the years following show that by that time Canterbury College was paying Oriel a yearly rent of 20s. and we know from other documents that it was Marre's tenement that they rented and that the prior of Christ Church Canterbury had agreed to the payment, in a deed which has now disappeared.[7] The Canterbury College accounts of the same period show a yearly receipt of rent from the letting of a 'tenement outside the great gate', which we may probably identify with Marre's tenement, especially as this receipt ceases at the same time as the rent paid to Oriel, as we shall see. When the northern range of the college buildings was built in 1439–40, the northern wall encroached a few feet upon Marre's tenement—according to one account, to the extent of 30 ft. by 4 ft.[8] The college continued to

[1] Mallet i. 288. [2] iii. 27. [3] iii. 28.
[4] iii. 33; Salter, *Survey*, S.E. 118. [5] iii. 38.
[6] C.L. Shadwell and H.E. Salter, *Oriel College Records* (1926) 217 ff., 458.
[7] Ibid., no. 232. [8] Ibid., no. 360 (4).

THE SITE

sublet the rest of the tenement for the time being. In 1442 Oriel transferred the rent of Marre's tenement with various other properties to the mayor and burgesses of Oxford, who in 1449 proceeded to take possession of the tenement and released Canterbury College from the payment of the annual rent for ever.[1] Evidently the college had to give up the use of the tenement. Accordingly, from 1448–9, the college accounts omit both the rent to Oriel and the receipt from the 'tenement outside the great gate'.

Canterbury College must have thought itself free, but Oriel seems to have thought otherwise. Before long it apparently got back Marre's tenement from the mayor and burgesses and, ignoring the perpetual acquittance made by the latter in 1449, it continued to regard Canterbury College as the tenant, both on the grounds of the original agreement with the prior of Canterbury and because part of the tenement was occupied by the northern wall of the college, in testimony of which there were certain great pieces of timber let into that wall.[2] Accordingly, the 20s. rent due from this tenement appears in the Oriel rentals of 1451, 1481 and 1482–3.[3] In 1479 Oriel was claiming 29 years' arrears of rent from Canterbury College and in 1495, 36 years (note the discrepancy).[4] In 1467–8 there was a lawsuit between Canterbury College and Oriel, when 'scrutatores ville predicte [Oxford] habebant visum super fundum muri nostri ubi est lis inter nos et Oryall.'[5] Evidently the overlapping of the northern wall was the crux of the matter, Oriel holding that it committed Canterbury College to the tenancy of Marre's tenement. Canterbury College seems to have succeeded in repudiating this tenancy, for it certainly never paid any more rent to Oriel. Perhaps at this time a piece of land like Marre's tenement was not of much value and was dear at 20s. a year—which would explain the attitude of both parties. Eventually Oriel united this tenement with St Edward's Hall, acquired in 1486, and the whole became the provost's garden and stables.

(2) South of Marre's tenement lay the eastern part of *Shitebarne Lane*,[6] now enclosed and rented from the city for 12d. a year.[7] The western parts were similarly enclosed in Ship Hall and Vine Hall. The lane was 13 ft. wide and marked the southern boundary of St Mary's parish. South of this was apparently St Edward's parish.

(3) *Godstow tenement*: perhaps the same as the Spaldyng tenement.

(4) *White Hall* (St Frideswide's). Of this there are two descriptions: (a) in 1343 as a tenement of Simon of Gloucester in St Edward's

---

[1] Ibid., no. 360; *Lit. Cant.* iii. 197. [2] *Oriel College Records*, no. 232.
[3] Ibid., 385, 397, 399. [4] Ibid., 397, 405. [5] ii. 189.
[6] *Oriel College Records*, no. 225 ff. [7] Salter, *Survey* i. 215.

parish, in Shidyard Street, between a tenement of Godstow (? north—possibly the Spaldyng tenement) and a tenement of St Frideswide's (? south—possibly Swynesford's entry);[1] (b) in 1364 as 'iuxta le Mariolhall' with an adjoining plot of land to the east.[2] It is rather difficult to reconcile the two accounts. Possibly White Hall was L-shaped, the main part lying back from the street and touching Mariol Hall on the south-east, while its western limb reached to Shidyard Street between the Godstow and St Frideswide's tenements. Or perhaps 'iuxta' does not mean 'adjoining', but only 'near'. White Hall may perhaps be the same as the house of William of Gloucester, immediately north of the site of the great gate of Canterbury College.[3] If so, it must have stood fairly close up to Shitebarne Lane.

(5) *Swynesford's entry*.

(6) *Fox Hall* (St Frideswide's), with Swynesford's entry, an empty plot to the north of it, as described in 1364.[4]

(7) *Mariole Hall* (St Frideswide's), described in the *Book of Wills*, no. 67, as between Fox Hall (north) and Staple Hall (south). According to the description of 1364, it had a vacant plot,

(7a) *Shelde Hall*, adjoining (? to the west).

(8) *Staple Hall* (Abingdon), the only Abingdon property that is known to have come to the college. It must be the tenement referred to in the licence of 1363 and the confirmation of 1373. The conveyance did not take place in the lifetime of Edward III and the licence was renewed on 6 May 1380;[5] but the hall had apparently passed to the college by 4 September 1380, the date of the acquisition of Chimere Hall. Apparently Abingdon gave the hall in exchange for two tenements in St Aldate's parish.[6]

(9) *Chimere Hall* (Balliol), the only Balliol property that is known to have come to the college.[7] It stood between an Abingdon tenement north (i.e. Staple Hall) and a St Frideswide's tenement south (perhaps the following). It was acquired by Canterbury College on 4 September 1380, by which time the ground to the north, west and south sides was already Canterbury property.

(10) *House of Joan Lavender*, with an adjoining

(10a) *vacant plot* at the corner (by St Frideswide's churchyard).[8]
On the St Edward's Street side the tenements were:

[1] *Cart. St. Frid.*, no. 157.
[2] Ibid., no. 158.　　　　　　　　　　　　　　　　　　　　　　　[3] Ibid., no. 97.
[4] *Cart. St. Frid.*, no. 158. For the earlier history of this hall see H.E. Salter, *The Cartulary of Oseney Abbey* i (1929) nos. 426 and 427.
[5] iii. 6, 30; 37, 57.　　　　　　　　　　　　　　　　　　　　　　[6] ii. 128.
[7] For its earlier history see H.E. Salter, *Oxford Balliol Deeds* (1913) no. 240 ff.
[8] *Cart. St. Frid.*, no. 158.

THE SITE

(11) *Vine Hall*. In 1364 Roger Compton, rector of Burghfield (diocese of Salisbury), confirmed Vine Hall to four persons, two of whom were William Duraunt and John de Bolton, chaplain.[1] Possibly Vine Hall was the tenement which these same two persons were going to convey to the college, according to the letters patent of 1 June 1363. The anachronism might be explained if they had already acquired, or intended to acquire the hall in 1363. By 1377 Vine Hall was in the hands of William Mydelworth, who in that year handed it over to Sir Geoffrey Lucy, kt., and others.[2] Mydelworth may probably be identified with the 'intruding' secular of that name and we may have here an example of the appropriation and alienation of former college property by the seculars of which the monks had earlier complained. The appearance of Lucy also deserves comment. By 1383–4 Vine Hall was apparently in the possession of the college[3] and it may have been presented by Lucy. He was certainly regarded as a very special benefactor, both to the priory and to the college.

The occupation of Vine Hall by the college cannot have lasted long. It is true that the city chamberlains' account of Michaelmas 1392—Michaelmas 1393 speaks of the 'venella inclusa in collegio de Cantuaria in le Vinehall';[4] but the college account of 1394–5 speaks of Vine Hall as being walled off[5] and in Twyne's extract about the 'venella inclusa' in 1396–7, 'Vynhalle' clearly belonged to New College[6] and it continued to do so until it was taken over by Henry VIII in 1546. Probably Vine Hall was given up about 1393, when the building of the quadrangle made it clear that the focus of the college was in the eastern, and not in the western part of the site.

Between Vine Hall and Ship Hall was the site of Shitebarne Lane.

(12) *Ship Hall*: a tenement belonging to Godstow, which was conveyed to Canterbury College on 11 April 1373.[7] It was in St Edward's Street between Vine Hall (north) and the existing property of Canterbury College (south). Attached to it was (12ª): an empty strip of land 80 ft. by 12 ft., also between Vine Hall and Canterbury College. One end of this (obviously the western) touched Ship Hall and the other touched a piece of Godstow property known as 'Spaldyngentre' (to the east), which may be the same as the Spaldyng tenement.

Ship Hall was at first used as college rooms, for the account of 1382–3 speaks of the chamber of Thomas Chillynden, formerly called Ship Hall;[8] but later it apparently fell into disuse, perhaps for the

---

[1] A. Clark, *Wood's City of Oxford* i (1889) 171, note 4, Cf. *Canterbury College* iii. 6, 30.   [2] iii. 33.   [3] iii. 49.
[4] H.E. Salter, *Munimenta Civitatis Oxonie* (1917) 276.   [5] ii. 141.
[6] iii. 57.   [7] iii. 28.   [8] ii. 131.

same reason that Vine Hall was given up altogether. There is no mention of it in the accounts, e.g. among the 'locaciones camerarum'. In 1503 it was back in the hands of the Abbess of Godstow.[1] On the other hand, the college went on paying the same rent to Godstow till the end.

(13) To the south of Ship Hall there was evidently a tenement or tenements belonging to Canterbury College.

There were also several tenements which have not been identified:

(14) A tenement to be given by *Thomas of Gloucester* in 1363.[2]

(15) *Spaldyng tenement*. This was held by Adam Spaldynges some time before 1286. It belonged to St Frideswide's, from whom Godstow held it at a rent of 2s. 3d. a year. Godstow was released from this rent in 1286 by virtue of a mutual agreement with St Frideswide's.[3] Later, the tenement was enclosed in Canterbury College and the old rent was paid by the college to St Frideswide's, but Godstow was still described as 'holding' the tenement. If this could by any stretch of language be described as a tenement of Godstow, we might identify it with 'Spaldynge-entre', which we know abutted on to the eastern extremity of the annexe of Ship Hall, and also with the Godstow tenement adjoining White Hall, probably to the north. Such an identification would bring it near to Shitebarne Lane and Marre's tenement, which had once belonged to Adam de Spaldynge.[4]

The 2s. 3d. rent occurs regularly in the college accounts (down to 1478, when it ceased), over and above the £2 rent paid for the tenements acquired from St Frideswide's in the deed of 20 July 1364. We cannot, therefore, identify the Spaldyng tenement with any of those named in that deed.

(16) *Bere Hall* and (17) *St Michael's Hall* appear among the halls acquired from St Frideswide's in 1364. They were presumably part of the Shidyard Street property.

The two following tenements appear for the first time in the college account of 1382–3:

(18) A tenement for which the college paid *Godstow* 2s. rent (and in after years 1s. 8d). This was evidently distinct from Ship Hall and the other Godstow property acquired in 1392.

(19) A tenement for which the college paid *University College* 2s. 6d. rent.[5]

(20) In 1382–3, the college bought from William Midilworth for

---

[1] Salter, *Munimenta* 289; id., *Survey*, S.E. 119.
[2] iii. 7, 30.   [3] *Cart. St. Frid.*, no. 142.
[4] *Oriel College Records*, no. 225.
[5] Note by H.E. Salter: 'apparently a quitrent.'

THE GENERAL PLAN

£6. 13. 4 a piece of land 57 ft. by 8 ft. called *Wyclyvislond*[1] and this was enclosed with a stone wall, together with another piece of college land adjoining eastwards towards the street. The latter may be one of the tenements already identified in Shidyard Street.

In 1392, the college was licensed to acquire the following tenements:

(21) From *William Savage*, clerk, one toft.
(22) From *John Tounysende* one toft.
(23) From *Godstow* a piece of land 80 ft. by 30 ft. The dimensions suggest a connexion with the annexe of Ship Hall, 80 ft. long; but we know that the latter was flanked by Vine Hall (north) and the existing ground of the college (south).
(24) From *John Colbrok* two pieces of land, one 68 ft. by 20 ft., the other 76 ft. by 14 ft. We learn from the *inquisitio ad quod damnum* that the latter piece was charged with an annual rent of 1s., to be paid to *John Spicer* and his heirs for ever. Accordingly, this Spicer rent appears regularly in the college accounts until 1501–2, when the rent is paid to New College. According to a New College document (Misc. 13), in 1427 John Spicer had a rent of 12d. from an enclosed place within Canterbury College which was once a tenement next to the land of John Wyclif.[2]

Before considering the particular departments of the college, it will be best to make an attempt at establishing the general plan from contemporary documents and from such later evidences as Loggan's view (1675) and the plan in Williams's *Oxonia Depicta* (1733). There are no existing remains. The college buildings consisted mainly of a quadrangle, entered from Shidyard Street through a gateway on the east. On the west, opposite the entrance, was the hall and on the south side was the chapel. Chambers formed the east and north sides of the quadrangle. Beyond the quadrangle, to the south and west, was apparently the garden. There is a good deal of uncertainty about the exact disposition of the kitchen buildings, in the north-west corner of the quadrangle and beyond, and of the library, apparently west of the hall.

In its general plan the college was not unlike Durham College (Trinity), except as regards the entrance, which was in each case determined by the position of the street.

---

[1] ii. 130. A connexion with the exiled seculars, Wyclif and Middelworth, at once suggests itself.
[2] Salter, *Survey*, S.E. 237. The licence for the acquisition of all these lands is in iii. 51.

The hall is not shown on Williams's plan, as it had been destroyed to make way for the new library of Christ Church. Loggan's view, however, shows it very clearly as a building of three bays lying north and south. Antony Wood, writing in 1687, speaks of 'the Chapell lately set up by the deane (viz., the old refectory standing north and south sometimes belonging to Canterbury College) in the quadrangle called Canterbury quadrangle'.[1] The view seems to show some kind of projecting building at the north-east angle, which may have been the porch to the hall, mentioned in 1504–5.[2] In any case the 'screens', the service and entrance end of the hall, must have been to the north, for it was in that direction, apparently, that the kitchen buildings lay.

At the other (south) end of the hall was a two-storeyed building, also shown in Loggan's view. Its southern wall, pierced by two windows, seems to survive in Williams's map. The axis of its roof was at right angles to that of the hall and it corresponds in position and appearance to the solar or great chamber of a private house. It is evidently the chambers in this building that are described in the accounts as the upper and lower chambers at the head of the hall. These were the best rooms in the college and perhaps the upper one was normally the lodging of the warden, who was directed by the statutes to take the principal chamber.[3] It seems to have been rather as an exception that these rooms were let, and then to very important people, such as an abbot or a dean or the archbishop's nephew.[4] Probably the *bassa camera ad finem aule*, let to the Reading monks 1459–63, was the lower room.

The chapel lay, of course, east and west. Its exact position can be determined from the account of 1487–8, in which the room occupied by the monks of Reading is described as being both south of the gateway and opposite to the room at the head of the chapel).[5] The latter room must therefore have been in the south-east corner and consequently the chapel itself must have been the building lying west of it, forming the greater part of the south range of the quadrangle. Agas's view, taken from the north, shows a lofty building in this position, with a door towards its western end and several large and elaborate windows. Loggan's view, being taken from the west, unfortunately shows nothing but the roof. The sequence of buildings on this side of the quadrangle, from west to east, is well illustrated from the account of the 'pale' or fence made in 1476–8 'ab ostio aule usque

[1] A. Clark, *Wood's Life and Times* iii (1894) 232.
[2] ii. 243.   [3] iii. 177.
[4] ii. 185, 190, 193, 231. Cf. the grant of the upper room at the west end of the chapel to a benefactor in 1381, before the rebuilding of the chapel: iii. 39.
[5] ii. 218, 219.

ostium capelle et ab ostio capelle usque ostium camere vocate Rochestyr Chambyr' (the lower room at the head of the chapel).[1]

William's plan shows the chapel to have been cut up into rooms: it was evidently not preserved after the suppression like the college hall. Its former character is still shown on the plan by the two large windows into the quadrangle and by the large number of buttresses, more numerous here than in any other part of the building then surviving. The western limit of the chapel seems to be clearly marked by the short return wall with the angle buttress and the western entrance was apparently through a kind of lobby. Owing to the subsequent remodelling, there is less certainty about the eastern extent of the chapel—i.e. the line of division between it and the chamber to the east. Both were under a single unbroken roof. Perhaps the dividing wall ran across on a level with the corner of the quadrangle.

There is a drawing by J.B. Malchair of Canterbury College in course of demolition in 1783.[2] As Tom Tower is shown in the distance on the right, a simple geographical calculation will show that this is most probably a view of the southern range, i.e. the chapel, from the quadrangle. The three great buttresses, the windows and the pointed door at the western end agree with the chapel building as shown on Williams's plan. The great square-headed windows probably represent an alteration made when the chapel was converted into rooms.

The eastern and northern ranges of the quadrangle were occupied by the chambers of the fellows and sojourners, arranged upon what seems to have been the customary plan—i.e. in groups consisting of two chambers on the ground floor with a single, straight, steep flight of stairs running up between them and leading to two similar chambers, one on each side, in the upper storey. This type of staircase still survives, for instance, at Merton in Mob Quad, east side, at Magdalen and in part of Tom Quad at Christ Church. Such a simple arrangement was quite adequate so long as rooms were built in two storeys only. It was after the close of the middle ages, when the third or attic storey came to be generally used for rooms, that a more complicated staircase was needed, such as can be seen inserted at New College.[3]

Loggan's view shows that by the seventeenth century at Canterbury College, the roof-space had been turned into a third storey of rooms. Perhaps this was the work of Dean Brian Duppa (1629–38). Williams's plan shows in the north-east rooms double-flighted stairs, no

[1] ii. 203.   [2] A. Vallance, *The Old Colleges of Oxford* (1912) 72.
[3] R. Willis and J.W. Clark, *Architectural History of the University of Cambridge* iii (1886).

doubt introduced to give access to the third storey, while apparently the original steep, straight stairs survive in the south-east rooms. The accounts of Canterbury College only speak of two storeys, the upper and the lower rooms, and there is no evidence that the roof-space above was used for inhabitable rooms in the medieval period. If the upper rooms were ceiled at all, the space above was evidently a mere loft. It seems that in Coventry Chamber there was a wood-store *above* the studies.[1]

It is probable that many of the partitions shown in Williams's plan were put in during the sixteenth or seventeenth centuries and that the original planning of the rooms was simpler. Judging from the evidence of the accounts and from contemporary usage, each chamber would have consisted of a large room, the *camera* proper, shared by several occupants, with separate studies adjoining. The studies are usually called *studia*, but in the later accounts there appears the more 'elegant' term *lucubratoria*, corrupted into *lugubratoria*![2] The usual number of occupants, and consequently of studies, was probably two: according to the statutes, each senior monk was to share his room with a junior.[3] Two studies could easily be formed by simply partitioning off one end of the chamber and dividing it into two. Williams's plan seems to show the remains of such an arrangement; Loggan's view shows two types of window, of which probably the larger lit the chambers and the smaller the studies. Judging from Williams's plan, the chambers in their original state would have measured about 20 ft. square in the eastern range, with studies about 10 ft. square, except that the studies of the room over the gateway must have been larger than usual. The northern range seems to have been on a smaller scale, measuring only about 15 ft. across.

This reconstruction of the chambers and studies is necessarily conjectural, but it seems to find support in a survey (c. 1544) of another monastic college, Durham College, which speaks of

> 'a chamber westward in length xxxvj fote, and in bredethe xvj fote, and at the west ende of the same chamber ij studies in length viij fote apece and eight fote in bredethe'

and

> 'a fayr chamber bynethe containing in length xxviij fote and in bredethe xviij fote, with ij studies and twoo woodhouses. Item over that a chamber seeled, with a studie, of the same lenght and bredethe, and a large woodhouse.'[4]

---

[1] ii. 219 (the wording is obscure). [2] ii. 229.
[3] iii. 177.   [4] H.E.D. Blakiston, *Trinity College* (1898) 22, 25.

THE GENERAL PLAN 141

There were three 'staircases' or groups of rooms, two forming the eastern range, with the gateway between them, and the third forming the northern range. As has been said, each staircase had four chambers, two upper and two lower. The accounts often speak of the chambers in pairs, one as *ex opposito*, opposite, to another across the staircase.

The accounts only begin to give particulars of the letting of rooms in 1455–6, but it is evident that the monks of the various monasteries had for some time been established in the constant occupation of certain rooms, which consequently took their name, as 'Rochester chamber' or 'Winchester chamber'. After about 1490, however, the traditional distribution is altered. At the south-east corner, at the head of the chapel, the lower room was the customary room of the monks of Rochester, the upper that of the monks of Evesham. North of these rooms, across the staircase, lay the 'opposite' pair of rooms, the upper being the Winchester chamber, the lower having various occupants—perhaps normally the monks of Reading. These rooms are usually described as being 'opposite' the rooms at the head of the chapel, but sometimes as being south of the gateway. Next, to the north, lay the great gateway, of which the western arch is seen peeping over the roof of the hall in Loggan's view and the eastern or external arch is shown in a view taken before the demolition in 1775. Of the adjoining rooms, the upper was normally occupied by Peterborough monks and had its studies over the great gateway, while the lower was not usually let. Probably it was occupied by the Canterbury monks, the fellows, themselves. The opposite rooms across the staircase occupied the north-east angle of the quadrangle. The lower chamber was assigned to the five secular *pueri collegii*; the upper was at first occupied by the monks of Coventry, but after about 1460 had a variety of occupants.

So far, it has been fairly easy to establish the sequence of the eastern rooms in two staircases with the gateway in the middle. There is more obscurity about the northern range. Williams's plan omits to mark the stairs (this part was already almost engulfed in the buildings of Peckwater Quad) but it seems most likely there was here a similar 'staircase' consisting of two opposite rooms on each floor. The difficulty is to identify these rooms of the northern range with the rooms mentioned in the accounts. The latter usually refer to an upper and a lower room 'near the kitchen' and an upper and a lower room 'near the cellar', and it is probable that these rooms were opposite to one another. Such a hypothesis would explain the accounts when they mention, in 1455–6 and 1459–60, a room 'opposite' the cellar room (i.e. ? the kitchen room)[1] and in 1476–8, 1504–5, 1505–6 and 1508–9, a room opposite or near the kitchen room (i.e. ? the cellar room).[2] We know from the account of 1502–3 that the cellar room was on the north of the quadrangle.[3] The simplest and most likely explanation seems that the cellar and kitchen rooms correspond to the two rooms mentioned. If, as we hope to show, the kitchen was in the north-west corner of the quadrangle, the kitchen room was presumably the western one and the cellar room the other. There is no evidence as to the exact position of the cellar: possibly it was the space otherwise unaccounted for between the cellar room and the room of the boys. The northern range may have extended further west than the kitchen room but not much further, for it would soon come up against the corner of Vine Hall, which seems to have projected awkwardly into the college at this point.

The kitchen, to judge from the repairs to its roof,[4] was probably a one-storeyed building, as was customary. It must have been connected with one end of the hall. As we have seen, Loggan shows the southern end occupied by a tall, solar-like building, which does not look like a kitchen and is much more likely to have been the best chambers at the head of the hall. The proximity to the chapel might also be against the placing of the kitchen there. More probably, then, the kitchen was at the northern end of the hall, in the space between it and the boundary of Vine Hall. In 1372–3, the monks bought from the nuns of Godstow a small *placea* on which to build a kitchen.[5] Now on 11 April 1373, Godstow conveyed to the college Ship Hall with a long narrow strip adjoining (? to the east).[6] If we may identify the *placea* with part of this acquisition, we have here another argument for placing the kitchen in the north-west. The kitchen may have been rebuilt later on, but it is not likely to have changed its place: it had to be at the lower end of the hall, which was one of the few parts of the college not rebuilt by Prior Chillynden.[7] The promptuary adjoined the hall, no doubt at the northern end, by the kitchen.

There must have been some sort of passage-way or slype between the kitchen and the hall, giving access to the parts of the college west of the quadrangle. During a popular rising in 1459–60, a substantial barrier of masonry with a door in it was erected between the hall and the kitchen, in order to protect the quadrangle, especially the chapel.[8] The north-west corner was evidently the weak place: on the other sides of the quadrangle there was a solid ring of buildings.

[1] ii. 179, 180.
[2] ii. 198, 199, 200, 201, 241, 244, 250.
[3] ii. 236.
[4] ii. 169, 246.
[5] Extract 3 below.
[6] iii. 28.
[7] *Lit. Cant.* iii. 116.
[8] ii. 181.

CHRONOLOGY

Of the position of the library, we only know that it adjoined the garden and that one of the rooms beneath it was described as being 'nearer to the hall'.[1] It was an afterthought and was probably built on part of the site to the west of the hall. In that case, the three buildings to the north of the library[2] may have been the same as the old buildings by Vine Hall (the northern boundary).[3] Near to the library, but separated from it by a stretch of paling and a gate, was the common latrine.[4] The room beneath the library, adjoining the garden, was let fairly regularly to various occupants—at one period especially to the monks of Bath.

There was probably a back entrance from St Edward's Street.[5]

The west side of the quadrangle—i.e. the hall and the two chambers, upper and lower, adjoining it at the south-west corner—was perhaps the part of the college to be built first, sometime about 1371–80: for the hall and two chambers were the only parts of the college not rebuilt by Prior Chillynden (1391–1411), who is stated to have rebuilt all the rest, including the chapel and chambers;[6] and the chamber at the west end of the chapel—i.e. one of the two at the south-west corner—is known to have been granted to Sir Geoffrey Lucy in 1381.[7]

Work seems to have followed (?c. 1379–97) on the south and east sides of the quadrangle, beginning with the south (chapel) and working round to the east (gateway and chambers). The account which belongs to either 1379–80 or c. 1383–5 shows the chapel on the south side already begun, with masons working on it and the roof timbers being assembled in the 'curtilage' of the college;[8] and in 1382–3 the purchase of land was recorded under *Novum opus*, perhaps in connexion with these building operations.[9] The statement already quoted that Prior Chillynden built the chapel must mean that he completed it, or else refers to the part he may have played at Oxford before becoming prior.

The most active period of the building of the college began after Chillynden became prior in 1391. One account of his works states that the 'novum opus' of the college was begun in his third year (1393–4) and lasted for three years (i.e. till 1396–7), at a cost of £340.[10] The accounts of 1394–7 show this 'novum opus' proceeding: first the finishing of the chapel, with its windows and the roofing with slates

---
[1] ii. 202.   [2] ii. 237.
[3] ii. 205.   [4] ii. 243. Cf. the room 'sub libraria prope foricam': ii. 252.
[5] ii. 243.   [6] *Lit. Cant.* iii. 116.   [7] iii. 39.
[8] iii. 126, 128.   [9] ii. 130.   [10] *Arch. Cant.* xxix. 66.

and 'daubing'; then work on the gateway, which was apparently vaulted; chimneys built, chambers 'daubed' and pargetting work done—all this probably completing the eastern range.[1]

The hall, chapel and gateway were probably entirely of stone; the partition walls and perhaps the upper exterior walls of the chambers would be timber-framed.

In 1439–40, part at least of the northern range of chambers was being built. Finally, about 1450 the library was built, somewhere on the western side of the college site.[2]

The hall is shown in Loggan's view with three windows looking on to the garden;[3] those on the other side looked on to the quadrangle. It appears to be early Perpendicular in character but, unlike most of the college buildings, it was not the work of Prior Chillynden:[4] it was probably built before his accession in 1391 as the beginning of the reconstruction after the great lawsuit and the monks' reconquest. The hall shared with the chapel and the library the distinction of having glass windows.[5] It was entered, apparently, from the quadrangle through a porch[6] and at the lower end, near the promptuary door, there was as usual a protecting screen or 'spere'.[7] It was warmed by a hearth, no doubt a central one, which was remade in 1506–7. The expense of the remaking is too small to suggest a removal to a proper fireplace at one side.[8] In 1501, there was a great 'ypoporgium' or andiron.[9] The accounts do not mention any rushes for the floor, but we know that it was found difficult to keep the hall clean in spite of the protecting 'pale' outside in the quadrangle.[10] There was little furniture: a cupboard, a counting table, three or four forms, a chair for the warden, a high table and a *mensa puerorum* for the five secular scholars are mentioned. The inventories speak of several 'mense' and a few supporting trestles, which were reserved for the high table.[11] The lower table must have been a 'table dormant'. Probably the sojourners dined at the high table with the warden and fellows.

The principal ornaments of the hall were the hangings, which were suspended from cords[12] and, apparently, wooden battens[13] fixed to the walls. A complete 'halling' or set of hangings consisted of a dorser[14] for the dais or high table end of the hall, costers for the sides and

---

[1] ii. 140 ff.   [2] ii. 157, 173.   [3] Cf. ii. 183.
[4] *Lit. Cant.* iii. 116.   [5] ii. 183, 223.   [6] ii. 243.
[7] i. 7.   [8] ii. 249.   [9] i. 38.
[10] ii. 237.   [11] i. 33, 38, 55.   [12] i. 155, 230.
[13] ii. 232.
[14] The word is also sometimes used loosely in the inventories to describe side-hangings.

THE HALL

bankers to cover the benches. Canterbury College possessed all these pieces, but not in a homogeneous set: the pieces were added from time to time and this process of development can be seen in the inventories. In 1443 the hall was not very rich in hangings. It had a dorser of woollen tapestry work, apparently decorated with beasts and foliage and lasting in a decrepit state down to 1534; a banker striped with alternate colours, red and blue, in defiance of the heraldic rule, but a scheme of decoration much used in these hangings; and a linen cloth stained or painted with the Cinque Ports and obviously of Kentish provenance. In 1459 there was an old hanging with ostrich feathers, which must have been a remnant of the great 'halling' of ostrich feathers of black tapestry with a red border of swans and ladies' heads, bequeathed by Edward the Black Prince to Christ Church Canterbury to be cut up into altar frontals and hangings for the choir.[1] Apparently some pieces were still in use there as floor coverings in 1540.[2] It was a strange fate that had brought the hangings of a great prince's hall to hang, old and 'nearly exhausted',[3] in a small monastic college. There were newer and smarter gifts from the priors of Canterbury. By 1459, Thomas Goldstone I had given for the upper end of the hall a new hanging of red and green stripes woven with the arms of the founders, together with one banker of the same suit, no doubt for the high table. These were supplemented by four handsome costers of red with the leopards of England given, probably in 1500–1, by Thomas Goldstone II,[4] who also at some time after 1510 gave a new dorser, apparently to go all round the hall.[5] It was decorated with 'apparitions of angels, with the images of prophets and patriarchs'—perhaps a Nativity scene with appropriate prophecies and 'types'.

The kitchen was apparently a single-storeyed building, for it possessed a slated roof of its own.[6] The accounts only speak of one door, which was strengthened with ironwork and furnished with a lock and key.[7] The fireplace is not described. There were certainly chimneys, which at first let in the rain but were ultimately protected by some device of stonework at the summit.[8] The kitchen contained several ovens,[9] a 'dressar' consisting of two tables[10] for dressing the meat with the aid of the dressing-knife[11] and apparently some stone-

---

[1] J. Wickham Legg and W.H. St John Hope, *The Inventories of Christ Church Canterbury* (1902) 96–7.   [2] Ibid., 91.
[3] i. 38.   [4] i. 33; cf. ii. 232.
[5] i. 64: 'ad ornatum tocius aule'.   [6] ii. 169, 246.
[7] ii. 156, 175, 192, 206, 222, 228, 234, 253, 257.   [8] ii. 249.
[9] ii. 138, 175, 205.   [10] ii. 148.   [11] i. 33.

work on which the food was spitted.¹ There were also cupboards and two small 'houses'—probably large cupboards. Poultry was kept, alive, in a coop within the kitchen itself. A subterranean channel or drain² ran from the kitchen, apparently across the quadrangle to the gate.³ It was covered by flags and in one place by a plank,⁴ and the opening from the kitchen was covered with an iron grating in order to prevent the channel from being choked with bones and other refuse.⁵

The inventories give lists of the kitchen utensils, which throw light on the methods of cooking. Fleshmeat was no longer forbidden entirely to the black monks in the fifteenth century, even in theory, and in any case the seculars would have demanded it. There were therefore several spits for roasting. They were turned upon a hook⁶ and one of the spits was a small one, used for birds and eels.⁷ For boiling there were pots of various sizes, a trivet to support them, hooks with which to lift or suspend them over the fire and a flesh-hook. There were also a gridiron and a frying-pan, a ladle, a 'scomer' or skimmer, a straining-basin full of holes (apparently a colander) for making potage of peas,⁸ a 'stoppe' or stoup for salt,⁹ a pepper-mill, a mustard-pot and several pestles and mortars of stone and metal, including one, apparently, for pounding flesh.¹⁰ Besides the pots there were various other vessels, pans, dishes, 'sawcers', 'podyngers' of brass, latten and tin, which were periodically mended by a tinker¹¹ or else exchanged for others (*pro cambio, commutacione*).¹² The college possessed several chafers or chafing-dishes for heating food or water, probably with the aid of charcoal. Some of these belonged to the kitchen, others could be used at table and were kept at first in the warden's room and afterwards in the promptuary. For cutting up wood for fuel there were a saw, an axe and iron wedges. There was a *domus carbonum*, presumably for charcoal. Even this was kept under lock and key.¹³

The promptuary was no doubt under the care of the *pincerna*, who kept his accounts there. It was a whitewashed room opening out of the hall¹⁴ and its door had a lock and two keys.¹⁵ While the more valuable pieces of plate, the *iocalia*, were kept in the warden's room, those

---

¹ ii. 178. For the objects mentioned in the next sentence see ii. 209, 205; 178, 243.   ² ii. 237.
³ ii. 220. This might, however, refer to the western or back gate.
⁴ ii. 253.   ⁵ ii. 156, 249.   ⁶ ii. 237.
⁷ i. 8.   ⁸ i. 70.   ⁹ i. 32.
¹⁰ i. 8.   ¹¹ ii. 220, 240.   ¹² e.g. ii. 155, 175.
¹³ ii. 169.   ¹⁴ i. 7; ii. 249.   ¹⁵ ii. 165, 181, 192, 202.

which were needed for everyday use in hall were kept in the promptuary: the mazer-bowls mounted with silver, with inscriptions and imagery on the 'print' at the bottom of the bowl—the martyrdom of St Thomas, for instance, or St Dunstan and the devil; the silver spoons; some salt-cellars of tin (the silver ones found their way into the warden's room); ewers and basins for washing at meals, one—'of nobler form'—being made, like monumental brasses, of latten of Cologne;[1] and to light the hall at supper time some candlesticks, one having two 'noses' or holders, in contrast to the more usual pricket form.[2]

The promptuary did duty both as buttery and as pantry. It contained barrels of beer, varying in number from six to twelve, with *storia* or coverings of straw or rushes,[3] a vessel for measuring out the beer and 'dropping tubs', into which, apparently, the leavings of beer were emptied.[4] There was also a barrel of verjuice. On one occasion, a 'pipe' was broken up and converted into smaller barrels.[5] The bread was kept in a chest[6] and cut up with a great knife, and after dinner the remnants of bread were gathered up and taken from the table in two great dishes, perhaps to be distributed in alms.

To the promptuary also belonged the linen, though it was kept in the *pincerna*'s chamber, which may have been adjoining. There were table-cloths and napkins for the hands and for the shoulder, some plain and some of diaper work.

It is not possible to determine the position and architectural character of the warden's room. It may have varied, in fact, from time to time since, according to the statutes, the warden was to choose what he considered to be the principal room in the college.[7] Perhaps this would normally be the upper room at the head of the hall, which was rarely let, though on one occasion at least a distinction seems to be made between the latter room and that of the warden.[8]

In accordance with the statutes, the warden shared his room with a junior monk-fellow. Consequently, the earlier inventories mention two beds, with testers. At a later time Dr Bockyng gave for the use of the warden a feather bed with a sparver or tester of Thornacles (dornick, from Tournai) and three curtains, together with hangings of red say and other furniture.[9] Perhaps by this time the warden had the room to himself, as there is no mention of a second bed. The warden and his companion (when there was one) had their own

---

[1] i. 17. [2] Ibid. [3] i. 8.
[4] i. 64. [5] ii. 155. [6] Or in a 'pipe': i. 8.
[7] iii. 177. [8] ii. 183. [9] i. 68.

studies, like the other members of the college.¹ At one time, the warden's *librariuncula* contained his only chair.² There were a growing number of chairs and stools, a table with two leaves, eventually used *pro familiaribus recumbentibus*³ (? a bed-table for the sick, or merely a classical phrase), a counting table, no doubt marked out for casting the college accounts,⁴ a round table and several cupboards. There were carpets for the table, the windows and the cupboards.⁵ The fire-place had an andiron⁶ and a pair of bellows.⁷ At first there was a plate (? or sconce) above the fire-place to hold candles;⁸ later there were candlesticks.⁹ On one occasion a pound and a half of wax was bought for the warden's study,¹⁰ but usually the accounts do not record the consumption of wax for lighting in the rooms, the hall or anywhere in the college except the chapel.

The warden's room naturally served as a kind of treasury. There were always several chests, holding *iocalia*, muniments, rolls, books etc., and from 1501 onwards there was a great chest for copes and the best vestments. Probably it was the sets of vestments recently given by Archbishop Morton and Prior Sellynge¹¹ that needed this special custody. In the warden's room also was kept the common chest of the college, mentioned in the statutes¹² though not described under that name in the inventories until 1510. In accordance with a usual precaution it had two locks, one key being kept by the warden and the other by the senior fellow. The common chest held the college seal, the yearly accounts, all money received by way of income and Dr Chaundler's fund for sick fellows.¹³ A new chest was bought for these purposes in 1481–2.¹⁴

The college plate was kept in the warden's room. It consisted chiefly of some silver salts, silver spoons and, above all, a considerable variety of drinking vessels: wooden mazer-bowls, nut cups (probably made from the cocoa nut) and 'pieces' or bowls of silver or silver gilt, some embossed, some with covers, some raised up on 'standing feet'. One mazer had a leather case.¹⁵ Pieces of plate, in some cases with distinguishing initials or inscriptions, were given by various priors (Thomas Goldstone I, Sellynge, Thomas Goldstone II)¹⁶ and by members of the college. Thus there was a 'Bokyngs pece' and a 'Henfelds cup'. 'Certain bachelors'—John Waltham, Roger Benett, John Henfylde (once more) and Robert Holyngbourne—joined together in giving eight silver spoons,¹⁷ apparently as a leaving

---

¹ ii. 156, 165. ² i. 37. ³ i. 63.
⁴ Probably *apocus* is intended for *abacus* and refers to this: i. 37.
⁵ i. 7, 68, 76. ⁶ ii. 209. ⁷ i. 7. ⁸ i. 7, 16.
⁹ i. 69. ¹⁰ ii. 161. ¹¹ i. 32. ¹² iii. 174.
¹³ *Lit. Cant.* iii. 269. Cf. *Canterbury College* ii. 228.
¹⁴ ii. 211. ¹⁵ i. 53. ¹⁶ i. 31, 37, 53 etc. ¹⁷ i. 37, 53.

THE CHAPEL

present. The first three men left Oxford about 1501 and the last became warden in that year. About the same time a fine silver-gilt cup with a foot and cover, weighing 40 oz., was bought by the college out of money in the common chest,[1] probably accumulated from Dr Chaundler's sick fund. In 1534 the covers of two lost bowls and some broken silver had been sold and the proceeds, £5, were kept in the common chest with a view to buying new bowls for the college.[2] Events were soon to teach the monks that cash was a better investment than plate, being less easily seized. In 1534 also, the warden's room housed some of the chapel plate, such as a thurible, a pax and the two silver basins of Prior Chillynden's gift, which were afterwards to be in the hands of the dean of the new foundation at Canterbury.[3]

It is difficult to reconstruct the general internal arrangements of the chapel, for the inventories are intended as a check upon the movable goods only and information from the accounts, though useful, is naturally casual. We have no straightforward description of the high altar, the windows, the choir-stalls or the screens.

One would naturally expect the chapel to follow the usual collegiate arrangement and to be divided into two unequal portions—choir and antechapel—by a screen of some kind.[4] That this was in fact the case seems evident from a reference to the rood over the entrance to the choir.[5]

The chapel contained altogether four altars: the high altar and three side-altars. The warden and fellows were of course bound, both by monastic legislation[6] and by the college statutes,[7] to say mass if not every day, at least frequently. Hence a number of altars were necessary, especially when the number of fellows increased at the end of the fifteenth century. The five secular scholars would not be in priest's orders but no doubt the sojourners, both regulars and seculars, were allowed the use of the altars. It must have been for their benefit that a missal of Sarum use was given to the college by Bourchier, many years before he became Archbishop of Canterbury.[8]

---

[1] i. 36.
[2] i. 75.
[3] Legg and Hope, *Inventories* 231 n., 225.
[4] Vallance, *The Old Colleges of Oxford*; Willis and Clark, *Arch. Hist. Cambridge*.
[5] ii. 222.
[6] *Chapters* i. 45, 70, 71, 78, 99, 241; ii. 32, 33, 46, 71, 83, 196, 197.
[7] iii. 181.
[8] i. 4, no. 21. Note that in 1429, though Bourchier had then been archbishop for some years, the scribe still calls him Bishop of Ely, copying either a previous inventory or an inscription in the book.

As to the position of the altars: the high altar would of course be at the east end of the choir. One of the side-altars was apparently in the vestry.[1] For the other two, the normal and most convenient place would be in the antechapel against the western face of the choir-screen, flanking the entrance to the choir. In that case, the celures over these side-altars, mentioned as newly painted in 1521, may have formed part of the coving of the screen.[2] If the two pictures or 'tables' mentioned in inventory C (1501)[3] are the same as the two in inventory D (1501),[4] then apparently the side-altar on the north was dedicated to SS. Thomas, Elphege, Benedict and Jerome—good Kentish, monastic patronage.

It seems that in 1443 (inventory A) there were only three altars: the high altar and two side-altars.[5] One entry in the inventory speaks of 'three minor altars',[6] but the word 'minor' is written above the line—whether in the same or a different hand it is hard to say. The altars at that time were of wood and so appear in the inventory. They do not appear in later inventories, for by the munificence of Dr Chaundler of New College stone altars were built and the chapel was consecrated sometime before 1473.[7]

There were a number of candles burning before the high altar. In 1443–4, wire was used for fixing them[8] and in 1480–1 they were on a beam supported by ropes.[9] This was probably the beam with five latten candlesticks given by Thomas Chaundler (inventory C, 1501)[10]—in which case the donor must have been Warden Chaundler of New College, not Warden Chaundler of Canterbury College. Ten years later, a new beam was made and painted.[11]

As regards the ornaments of the high altar: there was an alabaster image of Our Lady, given by J. Hampton, a monk of Winchester, probably a sojourner. It first appears in 1501 and by 1521 it had been placed by the warden, Hadley, in a gilt tabernacle over the altar.[12] There were also two large images of SS. Andrew and Dunstan, first appearing in 1501 and in 1521 described as being over the high altar.[13] They were of freestone, painted and gilt, though on one occasion they were described by mistake as of wood.[14] All three images had curtains to protect them from the dust.[15] There were also, in positions unspecified, alabaster images of the Blessed Trinity, St Thomas and

[1] i. 29.   [2] i. 58.   [3] i. 31.   [4] i. 35.
[5] i. 1–3.   [6] i. 3.   [7] iii. 114.
[8] ii. 164.   [9] ii. 208.
[10] i. 28. Cf. *five* candles as early as 1435–6: ii. 148.
[11] ii. 253.   [12] i. 28, 55.   [13] Ibid.
[14] i. 34.   [15] i. 58, 67, 73.

THE CHAPEL

St Katherine[1] and several pictures, including two of the four evangelists and the four doctors of the Church.[2]

On the high altar itself was a cross, usually described as of copper gilt, though in the last inventory, 1534, it is described as painted lead[3]—perhaps at that date it was more politic to err on the side of modesty in assessing one's treasures. There was also a painted cross of wood with a 'concave foot'[4] and seven latten candlesticks, four great and three small,[5] to go round among the four altars. There was a pyx of silver and another of ivory. Perhaps the pyx in use was suspended over the high altar, though there is no mention of any covering or canopy for it. The altars were provided with 'tables' for the Pax and with cruets. There was a tin vessel for keeping altar wine and a portable holy-water stoup of the same material. The silver plate of the chapel included two basins given by Prior Chillynden, a thurible, a pax and several chalices, varying in number from three to five. One of them was set aside for use on solemn feasts, while others were allocated to the permanent use of the warden or the senior fellow.[6]

The altars had their *apparatus* or hangings, a full set of which would comprise a dossal, frontal and two side curtains or riddels. The first inventory includes Prior Chillynden's gift of striped red hangings for three altars, some black sets for two altars and linen sets for three altars for Lent.[7] Of these Chillynden's sets alone survive, very old and worn, until the end; the others disappear after 1501. In the meantime, of course, there are fresh acquisitions: white hangings for the four altars, for instance, given by Warden W. Hadley I[8] and red hangings given by Warden Bockyng.[9] The inventory of 1521 shows some particularly splendid acquisitions: one set for the high altar of 'saten of Bryggys', striped red and green, with a crucifix and the arms of Christ Church, for use on St Thomas's day, Pentecost, Corpus Christi and All Saints; the other, complementary set, also of 'saten of Bryggys', this time striped blue and white, for Christmas, Easter, Ascension, Trinity and the Assumption. Besides these there were, for daily use, hangings of 'saten of Sypers', striped red and green, for the high and side-altars, including a cloth to cover the pictures which, it seems, adorned the high altar in addition to the three images already described.[10]

There were a number of *ambones* or lecterns standing in the choir: two in 1443, three in 1459–1501, four in 1510–24 and five in 1534.[11]

[1] i. 1, 9, 28, 34, 72. [2] i. 31, 58, 67, 73. [3] i. 1, 9, 28, 34, 50, 55, 65; 72.
[4] i. 3, 11, 30, 34, 52; 55. [5] i. 9, 28.
[6] i. 34. [7] i. 1–3. [8] i. 29.
[9] i. 57. [10] i. 57, 58. [11] i. 3; 11, 30, 36; 52, 58, 67; 74.

One of these, provided with a silk cloth, stood in the middle of the choir[1] at the place for the cantors, the *rectores chori*, who had a red carpet[2] and a seat with cushions.[3] The rest of the lecterns would no doubt be distributed on either side of the choir.[4] As this was a monastic choir, where the psalter was supposed to be known by heart, the lecterns would be intended chiefly for books of chant, like the four antiphoners and the five graduals mentioned in the inventories. The appearance of a 'book of pricksong' in 1510 and the more elaborate musical taste which this indicates may perhaps help to explain the gradual multiplication of the lecterns. There was also an organ, described in 1443 and 1459 as 'weak'. In 1499–1500 it was repaired and the bellows patched up with glue, and in the next inventory (C, 1501) the contemptuous epithet is removed; but in the second inventory of that year (D) it is once more 'valde debile'.

There is no mention of stallwork in the inventories and accounts. There is a reference to the *scamni* or forms in the chapel,[5] which may have been for the monks to sit on in place of stalls; or, as is more probable, they may have been low forms in front of the monks' seats or stalls, intended to support the monks when they knelt *prostrati super formas*. These *scamni*, in any case, were not meant for the secular scholars, for they were provided with stools, which varied in number but appear in every inventory except those of 1459 and 1501. The warden had a special seat, provided with cushions and decorated on great feasts with two cloths of red and green silk, which were also used for the Easter sepulchre.[6] In connection with the latter, there is mention of the 'painting of the holy cross'.[7]

In 1443 there were ten straw mats, *storia*, for the 'station' at masses and other services.[8] Six round mats (*storia*) had been bought in 1435–6 and five more (*stratoria*) in 1443–4.[9]

In 1501 there were eight stained cloths, *panni tincti*, of linen to hang on all sides of the chapel (*undique*)[10] and in 1521 they had been replaced by new *laquearia* or dossals for the choir.[11] These apparently corresponded to the costers or side-pieces of a hall, hanging at the back of the seats or stalls on either side—in effect, perhaps, rather like the contemporary wall-paintings of Eton chapel. They seem to exclude the possibility of any canopies or panelling to the stalls.

There was a great bell hanging outside the chapel door to ring for services[12] and three smaller sacring-bells.[13] Possibly the latter were fixed in a wheel, as was sometimes the practice.

[1] i. 56.   [2] i. 57.   [3] i. 57, 67.
[4] Cf. the illustration in P. Dearmer, *Fifty Gothic Altars* (1910) 159.
[5] ii. 205.   [6] i. 57, 66.   [7] ii. 148.
[8] i. 3.   [9] ii. 148, 164.   [10] i. 34.
[11] i. 58.   [12] i. 3, 11, 30, 36, 52, 58, 67, 73.   [13] Ibid.

THE CHAPEL

There are references to a vestry, which contained an altar and a picture of the Last Judgement.[1] Its position is not specified. If it had been on the north side, it would have projected awkwardly into the quadrangle, blocking up the doorway in the south-east corner. It is more likely that it either projected from the south side into the garden, or was a piece taken out of the ground-floor chamber east of the chapel. The chapel door was apparently protected by a porch.[2]

The liturgical books included from three to five missals, one of which was of the Sarum use; a book of rubrics and an *ordinale* from Canterbury, going back to the time of R. de Sancta Mildreda (c. 1290), to which Warden Bockyng added a new one of paper; two psalters and a book of day hours, *diurnale*; a small *legenda* for principal feasts, with another added by Reginald Goldstone; five graduals and four antiphoners; a small book for singing versicles and a book of pricksong or *cantus fractus* (from 1510); a book of sequences for the use of the celebrant (in 1524) and a book called trendlye or trenle, probably containing the trental of masses for the dead.[3]

[1] i. 29, 36.
[2] ii. 149.
[3] i. 68, 74.

7
THE LIBRARY

THE Constitutions of Benedict XII laid down the following general rule with regard to the supply of books to monk students:

> 'Volumus eciam, quod si in ecclesiis, monasteriis seu locis prefatis libri multiplicati fuerint, libris necessariis in ipsis ecclesiis, monasteriis et locis remanentibus, de ceteris libris per antistites in ecclesiis cathedralibus, et in monasteriis vel aliis locis predictis per eorum prelatos, et de consilio eorum cum quorum consilio studentes prefati sunt, ut premissum est, eligendi, fiat conveniens distribucio inter studentes eosdem; fiatque prius memorialis scriptura de personis studencium quibus dicti libri tradentur et librorum nominibus predictorum: que quidem scriptura in ecclesiis, monasteriis vel aliis locis huiusmodi conservetur.'[1]

In like manner, Courtenay's statutes for the college lay down that when a monk is sent to Oxford for the first time, the succentor (the second in command of the books at Canterbury) is to send to the warden of the college a 'note' of the books set aside for the use of the new student and these collections of personal books are to be inspected by the warden and two senior fellows once or twice a year. Even the warden's books are liable to the same inspection. These books, which are still regarded as the property of Christ Church, are not to be sold or pawned—e.g. to one of the university chests—without the special permission of the prior:[2] a necessary precaution, for the fellows of Merton, for instance, did not scruple to pawn books from their college library.[3]

In both these regulations, the books are considered as specially entrusted to each individual monk student. Such an individualistic arrangement was natural in the Constitutions of Benedict XII, probably contemplating a mixed society of monks from many different houses, like Gloucester College. It was less necessary in a close, united community like Canterbury College, but nevertheless it was repeated there, just as was the similar system of paying the students separate salaries. Down to the sixteenth century, we find surviving small lists of books granted by the prior for the private use of some of

---

[1] Wilkins, *Concilia* ii. 597.   [2] iii. 181.
[3] F.M. Powicke, *The Medieval Books of Merton College* (1931) 16.

the wardens and fellows, which are to be classed with their personal belongings, clothes and 'stuff'. On the other hand, we find a common stock of books, a college library, which is catalogued in each college inventory.

Naturally, the library of Christ Church Canterbury was the chief source or quarry for the collection of books at Canterbury College. On this point Leland has something to say when speaking of a copy of the Homelies of Hucarius the Levite (of St Germans, Cornwall):

> 'Pervenerat, quo nescio casu, Hucarii opus vel Durovernum usque Cantiorum; unde a monacho quodam translatum est ad Isidis Vadum et bibliothecae collegii Cantiani commendatum: id quod et aliis exemplaribus cum multis tum antiquis contingit. Tota enim huius bibliothecae supellex a fano Servatoris Duroverni translata est.'[1]

Leland's precise words suggest that the Hucarius went to Oxford as part of the outfit of a particular monk, in the manner prescribed by the statutes. However, it found its way into the common library of the college, apparently at the end of the fifteenth century, for it first occurs in the catalogue of 1501 (C 86).

Apart from the small private lists of books already mentioned, Canterbury has no general lists of books transferred to Oxford, like the list of books sent to Durham College.[2] We have to trace the transferences as best we can and we are hampered by the fact that Prior Eastry's great catalogue of the library of Christ Church (1284–1331)[3] fails to give the opening words of the second folios of the books (that method by which later medieval librarians identified their books) so that an exhaustive and certain comparison between the Christ Church and Oxford libraries is not possible. Still, some help is given by the manner in which the books of Eastry's catalogue are arranged under the names of donors[4]. Many of these were monks of Christ Church, who were bound to bring with them on entering the monastery any books they might already possess, and no doubt they found subsequent means of making or acquiring books. Sometime in the fifteenth century, perhaps when Archbishop Chichele rebuilt the Christ Church library, this arrangement gave place to a new subject-arrangement, recorded in William Ingram's list of 1508.[5]

[1] Leland, *Comm. de script. Brit.* c. 131, *De Hucario*. For this and the whole question of the relations of the libraries of the college and the monastery see James, *Ancient Libraries* xlvii ff.
[2] *Catalogi Veteres* (Surtees Society 1838) 39, 41.
[3] James, *Ancient Libraries* 13–142.
[4] Specially noticeable in the second *demonstratio*, but beginning much earlier.
[5] James lii–lv, 152–63.

THE LIBRARY 157

In the catalogues of the college library at Oxford, especially in the earlier ones, 1443 and 1459, a number of the books still bear the names of the original donors, who had figured in Eastry's catalogue. By means of these names, we can trace with more or less certainty the following Canterbury books in the Oxford collection:

Eastry 387 (?or 1489 or 1490) = A 64, H. de Depham (d. 1292).
    520 = A 31, W. de Neireforde (c. 1240).
    530 = A 5, T. de Stureya jr. (d. 1298).
    539A = B 24, C 154, T. de Leycester (d. 1290).
    555 = A 73, Hugo de Cretyng (c. 1250).
    603 = B 20, Adam the Prior (de Chillendon, d. 1274).
    722 = A 2, G. de Romenall.
    753 = A 67, G. de Romenall.
    839 = C 222, G 263, St Thomas (d. 1170).
    840 = C 215, G 261, St Thomas.
    846 = A 101, St Thomas.
    861 = C 172, Radulfus Remensis (d. 1188).
        This book is given in the Oxford catalogues as though Radulfus were the author rather than the donor.
    1047 = A 38, D 18, Mag. Humphredus (d. 1188).
    1053 = A 72, Mag. Humphredus.
    1088 = A 43, Nigellus Wireker (c. 1190).
    1176 = A 44, Simon Subprior (d. 1188).
    1440 = B 104, Thomas Prior (de Ringmere, d. 1285).
    1453 = A 59, W. de Refham (d. 1291).
    1523 = C 219, Reginaldus de Gessenbale (apparently for Robertus de Gressenhale).
    1606 = F 281, Martinus de Clyve (d. 1301).
    1641 = A 7, Archbishop R. Winchelsey (1292–1313).
    1685 = B 26, Mag. M. de Berham.
    1688 = A 12, D 57, Mag. M. de Berham.
    1700 = B 84, Mag. M. de Berham.
    1741 = A 57, Steph. de Faversham.
        Note that the Oxford description adds to the contents.
    1783 = A 51, B 17, W. de Lydbury or Ledebery (d. 1328).
    1795 = B 89, W. de Lydbury.
    1817 = A 75, W. de Norwyco (d. 1328).

From the list of Prior Henry of Eastry's own books (James, p. 143–5), 8 = A 13; 27, 28 or 29 = A 63; 57 = A 70. From the list of Prior Chillynden's books (James, p. 150), 1 = B 82, C 189, F 264. The Oxford library also had three books of Thomas Stoyl's (1299–1333), which no doubt came from Canterbury: A 10, A 42, A

61 (= C 167). He is just too late to appear in Eastry's catalogue; but cf. no. 12 in the list of 1337 (James, p. 147).

Besides the preceding list, it is possible to suggest the following conjectural identifications, mostly based on a particular combination of contents. The 'other contents' of the MSS are regularly given in the Eastry catalogue, but only occasionally in the Oxford catalogues—e.g. by accident, through the varying descriptions of the same MS.

Eastry 65 Proslogion Anselmi, lib. i; *in hoc vol. cont.* Anselmus de conceptu virginali et originali peccato, lib. i: perhaps = D 10, Anselmus de conceptu originali [*sic*]; = G 8, Proslogion. But of course such a combination of tracts would not be uncommon.
  128 Epistole Senece prime (with other contents) perhaps = C 305, Epistole Senece cum aliis contentis.
  165 Excepciones de partibus Haymonis (with other contents) perhaps = C 174.
  169 Tercia pars Haymonis (other contents include Sermo beati Maximi Episcopi etc.) probably = C 44, 3ª pars Haymonis et sermones Maximi.
  170 Opuscula Hugonis maiora (other contents, beginning with Didascalicon eiusdem) perhaps = C 177, Didascalicon de studio legendi; = D 51, Opera diversa Hugonis; = G 45, Opuscula Hugonis.
  182 Omelie Hucarii levite (etc.) = C 86.
  392 Priscianus iv magnus, libri xvi = C 330, Prescianus in maiori; = D 206, Prescianus quartus, 2° fo. In articulata. M.R. James conjecturally identifies 392 with Trinity College Cambridge MS. O. 2. 51, but the second folio does not correspond.
  415 Marcianus Capella secundus (with other, varied contents) perhaps = C 292, Marcianus Capella cum multis aliis contentis.
  427 Lucanus primus most probably = C 315, Lucanus primus, 2° fo. tota vacet.
  430 Lucanus quartus = C 300.
  431 Daret de bello Troiano versifice perhaps = C 301, Daretis yliados.
  560 Summa de casu et fortuna perhaps = A 83.
  940 Interpretaciones hebraicorum nominum (other contents begin with Sermo Stephani Archiep. Cantuar.) most probably = C 121.

THE LIBRARY 159

1139 Sermones diebus dominicis in gallica lingua et latina perhaps = C 147, liber parvus sermonum mixtim in latino et gallico.
1194 Liber de legibus et consuetudinibus Anglie perhaps = C 216.
1338 Cantica canticorum glos. (with Actus Apost., Apoc., Ep. canonice) perhaps = C 120.
1458 Summa magistri W. de rupella de viciis et virtutibus perhaps = G 207.
1495 Receptorium [Repertorium] iuris, with Summa Bernardi Compostelli super decretales imperfecta perhaps = B 79.
1585 Excepciones decretorum Graciani perhaps = C 209.

The book described as Gesta Alexandri Magni (A 89, B 102, C 295, E 128 etc.) is also described as Historie Langabarum (D 116). Did it perhaps consist of nos. 158 and 160 of Eastry's catalogue bound up together? A book in the catalogue of 1510 (E 215) is said to be of the gift of Prior Goldstone II. Was it perhaps specially bought for the college, and not a mere cast-off from the Christ Church library? Books were also given to the college library by Prior Sellynge in 1481.[1]

The books granted for the private use of the monk students did not as a matter of course pass subsequently into the college library; they might be given to other students, or even sold.[2] It seems likely, however, that in the case of the two wardens, Eastry (d. 1496) and Holyngbourne (d. c. 1508), some of their books went into the college's collection. Of Eastry's books,[3] no. 8 perhaps = F 233, G 235; no. 12 probably = F 293; no. 13 probably = F 289. Of Holyngbourne's,[4] no. 25 probably = F 285–6; no. 39 probably = F 297; no. 50 perhaps = E 185; no. 52 probably = F 299, G 290; no. 58 probably = F 284.

If Leland meant that the college library came entirely and directly from Canterbury, he was exaggerating, for it was partly furnished by other means. In the first place, some books were presented by wardens and fellows: Henry Wodehull (the first warden) A 18; John Waltham (warden 1438–41) B 105; William Thornden (warden 1454–9) B 111–3, 131–2; Robert Lynton (warden 1443–8) B 16, 18, 19, 23 (sermons of Wyclif), 110; J. Hedecron (scholar c. 1335–6) A 14; William Richemonde (fellow c. 1436–48) B 27. The *dicta Lyncolniensis*, B 22 (lent by the warden to Prior Sellynge and apparently never returned!),[5] was from H. Middelton. As there was no monk of Christ Church of exactly that name, he probably stands for William

[1] ii. 212; cf. ii. 206. [2] iii. 128.
[3] i. 82. [4] i. 85. [5] iii. 118.

Middelton or Milton (fellow c. 1379–83). To judge by the catalogues, Thornden must have given his books during his term of office, Lynton and Richemonde perhaps as a posthumous bequest, Waltham in neither manner—for his book does not appear in 1443, two years after the end of his wardenship, yet it is there in 1459, some years before his death.

Finally, there were books given by secular benefactors. According to a statement made by the seculars' party in the Roman process of 1369–70, Archbishop Islip gave some of his own books to the college, but these were detained by his successor, Langham.[1] In 1443, the college had two canon law books of Archbishop Arundel's, which were perhaps direct gifts to the college (A 15, 16). The same applies to the psalter of R. Courtenay, Bishop of Norwich (A 17): it is not one of the books bequeathed by him to Christ Church under the terms of the will of Archbishop Courtenay.[2] Two other donors who appear in the catalogues and were not monks of Canterbury—T. Acworth (A 74) and Mag. John de Wynbourne (B 83)[3]—were perhaps sojourners. Information about secular donors is scarce in the catalogues though, to judge from a surviving example, the books themselves had the name of the donor inscribed.[4] From other sources we have the names of two secular donors, W. Durant and T. Graunt. Their gifts evidently had to be fetched at the college's expense.[5]

The two fifteenth-century catalogues, A (1443) and B (1459), both represent roughly the same primitive arrangement, before the use of a special library building. A few standard works of theology and canon law, duplicates and books of reference were kept chained in the chapel;[6] the rest of the books were apparently kept in the warden's chamber (probably in the great chest which figures in later catalogues)[7] and were no doubt doled out according to need.

The catalogue A begins with the books chained in the chapel for reference, nos. 1–18 (nos. 19–26 are liturgical and do not concern us here). Then come the books of theology in the warden's study: nos. 27–44 mainly biblical exegesis and patristic, nos. 45–62 mainly scholastic: *questiones* and commentaries on the Sentences of Peter Lombard. Then follow canon law nos. 63–9, civil law nos. 70–6, philosophy 77–91, and logic (with sophistry and grammar) 92–102:

---

[1] iii. 185.   [2] James 498.
[3] The author seems to have changed his opinion on this point: see i. 100, no. 83.
[4] i. 112.   [5] ii. 189, 192; iii. 111.
[6] See the statutes of University College, Oxford (1292), which order that one book of every kind that the college has be placed in some common and secure place: *Mun. Acad.* i. 59.
[7] i. 63 etc.

THE LIBRARY

all these, presumably, in the warden's study, like the theological books. The library is really very small—only ninety-six books, if we exclude the liturgical books. At the beginning of the next century, Warden Holyngbourne had almost as many books for his private use.

The catalogue B (1459) heads the list, 'Books found in the chapel and in the warden's chamber' and says nothing about chaining. If we look closely, we shall see that nos. 1–14 correspond to chained books 1–12, 17 and 18 in the first catalogue and are probably still chained in the chapel. Four canon law books which were chained here for reference in 1443 (nos. 13–16) are now moved to the main section of canon law as nos. 69–72, while on the other hand, two theological books previously in the warden's chamber have now been shifted to the reference section in the chapel as nos. 17 and 24 and there are eleven new books here. Then come the liturgical books, 28–36, after which, presumably, we leave the chapel for the warden's chamber: 37–54 are biblical and patristic, 55–68 mainly scholastic, 69–84 canon law, 85–8 civil law, 89–114 philosophy, 115–132 logic etc. All follow closely the order of the first catalogue, with additions in appropriate places, except that the civil law section has shrunk. Philosophy and logic show the most growth, being nearly doubled.

The 'new library' (there is no evidence that it had a predecessor) already appears in the account of 1448–9, when stone for it was bought from Merton College;[1] and Thomas Goldstone I, Prior of Canterbury 1449–68, finding the library already begun, brought it to completion, as his obituary tells us:

> 'Preter hec in collegio Cantuarie Oxonie ad usum studencium, quos miro studio et benivolencia nutrivit et fovit, librariam quandam satis amplam, prius inceptam edificari, non sine magnis sumptibus ad perfeccionem duxit.'[2]

Thus, in 1454–5, when the prior was himself 'supervisor' of the affairs of the college, about £100 was spent on the 'new work of the library'.[3] In the next year, the work was sufficiently advanced for the new chamber under the library to be let to a sojourner.[4] This room is described as being in the garden, so that the library must have had a pleasant aspect, which would compensate for its proximity to the privies. The library then, as was customary, was raised up on the first-floor level and its floor was paved with stones,[5] so that the room or rooms beneath must have been vaulted, no doubt for dryness and

---

[1] ii. 173. Cf. J.E. Thorold Rogers, *Oxford City Documents* (1891) 315.
[2] MS. Arundel 68, fo. 3; Wharton, *Anglia Sacra* i. 145.
[3] ii. 176.   [4] ii. 179.   [5] iii. 111.

safety from fire.¹ Like the rest of the college, the library was roofed with stone 'tiles'. Repairs done to these on the *northern* and *southern* sides suggest that the roof-ridge and main axis of the building ran east and west, at right angles to the hall.² Like the hall and chapel, the library had glazed windows, which had to be repaired as early as 1459–60, the date of the catalogue B, when apparently the books were not yet moved in.³ The door, naturally, was furnished with a lock⁴ and there were brooms for sweeping:⁵ there were to be no such cobwebs as Leland found in the Greyfriars' library at Oxford.⁶

During the years c. 1460–1500, the books were moved into the newly-built library and, no doubt on account of the improved accomodation, their numbers increased enormously, from 132 (including liturgical books) in 1459 to 336 in 1501 (catalogue C). The acquisition and fitting-up of the new books are recorded from time to time in the accounts. Sometimes books had to be rebound, or provided with clasps or horn (to protect the title written on the front board of the book, as can be seen, for instance, on some of the older registers at Lambeth). More frequently still, chains had to be bought and fitted on to the books, apparently by the stationer.⁷ In a letter written probably about 1472 the warden, Chichele, asks Prior Sellynge to earmark the bequest of a certain priest for buying paving stones and chains for the college library: he has in his study forty good books, which he dares not put into the library until he can chain them.⁸ Evidently at this period, at least, the idea was that all books kept in the library should be chained—from which we may presume that the library was no mere store-room, but a place in which to work. There is no evidence as to the fittings. The libraries of the time were usually fitted with alternate benches and desks at right angles to the walls. The earlier 'lectern' system provided a single row of chained books; the later 'stall' system provided two or more rows and was adopted by the early sixteenth century at Oxford and probably in the library at Christ Church Canterbury.⁹ We must remember that the college library was on a comparatively small scale: 250 volumes could be accomodated in about 64 ft. of shelving, so that the simpler 'lectern' system may have sufficed here.

¹ Cf. the stone-built muniment-room at Merton College.
² ii. 222, 246.   ³ ii. 181, 209, 223.
⁴ ii. 209.   ⁵ ii. 220.
⁶ A.G. Little, *Greyfriars in Oxford* (1891) 62.
⁷ ii. 192, 196, 212, 214, 222.   ⁸ iii. 111.
⁹ For the whole subject of college libraries see Willis and Clark, *Arch. Hist. Univ. Cambr.*, pt. 3, sect. 7, ch. 1; J.W. Clark, *The Care of Books* (1909), ch. 4 and 6; James, *Ancient Libraries* lii ff.

THE LIBRARY

As an addition to the library regulations collected by J.W. Clark, it may be useful to give the following excerpt from the statutes of St Mary's College, Oxford, a college for Augustinian canons and so in some ways analogous to Canterbury College. We see some of the inconveniences of a monastic college library.

> 'De libraria
> Item ulterius statuimus quod nullus communarius ausu temerario ingrediatur librariam vestram in nocte cum candela studendo, nisi contingat ipsum facere aliquem solempnem actum, vel sermonem dicere, sic quod propter brevitatem temporis non datur sibi ocium: sub pena vj d. Addentes insuper quod nullus occupet unum librum vel occupari faciat ultra unam horam vel duas ad maius, sic quod ceteri retrahantur a visu et studio eiusdem, cum secundum canonica decreta, racio nulla permittit[1] ut quod pro communi utilitate datum esse cognoscitur propriis cuiusquam usibus applicetur.[2]

When we come, then, to the sixteenth-century catalogues (C-H), we find a change of system. Instead of the primitive arrangement, with a few books chained in the chapel and the rest kept in the warden's chamber, now the library contains the bulk of the books—that is evident from the catalogue headings—and they are apparently chained there, to judge from what has been said above and from a heading in the catalogue of 1524 (G),[3] while it is a minority of the books which are kept out in the chambers of the warden and fellows.

The catalogue C, made in 1501 when Warden Thomas Chaundler went out of office, records the greatly augmented collection of books, both those kept in the library and those for the time being kept in the chambers of the brethren; but it does not distinguish between the two classes, in the way that the later catalogues do. It begins, no doubt, in the library with the theological books. Nos. 1–67 are biblical and patristic, nos. 68–94 mainly scholastic, but the arrangement is not at all precise or orderly. With nos. 95–113, we seem to begin again with biblical commentaries and then the rest of the theological books, nos. 114–184, are so miscellaneous as to defy any classification. Some of these most probably are the books which were entered up as they were found in the chambers of the brethren. Then follow, as usual, the sections on canon law (185–211), civil law (212–224), logic (225–48),

---

[1] MS. apparently has 'committit'.
[2] Bodleian MS. Rawlinson Statutes 34, fo. 21. The quotation is from the Decretum, pars 2, causa 17, qu. 4, can. 1, palea.
[3] James 169.

philosophy (249–90), *libri poetrie*, classical authors and others (291–322), 'sophistry' (323–7) and grammar (328–36). All sections owe much to the acquisitions since 1459, especially the *libri poetrie*, of which all except three are new. This augmented library might be expected to owe something to two forces then beginning to make themselves felt: the revival of classical letters and the spread of printing; but in fact, neither seems to have operated. The classical authors here are such as might have been found in any good medieval library, while to the end, so far as one can see, printed books were an exception, in contrast to the contemporary library of Syon monastery.[1] Classics and printing were more evident in the private book-collections of the monks.

The next inventory, D, was made in the very same year as C, in 1501, when Robert Holyngbourne succeeded Chaundler as warden. One is the inventory of the outgoing and the other that of the incoming warden. They might be expected to be identical, but what a difference there is in the order and number of books. Instead of 336, catalogue D gives only 209—less by about a third. Some of the missing books have gone for good: possibly they were taken back to Canterbury. Others reappear in later catalogues, generally among the books 'out' in the brethren's chambers; so we may suppose that in this instance they had got stowed away and were overlooked by the cataloguer. Within the main subject-divisions, which remain much as before, the books have been arranged in quite a new order, as can be seen from the comparative table.[2]

The theological books at least are in rather better order: beginning with a new acquisition, the commentary of Nicholas de Lira in four volumes, nos. 1–85 are biblical and patristic, nos. 86–127 mainly scholastic. Canon law, with all that remains of civil law, comprises nos. 128–42, philosophy 143–61 and the cupboard devoted to grammar 204–9. Nos. 162–203 are the books in the chambers of the brethren, given separately for the first time: it is this distinction that helps to make the catalogue more orderly than C.

In the next catalogue, E (1510), within the main divisions the books are again rearranged, though the difference this time, perhaps, is not so great as that between the two catalogues of 1501. Nos. 1–89 are biblical and patristic, nos. 90–132 scholastic; law accounts for nos. 133–52, philosophy, logic and grammar for 153–87. Then follow the books in the chambers of the brethren. In all, there are 218 books, a very slight increase on D. With regard to the books kept in the library,

---

[1] *Catalogue of the Library of Syon Monastery*, ed. M. Bateson 1898.
[2] ii. 113.

the order settled in 1510 remained more or less fixed down to the last surviving inventory of 1534.

So far, we have been considering the books kept in the library. As to the books kept in the rooms of the warden and fellows: in catalogue C, these are not distinguished. In D, forty-eight such books are given, nos. 162–209; in E there are thirty-one, nos. 188–218: in both instances, theology and philosophy in no particular order.

Catalogue F, in 1521, is more specific: 30 books of theology, nos. 190–219, are in the great chest in the warden's room and 49 books, mostly of philosophy with some canon law, nos. 220–68, are in the same place. Then follow 35 miscellaneous books, nos. 269–303, in the warden's study (as distinct from his chamber) and 20 more, nos. 304–23, in a great chest in the room of William Pecham, the senior fellow.

Catalogue G, in 1524, so far as it goes, shows the same arrangement. There are the same 30 books of theology, nos. 192–221, in the great chest in the warden's room and there are 71 more books, nos. 222–92 (philosophy, law and miscellaneous), also in the great chest, to judge from the catalogue; but of these, nos. 270–92 correspond to the books described as in the warden's study in 1521 and we may suspect that they were still there. The books in the senior fellow's room are left out of account.

To sum up: at first a few books only were chained for reference in the chapel, while the rest were kept in the warden's chamber. After the building of the library in the middle of the fifteenth century, the bulk of the books were chained in the library but there was a growing body of books kept outside, in the chambers of the brethren. These outside books are separately described from catalogue D (1501) onwards and in catalogues F (nos. 190–323) and G (nos. 192–292) constitute by themselves quite a respectable collection, arranged according to subject: theology, canon law and philosophy, and miscellaneous. Thus there have grown up two libraries in the college.

If we examine the libraries of other colleges, we find a somewhat similar division: some books are kept chained in the library, while others are distributed among the fellows.[1] For Merton College, in particular, there is a great deal of evidence about the periodical *electiones* or distribution of theological or philosophical books among the fellows, each of whom received a *sors* or block of books more or less appropriate to the faculty in which he was studying.[2] How far is there a parallel between these *electiones* and the books kept outside the library in Canterbury College? It is true that these books are

[1] Willis and Clark, *Arch. Hist.* iii. 387 ff.; Clark, *Care of Books* 139 ff.
[2] Powicke, *Medieval Books*.

frequently described as *in cameris confratrum*; but when we are given more explicit information, as in the catalogues F and G, we find that they are kept in a chest in the warden's chamber, in his study and in another chest in the senior fellow's chamber. Moreover, they are given in a fairly regular sequence according to subject. This does not look like a general sharing-out among all the fellows. We suspect, rather, that these books were simply 'dumped' in places of security, because the college could not be bothered or could not afford to chain them in the library—in fact, they correspond to the 'forty good books' that Warden Chichele kept in his study. No doubt the fellows were free to borrow any of these unchained books, but what really corresponded to a share in an *electio* was probably the private collection of books which each fellow might hold with the permission of the prior.

8
EXTRACTS FROM ACCOUNTS

THE following extracts are taken from various monastic accounts of Christ Church Canterbury. They are intended chiefly to illustrate the affairs of the college, its fellows and the lectors, though some other entries of kindred interest, such as gifts to secular scholars and to the university, have also been included.

The information given mostly concerns incidental expenses such as travelling expenses, gifts, scholastic *cappae* etc. Occasionally, however, the full expenses of the maintenance of monk-scholars appear. Thus, the expenses of monk-scholars at Paris in 1304–6 and at Oxford immediately after the reconquest of the college, in 1370–5, are in the treasurer's account, and those of monk-scholars at Oxford in 1331–43 are in L 243. The prior's rolls also sometimes record large items: e.g. apparently the whole income and expenditure of the college in 1410–11 and 1472–3, the 'novum opus' of the college buildings in 1396–7 and an inception in 1410–11.

L. 242, fo. 22. Accounts 1274–5 (probably from Michaelmas to Michaelmas)
Item datum puero bedellorum Oxonie per priorem xij d.
fo. 22ᵛ
Item pro mantellis et cooportoriis et aliis ad opus fratrum, scilicet W. de Everel et socii sui ls. viij d.

L. 242, fo. 26ᵛ. Accounts 1275–6
Item puero fratrum minorum vj d. per preceptum prioris.
fo. 27ᵛ
Item scholaribus Oxonie per manus domini prioris c s.

L. 242, fo. 32. Accounts 1276–7
Item pro vestura W. Deverel et socii sui, per priorem xxxiiij s. iij d.
fo. 32ᵛ
Item socio lectoris xij d.
Item solutum pro minutis debitis fratris W. Deverel et socii sui et speciebus ad opus suum quando iter arripuit versus capitulum, per priorem vij s. xj d.
Item socio suo vj d.

fo. 33
Item datum scolaribus per priorem c s.

L. 242, fo. 38. Accounts 1277–8
Pro vestura lectoris et socii sui xxxij s.
Item pro una tunica ad opus magistri iiij s.
Item puero eorum, scilicet pro roba sua vij s. vj d.
Item pro diversis rebus in camera lectoris nostri v s. iij d. per manum domini Guidonis.
Item pro sotularibus ad opus pueri lectoris vj d.
Item fratri Philippo consorti lectoris nostri xij d.
Item pro sotularibus garcionis magistri nostri et aliis minutis ad opus magistri nostri ij s.
fo. 38ᵛ
Item pro minutis expensis lectoris nostri et socii cum sotularibus garcionis eorum ij s. vj d.
Item datum bedell' Oxonie per priorem xxj s.
Item cuidam scolari per priorem di. marc.
fo. 39ᵛ
Item cuidam garcioni eunti Dovoriam pro vestura lectoris nostri iij d.

L. 242, fo. 44. Accounts 1278–9
Item pro vestura lectoris nostri et socii sui xviij s.
Item pro roba pueri eorum xij s.
Item pro tunica fratris Philippi vj s. ob.
Pro uno potello olei ad opus magistri iiij d.
Item pro una tunica de blanket ad opus lectoris vj s.
fo. 44ᵛ
Item pro oleo ad opus magistri iiij d. per manus domini Guidonis.
fo. 45
Item pro sotularibus pueri magistri nostri a festo sancti Michaelis usque Pentecosten xxxiiij d.
Item datum fratri Philippo socio lectoris nostri xij d.
Item eidem ij s. ad parcamenum.
fo. 45ᵛ
Item Henrico de Depham eunti ad generale capitulum fratrum minorum pro lectore nostro x s.

L. 242, fo. 51. Accounts 1279–80
Item fratri Philippo consorti magistri nostri xij d.
Item pro oleo ad opus magistri nostri per I. de Beggebroke vj d.
Item fratri Philippo ij s. ad parcamenum emendum.
Item vestura magistri nostri et socii sui xxx s., empta per manus suas.

fo. 51ᵛ
Item pro medicina lectoris vij d.
Item datum magistro W. de Tremfeld per priorem et capitulum c s. ad exercicium scolarum.
Item pro iij ulnis de bleu ad opus garcionis magistri nostri v s. iij d.
Item pro cissura robe sue vj d.
Item pro sotularibus suis vj d.

L. 242, fo. 57. Accounts 1280–1
Item pro calciamentis et aliis minutis pueri lectoris nostri vj s. ij d.
Item fratri Philippo socio lectoris nostri ad parcamenum xv d.
Item puero lectoris nostri vj d. ad sotulares ad Pascha.
Item lectori nostro pro diversis rebus sibi necessariis x s. solut' per manum Rand*ulfi*.

fo. 57ᵛ
Item lectori nostro viij d.
Item pro vestura lectoris nostri et socii sui xxxvij s.
Item pro aliis necessariis ad opus eiusdem et socii sui vj s.
Item pro sotularibus pueri lectoris nostri xij d.
Item vj d. pro eodem.
Item xij d. eidem lectori.

L. 242, fo. 64. Accounts 1281–2
Item pro habitu lectoris nostri et socii sui xlv s. vj d., per manus eiusdem R.
Item puero eorum xij d.
Item datum Reynoldo bedello universitatis Oxonie di. marc.

fo. 64ᵛ
Item pro roba Thome Toting [?] pueri lectoris ix s. vj d.
Item socio lectoris nostri xviij d. ad parcamenum et alia.

L. 242, fo. 74. Accounts 1282–3
Item pro habitu lectoris nostri xxix s. ix d.
Item puero lectoris nostri iiij s. pro roba.

fo. 74ᵛ
Pro roba clerici lectoris nostri xij s. iij d.
Item pro parcameno lectoris nostri x d.
Item socio lectoris nostri ad parcamenum xij d.

L. 242, fo. 80. Accounts 1283–4
Item pro habitu lectoris nostri et socii sui xxv s.
Item pro parcameno ad opus lectoris nostri xviij d.
Item xviij d.
Item pro oleo in camera lectoris nostri viij d.
Item socio lectoris nostri xij d. ad parchamenum.

fo. 80ᵛ
Item pro parcameno ad opus lectoris nostri ij s.
Item datum lectori nostro xij d. per I. ad peticionem suam.
Datum bedell' universitatis Oxonie per priorem x s.

L. 242, fo. 86. Accounts 1284–5
Pro roba lectoris nostri et socii sui xxxij s.
Item valecto lectoris nostri ij s. in partem robe sue.
fo. 86ᵛ
Item lectori nostro per manus supprioris iij s.
fo. 87
Item clerico lectoris nostri pro roba sua vj s. sol' subpri'.
fo. 88ᵛ
Item puero portanti literas capituli ad capitulum fratrum minorum ij s.

L. 242, fo. 69. Accounts 1285–6
Fratri Willelmo socio lectoris nostri ad parcamenum xij d.
Item pro oleo ad opus lectoris nostri xiiij d. per H.
fo. 69ᵛ
Datum clerico lectoris nostri S. filio Sparuwe pro roba sua vij s.
Item vestura lectoris et socii sui xxvij s.

L. 242, fo. 92. Accounts 1286–7
Pro oleo ad opus lectoris nostri iij d.
Socio lectoris nostri ad parcamenum vj d.
Item pro oleo ad opus lectoris per vices vj d.
fo. 92ᵛ
Item pro roba pueri lectoris nostri vij s.
fo. 93
Item pro panno ad opus lectoris nostri et socii sui per manus P. de Hicham xiiij s. x d.
Item lectori nostro iij s. ad parcamenum.

L. 242, fo. 97ᵛ. Accounts 1287–8
Item pro duabus tunicis lectoris et socii vj s. di. d.
fo. 98
Item pro roba pueri lectoris nostri viij s. per subpriorem in vigilia sancte Margarete.
In donis per priorem diversis scolaribus xxxix s. viij d.

L. 242, fo. 105ᵛ. Accounts 1288–9
Pro robis lectoris nostri et socii sui xvj s.
Pro tunicis albis ad opus lectoris nostri et socii sui viij s.
fo. 106
Item pro parkameno ad opus lectoris nostri iij s.

EXTRACTS FROM ACCOUNTS

fo. 106ᵛ
Item solutum lectori nostro viij s. pro roba garcionis sui.
Item eidem pro parkameno iij s.
Pro habitu lectoris nostri et socii sui xxvij s. vj d.
Item datum per priorem duobus scholaribus vj s. viij d.
fo. 107
Item diversis scolaribus per priorem xxxv s.

L. 242, fo. 110. Accounts 1289–90
Pro parkameno ad opus lectoris nostri iij s.
Item pro roba garcionis lectoris nostri viij s.
fo. 110ᵛ
Item pannus ad opus lectoris et socii sui per I. de Hardres xxv s. ob. qua.

L. 242, fo. 153. Accounts 1290–1
Item liberatum lectori nostro vj s. pro parcameno et roba pueri sui.
Item liberatum lectori nostro v s.
fo. 153ᵛ
Item datum puero S. de Faversham pro autumno [sic] suo ij s.
Item pro vestura lectoris nostri et socii sui xxiij s. ix d.
fo. 154
Item eidem [*a messenger*] querenti dominum priorem Oxon' ij s.

L. 242, fo. 157. Accounts 1291–2
Item pro oleo empto ad opus lectoris viij d. ob.
Item pro parcameno ad opus lectoris nostri iiij s.
Item clerico lectoris nostri scilicet pro roba sua viij s.
Item datum socio lectoris nostri ad parcamenum xiiij d.

L. 242, fo. 163. Accounts 1292–3
Pro habitu lectoris nostri et socii sui xxj s. ij d. qua.
Item pro parcameno ad opus fratris R. lectoris nostri iiij s.
Item datum diversis scolaribus iiij li. xix s.
Item pro roba pueri lectoris nostri viij s.
Item xij d.

L. 242, fo. 169. Accounts 1293–4
Pro habitu lectoris nostri et socii sui xxij s. iiij d.
Item datum lectori nostro per preceptum supprioris iij s.
Item solutum eidem di. marc. ad opus clerici sui.
Item pro parcameno ad opus lectoris nostri iij s.
Item datum lectori nostro ij s. quando ivit ad generale capitulum.
fo. 169ᵛ
Item datum pauperibus scolaribus xliiij s.

L. 242, fo. 175. Accounts 1294–5
Item pro parcameno ad opus lectoris nostri ij s.
Item pro habitu lectoris nostri et socii sui xxj s. v d. ob.

L. 242, fo. 181. Accounts 1295–6, 33–4 Ed. I
Item datum lectori nostro ad parcamenum ij s.
Pro brevibus portandis pro Stephano de Faversam et Willelmo Vuicht viij d.
Item pro habitu lectoris nostri et socii sui xxiij s.
fo. 181ᵛ
Item clerico lectoris pro roba sua di. marc.
Item datum scolaribus lxxvj s. per priorem.

L. 242, fo. 186. Accounts 1296–7: anno Domini m°cc° nonagesimo sexto, regis Edwardi xxiiijᵗᵒ, incipiente vicesimo quinto
Item pro habitu lectoris et socii sui xxiiij s.
Item clerico lectoris nostri pro roba sua vj s. viij d.
fo. 186ᵛ
Datum lectori nostro ad percamenum ij s.

L. 242, fo. 192ᵛ. Accounts 1297–8, 25–6 Ed. I
Pro habitu lectoris nostri et socii sui xxiij s. vj d.
Item datum clerico lectoris nostri pro roba vj s. viij d.
fo. 193
Datum lectori ad perchamenum ij s.
Item datum lectori nostro ad perchamenum secundo ij s.
Datum ij scolaribus ij marc. per priorem.
Item datum Willelmo clerico lectoris nostri pro cura fratrum nostrorum vj s. viij d.

L. 242, fo. 199. Accounts 1298–9: anno Domini m°cc° nonagesimo octavo, regis Edwardi vicesimo septimo incipiente
Datum pro habitu lectoris nostri et socii sui xxiiij s.
fo. 199ᵛ
Solutum lectori nostro pro roba clerici sui vj s. viij d.
Item datum lectori nostro ad parcamenum ij s.
fo. 200
Item solutum Willelmo sirugico, clerico lectoris nostri, pro cura fratrum nostrorum xiij s. iiij d.
Fratri lectori nostro vj s. viij d.
Datum scolaribus Oxonie lxxiij s. iiij d.

L. 242, fo. 208ᵛ. Accounts 1299–1300
Datum lectori pro habitu suo et socii sui liiij s.
fo. 209
Datum lectori nostro pro roba clerici sui vj s. viij d.

L. 242, fo. 216ᵛ. Accounts 1300–1
Solutum lectori nostro pro habitu suo et socii xxx s.
Datum lectori nostro ad parcamenum iij s.
Solutum lectori nostro pro roba clerici sui vj s. viij d.
Datum bedell' universitatis Oxonie per manus Alexandri per priorem vj s. viij d.
fo. 217
Datum scolaribus per priorem vij li. xv s.

L. 242, fo. 223. Accounts 1301–2
Solutum lectori nostro pro roba clerici sui di. marc.
fo. 223ᵛ
Datum lectori nostro ad parcamenum emendum iiij s.
Solutum fratri R. lectori nostro pro habitu suo et socii sui xxviij s.

L. 242, fo. 229ᵛ. Accounts 1302–3
Liberatum ij scolaribus[1] admissis euntibus ad archiepiscopum ut videret eosdem vj s.
Datum lectori nostro pro roba clerici sui di. marc.
Solutum lectori nostro ad parcaminum iij s.
Pro habitu lectoris et socii xxx s.

L. 242, fo. 235ᵛ. Accounts 1303–4
Solutum lectori nostro pro roba clerici sui di. marc.
Solutum lectori nostro ad percaminum iij s.
Solutum lectori nostro pro habitu suo et socii xxviij . . .
Item eidem pro albo panno ad langel' xiiij s.

Acc. Bk. I. Treasurers' Accounts, 1303–4
In expensis fratrum Andree de Hardres et Stephani de Faversham studencium Parisius, cum passagio et apparatu eorundem, a festo sancti Mathie[2] apostoli anno regni regis Edwardi xxxij° usque ad festum sancti Valentini anno regni regis eiusdem xxxiij° xlvj li. xix s. iij d.

L. 242, fo. 241ᵛ. Accounts 1304–5
Datum Rad*ulfo* lectori nostro ad percamenum iij s.
Solutum lectori pro roba clerici sui di. marc.
Solutum lectori nostro pro habitu suo et socii sui xxviij s.
fo. 242
In expensis R. de Cherryng pro vinis nostris colligendis in regno Francie xx s.

[1] Perhaps scholars in the almonry.
[2] The word is hard to read and has perhaps been corrected from 'Mathei'. St Matthias (24 February 1304) and not St Matthew (21 September 1304) must surely be meant.

In expensis eiusdem R. de Cherryng alia vice portantis x marcas fratribus nostri studentibus Parisius vj s. x d.

Acc. Bk. I. Treas. Acc. 1304–5
In expensis fratrum S. de Faversham et G. Poterel studencium Parisius a festo sancti Valentini anno regni regis Edwardi xxxiij° usque ad festum natalis Domini anno regni regis eiusdem xxxiiij°,[1] cum passagio et apparatu domini G. xxxiij li. xix s.

L. 242, fo. 249ᵛ. Accounts 1305–6
Solutum lectori nostro pro roba clerici sui di. marc.
Item eidem ad parcamenum iij s.
Pro habitu lectoris nostri et socii sui xxxij s.
fo. 253ᵛ
Solutum duobus garscionibus euntibus pro fratribus nostris Parysius xiij s. iiij d.

Acc. Bk. I. Treas. Acc. 1305–6
In expensis fratrum S. de Faversham et G. Poterel Parisius a festo natalis Domini anno regni regis Edwardi xxxiiij° usque ad redditum eorundem domi xiij li. viij s.

L. 242, fo. 256ᵛ. Accounts 1306–7
Solutum lectori nostro pro roba clerici sui in festo sancti Barnabe apostoli per manus W. supprioris vj s. viij d.
Item eidem ad percamenum iij s.
Datum fratribus minoribus ad pitenciam die sepulture fratris Radulfi de Wodehey, per conventum x s.
fo. 257
Solutum fratri Roberto socio fratris R. de Wodehey lectoris nostri pro habitu suo precepto prioris xix s. vj d.

L. 242, fo. 114. Accounts 1307–8
Steph' de Faversham. Item solutum cuidam scolari, scilicet Ade Champenes de Sandwyco, pro domino S. de Faversham precepto prioris xx s.
fo. 114ᵛ
Item pauperibus scolaribus per priorem vj li.
Solutum lectori nostro ad parcamenum iij s.
fo. 115ᵛ
Pro habitu lectoris nostri et socii sui et coopertoriis et sagis ad lectos eorundem lij s.
Item solutum clerico lectoris nostri pro solidata vj s. viij d.
Item datum diversis scolaribus per priorem viij li. xiij s. iiij d.

[1] 14 February 1305—25 December 1305.

L. 242, fo. 264. Accounts 1308–9
Solutum domino Willelmo de Popering priori de Thrulegh pro domino S. de Faversham precepto prioris xx s.
fo. 264ᵛ
Datum lectori nostro per manus Alexandri precepto prioris iij s.
fo. 265
Solutum lectori nostro pro roba clerici sui di. marc.
fo. 265ᵛ
Item datum lectori nostro per priorem xl d.
Datum socio lectoris nostri xij d.
fo. 266
Pro habitu lectoris nostri et socii sui xxxvj s.

L. 242, fo. 273. Accounts 1309–10
Item datum lectori nostro per priorem vj s. per manus T. Stoyl.
fo. 273ᵛ
Datum socio lectoris nostri xij d.
Solutum lectori nostro pro roba clerici sui di. marc.
fo. 274
Item pro habitu lectoris nostri et socii sui xxxvj s. vj d.

L. 242, fo. 280. Accounts 1310–11
Item lectori nostro per manus eiusdem [sc. Alexandri capellani prioris] iiij s.
Pro habitu lectoris nostri et socii xxxvj s. viij d.
fo. 280ᵛ
Item solutum lectori nostro pro roba clerici sui vigilia nativitatis sancti Iohannis per manus clerici sui di. marc.

L. 242, fo. 122. Accounts 1311–12
Exp' pro abitu lectoris et socii sui xxx s.
 Datum lectori nostro per manus domini Alexandri per priorem vj s.
fo. 122ᵛ
Datum socio lectoris nostri xij d.
Datum lectori nostro per priorem per manus Alexandri capellani ij s.
Solutum lectori nostro pro roba clerici sui di. marc.
fo. 123
Datum diversis scolaribus per priorem quando prior fuit apud Newinton iuxta Oxoniam vj li. x s.

L. 242, fo. 287. Accounts 1312–13
Pro habitu lectoris nostri et socii xxxiiij s. vj d.
Datum lectori per priorem iiij s.

fo. 287ᵛ
Solutum lectori nostro pro roba clerici sui in festo Philippi et Iacobi di. marc.

L. 242, fo. 297. Accounts 1313–14
Pro habitu lectoris nostri et socii sui xxx s.
Datum fratri Roberto lectori nostro per priorem iij s.
fo. 297ᵛ
Solutum lectori nostro pro roba clerici sui vj s. viij d.
Item datum fratri Gilberto socio lectoris quando ivit ad concilium provinciale, per preceptum supprioris xl d.

L. 242, fo. 301. Accounts 1314–15
Pro habitu lectoris et socii sui xxxj s.
Datum fratri Roberto lectori nostro per priorem vj s. viij d.
Item pro tunica et corsetto ad opus domini S. de Favirsham lectoris x s.
fo. 301ᵛ
Item datum lectori nostro pro se et scriptore suo anno Edwardi octavo xx s.

L. 242, fo. 308. Accounts 1315–16
Item datum lectori nostro pro diversis necessariis xx s.

L. 242, fo. 316ᵛ. Accounts 1316–17
Item lectori nostro pro diversis xx s.

L. 242, fo. 325. Accounts 1317–18
Item pro pergameno empto ad opus lectoris iij s.

L. 242, fo. 331. Accounts 1318–19, 12–13 Ed. II
Item datum lectori nostro per ordinacionem supprioris[1] et capituli xxvj s. viij d.
Item pro j duodena parcameni empta ad opus domini S. de Feversham xviij d.
Item domino S. de Faversham pro clerico suo x s.
Item pro pergameno ad opus domini S. de Faversham lectoris xiiij s.
fo. 331ᵛ
Item pro pergameno empto ad opus lectoris iij s.
Item domino S. de Favirsham lectori pro salario suo xx s.

Acc. Bk. II. Treas. Ac. 1318–19
Item pro novis studiis xxxij li. ix s. vij d.

L. 242, Accounts 1319–20 (13–14 Ed. II) and 1320–1 (14–15 Ed. II) seem to contain no reference to the lector etc.; but see below.

---

[1] From other entries in the same year it seems that the prior was abroad, in France.

EXTRACTS FROM ACCOUNTS

L. 242, fo. 129ᵛ. Accounts 1321–2, 15–16 Ed. II
Datum fratri Roberto de Foleham per suppriorem ij s.
Item datum diversis scolaribus Oxon' et Paris' lxxvj s. viij d.

L. 242, fo. 135ᵛ. Accounts 1322–3, 16–17 Ed. II
Solutum domino S. de Faversham lectori nostro pro necessariis suis de anno regis Edwardi filii regis Edwardi xiiij°, xv° et xvj° iiij li. x s.
Item datum diversis scolaribus per priorem xlvj s. viij d.

L. 242, fo. 141. Accounts 1323–4, 17–18 Ed. II
Item datum fratri Stephano de Feversham lectori per N. de Burne de corona pro feodo suo, ut dicit, xx s.
Item datum universitati Oxon' per conventum lxvj s. viij d.
Item datum domino S. de Faversham lectori pro clerico suo x s.
Item datum fratri Roberto de Fulham quondam lectori nostro vj s. viij d.
fo. 141ᵛ
Item pro pergameno empto ad opus lectoris iiij s. iij d.

L. 242, fo. 147. Accounts 1324–5, 18–19 Ed. II
Item pro pergameno empto ad opus lectoris vij s. ij d.
Item pro pergameno empto ad opus lectoris v s.
fo. 147ᵛ
Item datum diversis scolaribus per priorem xlvj s. viij d.
Item datum lectori nostro per ordinacionem ad scaccarium xl s.

L. 242, fo. 352ᵛ. Accounts 1325–6
Item pro pergameno empto ad opus lectoris xj s. vj d.
Item datum lectori nostro pro se et clerico suo xl s.

L. 242, fo. 361. Accounts 1326–7
Item datum lectori nostro pro se et clerico suo xl s.

L. 243, fo. 2ᵛ. Accounts 1327–8
[Item domino H. de sancto Yvone pro feodo suo xx s.]¹
Item domino H. lectori nostro pro se et clerico suo de gracia conventus xl s.
Item datum diversis scolaribus per priorem xlvj s. viij d.

L. 243, fo. 10ᵛ. Accounts 1328–9
Item lectori nostro de gracia conventus pro se et clerico suo xl s.

L. 243, fo. 17. Accounts 1329–30
Item lectori nostro de gracia conventus pro se et clerico suo xl s.

---
¹ Struck through.

L. 243, fo. 25. Accounts 1330–1
Item domino H. de sancto Ivone lectori nostro pro se et clerico suo de gracia conventus xl s.

D.E. 3. Prior's accounts, 26 April 1331–2
Item fratribus nostris euntibus versus scolas l s.

D.E. 3. Prior's accounts, c. December 1331 seq.
Item missum H. de sancto Ivone et I. socio suo scolaribus rediuntibus de scolis pro suis expensis xx s.
Item liberatum pro expensis fratrum euntium versus Oxon' xxx s.

L. 243, fo. 32. Accounts 1331–2
Item pro panno de bourneto pro iij capis ad opus fratrum nostrorum missorum Oxoniis post festum sancti Michaelis lxij s.
fo. 32ᵛ
Scolares. Item in expensis dominorum H. de sancto Yvone, Rogeri de Godmersham, Iacobi de Oxene Oxoniis xxij li.
Item pro expensis eorundem versus Oxonias per preceptum domini prioris l s.
Item eisdem per dominum priorem xx s.
Item domino H. de sancto Ivone lectori nostro pro se et clerico suo de gracia conventus xl s.

D.E. 3. Prior's accounts, 26 April 1332—26 April 1333
Item missum scolaribus redeuntibus de Oxon' pro expensis suis xx s.
Item liberatum fratribus nostris euntibus versus Oxon' pro expensis suis xxx s.
Ibid., c. 25 November 1332
Item datum bedello universitatis Oxon' qui ad nos ex parte eiusdem universitatis accessit iij s. iiij d.

L. 243, fo. 41. Accounts 1332–3
Item datum domino Hugoni de sancto Ivone lectori nostro pro se et clerico suo de gracia conventus xl s.
Item in expensis dominorum H. de sancto Yvone, Iacobi de Oxene et Willelmi de Hethe Oxoniis pro tribus quarteriis xxiij li. x s.
Item in expensis eorundem pro necessariis suis c s.
Item in expensis eorundem versus scolas xxx s.
Item in expensis eorundem veniensium de Oxoniis xx s.

D.E. 3. Prior's accounts, 26 April 1333 seq.
Item datum cuidam scolari eunti versus Oxon' v s.
Item datum cuidam amico studenti in universitate Oxon' x s.
Item in donis fratrum euntium versus scolas xx s.

L. 243, fo. 49ᵛ. Accounts 1333–4
Item domino H. de sancto Ivone lectori nostro pro se et clerico suo de gracia conventus xl s.
Item in expensis dominorum Iacobi de Oxine et W. de Heth Oxoniis pro tribus quarteriis xiij li.
fo. 50
Item datum fratribus nostris euntibus Oxoniis per priorem xx s.
fo. 51ᵛ
Item cuidam garcioni misso apud Newynton pro I. de Oxne et socio suo in crastino passionis sancti Thome xij d.
fo. 52
Item Blebbe misso Oxoniis domino Willelmo de Heth ij s.

D.E. 3, p. xlvii. Prior's accounts 1333–4 (? c. 2 February 1334)
Newenton. Item memorandum quod prepositus de Newenton per ordinacionem custodis levabit contra festum Purificacionis x li.; sed tempore dicte ordinacionis ignoravit predictus custos quod haberemus scolares Oxon' et ideo scripsimus preposito de Newenton quod mittat nobis Cantuarie de dicta ordinacione c s. et residuum predicte ordinacionis reservabit pro fratribus nostris Oxon'. Scripsimus eciam sibi quod nobis mittat si possit totaliter dictam ordinacionem, ita tamen quod dicti fratres nostri nullum defectum paciantur.

D.E. 3. Prior's accounts, 26 April—20 December 1334
Item liberatum fratri R. de Icham pro carta regis impetranda pro domo empta Oxon' x s.
Item liberatum fratribus I. de Oxeneye et W. de Heth euntibus versus Oxon' xx s.

L. 243, fo. 57. Accounts 1334–5
Item domino Iacobo de Oxine et W. de Heth post festum sancti Michaelis pro necessariis suis v s. iiij d.
Item datum fratribus nostris euntibus Oxoniis x s. ...
fo. 57ᵛ
Item in panno empto pro capis dominorum Iacobi de Oxene et W. de Heth in festo sancti Michaelis, cum tintura xxix s. x d.
Item domino H. de sancto Yvone lectori nostro pro se et clerico suo de gracia conventus xl s.
In panno empto cum capis dominorum Iacobi de Oxene et W. de Heth sine tinctura et in tinctura eiusdem xij s. iiij d.
Item in expensis domini Iacobi de Oxene et W. de Heth pro mora eorundem apud Oxoniam [*sum blank*].

fo. 58
Item in expensis dominorum I. de Oxene et W. de Heth apud Oxoniam pro tribus quarteriis anni xv li.
Item datum fratribus nostris euntibus ad scolas per priorem xxv s.

D.E. 3. Prior's accounts, 26 April—1 August 1335
Item datum fratribus euntibus ad scolas xxv s.
Item datum cuidam pauperi scolari eunti ad scolas xiij s. iiij d.

L. 243, fo. 65. Accounts 1335–6
Item in panno burneto pro capis dominorum I. de Oxene, W. de Heth et I. de Hedecrone xxj s.
fo. 65^v
Item in expensis fratrum redeuncium de Oxoniis xxvj s. viij d.
Item in expensis dominorum Iacobi de Oxene, Willelmi Heth et Iohannis de Hedecrone pro mora eorundem apud Oxoniam xx li.

D.E. 3. Prior's accounts, 1338
Item Iohanni magistro puerorum domini archidiaconi [?] per vices v s.
Item liberatum quibusdam euntibus Oxon' xvj s.
Ibid., c. 12 June 1340
Item liberatum tribus garcionibus cum tribus equis euntibus Oxon' pro fratribus . . .
Ibid., c. 16 August 1340
Item scolaribus euntibus Oxon' xx s.
Ibid., c. 15 August 1341
Item liberatum fratribus euntibus ad scolas vij li. xiij s. iiij d.
Item liberatum fratri Iacobo de Oxene pro expensis suis et clericorum euntium ad dominum archiepiscopum xx s.
Ibid., c. 25 March 1342
Item datum cuidam scolari x s.
Ibid., c. 9 August 1342
Item receptum per manus fratris I. Frome iiij li. in partem solucionis xij li. nobis debitarum de domo nostra vendita in Oxon'.
Item liberatum fratri Iacobo de Oxene pro expensis suis et sociorum faciendis in scolis xl s.
Ibid., c. 8 April 1343
Item datum cuidam scolari Oxon' x s.
Ibid., c. 11 July 1343
Item per manus I. Frome pro domo nostra vendita in Oxonia iiij marc.
[*Accounts from 1343 to 1350 missing.*]

EXTRACTS FROM ACCOUNTS

L. 243, fo. 75ᵛ. Accounts 1350–1, 24 Ed. III
Item solutum domino I. Frome pro officio suo xiij s. iiij d.
Item solutum domino I. Frome pro officio suo per feretrarios xiij s. iiij d.

L. 243, fo. 78ᵛ. Accounts 1351–2, 25 Ed. III
Item solutum domino I. Frome lectori xiij s. iiij d.
fo. 79
Item domino Iohanni Frome lectori xiij s. iiij d.

L. 243, fo. 83ᵛ. Accounts 1352–3, 26 Ed. III
Item solutum domino I. Frome lectori xiij s. iiij d.
fo. 84
Item solutum I. Frome lectori pro officio suo xiij s. iiij d.

L. 243, fo. 88ᵛ. Accounts 1353–4, 27 Ed. III
Item solutum I. Frome lectori xij s. iiij d.
fo. 89
Item solutum domino I. Frome lectori xxvj s. viij d. per vices.
L. 243, fo. 92. Accounts 1354–5, 28 Ed. III
Item liberatum domino I. Frome lectori xiij s. iiij d.
fo. 92ᵛ
Item solutum I. Frome lectori xiij s. iiij d.

L. 243, fo. 97. Accounts 1355–6, 29 Ed. III
Item solutum domino I. Frome lectori xiij s. iiij d.
fo. 97ᵛ
Item solutum domino I. Frome lectori die transitus sancti Benedicti xiij s. iiij d.
fo. 98
Item solutum I. Frome lectori xiij s. iiij d.
fo. 98ᵛ
[Item in equis locatis apud Oxoniam pro domino Iacobo de Oxene et sociis suis x s.][1]
Item in equis locatis pro scolaribus et aliis per vices xvij s.

L. 243, fo. 102ᵛ. Accounts 1356–7, 30 Ed. III
Item liberatum I. Frome pro officio lectoris xiij s. iiij d.
Item I. Frome pro officio lectoris xiij s. iiij d.
[*Account 31 Ed. III missing.*]

L. 243, fo. 109. Accounts 1358–9, 32 Ed. III
Sol' serviencium anno E. xxxij^{do}. Magistro lectori xl s.
Solutum xiij s. iiij d. per feretrarios.

[1] Struck through.

Item xiij s. iiij d. per feretrarios.
Item xiij s. iiij d. per feretrarios.

L. 243, fo. 112. Accounts 1359–60, 33 Ed. III
Sol' serviencium. Magistro lectori xl s.
Solutum per feretrarios xiij s. iiij d.
Item xiij s. iiij d. per feretrarios.

L. 243, fo. 117ᵛ. Accounts 1360–1, 34 Ed. III
Equitantibus pro negociis ecclesie ... Item in equo conducto pro fratre Henrico Wodhell versus Magefeld ij s. vj d.
fo. 118
Sol' serviencium. Magistro lectori xl s.
Solutum per feretrarios xiij s. iiij d.
Item xiij s. iiij d. per feretrarios. Solutum totum.

L. 243, fo. 120ᵛ. Accounts 1362–3, 36 Ed. III
Item in panno de burneto empto pro W. Recolvere et I. Gloucestre scolaribus pro ij cappis scolasticis xlvj s.
fo. 122
Sol' serviencium. Magistro lectori xl s.
Solutum H. Wodhell xiij s. iiij d. pro primo termino per feretrarios.
Item eidem xiij s. iiij d. per eosdem.
Item I. Frome xiij s. iiij d. per feretrarios.

L. 243, fo. 124ᵛ. Accounts 1363–4, 37 Ed. III
Item datum domino H. Wodhell precepto domini prioris per feretrarios xx s.
fo. 126
Sol' serviencium. I. Frome xiij s. iiij d. per feretrarios.
Item xiij s. iiij d. per feretrarios.
Item xiij s. iiij d. per eosdem. Totum.

L. 243, fo. 129. Accounts 1364–5, 38 Ed. III
Item in uno equo conducto pro I. Bydindenne versus Oxoniam v s.
Item in panno de burneto empto pro I. Bydendenne pro cappa sua scolastica xxviij s.
Item in vj ulnis panni linei emptis pro I. Bidindenne vj s. vj d.
fo. 130
Item R. Stystede eunti Oxoniam xxvj s. viij d.
fo. 131
Sol' serviencium. Magistro lectori xl s.
Solutum totum. [*Some particulars, perhaps of payments by terms, erased.*]

L. 243, fo. 136. Accounts 1365–6, 39 Ed. III
Sol' serviencium. Magistro lectori xl s.
Inde solutum I. Frome pro termino natalis Domini xiij s. iiij d. per feretrarios.
Item H. Wodhull de termino Pasche xiij s. iiij d.
Item eidem termino sancti Iohannis xiij s. iiij d.

L. 243, fo. 139ᵛ. Accounts 1366–7, 40 Ed. III
Item fratri W. Richemund venienti de Oxonia x s.
Item datum cuidam scolari de Oxonia xiij s. iiij d.
Item in percameno empto Oxonie ij s. ij d.
Item in expensis Nicholai brevitour missi Oxoniam ij s.
Item in expensis domini H. Wodhell et socii sui missorum Londo*niam* per priorem pro diversis negociis lx s.
fo. 140
Magistro lectori xl s.
Inde solutum xiij s. iiij d. per feretrarios.
Item xiij s. iiij d. per feretrarios de termino Pasche.
Item xiij s. iiij d. per eosdem de termino sancti baptiste.

L. 243, fo. 143. Accounts 1367–8, 41 Ed. III
Item in expensis N. brevetour missi Oxoniam cum litteris iij s.
fo. 143ᵛ
Item proprio nostro nuncio misso Oxoniam ij s.
fo. 144ᵛ
Item in uno equo conducto versus archiepiscopum cum W. [?] Ferour pro domino H. Wodhell.
Item in expensis I. Redynggᵃt missi London*iam* pro negociis ecclesie vj s. viij d.
Item solutum Ade clerico misso ad curiam Romanam pro collegio Oxonie et aliis negociis ix li. xiij s. iiij d.
Item liberatum domino H. Wodhull misso archiepiscopo xl s.
fo. 145
Magistro lectori xl s.
Inde solutum xiij s. iiij d. de termino natalis Domini per feretrarios.
Item xiij s. iiij d. per eosdem. Solutum totum.

L. 243, fo. 148ᵛ. Accounts 1368–9, 42 Ed. III
Item in expensis domini prioris apud Dover quando cardinalis erat ibi xxvj s. viij d.
fo. 149
Item datum Nigello nuncio cardinalis deferenti litteras domini cardinalis de collegio Oxonie xl s.

Item in equis conductis pro fratribus nostris versus Oxoniam xx s.
fo. 150
Magistro lectori xl s.
Inde solutum xiij s. iiij d. per feretrarios.
Item xiij s. iiij d. per eosdem.

L. 243, fo. 153. Accounts 1369–70, 43 Ed. III
Item datum Nigello nuncio deferenti literas ad dominum cardinalem Cantuarie xl s.
fo. 153ᵛ
Item datum Coll brevytour misso Oxoniam fratribus nostris pro negociis ecclesie cum uno procuratore ij s.
Item datum Beryngario nuncio domini cardinalis in primo adventu suo vj s. viij d.
Item datum Berengario nuncio domini cardinalis Cantuarie deferenti literas ad dominum papam et cardinalem nostrum causa collegii xl s.
fo. 154ᵛ
Item I. Becford et R. Hatfeld euntibus versus cancellarium pro collegio lxiij s. iiij d.
fo. 155
Magistro lectori xl s.

1 *Acc. Bk. II. Treas. Acc. 1370–1*
Recepta de obvencionibus ... Item de xx li. receptis de fructibus sequestratis ecclesie de Pagham.
[*Expenses*] Item scolaribus studentibus Oxonie pro pensionibus eorum xx li.
Item in expensis fratrum versus Oxoniam xliiij s. vj d.

2 *Acc. Bk. II. Treas. Acc. 1371–2*
Recepta de obvencionibus ... De fructibus ecclesie de Pagham per manus domini Ricardi prioris iiij^{xx}vj li. xiij s. iiij d.
[*Expenses*] Item tribus scolaribus studentibus Oxonie pro pensionibus eorum xxix li.
Item in expensis eorum eundo et redeundo, equis conductis et cappis scolasticis emptis viij li.

L. 243, fo. 159. Accounts 1372–3, 46 Ed. III
Item solutum pro expensis nostris factis Dovorr' existent' ibidem cum domino cardinali xxx s.
fo. 161
Magistro lectori xl s. Nichil quia vacat.[1]

---

[1] The lector is put down as a matter of course every year in the list of salaried officials. When no particulars of payment are added, it *may* mean that the office was vacant.

EXTRACTS FROM ACCOUNTS

3 *Acc. Bk. II. Treas. Acc. 1372–3*
Recepta ... De fructibus ecclesie de Pagham de anno l li.
De fructibus eiusdem ecclesie sequestratis per dominum Simonem Langham archiepiscopum xl li. et non plus, quia in compoto precedenti inter obvenciones.
Reparaciones ... Item in reparacione aule collegii Cant' et camerarum una cum latrina et aliis necessariis inibi factis xxiij li. vj s. viij d.
Item in reparacione facta apud Pagham, Mundam et Berstede per Stephanum Monyngham custodem xxiiij li.
Novum opus ... In una nova domo facta apud Berstede per dominum S. Monyngham custodem et magistrum collegi x li.
Soluciones sine tall' ... Item eidem [sc. domino cardinali Cantuariensi] pro procuracione sua de ecclesia de Pagham lxxiij s. iiij d.
Item datum domino principi in prima peregrinacione ad beatum Thomam post aventum suum de Aquitannia iiij^{xx}xiiij li. xiij s. iiij d.
Item domino regi pro confirmacione advocacionis ecclesie de Pagham et aule Cant' cxxxiij li. vj s. viij d.
Item pro feodo carte et dupplicacione eiusdem xij li. xiij s. iiij d.
Item datum pro auxilio et amicicia habenda xxj li.
Item in expensis S. Monyngham custodis et aliorum Londoniis, Oxonie et Pagham eundo, redeundo, moram faciendo xxxij li. x s.
Item in bladis intrandis apud Pagham et Mundham cum utenciliis necessariis emptis xv li. xij d.
Item in una parva placea empta Oxonie de monialibus de Godistawe pro una coquina superponenda xxvj s. viij d.
Item in expensis trium fratrum studencium Oxonie in collegio nostro et duorum secularium scolarium cum expensis magistri collegii ibidem per vices xxxv li. xvj d.
Item in expensis eorundem eundo et redeundo, cariagio librorum et cappis scolasticis emptis iiij li. xv s. iiij d.

4 *Acc. Bk. II. Treas. Acc. 1373–4*
Item in expensis duorum fratrum studencium Oxonie in collegio nostro et duorum secularium scolarium cum expensis fratris Willelmi Woghop studentis in eodem per unum quarterium anni xxvj li. vj s. viij d.
Item datum magistro Rogero Croxton registrario domini cardinalis Cant' pro labore suo in curia Romana circa processum collegii nostri Oxonie xx s.

L. 243, fo. 165^v. Accounts 1374–5, 48 Ed. III
Item in expensis W. Woghope versus curiam xx li. xiij s.
fo. 166
Magistro lectori xl s.

5 *Acc. Bk. II. Treas. Acc. 1374–5*
[*Receipts*] De c li. receptis per manus domini Iohannis Wodhulle et Willelmi Topclyve executorum testamenti domini Willelmi Wyttleseye archiepiscopi de sequestro ecclesie de Pagham.
[*Expenses*] Et de viij li. x s. pro expensis fratrum nostrorum scolarium cum equis conductis pro eisdem versus Cantuariam pro eleccione celebranda, eundo et redeundo bina vice.
Et de xxx li. pro expensis quatuor fratrum studencium in collegio nostro Oxonie per tria quarteria.
L. 243, fo. 170^v. Accounts 1375–6, 49 Ed. III
Item in j equo empto pro domino W. Wohope versus curiam Romanam xxx s.
Item in expensis domini prioris versus Oxoniam et redeundo xvij li. v s.
Item in nuncio misso Oxoniam pro fratribus citandis ad eleccionem prioris[1] xl s.

6 *Acc. Bk. II. Treas. Acc. 1375–6*
[*Expenses*] Et de xviij s. solutis pro expensis domini I. Bertram de Oxonia usque Cantuariam.
Et de xiij s. vj d. solutis eidem pro expensis suis versus Londoniam pro ordine sacerdotali percipiendo.
Et de xxj s. iiij d. pro expensis domini Iohannis Aleyn versus Oxoniam.
Et de xx s. pro expensis domini I. Bertram versus Oxoniam.
Et de xx s. solutis domino Iohanni[2] pro capa scolastica.
Et de lx s. solutis pro cameraria vj fratrum Oxonie.
Et de v s. pro libris domini I. Estry querendis Oxonie.
Et de xiij s. iiij d. solutis pro expensis domini T. Wykyngge versus Oxoniam.
Et de xviij s. viij d. solutis pro expensis domini W. Gylyngham versus Oxoniam.

L. 243, fo. 172. Accounts 1376–7, 50 Ed. III
Magistro lectori xl s. Nichil.
fo. 172^v
Item domino I. Bydendenne eunti ad dominum archiepiscopum ad Saltwode pro literis impetrandis cause generalis capituli xx s.

---

[1] This would be on the death of Prior Richard Gillyngham, 31 August 1376: Searle 161.
[2] Either John Aleyn or John Bertram.

EXTRACTS FROM ACCOUNTS

7 *Acc. Bk. II. Treas. Acc. 1376–7*
[*Expenses*] Item de xvj s. viij d. liberatis domino W. Chert pro expensis suis versus Oxoniam.
Item de xxx s. pro expensis fratrum versus Oxoniam.
Item de vj s. viij d. pro expensis domini W. Gilyngham versus Oxoniam.
Item de lxvj s. viij d. solutis fratri W. Stone pro capa scolastica et expensis versus Oxoniam.
Item de xx s. datis dominis I. Aleyn et W. Stone pro expensis eorum versus Oxoniam.

8 *L. 243, fo. 175. Accounts 1377–8, 1 Ric. II*
Item in pergameno empto Oxonie ij s. iij d.
fo. 175^v
Item in factura indumentorum scolarium domini prioris' per feretrarios ij s.
Item datum domino W. Chert precepto domini prioris xiij s. iiij d.
Item datum domino I. Aleyn precepto eiusdem domini prioris xiijs. iiijd.
fo. 176
Magistro lectori xl s. Nichil.
fo. 176^v
Item Nicholao brevitori versus Oxoniam v s.
Item in expensis fratris W. Woghope missi ad dominum archiepiscopum ad Otteforde pro causa generalis capituli x s.

9 *Acc. Bk. II. Treas. Acc. 1377–8*
Item de xx s. solutis Thome Chylyndenne pro capa scolastica.
Item de vj s. viij d. solutis pro expensis nuncii nostri missi Oxoniam pro scolaribus contra eleccionem domini prioris.
Item de ix li. xiij s. ix d. solutis pro expensis scolarium veniencium de Oxonia pro eleccione domini prioris et rediencium ad scolas.

10 *Acc. Bk. II. Treas. Acc. 1378–9*
Item de vj s. solutis pro expensis garcionum et equorum a fratribus nostris de Oxonia redeuncium.
Item de xlj s. viij d. solutis pro ij urciolis factis pro collegio Cantuarie Oxonie.
Item de lxxiij s. iiij d. liberatis domino Iohanni Aleyn cum foret bacularius in theologia.
[*Mention of expenses of Thomas Chylyndenne* versus curiam Romanam.]

' Either the secular scholars at Oxford or the scholars in the almonry.

11 *Acc. Bk. II. Treas. Acc. 1379–80*
[Payments: fratri Thome Chylyndenne ad curiam Romanam.]
Item de cj s. viij d. solutis pro expensis fratris W. Dovore, Thome Everard et W. Miltone versus Oxoniam et capis suis scolasticis.

12 *L. 243, fo. 179ᵛ. Accounts 1380–1, 4 Ric. II*
Item in expensis pro harnasio W. Gylyngham de Oxonia iij s. iiij d.
Item in expensis in ostria pro scolaribus Oxon' ij s. j d.
fo. 180
Item in expensis Carre versus Oxoniam per dominum priorem xx d.
Item domino Iohanni Aleyn versus Oxoniam pro benediccione v s.
fo. 180ᵛ
Magistro lectori xl s.
Inde solutum xx s. per magistrum in criptis.

13 *Acc. Bk. II. Treas. Acc. 1380–1*
Item de xxvj s. viij d. pro expensis domini Thome Chilyndenne et equis conductis versus Oxoniam.
Item de l s. pro expensis domini Henrici Henfeld versus Oxoniam et capa sua scolastica.

14 *L. 243, fo. 188ᵛ. Accounts 1381–2, 5 Ric. II*
Domino Henrico Hevenfeld versus Oxoniam v s.
fo. 189
Item in expensis W. Stone versus London' cum doctore de Wynchestre et T. Chyllynden inceptore pro liberacione dicti Thome et I. Aleyn inceptorum xlij s.

15 *Acc. Bk. II. Treas. Acc. 1381–2*
Item de xx s. solutis domino Thome Dovorre pro capa sua scolastica.
Item de iiij li. solutis domino Thome Chillyngdene pro expensis diversorum fratrum versus Oxoniam ab eleccione archiepiscopi.
Item de vj s. x d. solutis domino Thome Chillyngdene pro expensis Thome Hwytpeys venientis de Oxonia.

16 *L. 243, fo. 183. Accounts 1382–3, 6 Ric. II*
Magistro lectori xl s.
Solutum Willelmo Gylyngham per feretrarios xx s.
Item per dominum ... custodem beate Marie in criptis x s.
fo. 183ᵛ
Item W. Dovor et W. Kenarton versus Oxoniam pro benediccione x s.
Item in expensis fratrum I. Glouc' et W. Chert versus dominum archiepiscopum pro W. Dover xxiiij s. viij d.
Item in expensis T. valecti nostri versus Oxoniam causa domini W. Dovore iconomi ij s. vj d.

EXTRACTS FROM ACCOUNTS

Item in expensis dominorum T. Chillynden et W. Chert versus dominum archiepiscopum causa W. Dovore x s.
Item in expensis T. Chilynden versus archiepiscopum existentem apud Otteford causa W. Dovorre v s. v d.
Item in expensis T. Chilinden et W. Chert versus dominum de Cobham pro eodem W. Dovere viij s.
Item in expensis domini prioris versus Londoniam et ibidem ad loquendum domino archiepiscopo pro W. Dovere iiij li. xv s.
Item in expensis domini T. Chyllynden versus dominum archiepiscopum existentem apud Otteford vij s. ij d.
Item in expensis domini Iohannis Aleyn versus Oxoniam xiij s. iiij d.
Item in expensis domini W. Gilyngham versus Londiniam causa collegii xviij s. iiij d.
Item in expensis domini T. Chylynden versus archiepiscopum xiij s. iiij d.
Item in expensis W. Dover versus Londoniam xxvj s. viij d.

fo. 185ᵛ
[Item in expensis dominorum I. Glouc' et W. Chert versus dominum archiepiscopum London' causa W. Dover ambientis custodiam collegii xxiiij s. viij d.]¹

fo. 186
Item pro munimentis collegii Oxon' cariandis xj s. viij d.

17 *Acc. Bk. II. Treas. Acc. 1382–3*
Soluciones debitorum sine tall' . . . Item de liij s. iiij d. pro expensis domini Iohannis Aleyn versus Oxoniam cum equis conductis.
Item xx s. solutis eidem pro capa sua scolastica.

18 *L. 243, fo. 192ᵛ. Accounts 1383–4, 7 Ric. II*
Magistro lectori xl s.
Solutum W. Gylyngham per feretrarios.
Domino Thome Everard versus Oxoniam v s.
Domino Henrico Henfeld versus Oxoniam v s.

fo. 193
Item in expensis domini Thome Chylynden versus dominum archiepiscopum xx s. Feretrar'.
Item in expensis eiusdem versus Oxoniam vj s. viij d. Feretrar'.

19 *Acc. Bk. II. Treas. Acc. 1383–4*
Soluciones debitorum sine tall' . . . Et de xxx li. xiij s. iiij d. solutis I. Schuluarde pro lib' domini Iohannis Aleyn et Thome Chyllyngden inceptorum.

L. 243, fo. 196ᵛ. Accounts 1384–5, 8 Ric. II
Magistro lectori xl s.

¹ Struck through because given above.

Inde solutum W. Gylyngham xxvj s. viij d.
Item Iohanni Aleyn xiij s. iiij d. per feretrarios.

20 *Acc. Bk. II. Treas. Acc. 1384–5*
Item de xxvj s. viij d. solutis pro expensis domini Thome Chyllyngdene venientis de Oxonia causa visitacionis.
Item de xlvj s. viij d. solutis pro expensis domini Henrici Henefelde et Willelmi Kenarton veniencium de Oxonia.
Item de cxiij s. iiij d. solutis Willelmo Dovorre pro statutis colegii Oxonie emendandis et causa ecclesie de Mepham.

L. 243, fo. 200^v. Accounts 1385–6, 9 Ric. II
Magistro lectori xl s.
Item Henrico Henfelde scolari Oxonie in festo natalis Domini anno ix° v s.
Item Willelmo Dovore pro benediccione versus Oxoniam v s.

21 *L. 243, fo. 204^v. Accounts 1386–7, 10 Ric. II*
Magistro lectori xl s.
In primis domino Henrico Evenefeld pro benediccione versus Oxoniam v s.
Item Henrico Chilham pro benediccione versus Oxoniam v s.
Item eidem ex presepto domini prioris xx d.

L. 243, fo. 208^v. Accounts 1387–8, 11 Ric. II
Magistro lectori xl s.
Inde solutum xiij s. iiij d. per feretrarios.
Item xiij s. iiij d. per custodem in criptis.

22 *L. 243, fo. 212^v. Accounts 1388–9, 12 Ric. II*
Magistro lectori xl s.
Solutum W. Gylyngham per feretrarios.
Item domino W. Dover scolari pro benediccione v s.
Item domino Thome Everard scolari v s.
Item domino Iohanni Berham versus Oxoniam v s.

L. 243, fo. 216^v. Accounts 1389–90, 13 Ric. II
W. Gyllyngham magistro lectori xl s.
Inde solutum xx s. per W. Richemunde custodem martirii.
Item xx s. per feretrarios. Totum.

23 *Prior's Rolls XVII, no. 4, 1396–7*
Expense officiariorum... In indumentis domini archiepiscopi, domini prioris et fratrum in conventu, cum camera v fratrum studencium Oxonie ac aliis expensis in eodem officio cxxxvij li. xj s. vj d. ob. Decima, quindecima soluta... In medietate unius decime solute pro

EXTRACTS FROM ACCOUNTS

... Pageham appropriata collegio Oxonie nichil causa predicta [sc. quia condonatur per dominum regem].
Novum opus collegii Oxonie ... In novo opere facto ad collegium Oxonie ut patet in compoto domini Willelmi Cherte custodis ac supervisoris dicti operis clxvij li. vj s. viij d.
Expense forinsece ... In expensis eiusdem [sc. Rob. William] bina vice versus Pageham pro firma querenda xxj s.

24 *Treasurers' Rolls, no. 8, 1407–8*
Forinceca ... Et pro capa domini Iohannis Langdone et expensis sociorum suorum versus Oxoniam xxxv s. xj d.

25 *Treas. Rolls, no. 9, 1408–9*
Forinceca ... In cariagio vestium fratrum Iohannis Wucton et Iohannis Dovorre cum expensis ab Oxonia xx s.

26 *Prior's Rolls, no. 2, 1410–11*
[*Receipts*] Fructus ecclesiarum et pensiones ... De ecclesia de Pageham iiij^{xx}vj li.
[*Expenses*] Collegium Oxonie. In expensis fratrum et secularium ibidem cum reparacione iiij^{xx} li.
Incepcio doctorum. In expensis incepcionis Iohannis Langedone in theologia et R. Godmersham in decretis cxviij li. iij s. v d. qua.

27 *Prior's Rolls, no. 1, March—September 12 Hen. IV, 1411*
Inde solutum per eundem dominum Iohannem [Wodnesbergh] priorem diversis creditoribus pro debito domini Thome [Chillynden] prioris.
Item fratribus studentibus Oxonie xlv li.
Item domino Iohanni Langdone custodi aule Oxonie c s.

28 *Treas. Rolls. no. 11, c. 1413; mutilated*
Item in expensis domini Willelmi Molasshe custodis ... in negociis ecclesie per vices cum expensis fratrum euncium ad studium cv s. iiij d.
Item pro ij cartis, videlicet de Selgrave et collegio Oxonie in cancellaria domini regis renovandis et sigillandis xxix s.

29 *Cart. Ant. X. 19. Accounts c. 1424*
Stipendia famulorum ... In stipendiis Iohannis Pocock servientis fratris Iohannis Wodenesberghe et custodis xv s.
Expense forinsece ... Et in expensis Iohannis Wodenesberghe ab Oxonia v s. j. d.
Et in expensis eiusdem procuratoris ecclesie in concilio generali apud Papiam hoc anno celebrato xx li.

30 *Treas. Rolls, no. 12, 1432–3*
In expensis Iohannis Waltham, Roberti Bynny et Ricardi Gravenay versus Oxoniam, eundo et redeundo per vices hoc anno, una cum equis conductis pro eisdem lxvij s. xj d.

31 *Acc. Bk. III, pt. 2. Weekly bills, Sun. after octave of Easter, 14 Hen. IV: 22 April 1436*
Item solutum Iohanni Wodonysberughe scolari Oxonie pro expensis versus Cantuariam et iterum versus Oxoniam xx s.

32 *Ibid. Trinity Sunday: 3 June 1436*
Item in cariagio vestium et aliarum rerum Iohannis Waltham scolaris Oxonie redeundo videlicet a Londonia per mare xviij d.
Item Roberto Lyntone pro expensis versus Oxoniam veniendo et redeundo xx s.

33 *Ibid. Sunday before Michaelmas, 15 Hen. VI: 25 September 1436*
In expensis W. Rychemunde et W. Thorndene xxx s.

34 *Ibid. 2 Sun. after St Peter ad Vincula, 15 Hen. VI: 4 August 1437*
Scolares. Item solutum T. Asshe pro capa scolari in transitu suo xv s.
Item in expensis eiusdem versus Oxoniam xx s.
Item expense Thome Assche versus Oxoniam xx d.

35 *Ibid. Sun. after Michaelmas, 16 Hen. VI: 6 October 1437*
Item in expensis scolarium Oxonie ij s. x d. ob.
Item in expensis Willelmi Thorndenne et Willelmi Rychemunde scolarium versus Oxoniam sine equis conductis eundo et redeundo xiiij s. iiij d.

36 *Ibid. 2 Sun. after Michaelmas, 16 Hen. VI: 13 October 1437*
Iohanni Broun pro vestibus studencium cariandis ad Londoniam x d.

37 *Ibid. Passion Sunday, 16 Hen. VI: 30 March 1438*
Item in expensis iiij^{or} scolarium redeundo et eundo Oxoniam propter eleccionem Iohannis prioris una cum equis conductis eadem causa lvj s. ix d.

38 *Ibid. St Matthew, 17 Hen. VI: 21 September 1438*
Item datum Roberto Lynton ex gracia speciali versus Oxoniam x s.

39 *Ibid. St Clement, 17 Hen. VI: 23 November 1438*
Item in expensis Iohannis Waltham versus Oxoniam cum equis conductis eadem causa xvij s. j d.

40 *Ibid. St Andrew, 17 Hen. VI: 30 November 1438*
Et solutum Iohanni Waltham pro capa scolari ex gracia domini prioris xv s.

EXTRACTS FROM ACCOUNTS 193

41 *Ibid. 4 Sun. after Michaelmas, 18 Hen. VI: 25 October 1439*
Item solutum Roberto Lyntone scolari pro costis suis versus Oxoniam xx s.

42 *Ibid. Sun. after Michaelmas, 19 Hen. VI: 2 October 1440*
Item solutum T. Prat pro pannis scolarium pro cariagio ad Feverysham xij d.

43 *Ibid. 3 Sun. after Michaelmas, 19 Hen. VI: 16 October 1440*
Item solutum pro expensis scolarium versus Oxoniam et pro conduccione equorum pro eisdem xliij s. x d.

44 *Ibid. 2 Sun. after octave of Easter, 19 Hen. VI: 7 May 1441*
Oxinford. Item Roberto Lyntun scolari pro expensis suis pro sermone faciendo xiij s. iiij d.
Item eidem eadem causa vj s. viij d.

45 *Ibid. 5 Sun. after Michaelmas, 29 October 1441*
Item Thome Aesche pro expensis veniendo de Oxoniis vj s. viij d.

46 *Ibid. 3 Sun. after All Saints, 19 November 1441*
Item Thome Assche redeunti ab Oxoniis usque Cantuariam vj s. viij d.

47 *Ibid. Easter, 1 April 1442*
Item fratri Roberto Lynton redeunti ab Oxoniis et venienti xx s.

48 *Ibid. Sun. in oct. St Benedict (translation), 15 July 1442*
Et solutum Roberto Lyntun pro v duodenis pargamini ab eo emptis iiij s.

49 *Ibid. Sun. after St Luke, 20 Oct. 1443*
Oxoniam. Item Roberto et Willelmo Chart euntibus Oxoniam pro expensis suis xx s.
Item Roberto Lintun custodi collegii Oxoniensis pro cappa sua xv s.
Item eidem [? Lynton] pro cariagio pannorum a Cantuaria usque Graystone xij d.

50 *Ibid. Vigil of SS. Simon and Jude, 27 October 1443*
Oxoniam. Item Willelmo Toryndenne cum sociis suis venientibus et redeuntibus ad Oxinis [sic] pro elexcione archiepiscopi xlvj s. viij d.

51 *Ibid. Advent Sunday, 1 December 1443*
Oxonia. Item pro cariagio pannorum Roberti Lyntone custodis collegii Oxonie ij s. viij d.

52 *Ibid. Sunday after Nativity of B.V.M., 13 September 1444*
Expense. Item solutum fratri Thome Asch pro expensis suis ab Oxonia usque Cantuariam xxiij s. iiij d.

53 *Acc. Bk. IV. Accounts ? September 1444—September 1445: 23 Hen. VI*
Expense generales ... dona. Et datum est Willelmo Thoryndene scolari rediunti ad studium xiij s. iiij d.

54 *Ibid. Accounts September 1445—September 1446: 24 Hen. VI*
Expense generales ... dona. Et datum Roberto Lyntone scolari Oxonie vj s. viij d.
Dona. Et datum monacho Ebor' pro sermone facto in ecclesia dominica 3^a Quadragesime vj s. viij d.
Dona. Et datum clericis Oxonie venientibus ab Oxonia ad eleccionem domini prioris xxxiij s. iiij d.
Soluciones forinsece. Et in denariis solutis custodi collegii in Oxonia ad reparacionem librarie eiusdem collegii cvj s. viij d.
Dona. Et datum Roberto Lyntone gardiano Oxonie venienti domino priori vj s. viij d.

55 *L.C.R. 74. Prior's roll, Michaelmas 1446—Michaelmas 1447*
Obvenciones... Et de vj s. viij d. receptis de peculio fratris Roberti Lynstede post mortem suam.
Oblaciones et dona ... Et datum scolaribus Oxonie ad diversas vices ut patet per librum prioris xiij s. iiij d.

56 *Acc. Bk. IV. Accounts September 1446—September 1447: 25 Hen. VI*
Expense generales ... forincece. Et datum Willelmo Richemunde scolari transseunti versus Oxoniam vj s. viij d.
Dona. Et datum Willelmo Thornbery eundo ad Oxoniam vj s. viij d.
Soluciones forinsece ... Et solutum fratri Roberto custodi collegii in Oxonia vj li. xiij s. iiij d.
Et fratribus ibidem in denariis xxx s.

57 *Ibid. Accounts September 1447—September 1448: 26 Hen. VI*
Expense generales ... dona. Et datum fratri Roberto Lyntone gardiano collegii Oxoniencis vj s. viij d.
Dona. Et datum fratribus Willelmo Pettham et Iohanni Holyngbourne pro expensis suis versus Oxoniam xiij s. iiij d.

58 *Ibid. Accounts September 1448—September 1449: 27 Hen. VI*
Expense generales ... Et solutum $iiij^{xx}ix$ fratribus die regressionis sancti Thome.
Datum. Et datum Christofero nuncio domini archiepiscopi portanti litteram custodi collegii Oxonie a domino Cantuariensi iij s. iiij d.

EXTRACTS FROM ACCOUNTS

Dona. Et datum Ricardo Graveney et ij scolaribus transseuntibus Oxon' xiij s. iiij d.

59 *Canterbury MS. 28. Prior's accounts September 1451—September 1452: 30 Hen. VI*
fo. 52
Scolares. Et solutum W. Petham et W. Hadlegh scolaribus pro termino natalis xx s.
Dona. Item datum fratri T. Aescheford eundo versus Romam vj s. viij d.

60 *Ibid., fo. 52^v*
Dona. Et datum Iacobo Goldwell doctori universitatis Oxonie xx s.

61 *Ibid., fo. 53*
Dona. Et datum priori studencium Oxonie ordinis nostri xiij s. iiij d.

62 *Ibid., fo. 53^v*
Dona. Et solutum W. Petham et W. Hadlegh scolaribus Oxonie pro termino sancti Iohannis baptiste xx s.
Item datum fratri W. Petham pro incepcione sua in bacall' iuris canonici xx s.
Et datum scolaribus euntibus ad scolas xiij s. iiij d.
Pensiones. Et solutum W. Petham et W. Hadley scolaribus Oxonie pro termino Pasche xx s.

63 *Ibid., fo. 54^v*
Scolares. Et solutum scolaribus Oxonie xx s.

64 *Prior's Rolls, XVII, no. 9, 1453–4: 32–3 Hen. VI*
Expense forinsece ... Et in expensis eiusdem domini prioris equitantis versus Oxoniam mense Augusti anno xxxij° [1454] una cum donis datis diversis monachis et familiaribus in collegio ibidem ut patet per librum dicti prioris ix li. iij s.
Oblaciones et dona ... Et datum scolaribus Oxonie ad diversas vices ut patet per librum domini prioris cvj s. iij d.

65 *Prior's Rolls XVII, no. 10, 1455–6: 34–5 Hen. VI*
Oblaciones et dona ... Et datum scolaribus Oxonie ad diversas vices ut patet per librum domini prioris vj li. xij s. j d.

66 *Treas. Rolls, no. 16, 1455–6: 34–5 Hen. VI*
Item in expensis scolarium ultra xl s. xiij s. iiij d.
Item pro indumentis ij^{orum} valectorum Oxonie x s. v d.

67 *L.C.R. 83. Treas. Roll 1456–7: 35–6 Hen. VI*
Forinceca ... Et in expensis Willelmi Thornden gardiani collegii Oxonie xlj s. viij d.

68 *Treas. Rolls, no. 17, 1457–8*
Et in expensis Willelmi Thornden, Willelmi Hadlegh et Willelmi Cellyng veniendo et redeundo Oxoniam l s. iiij d.

69 *L.C.R. 84. Treas. Roll 1459–60: 38–9 Hen. VI*
Forinceca ... Et in expensis Willelmi Hadleghe, Arnoldi Permysted et Willelmi Cellyng veniendo et redeundo Oxoniam lxxvij s. viij d.

70 *D.E. 52. Treas. Acc. 1460–1: 39 Hen. VI—1 Ed. IV*
Et de l s. vj d. pro expensis scolarium ab Oxonia usque Cantuariam eundo et redeundo.
Et pro indumentis duorum valectorum Oxonie xiij s. xj d.

71 *Treas. Rolls, no. 18, 1463–4*
Forinsece ... Et in expensis Willelmi Hadley, Willelmi Cellynge et Reginaldi Goldstone veniendo et redeundo Oxoniam xliiij s. viij d.

72 *Acc. Bks. 1467–9. Weekly bills, 1 Sun. April 7 Ed. IV: 5 April 1467*
Scolares. Item solutum pro expensis Reginaldi Goldstone eundo et redeundo ab Oxon' usque Cantuariam xx s.

73 *Ibid. 2 Sun. March 8 Ed. IV: 13 March 1468*
Scholares. Item solutum eidem pro expensis R. Goldstone et W. Chychele versus Oxoniam et Cantuariam pro sermonibus dicendis xxxiiij s. vij d.

74 *Ibid. 2 Sun. April 8 Ed. IV: 10 April 1468*
Scolares. Item solutum pro expensis Reginaldi Goldstone ab Oxon' usque Cantuariam xvj s. vj d.

75 *Ibid. 3 Sun. September 8 Ed. IV: 18 September 1468*
Scolares. Item solutum R. Goldstone et iij aliis scolaribus pro expensis versus Cantuariam pro eleccione xxxij s. iiij d.
Item solutum eidem, T. Chartham et W. Chychele versus Oxoniam xx s.

76 *Ibid. 3 Sun. February 8 Ed. IV: 19 February 1469*
Scolares. Item solutum Reginaldo Goldstone pro suis expensis veniendo et redeundo xxx s. iiij d.

77 *Ibid. 4 Sun. February 8 Ed. IV: 26 February 1469*
Scholares. Item solutum eidem pro conduccione j equi usque Oxoniam cum R. Goldstone iij s. iiij d.

EXTRACTS FROM ACCOUNTS

78 *Ibid. 2 Sun. October 9 Ed. IV: 8 October 1479*
Expense. Item solutum Reginaldo Goldstone pro expensis ab Oxon' usque Cantuariam v s.

79 *Ibid. 1 Sun. October 11 Ed. IV: 6 October 1471*
Item solutum domino W. Chychele pro expensis versus Cantuariam xiij s. viij d.
Item solutum domino Reginaldo Goldstone et domino Thome Umfray pro expensis versus Cantuariam xxvij s. vij d.

80 *Ibid. 2 Sun. October 11 Ed. IV: 13 October 1471*
Expense. Item solutum pro expensis domini W. Chychele gardiani collegii Oxonie et domini Thome Umfray socii cum conduccione equorum xxxviij s. viij d.

81 *Ibid. 3 Sun. March 12 Ed. IV: 15 March 1472*
Scolares. Item solutum Thome Umfray pro expensis versus Cantuariam ab Oxon' in parte solutis ij s. iiij d.

82 *Ibid. 2 Sun. April 12 Ed. IV: 12 April 1472*
Expense. Item solutum Thome Umfray pro expensis suis ab Oxon' versus Cantuariam in plenam solucionem vij s.
Expense. Item solutum eidem pro expensis famuli sui versus Oxoniam ij s. iiij d.
Scolares. Item solutum Thome Humfrey pro expensis versus Oxoniam x s.

83 *Ibid. 4 Sun. September 12 Ed. IV: 27 September 1472*
Scolares. Item pro iiij^{or} scolaribus et octo equis conductis versus Oxoniis lxxij s. x d.

84 *T.K., fo. 118. Prior's account, Michaelmas 1472—Michaelmas 1473*
Compotus domini Willelmi Sellyng S.T.P. ... ecclesie Christi Cantuarie a festo sancti Michaelis archangeli anno regni regis Edwardi quarti xij° usque idem festum extunc sequens anno regni eiusdem domini regis xiij per unum annum integrum.
[*Receipts*] Fructus ecclesiarum ... Et de lx li. ix s. viij d. ob. de fructibus et proventibus ecclesiarum de Pageham, Berstede et Mundham una cum redd' et ex'.
Et de lxxj s. x d. de cameris locatis in collegio Oxonie ut patet in compoto fratris Willelmi Chichele custodis ibidem.
Denarii liberati. Et in denariis liberatis Willelmo Chichele pro necessariis fratrum studencium Oxonie collegio xxviij li. iij s. viij d.

Et solutum custodi collegii Oxonie pro diversis expensis ibidem racione officii ut patet et cetera xxj s. j d.
Et eidem pro mensa puerorum collegii vij li. xij d.
Resolucio redditus. Et solutum pro collegio Oxonie diversis personis pro redditu ut patet per compotum custodis iiij li. xv s. j d.
Pensiones et feoda. Et solutum vicario de Berstede cum capellano de Bognore exeunt' de rectoria de Pagham lxvj s. viij d.
Reparaciones maneriorum et rectoriarum. Item in reparacionibus factis apud Pagham, Berstede et Bognore cj s. iij d. qua.
Item in reparacionibus factis in collegio Oxonie hoc anno x li. xv s.
Minuta. Et datum Willelmo Chichele ad gradum bacallarii in theologia suscipiendum xl s.
Et solutum Willelmo Thorndene pro sermone in die cinerum dicendo vj s. viij d.
Et fratri Willelmo Chichele pro sermone in die cene Domini vj s. viij d.
Et fratribus studentibus Oxonie pro uno apro erga festum natalis Domini ex consuetudine vj s. viij d.

85 *Treas. Rolls, no. 22: ? account c. 1471–4*
Forinceca. Et in expensis Willelmi Chycchele, Thome Umfrey, Iohannis Langdone et Thome Goldstone ab Oxonia veniendo et redeundo cum famulis et equis eorundem v li. x s. x d.

86 *Cart. Ant. X. 20: ? account c. 1472–4*
[*Receipts*] Et de xlvj li. iiij s. vj d. de claro profectu rectorie de Pageham cum Berstede et Mundeham hoc anno ultra repris' ut patet per compotum Willelmi Colman servientis ibidem.
Et de xliiij s. x d. de cameris locatis in collegio Oxonie hoc anno et non plus quia frater Willelmus Chichele[1] preventus non computavit.
[*Expenses*] Et fratri Willelmo Chichele ac Thome Humfrey pro necessariis fratrum studencium Oxon' xxx li.
Et eisdem pro mensa puerorum collegii x li.
Et eisdem pro expensis racione officii vj s. viij d.
Et datum scolaribus Oxonie xj s. viij d.
Et fratribus studentibus Oxonie pro uno apro empto erga festum natale Domini vj s. viij d.

---

[1] A word missing: perhaps 'morte'. That would place the account at about 1474, the probable year of Chichele's death. In any case it must be after 1472, as it refers to the tomb of Prior W. Pettham.

EXTRACTS FROM ACCOUNTS

87 *Acc. Bk. 1467–79; 3 Sun. February 12 Ed. IV: 21 February 1473*
Scolares. Item solutum W. Thorrynde pro capa scolar' pro Thoma Golstone Oxoniis x s.

88 *Ibid. 2 Sun. May 13 Ed. IV: 9 May 1473*
Expense. Item solutum pro expensis gardiani Oxonie versus Oxoniam xvj s.

89 *Ibid. 3 Sun. June 13 Ed. IV: 20 June 1473*
Et de lx s. receptis de dompno W. Chychele pro libris venditis.

90 *Ibid. 4 Sun. July 13 Ed. IV: 25 July 1473*
Equus. Item solutum pro uno equo furato in itinere ab Oxonia cum Iohanne Ive xvj s.

91 *Ibid. 3 Sun. October 13 Ed. IV: 17 October 1473*
Capa scolar'. Item solutum suppriori pro cappa Iohannis Langdon Oxonie x s.

92 *Ibid. 4 Sun. April 14 Ed. IV: 24 April 1474*
Expense. Item solutum Iohanni Ive pro expensis W. Chichele versus Oxoniam xv s.

93 *Ibid. 1 Sun. May 14 Ed. IV: 1 May 1474*
Expense. Item solutum pro conduccione equorum versus Oxoniam pro W. Chichele v s. viij d.

94 *Ibid. 1 Sun. October, 14 Ed. IV: 2 October 1474*
Expense. Item solutum pro expensis 2^{orum} scolarium versus Oxoniam xv s.

95 *Ibid. 4 Sun. October, 14 Ed. IV: 23 October 1474*
Expense. Item solutum Iohanni Ive pro expensis versus Oxoniam cum [?] fratribus ij s. viij d.

96 *D.E. 52. Short Account, Michaelmas 1475—Michaelmas 1476*
Item pro indumentis duorum valectorum Oxonie xiij s. iiij d.

97 *Acc. Bk. 1467–79. Weekly bills, 3 Sun. February, 15 Ed. IV: 17 February 1476*
Expense To'. Item solutum pro expensis Thome Wmffray versus Cantuariam xiij s. iiij d.
Expense To'. Item pro expensis famuli Thome Wmffray versus Oxoniam iij s. iiij d.

98 *Ibid. 3 Sun. April, 15 Ed. IV [sic, for 16 Ed. IV]: 21 April 1476*
Datum Willelmo. Item datum Willelmo Chartham pro capa sua x s.
Expense To'. Item solutum pro uno equo conducto versus Oxoniam v s.

Expense To'. Item solutum pro expensis To. Wmffray versus Oxoniam xx s.
Expense To'. Item solutum pro uno equo conducto Oxon' xij d.

99 *Ibid. 4 Sun. April, 16 Ed. IV: 28 April 1476*
Expense To'. Item datum in vino Thome Umfrey quando equitavit viij d.

100 *Ibid. 4 Sun. November, 16 Ed. IV: 24 November 1476*
Expense To'. Item solutum pro expensis Thome Wmfray equitando Oxoniam v s.

101 *Ibid. 2 Sun. February, 16 Ed. IV: 9 February 1477*
Expense. Item solutum famulo Thome Umfrey pro expensis versus Oxoniam iiij s.

102 *Ibid. 2 Sun. April, 17 Ed. IV: 13 April 1477*
Expense. Item solutum pro expensis Thome Wmfray versus Cantuariam xiiij s. vj d. ob.

103 *Ibid. 3 Sun. April, 17 Ed. IV: 20 April 1477*
Expense. Item solutum pro uno equo conducto versus Oxoniam pro gardiano v s.
Expense. Item solutum pro expensis Thome Umfrey versus Oxoniam xvj s. viij d.

104 *Ibid. 4 Sun. February, 17 Ed. IV: 22 February 1478*
Expense Thome Humfrey. Item solutum pro car' iij clothsaccar' Thome Humfrey ab Oxonia London' x s. iij d.
Item pro expensis eorundem versus Cantuariam ij s. ij d. ob.

105 *Ibid. 5 Sun. March, 18 Ed. IV: 29 March 1478*
Expense Thome Humfrey. Item solutum Thome Umfrey pro expensis versus Cantuariam xiiij s. xj d.
Item solutum Thome Humfrey pro expensis famuli sui versus Oxoniam iij s. iiij d.

106 *Ibid. 3 Sun. May, 18 Ed. IV: 17 May 1478*
Expense clericorum Oxon'. Item solutum Thome Goldstone et Roberto Eastry pro expensis eorum ab Oxonia versus Cantuariam x s.

107 *Ibid. 3 Sun. September, 18 Ed. IV: 20 September 1478*
Expense Oxon'. Item solutum Thome Goldston et Roberto Eastry pro expensis ab Oxonia versus Cantuariam ix s. vij d. ob.

108 *Ibid. 2 Sun. January, 18 Ed. IV: 10 January 1479*
Oxon'. Item solutum pro conduct' Thome Goldstone et Roberti Eastry versus Oxoniam xx s.

Oxon'. Item solutum Henrico Haloes pro uno equo conducto ab eo pro predictis scolaribus usque Oxoniam xx d.

109 *D.E. 52. Short Account, 1478-9*
Et pro indumentis duorum valectorum Oxonie x s. viij d.

110 *D.E. 52. Short Account, year ending 22 Ed. IV: 1481-2*
Et pro indumentis duorum valectorum, videlicet pincernarum [sic] et coci Oxonie x s. viij d.

111 *Treas. Rolls, no. 20: 1483-4*
Expense forinsece. Et in expensis veniencium ab Oxonia hoc anno nichil.

112 *D.E. 52. Short Account, 1484-5*
Et pro indumentis pincernarum [sic] et coci Oxonie xiij s. iiij d.

113 *D.E. 18. Travelling Accounts of Prior, 15 October—24 November, 2 Hen. VII: 1486*
[Payments at London] Item payd for j barell to trusse bokes in vj d. Item for j boke to Mr Langdon callyd Perottes gramer xij d.

T.K., fo. 209: 17 October 1490
Octobris 17 anno H. 7^{mi} 6to. Ego frater Robertus Estry recepi a T. Humfrey capellano pro expensis domini prioris eundo versus Calesiam in ambasia regis xiij li. vj s. viij d.

114 *R.E. 6. Accounts (? of Prior), Michaelmas 1492—Michaelmas 1493*
Scriptori domini prioris. Octobris 14° Iacobo Nele scriptori pro diversis per ipsum scriptis pro domino priore ix s. iiij d.
Item eidem pre manibus per assignacionem domini prioris iiij s.
Denarii soluti pro exhibicione Ricardi Tylle. Novembris 15to Thome Goldston pro denariis per ipsum deliberatis fratri Thome Chaundeler pro exhibicione Ricardi Tylle filii Willelmi Tylle studentis Oxon' xl s.
Sermo in cena Domini. Aprilis 24 Iohanni Langdon pro sermone domini prioris in cena Domini vj s. viij d.
Soluciones per fratrem Robertum Eastry in absencia Thome Goldstone custodis maneriorum in progressu suo termino Pasche anno regni regis Henrici vij octavo.
Et solutum fratri Iohanni Langdon custodi collegii Cant' Oxonie pro stipendio suo pro dimidio anno vj li. x s.
Et eidem pro communibus puerorum collegii ibidem per tempus predictum c s.
Et eidem ex assignacione domini prioris pro vino emendo erga gradum doctoratus suscipiendum xxx s.

Et eidem pro stipendio pincerne et coci ibidem per tempus predictum, videlicet pro dimidio anno xxx s.
Et eidem pro fratribus infirmis pro anno finiente festo Michaelis ultimo xxvj s. viij d.
Et fratri Thome Chaundeler pro stipendio suo pro dimidio anno iiij li.
Et fratri Iohanni Waltham ex assignacione domini prioris pro dimidio anno xl s.
Et eidem pro cameraria sua pro dicto dimidio anno xl s.
Et fratri Rogero Bennet ad assignacionem domini prioris pro dimidio anno l s.
Et fratri Roberto Holyngbourne eadem de causa l s.
Et fratri Thome Chaundeler pro Iohanne Assheton scolare domini prioris x s.
Theodorico scriptori i^a. Maii 6 Theodorico van Grembergh scriptori domini prioris per assignacionem domini prioris x s.
[*June*] Scriptores domini prioris. Item Roberto Estry pro diversis per ipsum expositis scriptoribus domini prioris xl s.
[*July*] Iohannes Sharpe scriptor domini prioris.
[*30 July*] Theodorico Grembergh scriptori domini prioris per manus Ricardi Copton x s.
[*September*] Expense circa Iohannem Dovor novicium domini prioris.
Item domino Roberto Estry pro expensis circa novicium domini prioris prout patet per billam manu domini prioris signatam xxx s. iiij d.

115 *Acc. Bks. III, pt. 1. Weekly bills, 5 Sun. March, 9 Hen. VII: 30 March 1494*
Expense fratris Thome Chawndeler versus Cantuariam. Et in expensis fratris Thome Chawndeler ab Oxoniis ad Cantuariam xviij s.

116 *Ibid. 1 Sun. May, 9 Hen. VII: 4 May 1494*
Expense scolarium versus Oxoniam. Et in expensis fratris Thome Chawndeler versus Oxoniam. Et pro equo conducto qui moriebatur per viam xxxvj s.

117 *Ibid. 1 Sun. July, 9 Hen. VII: 6 July 1494*
Custodi infirmarie pro summa missa Roberti Estry. Et fratri Reginaldo Goldston magistro infirmarie pro summa missa Roberti Estry thesaurarii xiij s. iiij d.

118 *Ibid. 4 Sun. August, 10 Hen. VII: 24 August 1494*
Expense versus Sandwicum. Et in expensis Roberti Estry versus Sandwycum ad videndum Monkynkey iiij d.

119 *Ibid. 5 Sun. November, 10 Hen. VII: 30 November 1494*
Robert Estry is treasurer.

120 *Ibid. 2 Sun. February, 10 Hen. VII: 8 February 1495*
Expense scolarium ab Oxonia usque Cantuariam. Et in expensis domini Iohannis Langdon et Thome Chaundler veniencium ab Oxonia post mortem domini Willelmi Sellyng prioris, causa nominacionis vel eleccionis novi prioris xxv s. x d.
Littera procuratoria scolarium existencium Oxonie tempore nominacionis vel eleccionis novi prioris. Item solutum pro littera procuratoria pro aliis sex fratribus ibidem studentibus, videlicet Iohanni Waltham, Rogero Benett, Iohanni Dunston, Iohanni Henfeld, Roberto Holyngbourne et Iohanni Boxwell ij s. vij d.

121 *Ibid. 3 Sun. February 10 Hen. VII: 15 February 1495*
Expense scolarium versus Oxoniam. Et in expensis fratris Thome Chaundeler redeuntis Oxoniam post eleccionem doctoris Thome Goldston prioris xvj s.

122 *Ibid. 1 Sun. April, 10 Hen. VII: 5 April 1495*
Equi conducti versus Oxoniam. Et Iohanni Hakenayman pro ij^{bus} equis conductis versus Oxoniam post eleccionem domini prioris v s. iiij d.
Equis conductis. Et in equo conducto versus Oxoniam xij d.
Expense scolarium versus Oxoniam. Et in expensis Roberti Estry gardiani versus Oxoniam xxvj s. vj d.

123 *Ibid. 1 Sun. June, 10 Hen. VII: 7 June 1495*
Et pro cariagio rerum Iohannis Landon ab Oxoniis usque Cantuariam.
Et domino I. Langdon pro cariagio rerum ab Oxoniis ad Cantuariam ix s. iij d.
Et pro cariagio rerum Roberti versus Oxoniam. Et pro vectura rerum domini R. Estry versus Oxoniam v s. iiij d.
Et in expensis eorundem xij d.

124 *Ibid. 2 Sun. July, 10 Hen. VII: 12 July 1495*
Equus conductus versus Oxoniam. Et Thome Wainflete pro uno equo conducto versus Oxoniam cum Roberto Estry et Iohanne Langdone in pro [sic] x^{cem} diebus iij s.

125 *Ibid. 1 Sun. April, 11 Hen. VII: 3 April 1496 (Easter)*
John Henfeld's first mass.

126 *Ibid. 2 Sun. April, 11 Hen. VII: 10 April 1496*
Robert Holyngbourne's first mass.

127 *Ibid. 1 Sun. May, 11 Hen. VII: 1 May 1496*
Expense scolarium versus Oxoniam. Et in expensis Thome Chaundeler venientis ab Oxon' usque Cantuariam xij s.
Et in expensis eiusdem cum Thoma Goldwell versus Oxoniam xxiij s. iiij d.
Regardys, nota bene. Et datum Iohanni Henfelde, Roberto Holyngbourne post celebracionem eorum primarum missarum ex speciali favore thesaurarii x s.

128 *Ibid. 2 Sun. July, 11 Hen. VII: 10 July 1496*
Equus conductus versus Oxoniam. Et Iohanni Hakeneyman pro uno equo conducto versus Oxoniam ij s. iiij d.

129 *Ibid. 2 Sun. October, 12 Hen. VII: 9 October 1496*
Cappa scolar'. Et Thome Goldwell pro cappa scolar' in plenam solucionem x s.

130 *Ibid. 4 Sun. February, 12 Hen. VII: 26 February 1497*
Brevigerulus. Et Roberto Newyngton brevitori differenti brevia fratrum Iohannis Langdone, Roberti Estry, Galfridi Glastyngbery, Willelmi Hartford ij s. viij d.

131 *Ibid. 1 Sun. April, 12 Hen. VII: 2 April 1497*
Expense gardiani Oxonie. Et in expensis Thome Chandeler venientis ab Oxonia versus Cantuariam causa predicacionis in xl^{ma} xxiij s. ix d. ob.
Regard Rogero Benet. Et datum Rogero Benett venienti ab Oxonia usque Cantuariam cum gardiano ex missione domini prioris ex speciali favore xv s.

132 *Ibid. 3 Sun. April, 12 Hen. VII: 16 April 1497*
Expense scolarium. Et expense scolarium versus Oxoniam xxij s. x d.

133 *Ibid. 4 Sun. April, 12 Hen. VII: 23 April 1497*
Expense scolarium versus Oxoniam. Et in expensis scolarium versus Oxoniam post Pasca x [blank].

134 *Ibid. Circa 12 Hen. VII: 1496-7*
Memorandum quod Ricardus Marchall thesaurarius recepit de domino priore liij s. iiij d. ad solvendum marbilario pro lapide domini Iohannis Langdong in officio thesaurarii. Et pro cariagio et wharfagio ij s.

135 *Ibid. 3 Sun. April, 13 Hen. VII: 15 April 1498*
Expense Iohannis Waltham studentis Oxonie. Et in expensis domini Iohannis Waltham ab Oxonia usque Cantuariam causa predicacionis erga xl^m in plenam solucionem xiij s. iiij d.

136 *Ibid. 1 Sun. May, 13 Hen. VII: 6 May 1498*
Expense scolarium. Et in expensis Iohannis Waltham versus Oxoniam post Pasca xij s. viij d.

137 *L.C.R. 86. Treas. Roll, 16–17 Hen. VII: 1500–1*
Minuta ... Et in diversis conductis in brasino in absencia Iohannis Wragge equitantis cum scolaribus versus Oxoniam et cum thesaurario versus Londoniam et Clyve ij s. ij d.
Expense forincice ... Et in expensis fratris Iohannis Waltham, Iohannis Dunstone, Rogeri Benett, Iohannis Henfeld et Iohannis Boxwell veniencium ab Oxonia et redeuncium lxxij s. vj d. ob.
Et in expensis doctoris Chaundeler venientis ab Oxonia usque Cantuariam xxvij s.
Et in expensis fratris Iohannis Waltham, Rogeri Benett et Iohannis Henfeld veniencium ab Oxonia cum pannis lx s. vj d.
Et brevigerulo deferenti brevia Thome Charte, Willelmi Vowle, Iohannis Sutton et Iohannis Otforde ij s. viij d.

138 *T.K., fo. 128^v. Treas. Acc., 1512*
Et in expensis fratrum Edwardi Bockyng, Willelmi Sellyng et Iacobi Hartey veniencium ab Oxonia usque Cantuariam xxx s. iiij d.
Et in expensis eorum et Willelmi Pekham a Cantuaria usque Oxoniam xxvij s. x d.
Et pro cariagio de le stuffe Iasparis Copton a Cantuaria usque Oxoniam iij s. viij d.
Et pro cariagio de le stuffe fratrum Willelmi Gyllingham, Iohannis Langdon, Iohannis Shepey et Iacobi Hartey ab Oxonia usque Cantuariam xxvj s. viij d.
Et in regardo dato Willelmo Courtoppe equitanti cum scolaribus versus Oxoniam xx d.

139 *L.C.R. 89. Treas. Roll, 9–10 Hen. VIII: 1517–18*
Expense thesaurarii ... Et in equis conductis versus Oxforde, Londoniam, Clyve et Longbeche infra tempus compoti xvij s. iiij d.
Minuta ... Et in diversis conductis in stabulis nostris in absencia Willelmi Snawdone et Vincencii Fantyng equitancium versus Oxforde, Clyve et alia loca infra tempus compoti ij s.
Expense forincece ... Et in expensis dompni prioris Goldstone causa nominacionis et electionis novi prioris liij s. iiij d.

Et in expensis domini Edwardi Bockyng et Willelmi Hadleygh veniencium ab Oxonia usque Cantuariam causa predicacionis et deinde versus Oxoniam iiij li. v s. xj d.
Et in regardo dato Christofero Taylour et Iohanni Starkey equitantibus cum scolaribus versus Oxoniam iij s. iiij d.

140 *L.C.R. 90. Treas. Roll, 10–11 Hen. VIII: 1518–19*
Expense thesaurarii ... Et in equis conductis versus Oxforde, London, Clyve et Longbeche infra tempus compoti xv s. ix d.
Oblaciones et dona ... Et Willelmo Brysell brevigerulo differenti brevia fratrum Ricardi Deryng, Henrici Addysham, Thome Anselme, Willelmi Farleygh, Willelmi Sellyng, Iohannis Elham, Guidonis Chillynden, Roberti Holden, Roberti Sutton, Iohannis Clement et Willelmi Petham vij s. iiij d.
Minuta ... Et in diversis conductis in stabulis nostris in absencia Willelmi Snowdone, Vincencii Fantyng equitancium versus Oxforde, Clyve et alia loca infra tempus compoti ij s. iiij d.
Expense forincece ... Et fratri Willelmo Hadleyghe pro expensis suis ab Oxonia usque Cantuariam causa predicandi xxxviij s. viij d.
Et fratribus Willelmo Hadleyghe, Laurencio Newnam et Iohanni Charte exeuntibus usque Oxoniam xlij s. vj d.
Et in regardo dato Ricardo Mokelle et Iohanni Ambrose equitantibus cum scolaribus versus Oxoniam cum scolaribus [sic] iij s. iiij d.

141 *T.K., fo. 130ᵛ. Treas. Acc. 1521*
Minuta ... Et in expensis fratrum Willelmi Peckham et Ricardi Thornden veniencium ab Oxonia causa predicandi et in expensis eorum iterum versus Oxoniam, cum expensis fratris Willelmi Hadley venientis ad Cantuariam causa predicandi in rogacionum diebus iiij li. ix s. vj d.

142 *Canterbury Chapter Accounts, Michaelmas 34 Hen. VIII— Michaelmas 35 Hen. VIII: 1542–3*
Reparacions at Canterbury Colledge. Item to M. Maisters for the surplusage of hys accompte in reparacions at Oxforth ix li. xvij s. iij d.
Expense necessarie. Item to M. Mylles for a jorney to Oxforth in a cause of the churche for the plate and to sett in ordre there wyth xiiij d.
for caryage of a vestyment from Oxforth to Caunterburye lxxvj s. xj d. ob.

143 *Christ Church Disbursements, 1580–1*
Term. 1, pt. 1. Primus terminus et pars prima.
Reparacions intrinsecall. To Matthew Atkins for slatting worke doen in Canterbury College ut per billam datam 29 Oct. xviij s. iij d.

16 Novemb. To Matthewe Atkins for slatting worke, parte in Peckwaters Inne, parte in Canterbury College, per billam xxxvj s. iij d.
Secunda pars secundi termini [sic]
Reparations intrinsecall. 24 Decemb. To Matthew Atkins for slatting work doen upon the hall in Canterbury College and the chamber at the ende thereof xxxiiij s. v d.
Secunda pars tercii termini
Rep. intrins. [April] 30. To Will. Pichaver ij dayes di. mendinge Canterbury College gate, the stilles in the buttery and one of the greate ladlers ... ix d.
For ... slitte by two sawyers ijs. x d.
Ibid. 1581–2, term 3, pt. 2
15 Julii. To W. Pichaver for a day and halfe about the plumpe in Canterberie Colledge, his former worke there not beyng sufficient, water fayling notwithstanding xv d.
Ibid. 1582–3, term 2, pt. 2.
Rep. intrins. 4 Januarii to John Elles for 10 lode of gravel layd to mend the way about Peckwaters Inne and Caunterburie Colledge, iiij d. the lode iij s. iiij d.
Term 3, pt. 2
Rep. intrins. 13 April. To John Elles by him p^d to Walter Dew for 14 lodes of clay spent about the vault in the kitchin yard and the wall made betweene Caunterburie Colledge and Peckewaters Inne iiij s. viij d.
Term 4, pt. 2
Rep. intrins. [27 July, to John Elles] Eodem. To him for his owne worke 5 dayes in mending eaves in Caunterbury Colledge fallen down and in Doctor Westfalinges woodhouse iij s.

9
DOCUMENTS CONCERNING MONASTIC STUDENTS BEFORE THE FOUNDATION OF CANTERBURY COLLEGE

1. *Prior Henry of Eastry to two monk students at Paris, 6 Sept. 1304*
Cambridge University Library, MS. Ee. v. 31, fo. 102^v

Littera clausa directa fratribus nostris studentibus Parysius

Henricus permissione divina etc. et eiusdem loci capitulum etc. dilectis fratribus suis A. de Hardr' et S. de Fevresham in universitate Parysius studentibus, salutem etc. Quia ex vestra suggestione nuper intelleximus quod pecunia quam ab Anglia vobiscum detulistis tota sit deducta, unde iam expense vobis deficiunt, quamquam nobis videatur quod adhuc sufficere debuisset: nolentes tamen, quantum in nobis est, vobis deficere in hac parte, mittimus vobis per R. de Cherringe, latorem presencium, decem marcas sterlingorum. Insuper et vina nostra, que per ipsum R. nomine nostro sunt in Francia colligenda, vel precium eorum quatenus commodius vendi poterunt, si hoc pocius eligere volueritis, ad presens decrevimus liberanda; iniungentes vobis pro indempnitate nostra et mutua honestate fraterna quatinus in annum futurum de utili familia et non excessiva vobis providere faciatis expensasque moderatas, statum scolarium et religiosorum honestatem specialiter contingentes, pro viribus vestris amplius deducere studeatis. Valeat vestra fraternitas in Domino. Dat' in capitulo nostro viij idus Septembr' anno Domini M°CCC° quarto.

2. *Prior Henry of Eastry to a monk-student at Paris, 15 Apr. 1305*
Cambridge University Library, MS. Ee. v. 31, fo. 103^v

Littera directa fratri Stephano de Feveresham studenti Parysius clausa

H. permissione divina prior ecclesie Christi Cant' et eiusdem loci capitulum dilecto sibi in Christo fratri Stephano de Feveresham studenti Parysius, salutem et fraternam in Domino caritatem. Cum loci latitudo nimia nos ab alterutro disiungat, quominus desolacionem tediosam quam attulit tibi fratris Andree de Hardres nuper a te urgens recessus consolacionis dulcedine possimus presencialiter relevare, fratrem Galfridum Poterel in laboris scolastici solatium et laudande conversacionis testimonium tibi duximus sociandum. De sumptibus vero vestris de cetero in studio faciendis ordinavimus in forma sequenti: videlicet, quod pro expensis vestris usualibus que statum scolasticum usualiter contingunt, pro quolibet mense duas marcas sterlingorum et pro aliis expensis vestris privatis pro instanti secundo studii anno quatuor marcas sterlingorum vobis decrevimus ministrare. Et volumus quod de expensis vestris ut premittitur ordinetis donec aliud inde duxerimus vobis mandare. Dat' in capitulo nostro xvij kal. Maii anno Domini M°CCC° quinto.

3. *Testimonial for Franciscan lector at Christ Church, 18 Nov. 1314*
Cambridge University Library, MS. Ee. v. 31, fo. 156^v
Litera fratris Roberti de Fulham quondam lectoris nostri, de conversacione sua

Reverende religionis viris, fratri R. fratrum minorum in Anglia ministro ceterisque fratribus eiusdem ordinis, H. permissione divina prior etc. et eiusdem loci capitulum salutem illam quam peperit puerpera singularis. Licet distancia localis amicorum presenciam quandoque inpediat corporalem, quod tamen tollit absencia suplet caritas, que absencium corda iungit eosque interne contemplacionis acie mutua recreat visione. Sane quia dilectus nobis in Christo frater Robertus de Fulham, ordinis vestri professor, quem ex speciali confidencia pre aliis magni nominis viris inter nos familiariter dudum admisimus pro lectoris officio exercendo, labores cathedrales in scolis nostris magno tempore sustinuit retroacto; cuius doctrina in urbe redolet Cantuarie ac plures nostre congregacionis fratres, ipsius sedulos auditores, ita sacre scripture aspersione intima fecundavit quod ipsos ad lectoris officium in scolis nostris subeundum ydoneos reputamus: nos unum de fratribus et commonachis nostris predictis loco dicti fratris Roberti ad huiusmodi ministerium exequendum duximus subrogare et, ne occasione premissa de prefato fratre Roberto aliqua opinio sinistra surrepat, nos certam mutacionis huiusmodi causam vobis innotescimus per presentes. Considerantes igitur condiciones laudabiles et mores imitabiles prefati fratris Roberti, cuius conversacionem omni honestati conformem, modum eciam legendi invenimus graciosum, ipsum tanquam benemeritum vobis omnibus et singulis specialiter recommendamus, sanctitatem vestram corditer deprecantes ut eundem favorabiliter recommendatum habere velitis devoto nostri rogaminis interventu. Et quia pium est veritati testimonium perhibere, fieri fecimus has litteras nostras patentes. Dat' in capitulo nostro xiiij kal. Decembr' anno Domini M°CCC° xiiij°.

BEFORE THE FOUNDATION

4. *To W. de Mondham on the acquisition of a hall for scholars, 1331*
Reg. L. fo. 10. Printed in *Lit. Cant.* i. 392.

Litera directa magistro W. de Mondham pro aula acceptanda Oxon' pro fratribus nostris mittendis ibidem ad scolas

Totaliter seipsum cum salute. Per literas vestras intelleximus quod ad instanciam confratris nostri H. de sancto Ivone quesivistis diligenter et explorastis unam aulam convenientem pro tribus fratribus nostris et invenistis eam situatam iuxta ecclesiam sancti Petri in oriente, ubi solebat dominus archiepiscopus manere. Cuius aule pensio vobis in presenti concessa est pro vj marcis sterlingorum et nos ipsam aulam cum cameris et deporto pro dictis fratribus acceptamus et predictam pensionem persolvemus. Valete etc.

5. *To Hugh of St Ives concerning his stay at Oxford, 6 Dec. 1331*
Reg. L, fo. 13. Printed in *Lit. Cant.* i. 414.

Litera missa fratri H. de sancto Ivone Oxon' studenti pro quibusdam actibus scolasticis contingentibus statum suum

Salutem. Lectis et intellectis literis vestris quas nuper recepimus nobis et singulis fratribus nostris nova placida de statu vestro continentibus habitoque super eisdem cum dictis fratribus nostris deliberato tractatu, sic ordinatum est: quod illa que graciose per vos inchoantur mediantibus nostris suffragiis oportunem finem laudabiliter ut proponimus sorcientur; ac eciam de pensione domus vestre et studiorum vestrorum reparacione una cum aliis statum vestrum contingentibus fiet secundum literarum vestrarum exigenciam nobis directarum. Valete in verissimo Doctore, sine quo nichil salubriter poterit edoceri. Dat' Cant' die sancti Nicholai sub sigillo nostro privato.

6. *To Hugh of St Ives at Oxford, 27 Dec. ?1331*
Reg. L, fo. 13^v. Printed in *Lit. Cant.* i. 417.

Litera directa fratri H. de sancto Ivone Oxon' studenti continens quedam contingencia ecclesiam nostram

Salutem. Recepimus literas vestras continentes nova de dilecto confratre nostro R. de Godmersham nobis et fratribus nostris dolorem inferencia, cuius anime propicietur Deus. Libros vero nostros, ciphos una cum parm' et alia iocalia, si que habuit penes ipsum[1] per vos inventa, custodite. De alio fratre mittendo ad scolas hoc anno non adhuc plene deliberavimus. Scripsimus servienti nostro de Newenton quod ipse ex parte nostra vobis iuxta discrecionis vestre indicium ministret pro introitu vestro ad lecturam de qua nobis alias

[1] Supplied from *Lit. Cant.*

nobis scripsistis. Et advertat circumspeccio vestra quod fratres nostri libenter aures suas inclinant ut audiant nova de vobis quoad expensas moderatas. Aliud contentum in literis vestris erat de caritatis diffusione, pro qua instanter laboramus ut inter fratres continuetur ac eciam augeatur. Valete in Christo, efficaciter cogitantes de ecclesia nostra ut ipsa personis ydoneis sive de Kancia sive aliunde traxerint originem felicius per sancte religionis habitum adornetur. Mittimus vobis ad quandam pitanciam duos cignos et xxx gallinas. Mittimus eciam vobis et socio vestro species quas recepimus ex parte vestra de corona et martirio; quem socium salutetis ex parte nostra, sibi dicentes ac eciam iniungentes quod cum effectu cogitet si valuerit de personis ydoneis supradictis. Iterum valete, de statu vestro per literas vestras nos frequenter informantes. Dat' Cant' die sancti Iohannis evangeliste sub sigillo nostro privato.

7. *To Hugh of St Ives and other students at Oxford, 1331*
Reg. L, fo. 13. Printed in *Lit. Cant.* i. 415.

Alia litera missa fratribus H., R. et I. ibidem studentibus, ut efficaciter cogitent de scolaribus ydoneis admittendis in religionem nostram

Salutem in ipso qui lumine doctrine sue mentes fidelium pre aliis gentibus illuminat pariter et illustrat. Recepimus literas vestras continentes quod vos salvis personis et rebus die sanctorum Symonis et Iude descendistis ad hospicium per nos Oxon' vobis provisum. Et quod pro victualibus vestris una cum aliis in via expendistis xxxvij s. de pecunia quam vobis tradidimus, et sic remanent penes vos de dicta pecunia xiij s. in partem solucionis domus vestre. Adhuc rogamus vos et in quantum possumus ortamur ut efficaciter cogitetis cum habueritis temporis oportunitatem de scolaribus pro nostra ecclesia ydoneis habitum suum secularem volentibus transmutare. Valete in Christo, ad memoriam vestram iugiter revocantes quod milites Christi estis et sub uno principe militatis, et ideo decet et expedit ut alter alterius onera supportetis. Et si forsitan ex condicione infirmitatis humane aliqua levis commocio inter vos subrepat, sequimini Pauli consilium exortantis: Sol non occidat super iracundiam vestram sed date locum ire, que de stirpe nascitur viciosa. Dat' Cant' ut supra.

8. *Temporary grant of St Augustine's chamber in Gloucester College to the monks of Christ Church, ? c. 1329–30: apparently a letter from the Abbot of St Augustine's Canterbury to the Prior of Gloucester College*
Bodleian MS. Rawlinson C 7, fo. 47ᵛ. Printed by W.A. Pantin in *Essays in Medieval History Presented to Bertie Wilkinson* (Toronto 1969) 212.

BEFORE THE FOUNDATION 213

MS. Rawlinson C7, fo. 1–50, contains a collection of letters connected with St Augustine's Canterbury known as *Epistole Mason*, compiled by a monk of the house, John Mason.[1] Other MSS of the same collection are Merton MS. 122, fo. 104–20 (mid-XIV century, nearly contemporary but less complete then Rawl. C 7) and Worcester Cathedral MS. F 80, fo. 120^v, 97–108 (XV century, incomplete). The dates, addresses and most names are omitted, but there are references to the succession to Abbot Thomas (Findon, ? 1310: Rawl. fo. 24); John of St Germans, monk of Worcester, lector at St Augustine's c. 1308 (Rawl. fo. 17^v, Mert. fo. 110^v; cf. Worcester Liber Albus, nos. 397–400); John de Northbourne, ex-abbot of Battle, resigned 1318; Edmund, Bishop of Ardfert c. 1331 (Mert. fo. 115^v); and the struggle against Archbishop Mepham over exemption c. 1329–33 (passim; cf. Thorne, col. 2039 ff.). The date of the collection thus roughly corresponds, perhaps, to the abbacy of Ralph de Bourne (1310–34). The letter here printed therefore probably dates from before 1331, when the hall near St Peter's in the East was hired, or possibly from after its sale in 1342.

Cum ab assumpte religionis ingressu nostre[2] intime voluntatis extiterit ea semper appetere per[3] que ordinis ipsius accrescat honoribus eaque semper pro viribus procurare que fratrum ordinis eiusdem in actibus studialibus proficere satagencium commoditatem respiciant et quietem: relacione fidedigna ad nostram noticiam iam deducto cameram illam infra mansum vestrum predictum[4] constitutam, quam monasterii nostri sumptibus constructam nos et confratres nostri[5] nobis quondam associati innabitantes iteratis fecimus sumptibus innovari, iam vacantem esse per venerabilis[6] viri fratris T. de N.[8]

---

[1] Cf. Tanner, *Bibliotheca* 518; James 298–9, nos. 953 (= Rawl. C 7), 954 (cf. Mert. MS. 122).
[2] nostro *MS*.　　　　　　　　　　　　　　　　　　　　　　[3] *om. MS*.
[4] 'predictum' would be explained if the opening salutation of the letter (now lost) referred to the addressee as Prior of Gloucester College.
[5] nostros *MS*.　　　　　　　　　　　　　　　　　　[6] venerabilem *MS*.
[7] Perhaps Thomas de Natindon, the monk of St Augustine's employed as proctor in the struggle with Archbishop Mepham c. 1329 (Thorne, col. 2040 ff.). Another letter, also evidently addressed to Gloucester College, explains that monk scholars had been withdrawn from the university in order to give counsel to the monastery during the struggle, but promises their return in the coming year and claims the right to reoccupy the St Augustine's chamber in the college (Rawl. fo. 102^v, Mert. 122, fo. 111; W.A. Pantin, *The Letters of John Mason* in *Essays in Medieval History presented to Bertie Wilkinson*, ed. T.H. Sandquist and F.M. Powicke (1969) 211). For a later dispute (1356) concerning the St Augustine's chamber at Gloucester College, cf. *Chapters* iii. 25.

revocacionem a studio, in qua palmitis fructiferi dolendam nimis precisionem a vite totum ordinem anxie ferre decet; quia cari nostri nobis fratres et commonachi ecclesie Christi Cantuarie studentes Oxonie, quamdiu ex permissione nostra processerit, desiderant et procurant dictam cameram occupare, nos specialis amoris intuitu quo ad fratres eosdem afficimur tamquam nostros benevolentes et vicinos, votis ipsorum duximus in hac parte amicabiliter annuendum, dummodo ipsi confratribus nostris et commonachis ad dictum studium proximo dirigendis in ipsorum adventum cameram eandem sine[1] molestia et contradiccione resignent consideracioneque gracie sibi prestite amicabiliter cedant eis. Quocirca fraternitatem vestram nobis semper gratissimam ex intimis deprecamur quatinus si coram vobis et tota vestra comitiva ad hoc specialiter convocanda dicti fratres ecclesie Christi Cantuarie nostris fratribus ad studium accessuris, quo ad occupacionem camere eiusdem, bona fide promiserint se[2] cessuros nobisque suas literas idipsum[3] continentes in testimonium fecerint premissorum, tunc ipsos dictam cameram interim inhabitare et libere ingredi permittatis.

[1] *om. MS.*
[2] *commiserunt et MS.*
[3] *ad ipsum MS.*

BIOGRAPHICAL DATA

THE details given below are not to be found in BRUO. They are not intended to complete the picture of the monks' careers at Christ Church: they are simply evidence that has been encountered casually and are used to show that the monk fellows took an important part in the life of the monastery.

The spelling of proper names was of course unfixed and subject to the caprice of the individual scribe. The forms used here are those given by W.G. Searle in the appendix to his *Chronicle of John Stone*, for it is probably through this list that most readers will already have made acquaintance with the monks of Christ Church.

With regard to the dates of tenure of fellowship or wardenship, it should be remembered that the office may have been held both before and after the limits mentioned, there being no evidence either to confirm or disprove. Dr Emden's dates in BRUO should be used with caution because of his habitual failure to distinguish between the cardinal and the ordinal numbers. If a man were said, for instance, to have died in his twenty-eighth year, Dr Emden would say that he died at the age of twenty-eight, instead of twenty-seven. Even apart from that, the materials assembled in the present volume sometimes invalidate the dates in BRUO.

The ordination dates, taken from the archiepiscopal registers at Lambeth, present plenty of gaps. It would be most unsafe to argue merely from the lack of evidence that a particular monk was never promoted beyond a certain order.

The dates in the extracts from the accounts are not always what they seem. The extracts are often from weekly bills, which can be dated exactly but, of course, the payment of the accountant might be behindhand, so that the journey or other item of expense might have taken place some time before; and sometimes there are two payments, separated by several weeks, for what was most probably the same journey (e.g. Extracts 45, 46; 81, 82).

There are certain dates in the sixteenth century at which it is possible to check the movements of members of the college:

9 September 1511, Archbishop Warham visited Christ Church. The names of the brethren at Canterbury, or studying at Oxford and Paris, are given by Miss M. Bateson in EHR vi. 18 f.

12 December 1534, the declaration renouncing the Pope's jurisdiction and acknowledging the royal supremacy, sealed with the convent seal and subscribed with the names of the monks of Christ Church; printed in *Report VII of the Deputy Keeper of the Public Records* (1846), appendix ii, p. 282. As the report points out, it is doubtful how far these signatures were autographs and it is obviously not to the present purpose to discuss the degree of spontaneity and of moral and legal responsibility incurred. Presumably the names subscribed at least represent the Christ Church Community present at that time and place. With these possible limitations understood, we describe them below for the sake of brevity as having signed the acknowledgement of royal supremacy. It may be noted that certain persons (W. Jerome, W. Sandwich, J. Waltham, J. Warham) who were undoubtedly at this date still monks of Christ Church, are missing from the list. Most probably they were absent at Oxford.

C. 1538 or later, a list of the monks of Christ Church with their offices, ages, etc.: printed above, iii. 151.

1540, two lists of the monks at the dissolution. One, dated 4 April 1540, gives those 'which ben appointed to depart the same House', with their pensions, and also includes a few monks who went on to the new foundation. The other list, which is undated, gives the whole community, with their monastic offices and their rewards and pensions, or the places assigned to them on the new foundation. See *Letters and Papers, Henry VIII* xv. 452. The two lists are printed in Somner-Battely, *Antiquities of Canterbury* (1703) part ii, appendix p. 51; Dugdale, *Monasticon*, i. 112. The actual deed of surrender has not come to light, but the house must have been surrendered about the beginning of April 1540. An inventory of the goods of the college was drawn up on 10 April 1540: J. Wickham Legg and W.H. St J. Hope, *Inventories of Christ Church Canterbury* (1902) 168 ff.

8 April 1541, the formal incorporation of the dean and chapter of the new foundation by letters patent: *Letters and Papers, Henry VIII* xvi. 779 (5). For the names of the prebendaries, see also Somner-Battely, *op. cit.*, p. 123.

I. Monk Students of Christ Church Canterbury Before the Foundation of Canterbury College

CLYVE, Richard de: not in BRUO. Professed 1286, d. 1326 (Searle 177). 1288 R. de Clyve, student at Paris, wrote to the prior concerning the Wine of St Thomas: Robert de Ponthoys called Anglicus recommended selling the wine (*Hist. MSS. Comm. Report, Various Collections* i. 277). This letter is evidently previous to the following: 7 April 1288 Robert Anglicus of Pontoise wrote to the prior that he had

BIOGRAPHICAL DATA

sold the Wine of St Thomas and was sending the money by Mr Richard de Clyve. 1292–1313 R. de C. regularly employed by the convent as proctor and commissary; 1298 proctor to the court of Rome (Cambridge University Library MS. Ee. v. 31 passim; cf. *Arch. Cant.* xxxii. 147, 161, 166). Before becoming a monk, he had probably been a master of arts and perhaps also a student of law: the books he left to Christ Church were mostly on canon law (M.R. James, *Ancient Libraries*, p. 140, nos. 1756–72). He was appointed subprior on 28 October 1317. For possible disputations by him at Oxford c. 1300, cf. A.G. Little and F. Pelster, *Oxford Theology and Theologians* (1934) 259. For the Wine of St Thomas see *Christ Church Letters*, p. xxiv.

FAVERSHAM, Stephen de: not in BRUO. Professed 1295 (Searle 178). 10 September ? 1324, letter of archbishop to prior and chapter concerning provision of salary, study and socius for S.F. as lector (*Reg. Hethe*, Cant. and York Soc. 1931, 341); 1337 his name down for a book (*Lit. Cant.* ii. 150); his books listed in James, *Ancient Libraries*, p. 139, nos. 1738–48; Letters from to Franciscans in *Lit. Cant.* i. 126, 142, 161, 169, 216, 313, 506, 572.

FROME, John de: BRUO ii. 730. Owned Cambridge University Library MS. Ff. 5. 31, *Legenda sanctorum*, xiii c. (1299), no. 1793 of the Eastry catalogue (James, *Ancient Libraries*, p. 141, 511). Canterbury Chapter Library MS. A. 1, Ricardus de Media Villa on the fourth book of the Sentences (early xiv c.), has a note added at the end of the colophon: 'de perquisito fratris I. de Fro.'. There are some marginal annotations and schemata in brown pencil and an incomplete alphabetical table at the end, which may be the work of J. de Frome. This MS. is no. 22 in Ingram's list (James, *Ancient Libraries*, p. 153).

GLOUCESTRE, J: not in BRUO. Professed 1361 (Searle 181); 1370 made a catalogue of the archives of Christ Church (*Hist MSS. Comm. Report* v. 435); 1376 one of a committee for infirmary regulations (*Lit. Cant.* iii. 4).

GODMERSHAM, Roger de: BRUO ii. 779. September 1331 went to Oxford (*Lit. Cant.* i. 414 ff.).

HARDYS, Andrew: not in BRUO. Professed 1294, d. 1305 (Searle 178). For his books see James, *Ancient Libraries*, p. 134, nos. 1621–3.

HEDECRON, John: BRUO ii. 900.

HETH, William de: BRUO ii. 924.

OXNEY, James de: BRUO ii. 1416. Sent to court of Rome in 1348 in connection with the archbishop's election (*Hist. MSS. Comm. Report* viii. 338).

POTERELL, Galfridus: not in BRUO. Professed 1298, d. 1328 (Searle 178); 1313 apparently sent to Rome in connection with the archbishop's election (Cambridge University Library MS. Ee. v. 31, fo. 262ᵛ, no. 822); 1317, 5 November penitenciarius; 1324, the prior in a letter to the archbishop speaks of his seditious machinations (*Hist. MSS. Comm. Report* ix. 4); 1326 sent as proctor to Convocation (Cambridge University Library MS. Ee. v. 31, fo. 262ᵛ, no. 1251); 1327 sent as proctor to parliament (*Hist. MSS. Comm. Report* ix. 96).

RECOLVER, William: not in BRUO. Professed 1361, d. 1408 (Searle 181).

SANCTO IVONE, Hugo de: BRUO iii. 1627. 13 July 1331, his opinion concerning the translation of St. Benedict is cited in a letter to the archbishop (*Lit. Cant.* i. 370); May 1333 asked by the university to incept, but not allowed to do so. Letters of apology were sent not only to the vicechancellor but also to Master John de Scapeya (Sheppey) S.T.P., an important Benedictine scholar and preacher who became prior and eventually Bishop of Rochester (cf. D.N.B. s.v. Sheppey; Tanner, *Bibliotheca* 666; Wharton, *Anglia Sacra* i. 371 ff.; BRUO iii. 1683). He may then have been the regent master of the black monks at Gloucester College and the master under whom Hugh of St Ives would have incepted. Probably the letter of excuse from the prior to the chancellor, 5 January 1333, was concerned with the same matter (*Lit. Cant.* i. 526).

II. Monks of Christ Church at Canterbury College

ALEYN, John: BRUO i. 22.

AMBROSE, John: BRUO 2. 8. In the list of those 'appointed to depart' at the dissolution, 1540, but became a canon on the new foundation, 1541.

ASSHE, Thomas: BRUO i. 63. March 1428, preached at the funeral of Prior Wodnesbrowgh on the text, *Inspiravit in faciem eius spiraculum vite* [Gen. 2.7] (Bodleian MS. Tanner 165, fo. 4ᵛ).

BENNET, Nicholas: BRUO 2. 42. Not among signatories to royal supremacy (perhaps because at Oxford) or in lists of c. 1538 and 1540.

BENETT, Roger: BRUO i. 166.

BERHAM, John: BRUO i. 174.

BERTRAM, John: BRUO i. 180.

BOCKYNG, Edward: BRUO 2. 54. At Oxford during Archbishop

BIOGRAPHICAL DATA 219

Warham's visitation, 9 September 1511; university preacher Ash Wednesday 1513 or 1514 (Oxford Univ. Archives, chancellor's reg. F, fo. 263); owned Trin. Coll. Cambridge MS. 61; draft of preface to book on Holy Maid of Kent printed by J.R. McKee in *Dame Elizabeth Barton* (1925) 60.

BOXWELL, John: BRUO i. 237.

BROWNE, Thomas: BRUO i. 286.

BYDENDEN, John: BRUO i. 331. One of the committee for regulating the infirmary at Canterbury, April 1376 (*Lit. Cant.* iii. 4).

BYNEE, Robert: BRUO i. 333.

CHARTE, John: BRUO 2. 112. Subdeacon 26 March 1513 (Reg. Warham, fo. 266ᵛ); first mass 1516–17 (*Arch. Cant.* xlviii. 69); acknowledged royal supremacy 12 December 1534; at dissolution, 1540, master of the table; petty canon on the new foundation 1541.

CHARTE, William I: BRUO i. 394. At election of archbishop 17 July 1381 (Bodleian MS. Ashmole 794, fo. 254); appointed penitencer 15 September 1382 (Reg. Courtenay, fo. 22).

CHARTE, William II: BRUO i. 394.

CHARTHAM, Thomas: BRUO i. 394. Received into religion 13 December 1457, professed 21 April 1458 (Searle 71); came to the *parvum servitium*[1] 11 February 1458; came to the *commune servitium* 26 February 1458 (Searle 189). See also Searle 116.

CHARTHAM, William: BRUO i. 394.

CHAUNDLER, Thomas: BRUO i. 399. Appointed penitentiary 27 July 1501 (Domestic Economy, no. 64); acted as commissary in the university September 1499, 1500 (*Reg. Canc. 1498–1506* ed. W.A. Pantin and W.T. Mitchell (1972) pp. 19, 56).

CHICHELE, William: BRUO i. 413.

CHILHAM, Henry: BRUO i. 415.

CHILLYNDEN, Thomas: BRUO i. 415. Preached at the election of Archbishop Courtenay 17 July 1381 and had been one of the original *compromissarii* (Bodleian MS. Ashmole 794, fo. 254); sent with W. Dover (warden) to the archbishop on behalf of the monks 9 June 1384 (Reg. G, fo. 233); letter of the prior and chapter 11 May 1389, defending him against calumnies apparently current among the monks of Rochester (British Library MS. Cotton Faustina C. v, fo. 39); accompanied archbishop on metropolitan visitation 30 September 1389 at Spalding Priory, where he preached on the text,

[1] Evidently some portion of the office. Cf. *parva cantaria* in the *Customary of St. Aug. Cant.*, ed E. Maunde Thompson (1902) 13.

Videamus si floruerit vinea [Cant. 7. 12] (Reg. Courtenay I, fo. 143ᵛ; cf. A. Hamilton Thompson, *Visitations of Lincoln Diocese* i, p. xxviii); was probably the *doctor legisperitus monachus Cantuarie* who in 1389 supported the archbishop's claim to visit the monks at Gloucester College (Walsingham, *Historia Anglicana* ii. 190); received letter of confraternity from Rochester September 1390–June 1391 (MS. Cotton Faustina C. v, fo. 53); preached in the synod (? Convocation) c. 1396, in the year of Archbishop Arundel's election, on the text, *Sacerdotes tui induantur iustitiam* [Ps. 131. 9] (Nich. Harpsfield, *Hist. Eccles. Angl.* (1622) 610); elected Bishop of Rochester (cf. John Langdon I) but refused, in the twelfth year of his priorate (*sic* Wharton, *Anglia Sacra* i. 143): this must have been on the death of Bishop W. de Botlesham, February 1400, or on the death of Bishop J. Botlesham, April 1404 (*ibid.* i. 379); made observations on the Cluniacs at the Council of Pisa (Martène et Durand, *Amplissima Collectio* vii. 1118; obituary *Anglia Sacra* i. 143: cf. *Lit. Cant.* iii. 116; epitaph in Somner-Battely, *Antiquities of Canterbury*, part i, appendix p. 62.

COLBROKE, Robert: BRUO i. 459. Sacrist 1444–6 (*Arch. Cant.* xlviii. 74).

COPTON, Jaspar: BRUO 2. 137. Acolyte 11 April 1506, subdeacon 3 April 1507, deacon 22 April 1508 (Reg. Warham, fo. 262ᵛ, 263ʳᵛ); Jespard Coptone was deacon at the mass in the chapel of Our Lady in the Crypt at Canterbury 15 August 1510 (*Arch. Cant.* xxxviii. 162 n.).

COPTON, Richard: BRUO i. 483. Appointed one of the archbishop's *auditores causarum in audiencia* 28 February 1503 (Reg. T (1), fo. 17); celebrated mass in the chapel of Our Lady in the Crypt 15 August 1510 (*Arch. Cant.* xxxviii. 162 n.); at Warham's visitation 1511; died c. 1520–1 (*Arch. Cant.* xlviii. 70).

CRANEBROKE, Henry: BRUO i. 509.

CROSSE, John: BRUO 2. 153. Signed acknowledgement of royal supremacy 12 December 1534; at dissolution, 1540, among those 'appointed to depart', with a pension of £30 (*sic*); scholar on the new foundation with same pension 1541.

DERYNG, John: BRUO 2. 168.

DOVER, John: BRUO i. 588. Promoted from refectorar to feretrar 15 February 1440 (MS. Corpus Christi Coll. Oxon. 256, fo. 119).

DOVER, Thomas: BRUO i. 589. *Magister ordinum* c. 1390 (Searle 184); for his death and devotion to St Mary Magdalen etc. see Cawston MS., fo. 20ᵛᵃ.[1]

[1] For this MS. see *Hist. MSS. Comm. Report* ix (1) 127.

BIOGRAPHICAL DATA

DOVER, William: BRUO i. 589. On the committee for infirmary regulations, 1376 (*Lit. Cant.* iii. 4); absolved from office of cellarer 15 September 1382 (Reg. Courtenay, fo. 21ᵛ). See also Cawston MS., fo. 20ᵛ.

DUNSTAN, John I: BRUO i. 610.

DUNSTAN, John II: BRUO i. 610. Probably a Morton exhibitioner; apparently signed acknowledgement of royal supremacy 2 December 1534, but the signature looks like *per me Iohannem Pamston*.

EASTRY, Christopher: BRUO 2. 184. Died of pestilence and was buried in the Lady chapel at St. Frideswide's (Cawston MS., fo. 35ᵛ).

EASTRY, John: BRUO i. 621.

EASTRY, Robert: BRUO i. 621. Carried letters to the archbishop on the death of the prior, January 1495 (Reg. S, fo. 393ᵛ).

EVERARD, Thomas: BRUO i. 654. Died 6 April 1398, buried in infirmary chapel (Cawston MS., fo. 17ᵛ).

GILLYNGHAM, William: BRUO ii. 770. Said to have written about the history of Christ Church and the writers of the Benedictine order: his work so pleased the monks that they set up paintings illustrating it in the choir, on the north side (Leland in Tanner, *Bibliotheca* 357; cf. 363). This style of writing—the compilation of catalogues of monastic saints, doctors, writers etc.—was very much in the air at the end of the fourteenth century: it was really part of a historical defence of the monastic order against the mendicants and the Wycliffites. Such catalogues are to be found in treatises from Bury St Edmunds (Vatican MS. Reg. Lat. 127, fo. 173ᵛ), Durham (British Library MS. Cotton Vitellius E. XII, fo. 58ᵛ, 62; Durham Chapter MS. B. III. 30, fo. 31), St Albans (MS. Cotton Claudius E. IV, fo. 324ᵛ, 326ᵛ). See W.A. Pantin, *Some Medieval English Treatises on the Origins of Monasticism* in *Medieval Studies presented to Rose Graham*, ed. V. Ruffer and A.J. Taylor (1950) 189 ff. At Durham too there were paintings of monastic saints and doctors set up in the church, at the altar of SS. Jerome and Benedict. The list is printed in *Rites of Durham*, ed. J.T. Fowler (1902) 124–36. It is a compilation from Durham Chapter MS. B. III. 30.

W.G. was at Oxford on 2 January 1377, at the time of the archbishop's visitation of Canterbury (Wilkins, *Concilia* iii. 110). Died ? c. 1409 or after 1410 (28 March, buried in crypt: Cawston MS., fo. 19). The 'doctor Gyllyngham' mentioned in iii. 67 may have been a secular.

GLASTYNBURY, Edward: BRUO 2. 234. At Canterbury at the dissolution.

GODMERSHAM, Richard: BRUO ii. 779. Known to have been *lector in scola claustrali* for many years c. 1412–41 (Cawston MS., fo. 24ᵛ). Was probably the 'doctor' and 'senior doctor' referred to in the accounts for the servants' liveries: in fact, in 1429 and in 1431 he is mentioned by name. In 1412 there preached at the synod (? Convocation) *eiusdem coenobii* (sc. Christ Church Canterbury) *monachus, Ioannes* (? error for Richard) *Godmershanus super illa verba: Diligite lumen sapientiae qui praeestis* [Sap. vi. 23] (Nich. Harpsfield, *Hist. Eccl. Angl.* (1662) 619).

GOLDSTONE, Reginald: BRUO ii. 782.

GOLDSTONE, Thomas: BRUO ii. 783. Offered S.T.P. in 1498 by Oxford (*Epist. Acad.* ii. 650: not chair of theology, as there stated); c. 1511–13 called by Erasmus *vir pius iuxta et prudens, neque scoticae theologiae rudis ... homo non stupidus (Peregr. relig. ergo)*.

GOLDWELL, Thomas: BRUO ii. 787. First mass c. 1499–1500 (*Arch. Cant.* xlviii. 66). *Hist. MSS. Comm. Report, Various Collections* i. 224 contains an *Inventorium librorum quos reverendissimus in Christo pater ac dominus, dominus Thomas Goldestone ecclesie Christi Cantuariensis prior, Thome Goldewell contulit*.

GRAVENE, Richard: BRUO ii. 803.

GROVE, James: BRUO ii. 833.

GUSTON, Thomas: BRUO ii. 838.

GYLLYNGHAM, William II: BRUO 2. 256. *In studio Parisiensi* 9 September 1511 (Warham's visitation).

HADLEY, William I: BRUO ii. 846. Had John Langdon II as novice c. 1465 (Searle 188); August 1468 described as D.D., bearer of letters to the archbishop on the death of Prior Goldstone I (Reg. S, fo. 231ᵛ); December 1468 Johannita Bely of Venice was granted confraternity of Christ Church in reward for kindness shown to Hadley and W. Sellynge in Italy (*Christ Church Letters*, p. xxxviii); 1475, *vir in sacra conversatione et vitae religiositate valde praecipuus* (*Lit. Cant.* iii. 291). British Library Arundel MS. 155, an xi or xii c. psalter, belonged either to W.H. I or W.H. II below.

HADLEY, William II: BRUO 2. 258. Subdeacon 25 March 1505, deacon 11 April 1506, priest 15 April 1511 (Reg. Warham, fo. 262ʳᵛ, 265ᵛ); at Oxford during Warham's visitation, 9 September 1511; gave Lambeth MS. 159 to John Sarysbury (M.R. James and C. Jenkins, *Catalogue* i. 249).

BIOGRAPHICAL DATA

HARTEY, James: BRUO 2. 272. Priest 3 April 1507 (Reg. Warham, fo. 263); not in the lists of 1534, 1538 or 1540—the signatory to the acknowledgement of the royal supremacy is J. Charte (q.v.), not J. Harte as printed; died ? before 1534. Owned Lambeth MS. 159, *Vitae Sanctorum*, paper and vellum, xvi c.

HATHFELDE, Richard, al. TURPYN: not in BRUO. Professed 1356 (Searle 181), formerly monk of Hatfield Regis; received into Christ Church with the consent of his former prior 23 January 1362 (*Lit. Cant.* ii. 413, but contrast with date given by Searle); on committee for regulations for infirmary, 1376 (*Lit. Cant.* iii. 4); nominated for cellarer 22 August 1383, but not chosen (*Reg. Courtenay*, fo. 43^v).

HENFYLDE, Henry: BRUO ii. 908. See also Cawston MS., fo. 17^v.

HENFYLDE, John: BRUO ii. 908. After 1511, licensed by Archbishop Warham to migrate to Battle Abbey. Still at Canterbury at Warham's visitation in 1511.

HETHE, John: BRUO ii. 923.

HOLDEN, Richard: BRUO ii. 947. See also Cawston MS., fo. 19^v.

HOLYNGBORN, John: BRUO ii. 955. Treasurer at Canterbury 1459–61 (Lambeth Court Roll 84, Cant. D.E. 52). Owned Lambeth MS. 558, a xiii c. psalter; Corpus Christi Coll. Oxon. MS. 189, *Viaticus Constantini* (medical treatises), xiii-xiv c. (fo. 1, 'de empcione Iohannis Holyngbourne'; no. 452 of the Eastry catalogue: James, *Ancient Libraries* 57, 509); Cotton Vespasian B. xxv: Solinus, Dares Phrygius etc., xii c. ('Liber dompni Iohannis Holyngbourne monachi ecclesie Christi Cant' emptus a quodam fratre anno Domini 1503 prec' xx d.': James no. 244, 2° fo. deinceps); Trinity College Dublin 829.

HOLYNGBOURNE, Robert: BRUO ii. 955.

HORDEN, Antony: BRUO 2. 299. Subdeacon 22 April 1508 (Reg. Warham, fo. 263^v; at Oxford at Warham's visitation, 9 September 1511; died 1511 or later.

HUMFREY, Thomas: BRUO ii. 983. Died 1494–5 (*Arch. Cant.* xlviii. 65).

ISLEPE, Simon: BRUO 2. 312. See also Cawston MS., fo. 36.

JEROM, William: BRUO 2. 316. See also Fox, *Acts and Monuments* (ed. Pratt) v. 429 ff.

KENNERTON, William (apparently = Kenardington): BRUO ii. 1036.

LANGDON, John I: BRUO ii. 1093. Preached at a 'synod' (Convocation) 1411 on the text, *Stellae dederunt lumen* [Baruch iii. 34], according to Nich. Harpsfield, *Hist. Eccl. Angl.* (1622) 619; appointed proctor of Christ Church Canterbury to the Council of Constance 1 November 1417 (Reg. S, fo. 77) in order to procure a bull for the indulgence of the jubilee of St Thomas of Canterbury for 1420 in place of a former bull said to have been lost: the prior and chapter 'transmiserunt ad predictum consilium Constanciense confratrem ... Iohannem Langdon, sacre pagine professorem, virum utique in sciencia preclarum, regi et regni proceribus multum acceptabilem, pro restauracione consimilis bulle, ut premittitur, aliisque ecclesie negociis exequendis' (P.R.O. E 36/196, fo. 35); one of the proctors for the Wine of St Thomas, 4 March 1419; present at Lambeth with Archbishop Chichele 14 February 1420 at the recantation of William Taylor, a heretic (Wilkins, *Concilia* iii. 405); called to the presence of King Henry V in France, Lent 1420 (P.R.O. E. 36/196, fo. 39); apparently with Archbishop Chichele in France 29 December ? 1420 and 'promoted' by him (*Lit. Cant.* iii. 139); at Convocation May 1421 and together with the chancellors of Oxford and Cambridge commissioned to examine and report on writings of William Taylor (Wilkins, *Concilia* iii. 406; Wylie and Waugh, *The Reign of Henry V* iii (1929) 282); epitaph in *Notes and Queries*, third series, ix. 274, from Bodleian MS. Rawlinson B. 155, fo. 16); notices in Tanner, *Bibliotheca* 465 and DNB s.v. *Langton* (but the latter is mistaken in repeating the statements that he was at Gloucester College and took his degree in 1400).

LANGDON, John II: BRUO ii. 1094. Novice of W. Hadley about 1465 (Searle 188). See also Cawston MS. 31^v.

LANGDON, John III: BRUO 2. 339.

LANGLEE, Peter: BRUO 2. 340. Scholar on the new foundation 1541.

LEE, Thomas: not in BRUO. Professed 1498 (Searle 192); priest 3 April 1507 (Reg. Warham, fo. 263); died c. 1523–4 (*Arch. Cant.* xlviii. 71).

LYNSTEDE, Robert: BRUO ii. 1195.

LYNTON, Robert: BRUO ii. 1195. Witness at an arbitration by the chancellor of the university, Thomas Gascoigne, 8 November 1445 (*Registrum Cancellarii*, ed. H.E. Salter, i (1932) 118).

MARCHALL, Edmund: BRUO 2. 380.

MILTON, William: BRUO ii. 1283. *Magister ordinum* c. 1391 (Searle 184).

BIOGRAPHICAL DATA

MOLASSHE, William: BRUO ii. 1288. Described 12 July 1415 as *custos* and chaplain to the prior; but this may mean 'warden of manors', not warden of the college (Somner-Battely, *Antiquities of Canterbury* (1703), pt. 1, app. 64).

MONGEHAM, Stephen: BRUO ii. 1293.

MORTON, John: BRUO 2. 403 confuses him with one who entered Christ Church in 1519. Professed 1502 (Searle 193); died c. 1516 or 1517 (*Arch. Cant.* xlviii. 69).

NEWNHAM, Lawrence: BRUO 2. 416. Subdeacon 26 March 1513 (Reg. Warham, fo. 266ᵛ); died or departed ? c. 1522–34 (not in lists of 1534 etc.).

OTFORDE, Roger: BRUO 2. 426. Subdeacon 26 March 1513 (Reg. Warham, fo. 266ᵛ); first mass 1520–1 (*Arch. Cant.* xlviii. 70).

OXFORDE, Thomas: BRUO ii. 1415.

PECKHAM, William: BRUO 2. 439. Deacon 19 April 1511 (Reg. Warham, fo. 265ᵛ).

PERMYSTEDE, Arnold: BRUO iii. 1429.

PETTHAM, William I: BRUO iii. 1470. Professed 20 July 1440 (Corpus Christi Coll. Oxon. MS. 265, fo. 119ᵛ); appointed proctor for Convocation 1 May 1460 (Reg. S, fo. 204ᵛ).

PETTHAM, William II: not in BRUO 2. Professed 1512 (Searle 194); subdeacon 26 March 1513 (Reg. Warham, fo. 266ᵛ); died 1518–19.

QUENYNGATE, Richard: BRUO iii. 1537. See also Searle 189.

RECOLVER, Thomas: not in BRUO. Professed 1381 (Searle 183); priest 23 December 1385 (Reg. Courtenay I, fo. 308).

REDYNGATE, John de: BRUO iii. 1563.

RICHEMONDE, William I: BRUO iii. 1575. On committee for drawing up infirmary regulations, 1376 (*Lit. Cant.* iii. 4); one of the *compromissarii* at the election of Archbishop Courtenay, July 1381 (Bodleian MS. Ashmole 794, fo. 254 f.). MS. no. 5 of the Bibliothèque Mazarine, a xiii c. Bible, 'liber eccl. Chr. Cant. cuius custos W. Rychemont monachus' (James, *Ancient Libraries*, p. 530), may have belonged to W.R. I or to W.R. II below. Died on St Hugh's day 1406 (Cawston MS., fo. 18).

RICHEMONDE, William II: BRUO iii. 1575.

SANDWYCHE, William: BRUO 2. 504. Subdeacon 26 March 1513 (Reg. Warham, fo. 266ᵛ); involved in the proceedings against John Thaycher 1 October 1537.

SARYSBURY, John: BRUO iii. 1631. Appointed proctor for Convocation 2 October 1434 (Reg. S, fo. 118); epitaph in Somner-Battely, *Antiquities of Canterbury*, pt. 1, app. 63.

SELLYNGE, Richard: BRUO iii. 1666. Acolyte 21 September 1476, subdeacon 22 March 1477, deacon 1 April 1480, priest 24 May 1483 (Reg. Bourchier, fo. 151^{rv}, 154, 156^v).

SELLYNGE, William I: BRUO iii. 1666. First mass 26 September 1456 (Searle 66); preached at the election of the prior at Canterbury 31 August 1468 on the text, *Quis ascendet contra Chananeum et erit dux belli?* [Iud. 1. 1] (Searle 105); December 1468, letter of confraternity to Johannita Bely of Venice in gratitude for her kindness to W.S. when in Italy (*Christ Church Letters*, p. xxxviii); 13 January 1471, letter of confraternity to John, Bishop of Urbino, in return for kindness shown (Reg. S, fo. 245^v); 1471, one of the chancellors of Christ Church: perhaps the fine italic handwriting in Reg. S, fo. 245^v–246, is his (cf. the italic handwriting in weekly accounts between October 1471 and September 1472: Acct. Bk. 1467–79); died 1494. See also *Materials for Hist. of Reign of Henry VII* (Rolls Series 1877) ii. 85, 114, 224, 240; *Hist. MSS. Comm. Report* v, app. p. 454.

SELLYNGE, William II, BRUO 2. 509.

SHEPAY, John: not in BRUO 2. Professed 1500 (Searle 193); first mass 1505–6 (*Arch. Cant.* xlviii. 67); departed or died ? c. 1512–34 (not in lists of 1534 etc.).

STONE, William: BRUO iii. 1789. Bearer of letters to the archbishop on the death of the prior, 1391 (Reg. S, fo. 1).

SUTTON, Henry: BRUO iii. 1819. Bearer of letter to archbishop concerning John Langdon I, 29 December 1420 (*Lit. Cant.* iii. 140).

SUTTON, Robert: BRUO iii. 1823.

THORNDEN, Richard, al. LE STEDE: BRUO 2. 564. Preached university sermon 1528, Ash Wednesday and the Ascension (Oxford University Archives, Reg. B reversed, fo. 362^v); 26 January 1534, mentioned as having been at Risborough and described as an enemy to the King's cause, harping against it in his sermons and conversation (letter of Richard Croke to Cromwell, *Letters and Papers, Henry VIII* vii. 101); 1540, Prior Goldwell complains to Cromwell that 'of late my brother the warden of the manors, Dr Thorneden, is called in my Lord of Canterbury's house "Dean of Christchurch in Canterbury"' (*Letters and Papers, Henry VIII* xv. 254).

THORNDEN, William: BRUO iii. 1865. See also Cawston MS., fo. 26^v.

BIOGRAPHICAL DATA 227

THROWLEY, Haymo: BRUO 2. 566. See also Cawston MS., fo. 35ᵛ.

THROWLEY, John: BRUO 2. 566. His name, 'John Trwley', is scribbled in a book once belonging to Canterbury College, Bodleian MS. Selden supra 65 (S.C. no. 3454), fo. 145.

TOKNAM, Thomas: BRUO iii. 1882. See also Cawston MS., fo. 20.

WALTHAM, John I: BRUO iii. 1974. Bearer of letter to archbishop c. February 1438 on death of Prior Molash (Reg. S, fo. 129).

WALTHAM, John II: BRUO iii. 1974. At Warham's visitation, 9 September 1511; died c. 1524–5 (*Arch. Cant.* xlviii. 71).

WALTHAM, John III: BRUO 2. 606 confuses him with the following, John Warham, al. Millys. Professed 1527 (Searle 195); not among those who acknowledged the royal supremacy 12 December 1534: he was perhaps absent at Oxford; January 1537 wrote to Cranmer informing him that certain of his fellow monks used the Pope's name etc. (*Letters and Papers, Henry VIII*, xii (i) 256); April 1538 fellow at Oxford, reported a dangerous conversation concerning More and Fisher: he was evidently of an informative disposition (*Letters and Papers, Henry VIII*, xiii (i) 845); c. 1538 student at Paris (iii. 153); as he is not in the list of 1540, he was probably allowed to depart, especially as he had been professed when under twenty years of age.

WARHAM, John, al. MILLYS: confused by BRUO 2. 606 with the foregoing, John Waltham III. Professed 1524 (Searle 195); first mass 1532–3 (*Arch. Cant.* xlviii. 73); fellow c. 1534; sued Agnes Maye for debt 20 March 1534 (iii. 268); mentioned in inventory 1534 as having lost or sold a chalice (i. 76); supplicated for B.D. November 1537, admitted to oppose 16 January 1538, B.D. 8 February 1538 (iii. 261–2); c. 1538 aged 30 and 'witty' (iii. 153); 1540 at the dissolution; 1541 on the new foundation, canon in the tenth prebend; died 1565.

WODEHULL, Henry: BRUO iii. 2073. 'Cuidam monacho de Abyngton incipienti in theologia apud Oxon. 40 s.', 1360–1 (*Durham Account Rolls*, Surtees Soc. 1899, iii. 562).

WODNYSBROWGH, John: BRUO iii. 2074. Perhaps succeeded J. Sarysbury as warden c. 1429. In that case, he would be the warden brought before the commissary because of the violence of his servants etc. in 1434 (*Registrum Cancellarii*, ed. H.E. Salter, i (1932) 8).

WOGHOP, William: BRUO iii. 2075. Priest 18 September 1367 (Reg. Langham, fo. 135ᵛ); one of the committee for the regulation of the infirmary in 1376 (*Lit. Cant.* iii. 4); one of the original *compromissarii* at the election of Archbishop Courtenay, July 1381 (Bodleian MS. Ashmole 794, fo. 254 f.). See also Cawston MS., fo. 17ᵛ.

WOOTTON, Antony: not in BRUO 2. Professed 1506 (Searle 193). Not at Warham's visitation, 1511. As his effects are listed with those of R. Holyngbourne c. 1508, he perhaps died at this time.

WOTTON, John: BRUO iii. 2091. Formerly a monk of Dover; died 11 September 1443 (Searle 33—but contrast obit date with Searle 184).

WY, John: BRUO iii. 2098. Deacon 2 April 1413 (Reg. Arundel II, fo. 101ᵛ); priest 10 April 1417 (*Reg. Chichele* iv. 328).

WYKYNG, Thomas: BRUO iii. 2114. At Oxford at time of archbishop's visitation 2 January 1377: being mentioned first in the list of students, he was perhaps the warden; absolved from office of penitentiary and made cellarer 15 September 1382 (Reg. Courtenay, fo. 21ᵛ–22). See also Cawston MS., fo. 18ᵛ.

WYLFRYDE, Thomas: not in BRUO 2. Professed 1521 (Searle 195); first mass 1526–7 (*Arch. Cant.* xlviii. 72); signed acknowledgement of royal supremacy 12 December 1534; at the dissolution, 1540, apparently received neither pension nor office.

LIST OF WARDENS

As far as it can be ascertained, the succession of heads of the college is as follows:

1363		H. Wodehull
1367	March	J. de Redyngate
	April	H. Wodehull
1371	July	J. Bydenden
	Sept.	W. Richemonde
1372		S. Mongeham
1377		T. Wykyng
1380		W. Dover
1382		J. Aleyn
		W. Dover (*yconomus*)
1383		W. Dover
1393		W. Charte
1401		T. Toknam (absolved)
		T. Wykyng
1403		R. Godmersham
1410		J. Langdon
1413		R. Holden
c. 1413		W. Molasshe
?		J. Grove
1428		J. Sarysbury
c. 1429		?J. Wodnysbrowgh
1435		J. Wodnysbrowgh
1437		T. Asshe
1438		J. Waltham
1441		J. Wodnysbrowgh
1443		R. Lynton
1448		J. Wodnysbrowgh
1449		R. Gravene
1454		W. Thornden
1459		W. Hadley
1466		R. Goldstone
1471		W. Chichele
1475		T. Humfrey
1478		J. Langdon

1486	R. Copton (vice-warden)
	J. Langdon
1495	R. Eastry
1496	T. Chaundler
1501	R. Holyngbourne
1504	J. Dunstan
1506	R. Holyngbourne
1508	W. Gyllyngham
1510	E. Bockyng
1521	W. Hadley
1524	R. Thornden
1534	W. Sandwyche.

INDEX OF NAMES

Abb..., Thomas, iii. 99; iv. 88
Abbotsbury, ii. 201; iv. 93
Abel, John, ii. 140, 141, 143–7
Abingdon, i. vii; ii. 128; iii. 6, 12–14, 21, 30, 37, 38, 57, 58; iv. 32, 37, 64, 71, 93, 131, 132, 134, 227
Aburton, iii. 225
Acerenza, iii. 197
Achab, iii. 70
Aclyn, John, iii. 133
Acworth, T., i. 6, 14; iv. 160
Adam, clerk, iv. 183
— prior, *see* Chillynden
Adams, dominus, iii. 243, 244
Adderbury, iv. 110
Addysham, Henry, iv. 206
Agas, R., iv. 138
Alan, magister, ii. 244
Alban Hall, iii. 237, 239
Albertolus, iii. 188, 189, 190, 191, 199; iv. 22, 25, 26
Alexander, iv. 173, 175
Aleyn, John, ii. 128, 129, 131; iii. 39, 40, 45; iv. 34, 41, 64, 65, 186–90, 218, 229
Alfred, John, iv. 53
Alkamar, W., iii. 134
All Souls College, iii. 111, 113, 126, 135, 227–33, 237, 238, 243, 244
Amblard, Peter, iii. 197
Ambrose, John, iv. 206
— John, monk, ii. 259; iii. 152, 218
Androin, *see* Roche
Anglicus, Robertus, iv. 216
Anselme, Thomas, iv. 53
— Thomas I, i. 91, 111; iv. 206
— Thomas II, iii. 153
Antony, John, iii. 146
— Robert, iii. 153
Appelton, iv. 8
Appilton, R., iii. 74
— William, iii. 101; iv. 88
ap Ryce, David, al. John, iii. 67
Aquitaine, iv. 37, 185
Ardfert, iv. 213
Arnold, *see* Permystede
Arundel, earl of, iv. 11

Arundel, Thomas, i. 4, 14, 97; iii. 59–61, 63, 68, 72; iv. 59, 160, 220
— W., iii. 143; iv. 54
Aschby, John, ii. 169
Asche, John, iii. 88, 92
— magister, ii. 224, 226
— Thomas, i. 2, 10; ii. 151; iii. 69, 72, 88, 91, 95, 97; iv. 78, 96, 192–4, 218, 229
Ascheford, J., iv. 54
— Thomas, iii. 91; iv. 79, 195
Ashridge, ii. 165; iv. 97
Askeby, Robert, iii. 221
Assheton, John, ii. 274; iv. 202
— Richard, iii. 96–8; iv. 96
Astell, Thomas, iii. 73; iv. 88
Astyn, Hugh, iii. 234–44
Athelney, iv. 2
Atkins, Matthew, iv. 206, 207
Atwater, William, ii. 224, 226, 229, 231, 238, 241; iv. 46, 98
Audoen, Henry, iii. 153; iv. 53
Auncell, *see* Anselme
Austen, John, ii. 271
— William, i. 91, 92; iii. 153
Avignon, iii. 33; iv. 39, 40
Awdroyn, *see* Audoen

Badcok, Robert, iii. 135
Bagwell, John, iii. 272; iv. 47
Baketon, Walter de, iii. 16, 204; iv. 30
Baldinton, John, ii. 128
Balliol College, ii. 140, 147, 151, 154, 161, 163, 167, 171, 174, 177, 182, 184, 187, 190, 192, 194, 197, 199, 206, 208, 212, 214, 217, 220, 223, 225, 228, 230, 232, 235, 238, 239, 243, 246, 249, 251, 254, 257, 258, 261; iii. 7, 30, 31, 37, 38, 49, 52–4, 57, 58; iv. 37, 106, 131, 132
Balsham, Hugh, iv. 12
Banbury, iii. 85
Barbour, John, iii. 10
Barnardcastell, Thomas, iii. 18
Barons, Thomas, ii. 258
Barrington, ii. 173
Barton, Elizabeth, iii. 147; iv. 49

Barton *(cont.)*
—John de, iii. 36
Basel, iii. 87, 89, 94; iv. 75, 79
Baskerville, Edward, iii. 271
Basshe, Edmund, iii. 212
Batell, John, ii. 198, 200
Bath, i. 2, 10; ii. 161, 165, 180, 186, 188, 189, 195; iii. 99; iv. 93, 95, 143
—William, monk of, ii. 173
Bathe, Henry, ii. 197
Battes Inn, iii. 55
Battle, ii. 179–81, 193, 195, 199, 200, 204, 207, 210, 213, 215, 218, 224, 226, 229, 231, 233, 236, 237, 239, 244, 247, 257; iii. 233; iv. 93–5, 213, 223
Baty, William, iii. 206
Bawdon, *see* Bowden
Beam Hall, iii. 227, 228
Beamunde, Peter, ii. 127, 131; iv. 125
Beaulieu, iv. 8
Becford, J., iv. 184
Becket, St Thomas, i. 6, 15, 61, 103; iii. 4, 9, 25, 45, 103, 159; iv. 150, 157
—— jubilee of, i. 102; iii. 74, 76, 108, 109; iv. 80, 103, 224
—Thomas, iii. 153; iv. 53
Beckley, iii. 55
Bedel, dominus, iii. 243, 244
Bedowhe, Richard, iii. 233, 235, 236, 243, 244
Bedynden, Thomas, iii. 101; iv. 88
Beeleigh, ii. 258; iv. 97
Beggebroke, John de, iv. 168
Beke's Inn, iii. 10, 11
Bekesbourne, iii. 120
Bekynton, William, ii. 201
Bely, Johannita, iv. 101, 222, 226
Benedict XII, iii. 33, 63, 144; iv. 1, 2, 6, 7, 12, 18, 19, 54, 55, 56, 59, 60, 107, 113, 116, 119, 155
Benet, dom, ii. 259
—Hugh, iii. 157
—Nicholas, i. 76; iii. 149, 150; iv. 74, 218
—Roger, i. 37, 91, 92; ii. 224, 226, 229, 232, 271, 274; iii. 149; iv. 202–5, 218
Benger, Richard, commissary, iii. 262
—Richard, proxy, iii. 16–18, 188–95, 198–202; iv. 17, 20, 21, 24–8, 33
Berde, John, iii. 225
Bere Hall, iii. 10, 49; iv. 136

Berengarius, iv. 184
Bergeneye, William, iii. 56
Berham, John, iv. 190, 218
—Michael de, i. 12, 14, 41, 97, 100; iv. 157
Bersted, ii. 127, 131, 151, 155, 156, 166, 170, 172–4, 176; iii. 6, 35, 156, 207ff.; iv. 122ff., 185, 197, 198
Bertram, John, iv. 67, 186, 218
Berwik, John, ii. 140
—William, ii. 143, 145, 146
Bery, Thomas, iii. 233
Beverley, i. 102
Birchington, Stephen of, iv. 11, 14, 131
Bisshop, William, iii. 100; iv. 88
Blake, Richard, iii. 116
Blank, John, iii. 210, 211, 212
—Thomas, iii. 211
Blaunkepayne, William, iii. 36
Blebbe, iv. 179
Blisse, Richard, iii. 265
Blodewell, John, iii. 76, 78
Bochar, Thomas, iii. 153
Bockyng, Edward, i. 45, 52, 55, 57, 58, 63, 64, 66, 68, 69, 75; ii. 241, 245, 248, 250, 252, 255, 271, 273; iii. 142, 143, 246–8, 256, 264; iv. 47, 49, 63, 64, 78, 107, 147, 148, 151, 153, 205, 206, 218, 230
—Thomas de, iv. 6
Bodi, John, iv. 6
Bognor, ii. 147, 151, 155, 162, 166, 168, 170, 173, 176; iii. 6, 35, 207ff.; iv. 122ff., 198
Bohemia, iii. 89
Bokbynder, William, i. 94
Bokyngham, John, iii. 93
Boldewell, John, *see* Blodewell
Boldon, Ughtred, iv. 30
Bolney, Richard, ii. 272
Bologna, iii. 130, 131; iv. 3, 80, 81, 83
Bolton, John de, iii. 6, 30, 31; iv. 131, 135
—Thomas de, iii. 58
Bonnyngton, Richard, iii. 152; iv. 54
Bosc, Matthew du, iii. 75
Bosqueto, Bernardus de, iii. 197, 198, 201, 202; iv. 29
Bossall, iv. 8
Boterwyc, Robert, ii. 137
Botlesham, John, iv. 220
—William, iv. 220

INDEX OF NAMES

Bourchier, John, ii. 190, 193–5, 197; iii. 117; iv. 98
—Thomas, i. 4, 12, 30, 52, 58, 67, 97; iii. 106, 109, 111, 116, 120, 208; iv. 92, 98, 103, 149
Bourer, John, ii. 127
Bourne, Bartholomew de, iii. 120
— Ralph de, iv. 213
Bowden, Edward, iii. 231–41, 243, 245
Bowyer, Richard, iii. 225
Boxley, iii. 243
Boxley, Robert, iii. 152; iv. 54
Boxwell, John, iii. 131; iv. 203, 205, 219
Boys, Roger de, iv. 16
Bradegare, Robert de, iii. 36
Brampton, iii. 70
Brasenose College, iii. 227–32
Braybrok, Alice, iii. 73
Brecknock, iii. 131
Breggar, William, iii. 43; iv. 43
Brightwalton, Berks., iii. 67
Bristol, ii. 213; iv. 97
Broadgates Hall, iii. 264
Broke, dominus; iii. 239–44
— William de, iv. 59
Browne, John, carrier, iv. 192
— John, wall-maker, iii. 210
— Thomas, monk, iii. 72; iv. 219
— Thomas, secular scholar, ii. 133, 135; iv. 88
— William, ii. 141, 142
Brudenell, Robert, iii. 214, 217
Brunnyng, Richard, iii. 228–32, 234
Brysell, William, iv. 206
Buccke, iii. 150
Burbrydge, John, iii. 56
Burfyld, John, iii. 264
Burghe, William, iii. 96; iv. 96
Burghfield, iv. 135
Burgundy, iii. 76
Burmarsh, iv. 7
Burne, N. de, iv. 177
Burnell's Inn, iv. 2
Burnham, iii. 73
Burton, ii. 177, 179, 188; iv. 93
Burton, James, ii. 213
— Thomas, iii. 234–42
Bury St Edmunds, iii. 61; iv. 93, 221
Buttlar, Walter, i. 93
Bydenden, John, iii. 18, 20, 21, 23; iv. 35, 182, 186, 219, 229
Byleth, ii. 258; iv. 97

Bynee, Robert, iv. 54, 192, 219
Byseley, Walter, iii. 63; iv. 88

Caermarthen, Edmund de, bp. of Ardfert, iv. 213
Calais, iv. 201
Calceto, de, see Wodelond
Calis, Thomas, i. 53, 68
Cambridge, iii. 131, 227; iv. 12, 49, 57, 81, 158, 224
— Peterhouse, iii. 131
Canner, iii. 149
Canterbury, Eastbridge Hospital, iii. 120
— St Alphege's, iii. 120
— St Martin's, iv. 104
— schools, iv. 69
Canterbury, archbishop of, ii. 195, 197; iii. 12, 83, 84; iv. 4, 6, 190, 211
— and alienations etc., iii. 168, 175, 181; iv. 106
— and election of prior, iv. 67
— and fellows, iii. 174, 187, 224; iv. 17, 56, 58, 64, 65
— and finances of college, iii. 181
— and Pagham, iii. 35, 168, 185, 199, 221–3; iv. 9ff.; 122, 123
— and pueri collegii, ii. 153, 164, 179, 184; iii. 98–120; iv. 85, 88, 89, 100
— and warden:— see Warden, appointment of
— chancellor of, iii. 8, 10, 36
— choristers of, iv. 52
— court of audience of, iii. 100
— crossbearer of, iii. 8
— election of, iii. 72, 105; iv. 67, 193, 218, 219, 220, 228
— jurisdiction of over college, iii. 9, 71
— knight of, iii. 8
— seneschal of, iii. 8
— servants of; ii. 251; iv. 66, 194
— visitation by of Christ Church, iii. 18; iv. 221–3, 227
—— of college, ii. 131; iii. 50
—— of province, iv. 219
— workmen, of, ii. 157
Canterbury, archdeacon of, ii. 254; iv. 180
— see also Chichele, Thomas
Canterbury, Christ Church, i. 3, 11, 30, 31, 57, 77, 80, 83, 88, 91, 96ff.; ii. 126, 149, 153, 154, 162, 168, 184, 196; iv. 2, 3, 5, 7, 14, 16, 17, 18, 29,

Canterbury, Christ Church *(cont.)*
31, 35, 39, 40, 49, 92, 105, 117, 145, 155
— almonry chapel, iv. 69, 70
— — school, iv. 52, 172, 187
— auditor, iii. 209, 210
— Black Prince's chantry, iv. 70
— brewhouse, iv. 204, 205
— cellarer, iii. 134, 173; iv. 41, 74, 77, 221, 223, 228
— chamberlain, iv. 41, 74, 117
— chancellor, iv. 74, 77, 84
— chapel of B.V.M., iii. 36
— chapter-house, iii. 83, 139–41; iv. 67
— choir, iv. 145, 221
— Christ Church gate, iv. 77
— cloister, iii. 142, 143
— compline, iii. 142, 143; iv. 69
— corona, iv. 6, 177
— court, iii. 142
— crypt, iv. 188, 190, 221
— — chapel, iii. 92, 93; iv. 220
— dinner, iv. 69
— dispenser, iii. 134
— Easter sepulchre, iii. 92, 93
— elections, iii. 50, 68, 82, 95, 102, 105, 108, 110, 131, 143; iv. 67, 186, 188, 192–4, 196, 203, 205, 218–20, 226, 228
— feretrars, iv. 181–4, 187–90, 220
— financial exhaustion, iii. 258.
— fourth prior, iii. 142
— infirmary, i. 88; iii. 38, 96, 112, 113; iv. 69, 100, 202, 219, 221, 223, 225, 228
— — chapel, ii. 194; iv. 110, 221
— larderer, iii. 133
— — Nicholas, servant of, iii. 133
— library, iv. 73, 156ff.
— list of monks and obediences, iii. 151; iv. 48
— magister operis, ii. 157
— magister ordinum, iv. 53, 68, 74, 77, 224
— martyrdom, iv. 190
— Morton scholars from, iii. 227; iv. 57, 63
— muniments, iii. vii, xi, 225; iv. 217
— novices, iv. 53–5, 69, 202, 222, 224
— obventions, iv. 184, 185
— Pagham, iv. 124ff
— patronage, iii. 156

— penitencer, iii. 68; iv. 41, 74, 77, 218, 219, 228
— precentor, iv. 41
— prior and chapter, i. 80, 100, 113 and passim
— prior's chapel, iv. 39
— — chaplain, iv. 110, 175, 225
— — horses, iii. 55
— — household, iii. 55, 111, 128, 129
— — scribe, iv. 201
— prison, iii. 91
— proclamation in chapter, iii. 143
— recruitment, iv. 5, 51ff., 212
— refectory, iii. 143; iv. 220
— Rule learned by heart, iii. 143; iv. 53, 54, 69
— sacrist, iii. 173; iv. 77, 220
— scholars, iv. 167ff.
— scrutators, iii. 143
— seneschal, ii. 251
— seniors, ii. 272, 274; iii. 142, 175; iv. 53, 54, 109
— sermons, ii. 149; iii. 119, 129; iv. 66, 67, 193, 194, 196, 198, 201, 204–6, 218–20, 226
— servants, iv. 168, 171, 174, 179, 180, 188, 191
— servitium commune, iv. 219
— — parvum, iv. 219
— stable, iii. 39
— studies, iv. 71, 176
— subcellarer, iii. 150; iv. 74
— subprior, ii. 263; iii. 36, 50, 67, 68, 83, 84, 88, 91, 94–6, 102, 108, 110, 111, 117, 131, 143, 148, 173; iv. 41, 67, 76, 77, 105, 170, 171, 174, 176, 177, 217
— succentor, i. 80; iii. 180; iv. 155
— table, master of, iv. 219
— treasurers, i. 103; ii. 271; iv. 7, 56, 66, 74, 85, 109, 125, 167ff., 223
— visitations, iii. 18, 41, 73, 100, 129, 183; iv. 6, 45, 190, 221–3, 227, 228
— warden of manors, ii. 195, 196, 206, 210, 217, 220, 223, 226, 228, 229, 231, 233, 235, 238, 241, 244, 247, 250, 252, 255, 257, 262ff.; iii. 120, 137, 142, 146–8, 209, 225, 227, 237; iv. 48, 56, 74, 108, 110, 117, 128, 225, 226
— wine of St. Thomas, iv. 78, 173, 209, 216, 217, 224

INDEX OF NAMES

Canterbury College, iv. 46
— name of, i. v
— new work, ii. 140, 144, 146, 172, 176; iii. 56
— reformatio, ii. 164
— satire on, iii. 68
— site of, ii. 128; iii. 56, 59; iv. 10, 14, 15, 32, 37, 38, 131ff.
— visitation of, ii. 131, 165; iii. 50, 98, 99
Canterbury, dean and chapter of, i. 78–9; iii. 155–7; iv. 48, 149, 219, 220, 227
Canterbury, diocese of, iii. 197
Canterbury, St Augustine's, i. 78; ii. 149, 224; iii. 69, 74; iv. 4, 7, 54, 72, 81, 82, 88, 93, 97, 212, 213, 219
— John, abbot of, iii. 82
Cantuaria, William de, iv. 6
Cardinal College, iv. 47
Carent, Nicholas, iv. 98
Carr, John, ii. 128; iv. 188
Cartar, Robert, iii. 270
Cary, T., ii. 143
Castellamare, iii. 197
Castiglioni, Branda, iii. 78
— James, physician of, iii. 79, 80
Catesby, William, iii. 116
Catrik, John, iii. 76
Caunterbury, William, iii. 153
Cawlyn, William, ii. 176
Cawston, William, iii. 153
Cellynge, *see* Sellynge
Cerne, ii. 221; iv. 93
Chace, Thomas, iii. 81, 84
Chaddesden, Nicholas de, iii. 8, 10
Champenes, Adam, iv. 174
Charing, iii. 9; iv. 14
Charte, John, fellow, ii. 258; iii. 153; iv. 206, 219, 223
— John, novice, iv. 54
— Robert, iv. 193
— Thomas, iv. 205
— William I, i. 32; ii. 126, 128, 132, 133, 135, 136, 138, 139, 142, 146; iii. 45, 53, 56; iv. 77, 187, 189, 191, 219, 229
— William II, iii. 101; iv. 53, 193, 219
Chartham, Thomas, ii. 185, 188; iv. 63, 116, 196, 219
— W., monk, ii. 272
— William, fellow, i. 32; ii. 204, 207, 211, 214, 216, 264–8; iii. 117,
128; iv. 56, 62, 75, 90, 105, 114, 119–21, 199, 219
Chaumpeneys, Hugh, iv. 6
Chaundler, Thomas, warden, i. 18, 28; ii. 221, 223, 225, 228, 231, 268–70, 274; iv. 62, 107, 150, 163, 164, 201–5, 219, 230
— Thomas, warden of New College, i. 28; ii. 201–3, 228, 263; iii. 110–14, 123–5; iv. 46, 76, 82, 90, 98, 101–4, 148–50
Chawdeler, doctor, iii. 232
Cherlew, John de, iii. 204
Cherryng, R. de, iv. 173, 174, 209
Chertsey, ii. 165, 173, 179; iv. 93
Chester, Hugh of, ii. 165
Cheyne, John, iii. 194, 195, 200; iv. 22, 28
Chichele, Henry, iii. 73, 75, 95; iv. 88, 156, 224
— Thomas, ii. 152, 162
— William, monk, iii. 142
— William, warden, i. 32; ii. 183, 185, 188, 190, 191, 193, 195, 197, 263; iii. 110, 112–15, 119, 121; iv. 75, 81, 94, 162, 166, 196–9, 219, 229
Chichester, ii. 155; iii. 8, 10, 22, 35, 184, 186, 188, 189, 191, 199, 204, 208, 209, 210; iv. 22, 30, 122
Chidley, George, iii. 267
Chilham, Henry, iii. 47, iv. 190, 219
Chillynden, Adam de, i. 12, 100; iv. 157
— Guy, iv. 206
— John, iii. 152; iv. 54
— Thomas, i. 1, 3, 9, 10, 14, 23, 28, 30, 34, 50, 51, 55, 56, 61, 65, 72, 75, 77, 100, 103; ii. 126, 129, 131, 206; iii. 34, 43, 45, 68; iv. 40, 43, 46, 55, 63, 65, 68, 72, 74, 79, 115, 135, 142–4, 149, 151, 157, 187–91, 219, 220
Chimere Hall, iii. 38; iv. 106, 132, 134
Chipping Norton, iv. 8
Christ Church, iii. 148, 155, 269, 270; iv. 50, 99, 138, 139, 141
Choperno, *see* Cheyne
Christopher, iv. 194
Chrysoloras, Manuel, iv. 79
Chyperley, magister, ii. 259
Cinque Ports, iv. 145
Clement, John, fifteenth-century, i. 28
— John, 1518; iv. 206

Clement, magister, ?1438; iii. 98
— Nicholas, iii. 152
Clerk, John, clerk of works, ii. 176
— John, merchant, iii. 113
— William, iii. 18
Cliffe, iv. 205, 206
Cluny, iii. 187; iv. 24
Clynt, William, iii. 62
Clyve, Martin de, i. 61, 70, 106; iv. 157
— Richard de, iv. 78, 79, 216, 217
Cobham, Lord, iv. 42, 189
Codessale, William, iii. 29
Coddiford, John, c. 1380, ii. 127
— see also Cottesford
Cok, John, iii. 55
Coke, Thomas, iii. 228–37
— William, iv. 91
— William, lawyer, ii. 161, 162
Cokkys, John, iii. 107; iv. 101
Colbroke, John, iii. 51; iv. 137, 220
— Robert, iii. 72, 88, 89, 91–3
Coldale, doctor, ii. 218, 221
Coldingham, iv. 107, 112
Coles, John, i. 93–5
Coll, iv. 184
Colman, Antony, iii. 228–37, 239–62
— William, iv. 198
Cologne, ii. 178; iii. 198; iv. 147
Colvyle, W., ii. 133, 135; iv. 88
Colyns, John, i. 93
Colynsun, John, i. 94
Combe, J., ii. 262
— W., ii. 207
Combys, Thomas, iii. 238–41
Compton, Roger, iv. 135
Conser, Thomas, iii. 238–44
Constance, iii. 73, 74, 76, 77, 79; iv. 76, 79, 224
Constantinople, iv. 79
Conwey, John, ii. 213
Cooe, Arthur, iii. 227–32
— see also Schowhe
Copton, Jasper, ii. 253, 272; iv. 205, 220
— Richard, ii. 213, 221, 266–70; iii. 128, 132; iv. 65, 117, 121, 202, 220, 230
Cornel Hall, iii. 122
Corner Hall, iii. 232, 237, 239, 243
Cornwall, iii. 90
Cornwall, Michael of, i. 42, 103; iv. 6
Corpus Christi College, iii. 59
Cottesford, John, commissary, iii. 266

— see also Codifford
Cottysmore, magister, ii. 227
Cotyngtun, iii. 2
Coulmer, John, iii. 235–7, 239–42
Couper, John, ii. 171; iv. 125
Courtenay, Richard, i. 2, 4, 12, 97; iv. 160
— William, ii. 131; iii. 39–48, 50, 158, 172, 178, 181–3, 222; iv. 13, 16, 19, 41–6, 58, 85, 86, 100, 106, 155, 160, 188–90, 225, 228
— — father of, iii. 43
Courtoppe, William, iv. 205
Coventry, ii. 179, 180, 199–202, 213, 221; iii. 115; iv. 93, 95, 97, 140
Coventry and Lichfield, diocese of, iii. 12
Cowensell, iii. 244
Crambroke, John, iii. 153
Cranborn, magister, ii. 168
Cranbrook, iii. 15
Cranebroke, Henry, i. 112; ii. 163; iii. 68, 103–5; iv. 83, 84, 103, 220
Cranmer, Thomas, iii. 146–8, 153, 154, 156; iv. 48, 49, 73, 227
Cratfield, William of, iii. 61
Cretyng, Hugh de, i. 6, 14, 99; iv. 157
Croke, Richard, iv. 226
Cromwell, Thomas, iii. 146–9, 151, 154, 155; iv. 47–9, 74, 226
Cronin, H. S., iv. 20
Crook, Thomas, iii. 12, 13
Crosse, J., novice, iv. 53
— John, cellarer, iii. 152, 225
— John, scholar, iii. 149, 150, 153, 220
Crowland, John, ii. 201, 202
Croxton, Richard (Roger) de, iii. 206; iv. 30, 31, 39, 185
Croydon, iii. 100
Cryppis, magister, ii. 271
Cryspyne, Richard, ii. 259
Culley, T., ii. 140
Culpeper, John, ii. 165
Cumbe, see Combe

Dabley, iii. 150
Dalby, John, iii. 227–35
— Thomas, iii. 227–31
Dalton, i. 112
Dandlyon, Marcellus, iii. 74
Daniel, iii. 162
Danyell, William, iii. 209–12

INDEX OF NAMES

Darknowlde, Robert, iii. 243, 244, 264
Dartford, iii. 127
Davyth, iii. 150
Deene, Robert, iv. 54
Deep Hall, iii. 99
Dele, Thomas, iii. 228, 229, 230
Dene, Peter of, iv. 72
Dennys, Quentin, iii. 153
Dens, Philip, iii. 236–42
Depham, Henry de, i. 5, 99; iv. 157, 168
Depyng, John, iii. 96
Derham, Thomas, iii. 116
Deryng, John, ii. 259; iii. 147, 248, 267, 268; iv. 47–9, 220
— Richard, iii. 209; iv. 206
Devenyshe, William, i. 79
Dew, Walter, iv. 206
Dey, Thomas, iii. 263
Donnington, iv. 21
Donton, John de, iii. 22; iv. 35
Doo, Adam, iii. 219
Dorset, iii. 131
Dover, iii. 69, 87, 90, 91, 109, 154; iv. 48, 81, 168, 183, 184
— Richard, bp. of = Richard Thornden, q.v.
Dover, James, i. 1, 9, 28, 56, 77
— John, 1408; iv. 191, 220
— John, novice, iv. 202
— Thomas, ii. 132, 133, 135, 136, 138, 140, 142; iii. 45–7; iv. 44, 68, 188, 220
— William, ii. 126, 129; iii. 36, 37, 39, 40, 41, 45, 46, 48, 50; iv. 41, 42, 44, 77, 78, 188–90, 219, 221, 229
Downyng, Adrian, iii. 228–37
Duke, John, iii. 227, 228
— Richard, iii. 229–34
Dunmow, John, iii. 131
Dunstan, John I, iv. 75, 221
— John II, i. 83; ii. 228, 233, 236, 239, 240, 244, 252; iii. 138, 143, 237–9, 242; iv. 203, 205, 221, 230
Dunstan, St., i. 110
Duppa, Brian, iv. 139
Durant, W., 1468; ii. 189; iv. 101
— William, 1363; iii. 6, 30, 31; iv. 131, 135
Durham, i. vii; iii. 71, 74, 206; iv. 1, 2, 107, 221
Durham College, iii. 144, 145; iv. 2, 8, 12, 30, 46, 67, 78, 85, 89, 91, 93, 96, 105, 109, 112, 113, 116, 137, 140, 156
Dygon, John, iv. 82
Dylmoth, John, ii. 170, 173; iv. 125

Eame, dompnus, ii. 259
Easton, Adam, iii. 206; iv. 30, 31
Eastry, novice, iv. 54
— Christopher, ii. 236, 239, 241, 245, 246, 248; iv. 75, 76, 221
— Henry of, i. 1, 4, 5, 10, 13, 14, 28, 96–8, 100; iv. 3, 31, 72, 78, 156–9; 209, 217
— John, iv. 186, 221
— Robert, i. 82, 106, 107; ii. 195, 202, 204, 207, 211, 214, 216, 218, 221, 263–70; iii. 121, 127; iv. 62, 75–7, 119, 121, 122, 200–4, 221, 230
Edmunds, James, iii. 266
Edward III, iii. 1, 4, 7, 19, 22, 23, 30, 37, 57, 159, 221, 223, 225; iv. 9, 11–13, 16, 32, 35, 36, 38; iv. 131, 134
Edward IV, iv. 101, 104
Edward the Black Prince, iv. 3, 31, 37, 70, 145, 185
Edward Hall, iii. 157; iv. 132
Edward, John sr., iii. 225
Edyngham, Thomas, iii. 61; iv. 88
Eggecombe, John, iii. 136
Egypt, iii. 172
Eleat, magister, ii. 251
— see also Elyatt
Elham, John, iv. 206
— John, prior, iii. 103
Elles, John, iv. 207
Ellffy (Elphe), John, iii. 152; iv. 54
Ellington, iii. 70
Elmswell, iii. 62
Elsmore, magister, ii. 190
Ely, i. vii; iii. 66, 131, 206; iv. 7, 18, 92, 103, 107, 118, 149
Elyatt, E., iii. 244
— see also Eleat
Emden, A. B., iv. 215
Englens, Richard, ii. 146
Epicurus, iii. 71
Erasmus, iv. 82, 83, 99
Esshford, see Ascheford
Eton, iv. 152
Eugenius IV, iii. 94
Evenefeld, see Henfeld

Everard, Humfrey, ii. 161; iv. 90
— Thomas, ii. 132, 133, 135–8, 140; iii. 45, 46, 54, 56; iv. 44, 68, 188–90, 221
Everel, William de, iv. 68, 167
Evesham, ii. 169, 179–82, 185, 186, 188, 190, 195, 196, 199, 200, 204, 206, 207, 210, 213, 214, 218, 221; iii. 81; iv. 93–5, 97, 141
— Richard, abbot of, iii. 81
Exeter, iii. 194, 198
Exeter College, i. vii, 93; iii. 49; iv. 8, 76, 98
Extone, William, iii. 97
Eydorne, W., i. 2, 10, 29
Eyon, iii. 207

Fahon, *see* Pfahon
Faith, monk, iv. 53
Fantyng, Vincent, iv. 205, 206
Farley, John, iii. 84
— William, iv. 206
Faryngton, iii. 31
Faversham, ii. 212; iii. 133, 150; iv. 66, 121, 193
Faversham, Stephen of, i. 5, 13, 42, 98; iv. 71, 78, 157, 171–7, 209, 217
— Thomas, iii. 153
— William, iii. 70
Feckenham, John, iv. 94
Feltham, Sussex, iii. 209
Ferour, W., iv. 183
Ferys, Eligius, iii. 254
Finchale, iv. 107, 112
Findon, Thomas, iv. 213
Fisher, John, iv. 227
— Walter, ii. 143, 145, 146
Fishlake, iv. 8
Flemyng; Richard, iii. 75, 76, 78; iv. 103
Fleshmonger, William, iii. 238–44
Flowyde, John, iii. 228–37
Foderby, Simon, ii. 226, 229, 241, 244; iii. 134; iv. 98
Fonteyn, Robert, i. 93; iv. 54
Fonteyn, William, i. 88
Ford, ii. 153; iv. 88
Fordham, John, iii. 62
Forestm', iii. 133
Forster, William, i. 112
— *see also* Foster
Forsyth, William, i. 112
Foster, John, iii. 75, 76, 78
— *see also* Forster

Fox Hall, iii. 10, 49; iv. 134
Frampton, iv. 8
France, iii. 76, 78, 79
Free, John, iv. 103
Freman, Henry, iii. 57
Frenshe, T., iii. 150
Fresnel, Peter, iii. 75
Freton, Roger de, iii. 188, 189, 192–7, 199–204; iv. 22, 24, 27–30
Frevell, George, iii. 153
Frome, John de, iv. 6, 180–3, 217
Fry, dominus, iii. 229
— John, of New College, iii. 228, 230–42
— John, of Pagham, iii. 209–12
— Robert, iii. 225
Fulham, Robert de, iv. 70, 71, 176, 177, 210
Fynche (Vynch), John, iii. 34, 36–8, 42–8, 50; iv. 40, 53
Fynes, magister, ii. 252
Fyton, John, iii. 74

Garradde, William, iii. 227, 229
Garrard, John, iii. 152; iv. 54
Garston, Richard de, iii. 56
Gascoigne, Thomas, iv. 224
Gasquet, Cardinal, iv. 79
Gaufridus, *see* Romenall
Gay, Christopher, iii. 209
— Humfrey, iii. 210
Geffrey, William, iii. 271, 272
Genington (?Barrington), ii. 173
Gentyll, Humfrey, iii. 109
Gilbert, doctor, ii. 200, 201
— lector's companion, iv. 176
Glassen Hall, iii. 33; iv. 132
Glastonbury, iii. 74; iv. 93, 113
Glastynbury, Edward, ii. 274; iii. 153; iv. 222
— Geoffrey, iv. 204
— William, iii. vii, 87–93; iv. 53, 117, 118
Glasyer, Hugh, i. 79
Gloucester, iii. 210; iv. 8, 93
Gloucester, J., iv. 182, 188, 189, 217
— Simon of, iv. 133
— Thomas de, iii. 7, 30, 31; iv. 131, 136
— William of, iv. 134
Gloucester College, i. vi; iii. 21, 50, 121; iv. 1–4, 6, 30, 35, 36, 68, 78, 93–7, 113, 116, 155, 212, 213, 218, 220, 224

INDEX OF NAMES

Glover, John, iii. 238, 240, 241, 243, 245
Godfery, John, iii. 234–43, 245
— William, iii. 227–32
Godmersham, John, iv. 222
— Richard, 1457, iv. 54
— Richard, 16th. c., iii. 143, 152
— Richard, warden, ii. 132, 133, 135, 136; iii. 60, 63, 68; iv. 64, 65, 71–3, 77, 80, 191, 222, 229
— — servant of, iv. 72, 73
— Roger de, iv. 5, 178, 211, 212, 217
Godstow, ii. 130, 140, 147, 151, 154, 161, 163, 167, 171, 174, 176, 182, 184, 187, 190, 192, 194, 197, 208, 212, 217, 220, 223, 225, 228, 230, 232, 235, 238, 243, 246, 249, 251, 254, 257, 259, 261; iii. 7, 28–31, 51, 57, 120; iv. 37, 131–7, 142
Goldstone, Reginald, i. 30, 35, 36, 51, 56, 65; ii. 180, 183, 184, 187, 190, 192; iii. 108–11, 123; iv. 55, 62, 77, 80, 153, 196, 197, 202, 222, 229
— Thomas I, i. 10, 16, 17, 28, 33, 34, 50, 54–6, 63, 65, 66, 69, 77; ii. 173; iii. 92, 108, 208; iv. 127, 145, 148, 161, 222
— Thomas II, i. 31, 33, 37, 38, 50, 51, 53–7, 63–6, 68, 69, 72, 73, 80, 81, 83; ii. 195, 200, 202, 204, 207, 211, 247, 263–8; iii. 117, 122–5, 127, 130, 136–41, 143, 210, 211, 215, 237, 239; iv. 54, 74, 79, 81–3, 102, 110, 145, 148, 159, 198–201, 203, 205, 222
— Thomas III, iii. 142, 143; iv. 54
— Thomas IV, iii. 153
Goldwell, James, iii. 126
— John, iii. 70
— Thomas I, iii. 92
— Thomas II, i. 68, 81, 107; ii. 224, 226, 229, 232, 233, 236, 239, 241, 245, 248, 271, 272; iii. 140–2, 146, 147, 151, 155, 214ff.; iv. 74, 82, 222, 226
— Thomas III, iii. 265; iv. 63, 81, 117, 204
— Thomas, bp., iii. 147
— William, iii. 152
Goli, iii. 69, 72
Goodneston, J., 14th c., i. 7, 9, 16, 28, 56, 77
— John, 16th c., iii. 152
Googen, John, ii. 197

Goore, Thomas, i. 8
Gosebourne, Robert, iii. 119, 120
Gover, Walter, ?ii. 260; iii. 267
Gower, iii. 268
— John, ii. 137
Grant, Thomas, i. 112; ii. 192; iii. 111; iv. 101
— Thomas, of Oriel, iii. 82
Gravene, Richard, i. 11, 29, 80; ii. 170, 173, 174, 176, 179; iii. 97, 103, 106, 249; iv. 63, 77, 127, 192, 195, 222, 229
Gravesend, iii. 127, 150
Gray, William, bp. of Ely, iv. 103
— William, of Feltham, iii. 209
Graystone, iv. 193
Greenhurst, Ralph, iii. 67
Gregory XI, iii. 32
Gregory, William, iii. 153
Grembergh, Theodoric van, iv. 202
Gressenhale, Robert de, i. 24, 103; iv. 157
Grocyn, William, iv. 103
Grogge, iii. 71
Grove, James, i. 7, 8, 16, 17, 32, 38, 77; iv. 222, 229
— John, iii. 227–9
— William, iii. 227–32, 234–7
Guido, iv. 168
Gunthorpe, John, iv. 103
Gurgayne, Guy, iv. 75
Guston, John, i. 17
— Thomas, iii. 72, 76; iv. 222
Gwynne, Maurice, ii. 231, 236, 241, 244, 247, 250
Gybbes, John, iii. 29
Gyfforde, Hugh, iii. 227–30
Gyles, John, iii. 67
— Stephen, iii. 153
Gyllyngham, doctor, iii. 67; iv. 221
— Richard, iv. 31, 186
— William I, ii. 126, 127; iii. 54, 67; iv. 68, 71, 186–90, 221
— William II, i. 84; ii. 244, 249, 255, 272; iii. 137, 140, 141, 152, 242, 250, 263; iv. 57, 77, 81, 205, 222, 230
— William III, iii. 148
Gynibis, John, iii. 54

H., iv. 170
— prior = Henry of Eastry, q.v.
Hackneyman, John, iv. 66, 203, 204

Hadley, William I, i. 29; ii. 174, 176, 179, 180, 182, 183; iii. 105, 108; iv. 73, 77, 80, 101, 150, 151, 195, 196, 222, 224, 229
— William II, i. 55, 110; ii. 250, 253, 256, 257, 272, 273; iii. 152; iv. 49, 117, 206, 222, 230
Haghe, Thomas, iii. 88–91
Hales, Baron, iii. 226
Hall, Thomas, ii. 271, 272
Haloes, Henry, iv. 201
Hampden, Thomas, ii. 189
Hampton, John, i. 28; iv. 150
— Thomas, iv. 81, 82
Hanney, John, ii. 202
— Peter de, iii. 37
— Thomas de, iii. 12, 13
Haralde, magister, ii. 223
Hardres, Andrew de, iv. 78, 173, 209, 217
— John de, i. 103; iv. 171
Harleton, John, iii. 16
Harper, Thomas, ii. 224, 226
Harrys, William, iii. 263, 264
Harste, *see* Herst
Hartey, James, i. 110; ii. 250, 253, 255; iii. 143; iv. 55, 205, 223
Hartford, William, iv. 204
Hastar (Hafter), John, ii. 236, 239, 241
Hatfield Regis, iv. 223
Hathbrand, Robert, iii. 18, 19; iv. 31
Hathfelde, Richard, al. Turpyn, iii. 15, 18; iv. 184, 223
Hautrive, doctor, ii. 161, 162
Hawkherst, John, iii. 82
Hedecron, John, i. 4, 13, 97; iv. 159, 180, 217
Helder, Robert, ii. 176
Henfylde, Henry, iii. 45; iv. 64, 188, 189, 190, 223
— John, i. 37, 75; ii. 226, 229, 232, 271; iv. 148, 203–5, 223
Hengstrych, John, ii. 207
Henley, ii. 143–6; iii. 54
Henry, *see* Sutton
— carpenter, *see* William
— servant of William Sellynge I, iii. 111
Henry IV, iii. 57
Henry V, iii. 75, 76, 78–80; iv. 74, 224
Henry VII, iii. 226; iv. 201
Henry VIII, iii. 146, 147, 156, 157, 217; iv. 47, 226
Henslade, William, ii. 147

Hereford, ii. 157; iii. 123–5; iv. 98, 102, 128
Herne, Thomas, iii. 88–91
Herst, Nicholas, i. 110; iii. 143, 152; iv. 54
Hertwelle, John, iii. 29
Hethe, John, ii. 136, 138; iv. 223
— William de, iv. 178–80, 217
Hicham, P. de, iv. 170
Hieyne, William in the, iv. 15
Hille, N., iii. 78
Hinksey Hall, iii. 228–33, 237, 239
Holden, Richard, i. 7; iv. 75, 77, 223, 229
— Robert, iv. 206
Holond, Richard, ii. 137
Holwey, J., i. 30
Holyngborn, John, fellow, ii. 167, 171; iv. 194, 223
— John, novice, iv. 54
— Robert, i. 34, 37, 39, 80, 83, 84, 96, 106, 107; ii. 224, 226, 228, 229, 232, 233, 235, 238, 241, 244, 247, 271, 274; iii. 138–40, 227, 229, 234, 237, 239, 244, 250–2; iv. 62, 75–7, 101, 107, 119–21, 148, 159, 161, 164, 202–4, 230
Holy See, *see* Rome
Homer, iv. 83
Hopton, Robert, iii. 243, 244
Hordern, Trinity Hall, iii. 243, 245.
— Antony, monk, ii. 250, 255; iv. 223
Hore, Richard, ii. 168
— Robert, i. 7, 16
Hornsea, iv. 8
Horsepath, Helen of, iii. 69, 72
Howhyn, Thomas, iii. 227–30
Hubbard, Alexander, iii. 120
Hugeson, William, iii. 243, 244
Humfrey, esquire, ii. 189
— master, i. 4, 6, 14, 40, 61, 98; iv. 157
— Robert, iii. 225
— Thomas, ii. 188, 191, 193, 195, 197, 198, 200, 263, 264; iii. 115–18, 121; iv. 55, 74, 78, 94, 197, 198, 200, 201, 223, 229
Hunt, John, juror, iii. 219
— manciple, iii. 265, 266
Hurstbourne Priors, iii. 22
Husey, Henry, iii. 213
Hwytpeys, Thomas, iv. 188
Hyberden Richard, iii. 225
— Wilham, ii. 258

INDEX OF NAMES

Hyckham, Thomas, iii. 153
Hyde, ii. 188, 193, 207, 210; iv. 93, 94
Hyghwoode, John, iii. 209–12
Hynde, Roger, iii. 225

I, iv. 178; ?– James de Oxney, q.v.
Icham, R. de., iv. 179
Ingram, William, iv. 156, 217
Innocent III, i. 103; iv. 124
Islip, Northants., iv. 15
— Oxon., iv. 15
Islip, Simon, archbishop, iii. 1–5, 7–9, 11, 14–17, 19, 20, 23, 26, 30, 35, 36, 57, 158, 159, 172, 173, 179, 181, 182, 184–6, 221, 222, 224, 225; iv. 1, 2, 8–25, 27, 32, 33, 37, 39, 40, 45, 46, 55, 100, 131, 160, 183
— Simon, monk, ii. 248; iv. 75, 223
— William, archbishop's crossbearer, iii. 8
— William de, archbishop's nephew, iii. 4, 7, 8; iv. 14, 15
Israel, iii. 70.
Iudice, Marinus de, iii. 197
Ive, John, iv. 199

James, physician, iii. 79
James, M. R., iv. 83
Jamis, Robert, iii. 265
Jarrow, iv. 107, 112
Jerom, William, i. 76; ii. 259; iii. 148, 252, 269; iv. 48, 49, 53, 216
Jezabel, iii. 70
Jezrahel, iii. 70
Jocelyn, J., i. 112
John, clerk of John Langdon I, iii. 74
— master of the boys, iv. 180
— prior, iv. 192
John, King, iii. 223
Johnsons, P., iii. 150
Jordayne, Oliver, iii. 227–32, 234–7, 239, 240, 242
— see also Olyver

Kelseham, Richard, iii. 210
Kembar, iii. 243, 245
Kemp, John, iv. 103
Kenarton, William, iii. 47; iv. 188, 190
Kenelm, William, ii. 231
Kent, iii. 71; iv. 18, 52, 145, 150, 212
Kidderminster, Richard, ii. 224, 253; iii. 252, 262; iv. 59, 90, 101
King's College, iv. 47, 49, 50

Knole, iii. 141
Knygthe, Richard, iii. 82
Kyngston, R., i. 17, 77; ii. 148
Kynth, Robert, iii. 269
Kynton, John, iv. 52
— Thomas, ii. 179
Kyppyng, John, 1396, ii. 143
— John, c. 1473, iii. 113
Kyrton, John, ii. 199, 201

Lambarherst, John, iii. 152; iv. 54
Lambe, John, iii. 234–6, 238–44
Lambeth, iii. 39–41, 83, 100, 102, 106, 139, 148, 221; iv. 162, 215, 224
Lancastre, Roger, iii. 131
Lane, William, ii. 178
Lanfranc, iv. 51
Langdon, John I, i. 8; iii. 63, 68, 72–8, 80, 84; iv. 65, 74, 79, 191, 220, 224, 229
— John II, i. 31, 35, 36, 52, 58, 67, 109; ii. 195, 203, 206, 210, 215–18, 220, 263–6, 268–70, 272, 274; iii. 119, 120, 123, 128, 129, 131; iv. 63, 75, 77, 78, 90, 121, 198, 199, 201, 203, 222, 229, 230
John III, ii. 234, 236, 239, 250, 253; iii. 152, 242; iv. 54, 57, 204, 205, 224
— Thomas, iii. 154
Langham, Simon, iii. 11, 14–18, 24, 30, 31, 181, 184–93, 198, 206; iv. 17–27, 30–4, 36–40, 43, 45, 59, 100, 124, 160, 183–5
Langley, Peter, iii. 149, 150, 153; iv. 224
— Thomas, iii. 74
Langton, Robert, iii. 131
— Thomas, iii. 131
Larcomb, Thomas, iii. 267, 268
Lateran Council III, iv. 122
— IV, iv. 123
Latimer, William, iv. 82, 99, 104
— see also Lotomer
Laurence, see Newnham
Laurence Hall, iii. 237, 239
Laurens, Thomas, iii. 233
Lavant, iii. 221
Lavender, Joan, iii. 10; iv. 134
— John, iii. 49
Lawford, iii. 10
Leades, Edward, iii. 268
Leah, iii. 5, 172
Ledok, Philip, ii. 174, 176; iv. 125

Lee, N., iii. 129
— Thomas, monk of Christ Church, ii. 234; iv. 53, 224
— Thomas, monk of Milton, ii. 199, 201
Leeds, Kent, ii. 221; iv. 97
Leeff, John, ii. 257
Leland, John, iv. 72, 79, 80, 156, 159, 162
Lemstar (?Leominster), vicar of, ii. 244
Len, John, iii. 212
Le Stede, *see* Thornden
Lewes, ii. 213, 215, 229, 231, 250, 252, 256, 259; iii. 204; iv. 30, 93, 95
Leycestria, Thomas de, i. 12, 100; iv. 157
Lichfield, iii. 10, 12, 76, 194
Lillysden, ii. 137
Linacre, Thomas, iv. 46, 82, 83, 99, 100, 104
Linborne, William, iii. 228, 229, 235–7, 239–41, 243–5
Lincoln, diocese of, iii. 4, 12, 17, 33, 35, 60, 73, 75, 80, 93, 107, 184, 188, 191, 194, 198, 201, 202, 206, 266; iv. 4, 14, 39, 98, 101
Lincoln College, iii. 243
Lisieux, iii. 74–6, 78, 79; iv. 75
Litylwode, William, iii. 109
Loggan, David, iv. 50, 137, 138, 140, 142, 144
London, i. 109, 112; ii. 148, 149, 176, 181, 189, 206, 212; iii. 10, 36, 54, 64, 66, 67, 70, 76, 78, 80, 96, 111, 113, 127, 133, 137, 198, 255; iv. 29, 42, 66, 183, 185, 186, 188, 189, 192, 205, 206
— Paternoster Row, i. 112
— St. Bartholomew the Less, iii. 109
— St. Paul's, iv. 101
— — cross, iii. 151; iv. 48
— *see also* Southwark, Westminster
London, John, iii. 268
— William, iii. 153
London College, iii. 238
Longbeach, iv. 205, 206
Longland, John, iii. 266
Longworth, iii. 12
Lotomer, magister, ii. 256, 257, 259; iv. 98
— *see also* Latimer, William
Louvain, iii. 141, 142; iv. 81, 82, 95
Lovell, William, iii. 131

Lucca, iii. 109
Lucy, Geoffrey de, ii. 126, 128, 129, 131; iii. 38, 113, 181; iv. 32, 100, 102, 135, 143
Luke, i. 112
Lychefeld, Edmund, ii. 195
— W., iv. 54
— William, iii. 152
Lydbury, W. de, i. 12, 14, 98, 100 (89); iv. 157
Lynder, William, ii. 149; iv. 125
Lyndesey, Martin, i. 93; iii. 266
Lyndwood, William, iv. 124
Lynstede, Robert, ii. 160; iv. 194, 224
Lynton, Robert, i. 1, 12, 15, 100; ii. 147, 153, 154, 156, 160, 162, 163, 167, 173; iv. 75, 76, 107, 159, 160, 192, 193, 194, 224, 229

Magdalen College, iii. 134, 228–32, 237, 238, 243; iv. 65, 98, 139
Magium, Hugh, iii. 197
Maidstone, iii. 61, 103, 139
Maisters, Richard, iii. 156; iv. 49, 206
Malchair, J. B., iv. 139
Malinis, Peter de, iv. 101
Mallet, C. E., iv. 17
Malmesbury, iii. 21; iv. 93
Mandeville, John, iii. 69
Mantes, iii. 75
Marchall, Edmund, ii. 273, 274; iv. 224
— Richard, deacon, iii. 154
— Richard, treasurer, iv. 204
— Richard, warden of manors, ii. 235; iii. 227
Marcham, John, iii. 12, 13
Mare, Thomas de la, iii. 198; iv. 29
Mariole Hall, iii. 10, 11, 69; iv. 134
Markwyk, William, ii. 170, 174, 175; iv. 125
Marlow, iii. 66
Marre's tenement, iv. 132, 133, 136
Martin V, iii. 76, 78, 80
Martyn, Richard, iii. 245
Mary, B. V., iv. 31
Mason, John, iv. 213
— Roger, *see* Roger
— William, ii. 128
Mathew, John, ii. 132, 136, 137, 146
Maupas, Henry, iii. 59
May, Agnes, iii. 268; iv. 227
— John, ii. 172, 173
Maycot, Robert, iii. 215, 218

INDEX OF NAMES

Mayfield, iii. 3, 4, 8, 11, 15, 16, 60; iv. 13–15, 182
Meller, William, iii. 133
Menys, John, i. 79; iii. 131, 132, 152
Mepham, iv. 190
Mepham, Simon, iv. 213
Mereden, William, iii. 73; iv. 88
Merstone, John, iii. 54
Merton College, i. 93, 99; ii. 137, 173; iii. 49, 59, 68, 98, 158, 167, 237, 238; iv. 98, 139, 161, 162, 165
Mézières, Philippe de, iii. 197
Michael, magister, ii. 161
Michaeas, iii. 70
Middelton, H., i. 12; iv. 159
— John de, i. 100
— Thomas, i. 100
— William, al. Milton, i. 100; ii. 129; iii. 45; iv. 159, 160
Middilworth, William, ii. 130; iii. 33, 198, 201, 202; iv. 17, 20, 21, 32, 33, 135–7
Milan, iii. 188–91, 199; iv. 22, 25
Mildred Hall, iii. 229–33
Millys, *see* Warham, John
Milton, iii. 12
Milton abbey, ii. 201, 204, 207, 210; iv. 93
Milton, T., iii. 143; iv. 54
— William, iii. 45; iv. 188, 224
— *see also* Middelton
Minster, i. 110
Missenden, iv. 91
Missinden, John, ii. 197, 202; iv. 91
Mochelne, William, ii. 127
Mokelle, Richard, iv. 206
Molasche, W., monk, iv. 54
— William, prior, i. 2, 10, 29; ii. 153; iii. 72, 95; iv. 74, 77, 193, 225, 227, 229
Monday, Thomas, iii. 267
— William, iii. 267
Mondham, William de, iv. 4, 211
Mongeham, Stephen, iii. 28; iv. 34, 35, 74, 185, 225, 229
Monkynkey, iv. 202
Mons, duke of, iii. 75
Montefiascone, iii. 194–7, 206; iv. 28, 29, 31
Monyngham, *see* Mongeham
Mordant, magister, iii. 232
Morden, Thomas, iii. 74
More, Cressacre, iv. 99
More, John, ii. 189; iv. 100

— Thomas, iii. 225; iv. 46, 82, 99, 100, 104, 227
Morell, Richard, iii. 211, 212
— Thomas, iii. 211, 212
Morgan, Philip, iii. 66, 67
Morton, John, cardinal, i. vi, 31, 35, 51, 56, 65, 72, 78, 83; ii. 271, 273, 274; iii. viii, 120, 139, 225, 227ff.; iv. 46, 57, 63, 77, 99, 101, 148, 221
— John, monk, ii. 272; iii. 152; iv. 225
Morwen, Robert, ii. 258
Motlowe, Thomas, iii. 62
Muchelney, ii. 179, 191, 193, 207, 210, 221; iv. 93, 95
Mundham, South, ii. 171–4, 176; iii. 156, 209; iv. 125, 185, 197, 198
Muskham, Wiliam de, iv. 4
Mylle, John, iii. 225
Mylles, iv. 206
Mynnes, *see* Menys
Mysden, *see* Missinden

N., John, iii. 136
Naboth, iii. 70
Naples, iii. 74
Napper, John, iii. 225
Natyndon, Henry de, i. 12, 30, 52, 58, 100
— Thomas de, iv. 213
Nawnt, David, iii. 84, 86
Neirefordé, W. de, i. 4, 12, 97; iv. 157
Nekton, Roger, iii. 97
Nele, James, iv. 201
Neville, George, iv. 65
— John, ii. 247
— Robert, i. 79
Neville's Inn, iii. 228–33, 237
New College, ii. 126, 240, 251, 257, 261; iii. 51, 57, 67, 112, 228–33, 237, 238, 243; iv. 46, 90, 98, 101–3, 135, 137, 139
New Inn Hall, iii. 228, 230–3, 237, 239, 243
Newbery, John, iii. 152
Newington, ii. 137, 251, 271, 274; iii. 29, 52, 53, 120, 121, 123; iv. 5, 75, 175, 179, 211
Newnham, James, iii. 153
— Lawrence, ii. 258; iii. 143; iv. 54, 206, 225
— Richard, ii. 196
Newport, John, ii. 133, 135; iv. 88
Newton, John, ii. 173; iv. 53

Newyngton, Robert, iv. 204
— Thomas, ii. 231
Nicholas IV, iv. 123, 127
Nicholas, larderer's servant, iii. 133
— letter-carrier; iv. 183, 187
Nigel, messenger, iv. 183, 184
— Wireker, i. 5, 13, 22, 59, 98; iv. 157
Nixon, iii. 266
— widow, iii. 269
Noble, John, iii. 264
Noke, ii. 196
Normandy, iii. 75, 76, 78, 79
Northampton, ii. 129; iii. 96, 97
Northbourne, John de, iv. 213
Northon, Richard, ii. 143 (?also 141)
— William, iii. 29
Norton, John, 1373, iii. 29
— John, chancellor of Salisbury, iii. 204; iv. 30
Norwich, iii. 91, 126, 206; iv. 7, 8, 31, 93, 160
Norwyco, Walter de, i. 6, 14, 99; iv. 157

Oake, iii. 206
Odyngell, see Orynshals
Ollyar, ii. 274
Olyver, magister (?=Oliver Jordayne), iii. 243, 244
Olyver, John, iii. 269, 270
Orgarswick, iii. 135
Oriel College (aula regalis), ii. 143, 147, 151, 154, 163, 167, 187, 189; iii. 49, 82, 102, 111, 227-33, 239, 243; iv. 8, 91, 101, 132, 133
— John, manciple of, iv. 91
Orleans, iv. 3
Orynchals, John, iii. 271, 272
Osney, iii. 55; iv. 50
Otford, iii. 16, 18, 46, 48, 76, 143, 146; iv. 20, 187, 189
Otforde, Bartholomew, iii. 153
— John, iv. 205
— Roger, ii. 272, 273; iii. 252, 253, 257; iv. 57, 64, 225
Overbury, iv. 7
Oxford, archdeacon of, iii. 198, 201; iv. 29, 39
Oxford, city of, aldermen of, iii. 102
— All Saints, ii. 189
— bailiffs, ii. 130, 148, 151, 154, 238; iii. 6, 7, 56, 102
— Bear Lane, iv. 131, 132
— Carfax, iii. 55

— chamberlains, ii. 163, 167, 171, 174, 199, 208, 212, 217, 220, 223, 225, 228, 231, 232, 235, 243, 246, 252; iii. 57, 102
— domus Dei, ii. 128
— iurati, ii. 182, 184, 197
— mayor, ii. 130, 189; iii. 29, 56, 102; iv. 133
— St Aldate's, ii. 128; iii. 38
— St Edward's parish, iii. 10, 33, 49, 59; iv. 133
— St Edward's St., iii. 28, 33; iv. 131, 132, 134, 135, 143
— St Mary's, iii. 144, 145, 156, 247, 248, 253, 255-7, 260, 262; iv. 133
— St Peter's in the East, iv. 2, 4, 113, 211, 213
— School St., iii. 170
— Shidyard St., iii. 56; iv. 131, 132, 134-7
— Shitebarne Lane, iv. 131, 133-6
— Stockwell St., iii. 21, 50
— sureties from, ii. 189
— town clerk, ii. 128
Oxford, Council of, iv. 123
Oxford, diocese of, iii. 157
Oxford, university of
— and council of Basel, iii. 89
— scholars of, ii. 161
Oxforde, Thomas, ii. 138, 140; iv. 225
Oxney, James, de, iii. 38; iv. 5, 6, 72, 178-81, 212, 217
— John, prior, ii. 264; iii. 108, 110
— John, treasurer, iii. 152

Padua, iv. 103
Pagham, ii. 126-9, 131, 147-50, 153-5, 160, 162-4, 166-70, 172, 174-6, 262; iii. 1, 5, 9, 16, 17, 19, 20, 22-6, 31, 32, 34, 35, 41, 43, 156, 172, 175, 181, 184-7, 189-91, 199, 207ff.; iv. 8-12, 14-16, 20-5, 28, 30, 32-5, 37-40, 42, 43, 49, 66, 85, 90, 108, 111, 112, 114, 122ff., 184, 185, 191, 197, 198
Paleologus, Manuel, iv. 79
Palestine, iv. 104
Pamfield, iv. 101
Pantin, W. A., i. viii; iv. 1ff.
Paris, i. 98; iii. 89, 130, 153; iv. 3, 71, 78, 79, 81, 82, 95, 167, 173, 174, 209, 215, 216, 222, 227
Parkehurst, Richard, i. 78
Parker, Matthew, i.112

INDEX OF NAMES

— parson, iv. 49
Paul Hall, iii. 86
Pavia, iv. 63, 79, 191
Payne, dominus, iii. 235–42, 244
Pecham, John, iv. 123
— William, i. 62; ii. 256, 258, 272–4; iii. 253, 254; iv. 63, 108, 165, 205, 206, 225
Peckwater Inn, iii. 157, 230, 239, 267; iv. 47, 207
Pekoke, magister, ii. 251; iii. 243
— William, son of, iii. 243, 244
Pelle, Stephen, iii. 228–37, 239–41
Penshurst, iii. 120
Perham, William, iii. 228–34
Permystede, Arnold, ii. 174, 176, 180, 183; iii. 105, 254; iv. 61, 62, 75, 196, 225
Perne, Thomas, ii. 178
Pershore, iii. 70; iv. 93
Persons, John, ii. 229
Perys, iii. 150
Peter, dauber, ii. 144, 145
— Sir, ii. 127; *see* Beamunde
Peterborough, ii. 175, 179, 180, 182, 185, 188, 190, 193–5, 198, 200, 201, 204, 207, 210, 212, 213, 215, 218, 221, 222, 224, 252; iii. vii, 64, 67, 96, 121; iv. 92–7
— seneschal of, iii. 96, 97
— William, monk of, iii. 96
Pettham, J., i. 2, 10
— William I, i. 29, 51, 56, 72; ii. 171, 172, 176; iii. 110, 254; iv. 64, 74, 194, 195, 198, 225
— William II, ii. 256, 272, 274; iv. 206, 225
Petyr, John, ii. 207
Peveher, Richard, iii. 227–32, 235–8, 240–4
Pfahon, Richard, iii. 227–31
Phasaninus, Nicolaus, iii. 131
Philip, carpenter, ii. 141–3
— friar, iv. 168, 169
Phissher, *see* Fisher
Piacenza, iii. 78
Piard de Buciaco, Iohannes, iii. 197
Pichaver, W., iv. 207
Piddington, iii. 206
Pisa, iv. 220
Playford, John, iii. 126
Pocock, John, iv. 191
Poggio, iv. 104
Poissy, iv. 78
Poitiers, iv. 31
Pole, Thomas, iii. 84–6
Politian, iv. 80, 82
Polsted, Henry, iii. 214, 219
Polton, Thomas, iii. 76
Polyng, Henry, iii. 225
Ponet, Henry, iii. 219
Pont, Hugh, iii. 232
Ponthoys, Robert de, iv. 216
Pontoise, iii. 75
Popering, William de, iv. 175
Poterel, Geoffrey, iv. 174, 210, 218
Potkyn, James, iii. 230, 231, 233, 234, 237
— Peter, iii. 228, 230, 232, 235, 236, 239–43, 245
— William, iii. 263
Poucin, Robert, i. 4, 11, 97
Powden, *see* Bowden
Poyns, magister, ii. 256
Prat, T., iv. 193
Prester John, iii. 68ff.
Preston, William de, iii. 206
Prignano, Bartholomew, iii. 197
Prophete, T., ii. 133, 135; iv. 88
Proteus, iii. 69
Pryse, *see* ap Rhys
Pulton, Giles, iii. 136
— Katherine, iii. 136
— Margaret, iii. 136
— W., ii. 208
Pyel, John, iv. 16
Pygot, Henry, iii. 110
Pyrry, Thomas, iii. 214–20, 223

Queen's College, i. 101; iii. 49; iv. 4, 33
Quenyngate, Richard, i. 16, 32, 38, 77; iv. 75, 76, 225
Quylter, John jr., iii. 238–42, 244, 245
— John sr., ii. 272; iii. 234–6, 238, 240–2

R., lector, iv. 171, 173; = Radulphus and perh. Randulfus, q.v.
Rachel, iii. 5, 172
Radulphus (R.), lector, iv. 171, 173; *see also* Randulphus
Ramsey, iv. 93
Ramsey, William, iv. 94
Randulfus, iv. 169; *see also* Radulphus
Rashdall, H., iv. 45
Raulens, John, iii. 239

Raven, John, iii. 131
Raynold, John, ii. 225
Reading, ii. 155, 175, 179, 180, 182, 189, 199, 200, 204, 213, 215, 218, 219, 221, 223, 224, 229, 236, 239, 240, 245, 250, 252, 259; iv. 93-5, 138, 141
— Edward, monk of, ii. 175
Recolver, Thomas, iii. 45, 47; iv. 225
— William, iv. 182, 218
Rede, John, ii. 178, 196
Redyng, Henry, ii. 223, 226, 231
Redyngate, John de, iii. 2, 14-16, 20, 22; iv. 12, 19, 35, 183, 225, 229
Refham, William de, i. 5, 13, 98; iv. 157
Repyngdon, Philip, i. 101
Respese, magister, iii. 238-41
Rever, A. de, iii. 66
Reynham, John de, iii. 12-14, 58; iv. 32
Reynold, John, i. 69
Reynolds, Walter, iv. 69
Reynoldus, bedel, iv. 169
Rheims, Ralph of, i. 23, 47, 103; iv. 157
Ricardus, *see* Godmersham, ii. 135
Richard II, iii. 37, 49, 51, 52, 57, 59
Richard, dauber, ii. 144, 145
— mason (?= Richard Northon, q.v.) ii. 141
— prior, iv. 184
Richemonde, William I, iii. 2, 15, 22; iv. 12, 35, 190, 225, 229
— William II, i. 12, 16, 77, 100; ii. 154, 160, 163, 167, 173; iii. 96-8, 101; iv. 75, 76, 96, 159, 160, 192, 194, 225
Ringmere, Thomas de, i. 15, 100; iv. 157
Risborough, ii. 141, 153, 274; iii. 28; iv. 75, 125, 226
Roberd, John, i. 112
Robert, lector, iv. 176; = Robert de Fulham, q.v.
Roche, Androin de la, iii. 184, 187-202; iv. 24, 26-9
Rochester, ii. 179, 180, 182, 185, 186, 188, 195, 199, 200, 203, 204, 206, 210, 215, 218, 221, 247; iii. 10, 55, 63, 127; iv. 65, 75, 93, 95, 139, 141, 218-20
— bishop of, iii. 8, 10, 84
Rochester, John, ii. 165; iii. 97

Roger, carpenter, ii. 145
— mason, ii. 141, 143, 144; iii. 56
Rogers, John, iii. 265
Rome, i. 98, 103; ii. 126; iii. 16-18, 34, 36, 73, 74, 76, 77, 81, 94, 108, 109, 166, 184ff.; iv. 2, 7, 15-18, 20-3, 25, 29, 30, 33-5, 38-40, 79, 80, 82, 101, 123, 183, 185-8, 195, 217, 218
Romenall, G. de, i. 3, 5, 11, 14, 40, 97; iv. 157
Romney, iii. 112; iv. 76, 102
Roo, Richard, iii. 219
Roper, iii. 225, 226
Rosell, T., iii. 78
Ross, iv. 67
Rouen, William de, iii. 197, 198
Rowchester, *see* Rochester
Roydam, Geoffrey, iii. 197
Ruddington, iv. 8
Rugge, Robert, ii. 126, 127; iv. 98
Rumsey, Richard, ii. 207

S., filius Sparuwe, iv. 170
St Albans, iii. 198; iv. 7, 8, 29, 71, 93, 221
St Asaph, iii. 147
St Benedict, iii. 149; iv. 150, 218, 221
St Bernard, iv. 55
St Edward's Hall, iii. 157; iv. 133
St Elphege, iv. 150
St Frideswide's, ii. 128, 130, 140, 147, 151, 154, 161, 163, 167, 171, 174, 176, 177, 182, 184, 187, 190, 192, 194, 197-9, 202, 206, 208, 212, 217, 220, 223, 225, 228, 230, 232, 235, 237, 239, 243, 246, 249, 251, 254, 257, 258, 261; iii. 6, 7, 10, 27, 28, 31, 49, 50, 156, 157; iv. 5, 15, 32, 37, 47, 131, 132, 134, 136
— cemetery, iii. 11; iv. 131, 132
— church, iii. 59; iv. 76, 221
— clerk, ii. 139
— cross, iii. 261
— Nicholas, prior, iii. 10
— sacrist, ii. 217; iv. 91
St Gabriel, iii. 72
St Germans, John of, iv. 213
St Gregory, iii. 149; iv. 55
St Gregory's, prior of, ii. 130
St Ives, Hugh of, iv. 5, 71, 177, 178, 211, 212, 218
St Jerome, iv. 150, 221
St Mary College, iv. 97, 163

INDEX OF NAMES

St Mary Hall, iii. 237, 238, 243, 245, 265, 266, 271
St Mary Magdalen, iv. 220
St Michael's Hall, iii. 10, 49; iv. 136
St Paul, iii. 71, 104
St Thomas of Canterbury, *see* Becket
— More, *see* More
Salisbury, iii. 64, 74, 194, 198, 204; iv. 30, 135
Salter, H. E., iii. 68, 263
Saltwood, iii. 23, 60; iv. 186
Sancta Mildreda, R. de, i. 4, 12, 30, 97; iv. 153
Sancto Nicholao, Thomas de, i. 6, 15, 99, 100
Sandwich, iii. 135; iv. 174, 202
Sandwyche, William, i. 72; ii. 256, 258, 272; iii. 148, 151, 152, 154, 155, 255, 269, 270, 271; iv. 48, 77, 107, 216, 225, 230
Sarysbury, John, early 15th c., i. 2, 7, 8, 10, 16, 29, 77; iii. 69, 71, 83, 84, 88, 91, 94; iv. 54, 65, 74, 79, 226, 227, 229
— John, 16th c., i. 110; iii. 152; iv. 54, 222
Saul, iii. 71
Sautri, William, ii. 141
Savage, William, iii. 51; iv. 137
Savine, A., iv. 124
Sawyer, Roger, ii. 163; iv. 125
— William, iii. 211, 212
Scarle, iii. 53
Scarlet, John, iii. 272
Schamerege, iii. 153, 168
Schowhe, Arthur, iii. 227–9
— William, iii. 227, 228
Sclapple, John, ii. 140, 144–6
Sclepynden, John (William), iii. 228–37, 239–43, 245
Scot, John, ii. 197
Searle, W. G., iv. 51, 215
Segninus, iii. 188, 190–2
Selby, William, iii. 198, 201, 202; iv. 17, 20, 21, 33
Selgrave, iii. 59; iv. 191
Sellynge, Richard, ii. 267, 269, 270; iii. 126, 127; iv. 56, 64, 226
— William I, i. vi, 31, 109, 113; ii. 174, 176, 180, 183, 212, 267; iii. viii, 105, 107–9, 112, 113, 116–20, 122–6; 128, 129, 131, 135, 255; iv. 46, 55, 56, 67, 73, 74, 77, 79–84, 99–104, 148, 159, 162, 196, 197, 203, 222, 226
— William II, ii. 241, 245, 248, 250, 253, 256, 271–3; iii. 136–8, 247, 256; iv. 61, 63, 75, 205, 206, 226
Sentleger, Arthur, i. 78
Shakeston, dominus, iii. 238–44
Sharpe, John, iv. 202
Shaw, iii. 64
Shawe, Alexander, iii. 212, 213
Sheffield, Robert, iii. 111
Shelde Hall, iii. 10, 69; iv. 134
Shepeye, John, iv. 54, 205, 226
Sheppard, J. B., iii. 18, 31; iv. 13, 45, 51, 52
Sheppey, John de, bp. of Rochester, iv. 218
Sherborn, Robert, iii. 210
Sherborne, ii. 191, 201, 204, 207, 210, 218, 221; iv. 93, 95
Ship Hall, ii. 131; iii. 28, 29, 33, 49, 56; iv. 131–3, 135–7, 142
Simon, dauber, 144–6
— subprior, i. 5, 13, 98; iv. 157
Sittingbourne, iii. 128
Skelton, William, ii. 152
Slinfold, Sussex, iii. 213
Smyth, John, O.F.M., iii. 252
— John, poor scholar, iii. 101
— M., iii. 141
— Richard, iii. 272
— Thomas, ii. 153–5, 160, 166, 170; iv. 125
Snawdone, William, iv. 205, 206
Soper, Nicholas, iii. 211, 212
— Thomas, iii. 209
Southam, Thomas, iii. 198, 201, 202, 206; iv. 29, 30, 34, 39, 40
— William, iii. 56
Southampton, iv. 37
Southchurch, ii. 200
Southwark, ii. 126; iii. 211; iv. 128
Spain, ambassador of, ii. 254; iv. 101
Spalding, iv. 219
Spaldyng tenement, iii. 28; iv. 133, 134, 135, 136
Spaldynges, Adam de, iv. 136
Sparuwe, iv. 170
Spicer, John, ii. 140, 148, 151, 154; iii. 51, 56; iv. 137
— heirs of, ii. 177, 182, 184, 187, 190, 192, 194, 197–9, 206, 208, 212, 215, 217, 220, 223, 225, 228, 231, 232, 235, 238, 243, 246, 249, 254, 257, 259; iii. 51

Spilman, iii. 225
Spragat, Richard, iii. 102
Spryng, Agnes, i. 95
Stafford, John, iii. 98–103; iv. 88, 193
Standwyche, Edward, iii. 227–9, 231, 232, 234–42
Stanton, Roger, iii. 56
Stapilton, John, iii. 225
Staple Hall, iv. 106, 132, 134
Stapyll, Alexander, iv. 53, 54
Starkey, John, iv. 206
Stepney, iv. 48
Stevenirs, John, iii. 74
Stevenys, Thomas, iv. 101
— William, ii. 187, 189
Stillington, Robert, iii. 99; iv. 88
Stok, John, ii. 127
Stokes, John, iii. 74, 75
— John, warden of All Souls, iii. 111
Stone in Oxney, iv. 7
Stone, John, iii. 153
— Richard, i. 88, 108, 110
— William, iv. 187, 188, 226
Stonor, John, ii. 180, 181
Stonys, Richard, ii. 204, 207
Story, T., i. 3, 11, 97; iv. 157
Stoyl, Thomas, i. 4, 5, 11, 13, 22, 42, 97, 98, 105; iv. 157, 175
Stretelegh, Agnes de, iii. 28
Stureya, *see* Story
Style, John, i. 80; iv. 87
Stystede, R., iv. 182
Suardeby, iii. 18
Sudbury, John, iv. 54
— Simon, i. 1–3, 10, 28, 34, 51, 56, 65; iii. 34, 36, 45, 181, 198; iv. 29, 40, 41, 42, 46, 100, 186
— William, iii. 153
Suffolk, Michael, fourth earl of, iii. 85
Surrey, iii. 75
Sussex, iii. 155, 219, 223; iv. 122
Sutton, iii. 17
Sutton, Henry, ii. 132, 133, 135, 136, 138, 140; iv. 226
— John, iv. 205
— Robert, 1438; iii. 95; iv. 226
— Robert, 1518; iv. 206
Swalowe, John, iii. 82
Swambour, John, iii. 54
Swan, William, iii. 73, 75–7, 80
Swyndon, Thomas, ii. 127
Swynesford's entry, iii. 10, 49; iv. 134
Sylksted, Thomas, ii. 253
Syon, i. 96; iv. 164

Syvyer, *see* Whytwey

T., prior = Thomas de Ringmere, q.v.
Talbot, John, ii. 229, 231, 236, 237, 239, 241, 244, 247, 249
Tankervile, William, iii. 10
Taupener, Thomas, ii. 163; iv. 125
Tavistock, ii. 180, 182; iv. 93
Taylour, Christopher, iv. 206
— William, iv. 224
Teb, Agnes, iii. 267, 268
— Robert, iii. 267, 268
Temple, John, 1443, i. 2, 10
— John, 1477, ii. 199, 201
Tetsworth, iii. 127
Tewkesbury, iv. 93
Thames, iv. 66, 93, 121
Thaycher, John, iii. 270–2; iv. 47
Theodoric, *see* Grembergh
Thomas, glasier, ii. 143, 145
Thoralby, John, iii. 59
Thore, magister, ii. 213
Thornbery, William, iv. 194; = Thornden, William, q.v.
Thornden, Richard, al. Le Stede, i. 65, 72, 75, 78; ii. 259, 272–4; iii. 146, 147, 152, 154, 213, 253, 257–9, 265–9; iv. 48, 61, 64, 65, 74, 77, 78, 82, 107, 206, 226, 230
— William, i. 9, 15, 16, 101; ii. 154, 160, 163, 165, 167, 171, 174, 176, 178, 179; iii. 98, 100, 259; iv. 61, 62, 77, 107, 127, 159, 160, 192, 194, 196, 198, 199, 226, 229
Throwley, iv. 175
Throwley, Haymo, ii. 234, 236, 239, 241, 244, 246; iv. 75, 76, 227
— John, i. 112; ii. 256, 258; iii. 152, 260, 261; iv. 227
Thurstan, provost of Beverley, i. 102
Tille, iii. 109
Tiptoft, John, iii. 103, 104; iv. 79, 82, 84, 103, 104
Titchfield, i. 99
Tokenham, Thomas, ii. 132, 133, 135, 136, 138, 140; iii. 59; iv. 227, 229
Toller, John, ii. 266
Topclyve, William, iv. 186
Toryndenne, William, iv. 193
Toting, Thomas, iv. 169
Totnes, iv. 128
Tounysende, John, iii. 51; iv. 137

INDEX OF NAMES

Tournai, iv. 147
Tredcroft, William, iii. 225
Tregeran, John, ii. 163, 167, 171, 174, 192, 194; iii. 136
— Margaret, iii. 136
Tremfeld, W. de, iv. 169
Tresham, William, iii. 266, 267, 269, 271
Trinity College, iv. 137
Trinity Hall, iii. 228–30, 237, 239, 243
Turpyn, see Hathfelde
Twayt, Thomas, iii. 269
Twyne, Brian, iii. 263; iv. 135
Tyll, Richard, ii. 262, 266, 267; iii. 122; iv. 83, 100, 201
— William, iv. 201
Tylneye, John, iii. 17.
Tyndall, Henry, iii. 262
Tyrwhit, Thomas, iii. 53, 54
Tystede, Thomas, iii. 149, 150
Tyverton, T., ii. 207

Umfray, see Humfrey
University College, ii. 130, 140, 148, 151, 154, 161, 163, 167, 171, 174, 177, 182, 184, 187, 190, 192, 194, 197–9, 206, 208, 212, 217, 220, 223, 228, 231, 232, 235, 238, 239, 243, 246, 249, 251, 254, 257, 259, 261; iii. 49; iv. 136, 160
Upton, John de, iii. 16, 206; iv. 20
Urban V, iii. 8, 9, 24, 184, 187, 189–91, 197, 198, 202, 206; iv. 22, 24–7, 29, 184
Urban VI, iii. 34, 173, 197; iv. 40
Urbino, iv. 101, 226
Ursins, Jordan des, iii. 74
Uxbridge, iii. 127

Valla, Lorenzo, iv. 104
Vaughan, see Pfahon
Venice, iv. 101
Verity, monk, iv. 53
Vestynden, John, ii. 156
Videan, Richard, iii. 139
— Roger, iii. 139, 244, 245
Vienne, iii. 33
Vincentius de Castro Novo, iii. 130
Vine Hall, ii. 141, 156, 186, 202, 205; iii. 28, 33, 49, 56, 57, 157; iv. 32, 100, 131–3, 135–7, 142, 143
— houses by, ii. 205, 222
Vitelli, Cornelio, iv. 103

Viterbo, iii. 194, 195, 199–202; iv. 28
Vives, J. L., iv. 82
Vowle, William, iv. 205
Vuicht, William, iv. 172
Vynch, see Fynche

W., prior, see Molasche
— subprior, iv. 174
— treasurer, i. 103
W. B., magister, iii. 12
W. R., poor scholar, iii. 101
Waddon, John, ii. 142, 143, 146
Wainflete, Thomas, iv. 203
Wakering, Thomas, i. 10, 77
Walden, iv. 2
Walden, John, iii. 61
Wales, iii. 130
Waleys, John, iii. 8
Walker, Thomas, iv. 46
Wallingford, magister, ii. 187, 190
Walter, mason, ii. 146
Walter, William, iii. 130
Waltham, John I, i. 15, 101; ii. 147, 154, 159, 162, 166; iii. 87, 90, 91, 93, 95, 97, 113; iv. 96, 159, 160, 192, 227, 229
— John II, i. 37; ii. 224, 226, 228, 229, 232, 270, 271, 274; iv. 148, 202, 203, 205, 227
John III, iii. 153; iv. 81, 216, 227
Walton, Thomas de, 1380, iii. 38
— Thomas, vicar of Bersted, iii. 207, 208; iv. 124
Ward, Richard, iii. 135
— Thomas, iii. 67
— Thomas, scholar, iii. 61; iv. 88
Warham, John, al. Millys, i. 76; iii. 151, 153, 261, 262, 268; iv. 49, 216, 227
— William, archbishop, iii. 138, 139, 141, 143, 144, 146, 262, 266; iv. 215, 219, 220, 222, 223, 227
— William, clerk, iii. 136
Warneham, iii. 156
Warton, John, iii. 227–32, 234–7
Wearmouth, iv. 107, 112
Webbe, John, ii. 146
Wells, ii. 185; iv. 98, 101
Wellys, Robert, iii. 67
Welwyke, John de, i. 42, 105
West, Nicholas, iii. 131
Westfaling, Herbert, iv. 207
Westfylde, Clement, ii. 241
Westgate, John, iii. 91

Westminster, iii. 2, 21, 22, 26, 31, 50, 53, 59, 127, 214, 217–20, 226; iv. 4, 7, 18, 35, 36, 53, 66, 93, 114, 122
— St Stephen's, iv. 101
Whatlyngton, Godfrey, ii. 174, 176; iv. 125
Whitby, iv. 93
White, John, ii. 196
— Philip, iii. 212
— Thomas, ii. 257
White Hall, iii. 266
— part of college site, iii. 10, 49; iv. 133, 134, 136
Whittlesey, William, iii. 8, 10, 20, 22, 26, 225; iv. 33–5, 37, 186
Whytwey al. Syvyer, William, iii. 209
Wibert, iv. 102
Wilkins, D., iv. 12, 13, 24, 45
Willesborough, iv. 7
William, carpenter, ii. 145
— carrier, iii. 133
— friar, iv. 170
— ironmonger, ii. 143, 146, 147
— surgeon, iv. 172
William, Henry, ii. 140, 141, 143, 144, 146
— Robert, iv. 191
Williams, John, iii. 265, 266
— W., iv. 137–41
Wilson, Margery, iii. 268
— Ralph, iii. 268
Winchcomb, ii. 224, 226, 229, 231, 236; iv. 59, 90, 93, 101
— abbot of, ii. 253; iii. 252, 262; *see also* Kidderminster, Richard
Wincheap, William, i. 91; iii. 182
Winchelsea, iii. 34; iv. 40, 53
Winchelsey, John, iii. 143; iv. 54
— Robert, i. 3, 11, 97, 100; iv. 69, 157
Winchester, i. vii, 28; ii. 175, 179, 180, 182, 185, 188, 190, 193–5, 198–202, 204, 207, 210, 212, 213, 224, 226, 229, 236, 237, 239, 241, 244, 247, 249, 250, 252, 256, 257, 259; iii. 149; iv. 7, 93–5, 118, 121, 141, 150, 188
— bishop of, ii. 128
— prior of, ii. 253; iv. 101
— warden of college, iii. 112; iv. 101
Windsor, iii. 52; iv. 98
Wingham, iii. 36
Wireker, *see* Nigel
Witney, iii. 107; iv. 101
Wmffray, *see* Humfrey

Wodehey, R., iv. 174
Wodehull, Henry, i. 4, 12, 97; iii. 2, 3, 15, 16, 158, 185–7, 192–6, 198, 200–3; 205; iv. 12, 13, 17–20, 22, 23, 25, 27, 28, 30, 35, 52, 64, 71, 77, 159, 182, 183, 227, 229
— John, iv. 186
Wodeland, Richard, iii. 8, 10
Wodnysbrowgh, John, prior, ii. 137; iii. 55, 83; iv. 118, 191, 218
— John, warden, ii. 147, 150, 151, 162, 163, 170; iii. 82–4, 86–93, 95, 102, 263; iv. 54, 63, 65, 73, 77, 79, 191, 192, 227, 229
Woghop, John, ii. 133, 135; iv. 88
— William, iii. 18, 28; iv. 185, 187, 227
Wokyngham, Richard, ii. 203
Wolgere, Thomas, iii. 209
Wolton, Thomas de, iii. 8, 12, 13, 14, 58; iv. 32
Wood, Antony, iii. 266, 267; iv. 138
Woodford, iii. 4, 7, 8; iv. 14, 15, 16, 24
Woodman, Robert, iii. 265; iv. 91
Woodstock, iii. 56, 67
Worcester, i. 98, 99, 101; ii. 185, 188, 189; iii. 62, 66, 81, 91, 206; iv. 7, 93
— earl of, *see* Tiptoft
Worcester, Thomas, ii. 241, 247
— William, iv. 83
Workman, H. B., iv. 18, 30, 34
Wootton, Antony, i. 84, 87, 106, 109; iv. 119, 120, 228
— John, iii. 7; iv. 228
— Nicholas, iii. 156
Wragge, John, iv. 205
Wucton, John, iv. 191
Wultrop, William, ii. 207
Wurthiall, John, iii. 264
Wy, John, i. 3, 7, 11; iv. 75, 76, 228
Wyclif, John, iii. 11, 16, 158, 184–7, 193–6, 198–204; iv. 17–25, 28, 29, 33, 34, 39, 71, 98, 137
Wyclivislond, ii. 130; iv. 32, 137
Wycomb, iii. 64, 127
Wykeham, William of, ii. 126, 128; iv. 132
Wykyng, Thomas, i. 10, 29; iii. 60, 77; iv. 228, 229
Wylde, John, iii. 262
Wylfryde, Thomas, iii. 143, 153; iv. 54, 81, 228

Wynbourne, John de, i. 14, 100; iv. 160
Wynchecombe, Thomas, iii. 81
Wyngham, William, iii. 152; iv. 54
Wynnesbury, Margaret, iv. 4
— Thomas, iv. 4
Wyse, ii. 259

Wystowhe, Humfrey, iii. 227–30
— Richard, iii. 227–32, 234–7, 239–42, 244
— Stephen, iii. 227–30, 238

York, i. 98, 103, 106; iii. 70, 72, 76, 198; iv. 8, 66, 93, 101, 194

INDEX OF SUBJECTS

Abacus, i. 37, 38; iv. 144, 148
— *see also* Counter-boards
Abstinence, *see* Meat
Accounts, i. vii, 8, 32; iii. 169, 170, 175; iv. 5–8, 56, 57, 63, 64, 67, 85, 90–5, 107, 108ff., 125, 127, 128, 140, 141, 144, 146, 148, 162, 167ff., 215, 226
Act, iii. 253, 255, 258
Administrator, iii. 39, 40, 41
Alabaster, i. 1, 9, 28, 34, 50, 53, 55, 63, 65, 68, 70, 75, 108; iv. 150
Albs, i. 1, 2, 10, 11, 28, 29, 30, 31, 35, 51, 52, 56, 57, 58, 65, 66, 72, 73, 78, 89; ii. 171, 175, 208, 211, 219, 222, 224, 227, 230, 232, 240, 248, 250, 258; iv. 170
Alienations, iii. 168, 175
Alms, ii. 129, 131; iv. 147
Almuces, iv. 119
Altar-cloths, i. 2, 3, 52, 58, 67, 74, 171, 181; ii. 224, 230, 232
Altar-covers, i. 30, 35, 58, 67, 73; ii. 230
Altar-hangings, i. 1–3, 9–11, 28–31, 34, 51, 52, 56, 57, 65, 67, 72, 73, 89; ii. 196, 219; iv. 145, 151
Altars, i. 1–3, 9–11, 29–31, 34–6, 51, 52, 55–8, 65, 67, 70, 73, 74; ii. 131, 164, 181, 230; iii. 112, 114; iv. 102, 108, 150, 151, 153
Amber, i. 83, 87, 90
Amercements, ii. 149, 173; iv. 126
Amices, i. 78, 84, 87, 90; ii. 175; iv. 118, 119
Andirons, i. 37, 38; ii. 209; iv. 144, 148
Andwene, ii. 134
Antiphons, i. 36; iii. 170, 180, 182
Appropriation, iv. 7, 8, 10–12, 14, 15, 24, 39, 112, 122, 123ff., 185
Archdeacon, ii. 157, ?= Thomas Chichele, q.v.
Arrows, i. 90
Arts, iii. 126, 127, 144, 145, 160, 161, 165, 169, 170, 249, 254, 260; iv. 58, 59, 60, 63, 64, 87, 91
Aumbry, ii. 178
Axes, i. 17; ii. 152, 186; iv. 146

Bachelors, i. 53, 63, 68; iii. 113, 144, 145, 168, 262; iv. 73, 113, 119, 187, 198
Bags, i. 90; iii. 88
Baking, ii. 168; iv. 47
Bankers, i. 7, 16, 33, 37, 55, 69, 74, 92; ii. 128, 216; iv. 145
Banners, i. 3, 11, 30
Banquets, iii. 54, 63, 86, 132, 163; iv. 65
Barbers, ii. 133, 135, 139, 140; iii. 128; iv. 90, 114, 118
Barley, iii. 55, 133
Barns, ii. 127, 131, 166, 169, 170, 172, 173; iv. 126
Barrels, i. 8, 32, 38, 54, 64, 69, 75; ii. 155, 228; iii. 54, 56; iv. 147, 201
Basins, i. 1, 7–9, 16, 17, 28, 32, 34, 38, 50, 53–5, 63–5, 68, 69, 74, 75, 77, 83, 94; ii. 128, 152, 178, 186, 189, 193; iv. 118, 147, 149, 151
— *see also* Bowls
Batells, i. 133, 135, 138–40; ii. 218; iv. 115
Battens, iv. 144
Beams, i. 28; ii. 208, 209, 219, 253; iv. 150
Bedels, i. 93, 94; ii. 135, 162; iii. 65–7, 85, 86, 145, 252, 253; iv. 65, 116, 126, 167–70, 173, 178
— Boterwyc, Robert, ii. 137
Beds etc., i. 7, 16, 53, 68, 80, 82, 84, 87, 94; ii. 161, 165, 169, 175, 184, 186, 192, 194, 202, 217, 222, 225, 230, 246; iii. 87, 90–2, 150, 168; iv. 69, 92, 117, 118, 120, 121, 147, 167, 174
— *see also* Coverlets
Beer, i. 7, 8, 16, 32, 38, 54, 64, 69, 75; ii. 148, 158; iii. 54, 64, 85, 263; iv. 147
Bellows, i. 7; iv. 148, 152

Bells, i. 3, 11, 30, 36, 52, 58, 67, 73; ii. 171, 175, 181, 183, 184, 222, 230; iii. 99; iv. 152
Benches, iv. 162
Benedictines, agreement about studies of, iii. 61–3
— chapters, provincial and general, iii. 32, 61, 62, 174; iv. 1–4, 19, 29, 39, 40, 65, 68, 93–6, 186, 187
— names, iii. 149; iv. 6, 215
— poverty, iv. 70, 107, 112, 116, 120-2, 155–6, 166, 194
— privileges, iii. 144, 262
Benefactors, iv. 100ff., 135
Benefices, iii. 166
— taxes on, iii. 221
Bevers, ii. 191, 194, 206, 212, 220, 223, 225; iii. 127, 179, 180
Bible-clerk, ii. 133; iii. 162, 176, 182; iv. 90
Birds, i. 8, 17, 38, 54, 64, 70; ii. 178; iv. 146
Bitterns, iii. 65, 133
Blacksmiths, ii. 131, 184, 196, 209, 219, 220, 222, 227, 240
Blankets, i. 80, 82, 84, 87, 94; iii. 265; iv. 118, 168, 173
Boards, ii. 127, 134, 140–3, 146, 161, 169, 172, 181, 184, 209, 219, 230, 235, 246, 256; iii. 56; iv. 121
— See also Planks
Boars, ii. 184, 191, 263–9, 272, 273; iv. 198
Bolsters, i. 84, 87, 94; iv. 118
Bolts, ii. 202, 211
Bonshommes, iv. 97
Books, ii. 189, 192, 193, 212; iii. 118, 128, 129, 150, 167, 181, 182, 185; iv. 5, 49, 101, 106, 108, 120, 121, 155ff., 185, 186, 199, 201, 211, 217ff.
— binding of, ii. 181, 192, 212, 222, 246; iii. 181; iv. 162
— chaining of, i. 3, 32, 71; ii. 192, 193, 196, 222; iii. 111; iv. 162, 163
— sellers of, iii. 121, 128
Bottles, i. 85; iii. 150; iv. 121
Bowls, i. 33; ii. 133, 148, 186, 212; iv. 148, 149
— see also Basins
Bows, i. 90
Brass, i. 17, 32, 33, 39; ii. 192, 209; iii. 266; iv. 146

Bread, i. 8, 32, 38, 54, 64, 69, 74; ii. 158, 178, 209; iii. 54, 64, 85, 266, 267; iv. 147
Breeches, i. 80; iv. 118
Bricks, ii. 225, 260
Bronze, i. 1, 7–11, 17, 28, 30, 32–4, 36, 38, 39, 51, 52, 54, 56, 58, 64, 65, 69, 70, 73, 74; ii. 156, 178, 181, 183, 186, 192, 202, 206, 222, 230, 240
Brushes, ii. 220, 227; iv. 162
Buckets, i. 39; ii. 133, 149, 165, 172, 181, 183, 184, 186, 223, 227, 240
Buckram, i. 84; ii. 196
Bucks, iii. 133, 134; iv. 65
Burnet, iv. 178, 180, 182
Bursar, iii. 163, 168, 169, 170
Burses, i. 52, 58, 67, 74
Butcher, iii. 67
Buttery, iv. 207
— book, iii. 272; iv. 47, 90
Buttons, iii. 150
Buttresses, iv. 139

Cades (lambskins), i. 90
Camera, apostolic, *see* Swan, William
Cameraria, ii. 266–71, 273, 274; iii. 175; iv. 56, 113, 114, 116, 117, 120, 186, 190, 202
Canamas, iv. 118; ?=canvas, q.v.
Cancellarius natus, iii. 62, 266
Candles, i. 7, 16, 56; ii. 148, 151, 155, 161, 164, 166, 168, 171, 174, 196, 201, 208, 209, 211, 219, 227, 230, 232, 234, 237, 240, 242, 245, 250, 260; iii. 55, 92, 93, 127, 129, 169, 180; iv. 148, 150, 163
— *see also* Wax
Candlesticks, i. 1, 7, 8, 9, 17, 28, 32, 34, 38, 51, 54, 56, 64, 65, 69, 73, 75, 85, 90, 95; ii. 169, 175, 189, 192, 193, 209; iv. 121, 147, 148, 151
Canon law, iii. 34, 63, 67, 80, 84, 89, 126, 127, 161, 164, 170, 174, 177, 179, 180, 249, 254; iv. 58–60, 63–5, 72, 73, 78, 87, 91, 113, 119, 191, 217
— schools, iii. 86
Canons, ii. 218; iii. 174; iv. 52, 97
— *see also* Byleth, Leeds
Canvas, i. 2, 10; iii. 55, 65; ?iv. 118
Capacities, iii. 116
Cape (rotondellus), iv. 119

INDEX OF SUBJECTS

Capons, ii. 137, 178, 243; iii. 55, 65, 132, 133
Caps, i. 83; iii. 65, 66; iv. 118, 119
Carpenters, ii. 141–6, 148, 152, 156–8, 161, 166, 168, 172, 173, 175, 177, 178, 181, 183, 196, 203, 205, 209, 211, 212, 216, 217, 219, 220, 222, 230, 232, 234, 237, 240, 242, 243, 246, 249, 256, 260; iii. 55
Carpets, i. 3, 7, 11, 31, 36, 52, 57, 58, 67, 68, 73, 76, 84, 94; ii. 164; iii. 266; iv. 121, 148, 152
Carrels, i. 90
Carriage, ii. 140–8, 153, 156–8, 165, 168, 172, 173, 177, 181, 184, 186, 189, 192, 196, 197, 205, 206, 208, 209, 212, 227, 232, 237, 242, 254, 258, 260, 272; iii. 54, 65, 66, 127, 133; iv. 66, 91, 160, 185, 186, 189, 191–3, 200, 203–5
Carts, ii. 127, 141–8, 152, 157, 158, 165, 166, 169, 172, 181, 186, 189, 191, 194, 196, 202, 203, 205, 212, 225, 227, 230, 234, 242, 243, 245, 248, 251, 253, 254, 260; iii. 55, 65
Casket, i. 85
Catches, ii. 156
Cellar, ii. 175, 186, 202; iv. 142
— beer-cellar, ii. 209
— *see also* Chambers
Celure, i. 58, 84; ii. 170
Chafing-dishes, i. 7, 16, 32, 33, 38, 54, 64, 69, 74, 94; ii. 211; iv. 146
Chairs, i. 7, 32, 37, 54, 55, 63, 64, 68, 69, 74, 75, 95; ii. 189; iv. 144, 148
Chalices, i. 1, 9, 10, 13, 28, 31, 34, 50, 55, 65, 76, 77, 83; ii. 230; iv. 49, 151, 227
Chalk, burnt, ii. 225, 227, 234, 240, 248, 251, 254, 260
Chambers, i. 18, 43, 45, 49, 59; ii. 127, 129, 131, 137, 147, 149, 150, 152–4, 160, 162, 163, 165–75, 177, 179, 182, 183, 185, 186, 188, 189, 193–6, 198–203, 209, 217, 224, 226, 229, 237, 247, 249, 259, 260; iii. 99, 113, 137, 167, 175, 177; iv. 4, 6, 92–4, 97, 102, 108, 111, 127, 135–7, 139–41, 148, 163–6, 185, 197, 198
— designated by focal points: Boys, i. 68; ii. 156, 165, 166, 175, 177, 212, 214, 243; iii. 179; iv. 86, 141, 142, 144
—— above, ii. 166, 179, 180, 183, 185, 188, 190, 204, 205, 211–13; 216, 218, 219, 221, 222, 226, 229, 231, 233, 235–8, 241, 243, 244, 246, 248, 250, 252, 256, 257; iv. 92
—— opposite chamber over gate, ii. 239
—— opposite or before, ii. 244, 247
— Cellar, beside, ii. 179–82, 184, 185, 204, 207, 210, 213, 215, 218, 219, 221, 223; iv. 92, 141, 142
—— north of, ii. 233, 236
— Chapel, at end of, ii. 182, 206, 207
—— at head of, ii. 179, 180, 185, 186, 188, 190, 203, 204, 206, 210, 212–16, 218, 221, 223, 225, 226, 227, 229, 231, 233, 234, 236, 237, 239, 241, 242, 244, 246, 247, 249–52, 256, 257, 259; iii. 56; iv. 92, 138, 139, 141, 153
—— west of, ii. 202; iii. 39, 100; iv. 143
— Gate, above, beside studies, ii. 179, 180, 185, 188, 190, 193, 204, 207, 209, 210, 213, 215, 218, 221, 226, 229, 231, 239, 241, 254, 259, 260; iv. 140
—— lower chamber, ii. 179, 188, 222, 241, 259, 260
—— opposite boys, ii. 239
—— outside or beside, ii. 147–50, 153, 154, 160, 163, 165, 167; iv. 111, 132, 133
—— on either side of, iv. 141, 143
—— left of, ii. 246
—— north of, ii. 251; iv. 141
—— south of, ii. 182, 219, 257, 259; iv. 138, 141
— Hall, at head of, ii. 185, 190, 193, 194, 196, 202, 206, 209, 212, 216, 217, 231, 233, 243, 253; iv. 98, 138, 142, 143, 147
—— at end of, ii. 180, 182, 183, 185; iv. 100, 138, 207
—— behind, ii. 165
— Kitchen, ii. 179, 182, 185, 188, 191, 193, 195, 198–200, 203, 204, 207, 210, 213, 218, 221, 223, 230, 241, 250, 251, 258, 260; iv. 92, 141, 142
—— west of, ii. 244

Chambers *(cont.)*
— Library, under, ii. 191, 239, 240, 256, 258
—— garden chamber, ii. 179, 180, 195, 199–201, 204, 207, 210, 212–14, 218, 221, 226, 229, 231, 233, 236, 245, 247, 250, 259; iv. 143, 161
—— hall chamber, ii. 202, 211
—— near privies, ii. 241, 252
— New, ii. 146
— Quadrangle, north of, ii. 157, 158, 231, 247, 248, 256, 258, 259
—— south of, ii. 226, 229
— Warden's, i. 4, 7, 11, 16, 18, 31, 37, 45, 53, 59, 61, 68, 71, 75, 76, 82, 84; ii. 134, 152, 156, 161, 165, 169, 175, 177, 178, 183, 186, 189, 194, 209, 227, 230, 234, 246, 251, 253; iii. 111, 167, 177; iv. 108, 138, 146–9, 160, 161, 163, 165, 166
—— beside, ii. 156, 184, 189, 191, 193
—— at steps of, ii. 250, 252
— *see also* Cooks, Manciples, Porters
Chamlet, i. 30, 51, 56, 72
Chancellor, iv. 184
Chancellor, university, ii. 161, 162, 203; iii. 9, 62, 81, 84, 86, 114, 144, 145, 171, 246ff., 263ff.; iv. 46, 47, 65, 98, 102, 104, 224
— gentleman and servant of, iii. 85
Chantries, iii. 111, 116, 119, 120
Chapel, i. 3, 9, 11, 28, 34, 36, 50, 55, 65, 72, 77; ii. 126–8, 133, 140–3, 148, 151, 152, 155, 156, 164, 165, 168, 169, 171, 174, 175, 177, 178, 181, 184, 186, 188, 189, 193, 194, 196, 198, 201, 203–5, 208, 209, 211, 216, 219, 222, 224, 227, 228, 230, 232, 234, 237, 240, 242, 245, 248–50, 253, 256, 258, 260, 266; iii. 9, 99, 112, 114, 160, 166, 168, 179, 181, 182; iv. 16, 46, 92, 98, 102, 108, 112, 137, 138, 139, 142, 143, 144, 148, 149ff.
— bell, i. 3, 11, 30, 36, 52, 58, 67, 73; ii. 181, 183, 184; iv. 152
— books, iv. 160ff.
— choir, i. 56, 58, 65, 67; ii. 222; iv. 149–52
— door, ii. 201; iv. 139, 152
— porch, ii. 149, 184

— roof, ii. 128, 141, 225, 227; iv. 139, 143
— screens, iv. 149, 150
— stone floor, i. 30
— windows, ii. 187, 201, 223, 227, 228, 243, 246; iv. 138, 139, 143, 149, 162
— *see also* Chambers
Chaplain, college, iii. 160, 168, 169
— private, ii. 192
— university, iii. 85
Charcoal, iv. 146
Chargers, i. 8, 17, 33, 95; ii. 133, 178
— *see also* Dishes
Chasubles, i. 2, 10, 11, 29, 35, 51, 52, 56, 57, 66, 72, 73, 78; ii. 184, 266
— mending of, ii. 171, 175
Cheese, iii. 55, 85
Chests, i. 9, 37, 90; ii. 175; iii. 181; iv. 121
— chapel, iii. 168
— common, i. 36, 37, 53, 63, 68, 75; ii. 154, 167, 238, 243, 244, 246, 252, 255, 259, 261, 271, 274; iii. 169, 174, 175; iv. 76, 108–11, 122, 148, 149
— Danvers, iii. 256
— J. Grove's, i. 7, 16
— kitchen, i. 9
— university, iv. 106, 155
— for books, i. 59, 62; iv. 108, 148, 160, 165
— for books in manuscript, i. 63, 71, 76
— for bread, i. 8, 32, 38, 54, 64, 69, 74; iv. 147
— for linen, i. 32, 38, 54, 64, 69, 75; iv. 90, 108
— for manciple's accounts, i. 8
— for muniments, i. 7, 16, 32; ii. 211; iv. 148
— for plate, i. 7, 16, 54, 63, 68; ii. 222; iv. 148
— for rolls, i. 32, 53, 75; iv. 148
— for vestments, i. 32, 53, 63, 68; iv. 148
Chimneys, ii. 142, 143, 145, 157, 222, 249; iii. 56; iv. 144, 145
Choir, rulers of, i. 57, 67, 73; iv. 87, 152
Circuitus, iii. 85
Civil law, iii. 84, 86, 161, 170, 179; iv. 63, 87, 100
Clasps, iii. 65

INDEX OF SUBJECTS

Classics, iv. 83, 103, 164
Clay, ii. 127, 155, 156, 165, 166, 170, 186, 194, 203, 212, 258, 260; iv. 207
— *see also* Earth
Cleaning, ii. 168, 186, 187, 189, 211, 212, 220, 227, 237, 243; iv. 90
Clerks, iii. 66
Cloaks, iii. 163; iv. 119
Cloth, iii. 66; iv. 169–71, 173, 179, 188, 200
— *see also the various fabrics*
Cluniacs, iv. 220
Coal, i. 33; ii. 138; iii. 55, 65
— house, ii. 156, 168, 169, 175, 256; iv. 146
Coats, i. 84, 87, 88; iv. 119
— petticoat (waistcoat), i. 87; iii. 129
Coffers, i. 95; iii. 150
Coffin, i. 93
Coins, iii. 267
Comb, iv. 118
Comitia, *see* Act
Commissaries, i. 93; ii. 187, 189, 190, 235, 238; iii. 62, 145, 262, 263, 266–8, 271, 272; iv. 98, 102, 218, 219, 227
Common Pleas, iii. 213–15, 217, 218
Commons, ii. 132, 135–9, 142, 152, 156–9, 168, 169; iii. 56, 67, 86, 127, 128, 162–4, 169, 265; iv. 115
Compounding, iii. 247, 251, 253, 258–60
Confectionery, iii. 55, 65, 67
Confraternity, iii. 107, 116; iv. 101, 104, 220, 222, 226
Congregation, iii. 62, 163, 246
— house, iii. 86, 253
Consumption, iv. 75
Contributions, for fellows, ii. 133, 135, 138; iv. 116
— for servants, ii. 264, 265, 270
— *see also* Cooks, Manciples
Convocation, iii. 144, 263
— clerical, iv. 214, 220, 222, 224–6
Cooks, ii. 197; iii. 168, 169; iv. 89–91, 201
— chamber, ii. 168, 181
— livery, ii. 153, 156, 161, 172, 223; iii. 85; iv. 91

stipend, ii. 195, 196, 199–201, 204, 207, 208, 210, 211, 216, 218, 219, 221, 224, 226, 229, 232, 234, 236, 239, 242, 245, 248, 251, 253, 256, 258–60, 266–74; iii. 55, 66, 86, 112, 114; iv. 90, 102, 202
— *see also* Contributions
Copes, i. 1, 2, 10, 28, 29, 31, 32, 34, 51, 56, 57, 65, 66, 72, 73, 77; ii. 196; iv. 148
— regent, i. 84; iv. 119
— riding, i. 84, 90; iv. 119
— scholastic, iii. 144; iv. 119, 167, 178–80, 182, 184–9, 191, 192, 199, 204
Copper, i. 1, 9, 28, 34, 50, 55, 65; iv. 151
Cords, ii. 140, 155, 167, 171, 172, 175, 181, 183, 184, 186, 192, 194, 208, 209, 222, 230; iv. 144, 150
Corn, iii. 55, 211, 212; iv. 185
Cornel Hall, iii. 122
Corporals, i. 2, 10, 30, 35, 52, 58, 67, 74
Correction, iii. 165, 177, 178
Corsettus, iv. 176
Costers, i. 7, 16, 38, 55, 63, 69; ii. 155, 196; iv. 144, 145, 152
Counter-boards, i. 7, 37, 53, 63, 68, 75; iv. 144; 148
— *see also* Abacus
Coverlets, i. 68, 84, 87, 94
— *see also* Beds
Cowls, i. 83, 87, 90, 93; iii. 129; iv. 119
Cranes, iii. 133
Cream, iii. 55, 65
Cresset, ii. 209, 227
Cresting, ii. 127, 141, 143, 157, 158, 169, 178, 203, 205, 212, 243, 246; iii. 56
Crosses, i. 1, 3, 9, 11, 28, 30, 34, 50, 52, 55, 65, 70; ii. 148, 151, 222; iv. 151, 152
Cruets, i. 9, 28, 34, 36, 50, 51, 54, 55, 65, 69, 73–5, 77; ii. 148, 168, 175, 189; iv. 151, 187
Cuffs, i. 83, 90
Culets, iii. 145; iv. 116
Cupboard cloths, i. 69, 85; iv. 118, 121
Cupboards, i. 7, 16, 31, 33, 38, 54, 55, 68, 74, 76, 95; ii. 178, 209; iv. 144, 146, 148

Cupboards, *(cont.)*
— for grammar books, i. 44
Cups, i. 8, 31, 32, 36, 37, 63, 82, 87, 90; ii. 172, 178, 222, 227, 230, 240; iii. 55, 66, 266; iv. 149, 211
Curtains, i. 7, 29, 34, 52, 56, 57, 58, 65, 67, 68, 72, 73, 84, 87, 89, 92; iv. 118, 147, 150, 151
Cushion covers, i. 34
Cushions, i. 3, 7, 30, 34, 52, 56, 65–8, 72, 73, 76, 82, 85, 94; ii. 209, 222, 230; iii. 266; iv. 121, 152
Cygnets, iii. 133

Dalmatics, i. 1, 2, 10, 11, 28, 29, 31, 35, 51, 56, 57, 65, 66, 72, 73; ii. 175
Damask, i. 31, 35, 89
Damp, ii. 127
Daubing, ii. 142, 144, 145, 146, 148, 149, 152, 165, 166, 170, 172, 196, 205, 216, 222, 234, 237, 260; iv. 144
Dead, prayers for, iii. 112, 114, 167, 181, 182; iv. 100, 102, 153
Dedications to SS. Thomas, Alphege, Benedict and Jerome, i. 35; iv. 150, 221
— B.V. Mary and St. Thomas, iii. 9; iv. 16
Deponing, iii. 84
Deportum, iv. 4
Desks, iv. 162
Determination, iii. 165, 170
Diaper, i. 32, 38, 52, 58, 64, 67, 69, 82, 84, 85, 90, 94; iv. 147
Dice, iii. 98; iv. 96
Dishes, i. 39, 54, 65, 74, 95; ii. 148, 152, 175, 192, 227; iv. 147
— *see also* Chargers, Platters, Vessel
Disputations, iii. 169, 170, 180
Ditches, ii. 166; iv. 126
Divinity school, iii. 145
Doctors, ii. 128, 144; iii. 174; iv. 65, 73, 98, 113, 119
Dogs, iii. 177
Doors, ii. 127, 141, 149, 152, 156, 165, 166, 168, 169, 175, 181, 186, 189, 192, 202, 203, 206, 209, 211, 222, 225, 230, 232, 234, 243; iv. 145, 146, 162
Dornick, i. 68; iv. 147
Dorsers, i. 7, 16, 54, 55, 58, 63, 64, 69, 74, 216; iv. 144, 145
Dovecote, ii. 166

Drain, ii. 156, 196, 230, 249, 253; iv. 146
Drawers (garments), iv. 118
Dress, academic, i. 83, 84; iii. 144, 251, 262; iv. 5, 56, 119, 121
— of fellows and monks, iii. 163, 168; iv. 5, 116ff., 187, 191
— of Franciscan lectors, iv. 167–76
Dressers, ii. 148; iv. 145
Dropping-tubs, i. 8, 64, 69; iv. 147
Ducks, iii. 55
— mallard, iii. 133
Dyeing, iv. 179

Earth, ii. 141, 148
— red, ii. 157
— terra tenax, ii. 227, 230, 242, 253
— *see also* Clay
Easter communion, ii. 131
— sepulchre, i. 57, 66, 73; ii. 148, 151, 222; iv. 152
Eels, i. 8; iv. 146
Eggs, iii. 56, 65
Embossing, i. 53, 63, 68
Enclosures, ii. 131; iii. 211
Eschaetor, ii. 128
Ewers, i. 7–9, 16, 17, 32, 38, 64, 69, 94; ii. 152, 165, 174, 186, 189, 193; iv. 147
Examination, iii. 33
Exchange of goods, ii. 148, 152, 155, 168, 175, 178, 181, 192, 211, 227, 246; iv. 146
Exchequer, iii. 221

Faggots, *see* Firewood
Fair, i. 70
Feathers, i. 82
Fees, iv. 64, 65, 115, 116
Fellows, ii. 128, 129, 133, 135, 138, 176, 187; iii. 32, 57, 58, 69, 71, 72, 86, 99, 105, 120, 129, 172, 183–205, 222, 224; iv. 9, 10, 12–14, 16, 17, 19, 20, 23, 32–4, 36, 38, 40, 43, 44, 46, 51ff., 105, 108, 109, 121, 144, 147, 156, 184ff.
— appointment, iii. 42, 44–7; iv. 17, 58
— commons, ii. 132, 133, 135–9; iii. 56
— elections, journeys, to, iii. 50, 68, 82, 83, 95, 102, 103, 108, 110, 131, 143

INDEX OF SUBJECTS

—salaries, ii. 129, 130, 147, 150, 154, 160, 163, 171, 174, 176–8, 180, 183, 185, 188, 191, 193, 195, 204, 207, 210, 211, 216–18, 221, 223, 224, 226, 229, 231, 233–6, 238, 239, 241, 244, 245, 247, 248, 250, 252, 253, 255–9, 262ff.; iii. 113; iv. 90, 112ff.
—senior, i. 34; iii. 112, 160, 165, 167, 174, 178, 180; iv. 76, 108, 109, 148, 151, 165
—second senior, ii. 260, 274; iii. 47, 177, 180
—seniors, iii. 161, 181
—statutes concerning, iii. 160, 161, 165, 167–70, 173–5, 178–82; iv. 60
—see also Batells, Cameraria, Contributions, Sickness
Feltr', i. 90
Fences, see Paling
Fever, ii. 244
Fifteenths, iii. 49
Fire-places, i. 7, 16, 37; ii. 127, 189, 192, 209, 212, 227, 243, 246, 260; iv. 144, 145, 148
Firewood, i. 9; ii. 127, 138; iii. 55, 65, 127
Fish, i. 9, 33; iii. 55, 64, 66, 80, 169
—see also Eels, Pike, Tench
Flesh-hooks, i. 33, 39; iv. 146
Floors, i. 30; ii. 166; iv. 161
Flour, iii. 266
Footwear, i. 94; iv. 69, 116, 118, 168, 169
Forks, i. 17; ii. 134, 165, 192
Forms, i. 7, 16, 32, 33, 38, 54, 55, 64, 69, 74, 75; ii. 205, 209; iii. 56; iv. 144, 152
Friars, i. 93, 98, 106; ii. 185; iii. 92; iv. 1, 3, 6, 58, 68, 70, 174, 217
Frith, ii. 166, 169, 172
Frocks, i. 90, 92, 94; iv. 119
Frying-pans, i. 17, 33, 39, 54, 64, 70, 74; ii. 134, 135, 148, 220, 222; iv. 146
Fumigation, ii. 255
Funeral expenses, i. 93; ii. 274; iv. 76
Fur, i. 84, 90, 94; iii. 66, 163; iv. 118, 119
Fustian, i. 84

Gable, ii. 209
Gallon measure, iii. 266
Game, iii. 55, 56, 67

Garden, i. 33, 39; ii. 127, 128, 131, 134, 152, 153, 156, 158, 172, 175, 179, 180, 186, 189, 192, 203, 204, 207, 225, 227; iii. 59, 156, 168; iv. 90, 137, 143, 144, 153, 161
—see also Chambers
Garlic, i. 9
Garter, order of, iv. 98
Gate, ii. 134, 137, 141, 143–6, 181, 191, 194, 196, 212, 220, 260; iii. 66; iv. 143, 207
—back or west, ii. 181, 209; iv. 146
—garden, ii. 203
—little, ii. 128
—old, near Vine Hall, ii. 186, 222
—pale, ii. 214, 243; iv. 143
—postern, ii. 224, 260
—see also Chambers
Gaudies, ii. 136, 139, 149, 153, 155, 161, 166, 169, 171, 177, 178, 180, 183, 185, 188, 191, 193, 195, 196, 198, 199, 201, 204, 207, 208, 211, 214, 216, 218, 219, 221, 224, 226, 229, 232, 234, 236, 238, 242, 245, 248, 251, 253, 256, 258, 260; iv. 112, 115
Geese, iii. 54, 65
Gentlemen, iii. 65
Gifts, iv. 167ff.; see also Tips
Gilding, ii. 1, 9, 10, 28, 31, 34, 36, 50, 53, 55, 58, 62, 63, 65, 68, 75, 76, 77, 83, 84, 87, 90; ii. 177; iii. 266; iv. 148, 149, 151
Girdles, i. 89; ii. 133, 151, 168, 250, 253; iii. 65, 150, 268; iv. 118
Glasiers, ii. 142, 143, 145, 146, 201, 209, 212, 243, 246, 253
Glass, see Windows
Gloves, i. 87; ii. 144, 152, 158, 192, 217; iii. 65, 85, 86, 132, 150; iv. 65, 91
Glue, ii. 230; iv. 152
Goblet, i. 87
Gold, i. 29, 31, 95; iii. 133
—cloth of, i. 1, 2, 10
Goldsmiths, ii. 227, 234, 240
Gowns, i. 80, 94; ii. 223; iii. 123, 265
Graces, iii. 84–6, 111, 132, 246ff.; iv. 58–63, 72
Graduation, ii. 273; iii. 111, 174, 177, 246ff.; iv. 5
—see also Inception
Grain, ii. 173
Grain (cloth), i. 84

Grammar, i. 44; iii. 61, 101, 179; iv. 52, 60, 87
Grass, iii. 212
Grate (?grater), i. 9, 17; ii. 175
Gratings, ii. 205, 227, 249; iv. 146
Granary, ii. 166
Gravel, iv. 207
Graves, i. 93; iv. 204
Greek, iv. 83, 103
Grills, i. 9, 17, 33, 54, 64, 70, 74; ii. 134, 135, 156, 175, 220, 232; iv. 146
Guests, ii. 149, 153; iii. 164, 165, 176, 177
Gutters, ii. 143, 152, 165, 173, 183, 191, 194, 211, 212, 216, 220

Habits, religious, iv. 69, 118, 169, 171-5
Haircloth, i. 30, 52
Hall, i. 7, 16, 33, 37, 54, 63, 69, 74; ii. 134, 143, 155-7, 161, 164, 169, 175, 178, 181, 183, 189, 191, 192, 203, 205, 209, 211, 212, 216, 223, 230, 232, 237, 243, 245, 249, 257; iii. 162, 165, 180; iv. 98, 108, 137-9, 142-8, 162, 185, 207
—see also Chambers
Hallings, iv. 144, 145
Halls (academic), iii. viii; iv. 2, 4, 5, 6
Halls (tenements), ii. 128, 131; iii. 19, 25, 27, 30, 37, 38, 49, 52, 53
Hammer, ii. 152
Handcarts, ii. 152, 168, 181, 205
Handkerchiefs, i. 84, 87, 90; iv. 121
Handwriting, iv. 84, 226
Hangings, i. 16, 33, 37, 38, 68, 94; ii. 186, 231, 232, 257; iii. 137; iv. 147
Hay, ii. 137, 145; iii. 55, 211, 212
Head-sheets, i. 84, 87
Hearth, ii. 249; iv. 144
Hedges, ii. 173; iv. 126
Hen-house, ii. 149, 178
Hens, iii. 65; iv. 212
Heresy, iii. 89; iv. 48, 224
Herons, iii. 55, 65, 133
Hinges, ii. 166, 168, 243, 260
Holy-water buckets, i. 3, 11, 36; ii. 151, 183; iv. 151
— sprinkler, ii. 219
Honey, iii. 65
Hoods, i. 83; iii. 66, 163; iv. 119
Hooks, i. 54, 64, 70; ii. 140-3, 146, 156, 166, 168, 203, 237, 249; iv. 146
Hoops (on barrels etc.), ii. 155, 172

Horn, ii. 192
Horse-bread, iii. 55, 128
Horses etc., ii. 128, 129, 140, 148-50, 153, 155, 162, 164, 168, 172, 189; iii. 39, 55, 56, 67, 87, 109, 127, 128, 132, 133, 211; iv. 66, 100, 181-4, 186-9; 192, 193, 196-206
Hose, i. 84; iii. 129; iv. 118
Hosts, ii. 131
Hours, canonical, iii. 99, 100
Hurdles, i. 140; ii. 157, 169, 202
Hutches, ii. 205

Illegitimacy, iii. 73
Images of angels, i. 52, 64, 67, 69, 74, 78; iv. 145
— Christ, i. 2, 10, 29, 30
— Crucifix, i. 29, 50, 55-7, 65, 90; iv. 149, 151
— doctors, i. 58, 67, 73; iv. 151
— evangelists, i. 58; iv. 151
— holy sepulchre, i. 92
— last judgement, i. 3, 30; iv. 153
— magi, i. 90
— passion, i. 2, 51, 56, 66
— patriarchs and prophets, i. 64, 69; iv. 145
— Trinity, i. 1, 9, 28, 29, 34, 50, 72; iv. 150
— St Andrew, i. 28, 34, 50, 55, 58, 65, 67, 73; iv. 150
— St Denis, i. 52, 58, 66
— St Dorothy, iii. 150; iv. 121
— St Dunstan, i. 8, 28, 34, 50, 55, 58, 65, 67, 73, 89; iv. 147, 150
— St Gregory, i. 3, 11, 29, 90
— St James, i. 8, 17, 77
— St John Baptist, i. 92
— St John Evangelist, i. 2, 8, 10, 17, 29, 77
— St Katherine, i. 1, 8, 9, 28, 34, 50; iv. 151
— St Mary the Virgin, i. 2, 10, 28, 29, 34, 35, 50, 53, 55, 58, 63, 65, 67, 72, 73, 75, 90; iv. 150
— St Peter, i. 2, 10, 29
— St Thomas of Canterbury, i. 1, 8-10, 29, 51, 57, 66, 73, 90; iv. 147, 150
Incense, ii. 155, 168, 171, 175, 177, 181, 183, 185, 188, 193, 208, 219, 222, 224, 227, 230, 234, 242, 245, 256
Incense-boats, i. 2, 11, 30, 52, 58, 67, 74

INDEX OF SUBJECTS

Inception, ii. 142, 157, 273, 274; iii. 54, 63, 69, 84, 124, 132, 142, 160, 165, 170, 176, 247ff.; iv. 1, 5, 63–6, 167, 188, 191, 195, 201, 218, 227
Indians, iii. 70, 71
Indulgences, iii. 109, 112; iv. 102, 224
Inkpot, i. 83
Insurrection, ii. 181
Inventories, iii. 167, 175; iv. 107, 119, 121, 144, 145, 147, 148, 150, 151, 152, 156ff.
Iron, i. 8, 9, 17, 33, 39, 54, 64, 70, 74; ii. 131, 140, 141, 143, 146, 149, 151, 152, 156, 157, 165, 172, 175, 178, 181, 184, 186, 192, 202, 203, 205, 209, 211, 222, 223, 225, 227, 228, 230, 234, 236, 249; iv. 145
Ironmongers, ii. 143
Ivory, i. 3, 11, 28, 51, 56, 65, 76; iv. 118, 151

Jacket, i. 84
Jasper, i. 87

Keys, i. 8; ii. 127, 134, 143, 148, 156, 165, 169, 172, 175, 177, 181, 183, 186, 189, 191, 193, 196, 201, 202, 205, 206, 209, 212, 219, 224, 227, 228, 230, 251, 253, 257; iii. 150, 168, 169, 174, 175, 266; iv. 92, 145, 146, 148
— chain of, ii. 212
King's Bench, iii. 213, 217
Kitchen, i. 8, 17, 32, 38, 54, 69, 74; ii. 127, 133, 134, 138, 148, 152, 155, 156, 169, 175, 178, 181, 183, 186, 189, 192, 194, 202, 205, 206, 209, 211, 212, 220, 222, 227, 228, 230, 232, 234, 240, 243, 246, 249, 253, 257, 258; iii. 55; iv. 108, 138, 142, 145, 146, 185, 207
— see also Chambers
Knives, i. 8, 32, 33, 38, 39, 54, 64, 65, 69, 70, 74, 83, 87, 93; ii. 209; iii. 90, 91, 92, 118; iv. 145, 147

Labourers, ii. 140–5, 152, 156–9, 165, 178, 186, 187, 206, 212, 220, 223, 237, 242, 243, 251, 253, 254; iii. 55
— see also Workmen
Ladders, i. 39; ii. 149, 177, 183, 184, 211, 220, 254
Ladles, i. 9, 33, 39, 54, 64, 70, 74; ii. 192, 209, 230; iv. 146, 207

Lamps, i. 56, 90
Langel', iv. 173
Latches, ii. 156, 220
Laths, ii. 140, 141, 144–6, 149, 152, 165, 169, 172, 202, 205, 234, 242, 253, 254, 258, 260
— contra lath, ii. 158
— eve laths, ii. 225
Latin, iii. 164, 177; iv. 103, 104
Latten, i. 17, 54, 64, 69, 74, 75; ii. 178; iv. 146, 147, 150, 151
Lattices, ii. 168, 193, 209, 212, 222, 223
Lead, i. 72; ii. 127, 156, 165, 183, 186, 216, 234, 240, 243; iv. 151
Leather, i. 63, 68, 85, 90–2; iv. 121, 148
— kid, i. 87; iii. 150
Lecterns, i. 1, 3, 10, 11, 30, 36, 52, 56–8, 65, 67, 72, 74; ii. 219; iv. 151, 152
— cloths for, i. 1, 10, 30, 36, 52, 56–8, 65, 67, 72, 74; iv. 152
Lectors, i. 98; ii. 126; iv. 3, 5, 55, 64, 68ff., 77, 83, 167ff., 210, 217, 221
Lectures, iii. 85, 99, 100; iv. 116
Legible days, iii. 182
Lenten array, i. 3, 11, 34; iv. 151
Letter-carriers, ii. 142; iv. 76, 170, 172, 183, 187, 204–6
Library, i. 18, 39, 45, 48, 59, 70, 76; ii. 173, 176, 181, 183, 187, 196, 209, 220, 222, 223, 243, 246, 253, 254, 256; iii. 111, 167, 168; iv. 46, 60, 63, 64, 108, 120, 143, 144, 155ff., 194, 199
— houses north of, ii. 237
— see also Chambers
Lime, ii. 127, 130, 131, 140, 141, 143–7, 245
— burnt, ii. 151, 165, 169, 172, 181, 186, 203, 205, 212, 222
— quick, ii. 157
Linen, i. 1, 3, 7, 10, 11, 29–31, 34–6, 52, 54, 58, 64, 67, 69, 74, 82, 84, 85, 87; ii. 168, 175, 192, 196, 219, 240; iii. 55, 67; iv. 90, 120, 122, 145, 147, 152, 182
— holland, ii. 181
— see also Vestments, washing of
Litigation, ii. 161, 187, 189, 251; iii. 184ff., iv. 112, 123, 144
Litter, iii. 55

Liturgy, iii. 99, 100, 166, 168, 179, 182, 247, 248, 251, 253, 257, 260; iv. 2, 87, 89, 92, 100, 102, 149
— Epiphany, ii. 254
— Good Friday, i. 57, 66, 73; ii. 151
— ferias, i. 2, 9, 29, 30, 52, 57, 58
— greater feasts, i. 2, 57
— principal feasts, i. 1, 10, 11, 28, 29, 57
— Saturdays, i. 2, 10, 29
— secondary feasts, i. 56, 66
— Sundays, i. 2, 10
Liveries, ii. 148, 153, 156, 161, 169, 172, 181, 223; iii. 56, 66, 67, 84-6, 168, 169; iv. 64, 65, 69, 72, 91, 117, 125, 126, 167ff., 222
Locks, i. 9; ii. 128, 134, 143, 148, 152, 156, 165, 169, 172, 175, 177, 181, 186, 189, 191-3, 201, 205, 206, 209, 211, 212, 222, 224, 227, 228, 230, 243, 253, 257; iii. 168, 169, 175; iv. 92, 145, 146, 148, 162
Lodgings, iii. 56
Logic, iii. 145, 174, 177, 246ff.; iv. 55, 60, 61, 99

Male (bag), i. 90
Manciples, i. 8, 30, 58, 67, 112; ii. 134, 153; iii. 134, 150, 168, 169, 263, 265, 272; iv. 86, 89-91, 108, 114, 146, 201
— chamber, i. 32, 38, 54; ii. 189; iv. 108, 147
— livery, ii. 153, 156, 161, 172; iii. 85; iv. 91
— stipend, ii. 195, 199-201, 204, 207, 210, 211, 216, 218, 219, 221, 223, 224, 226, 229, 232, 234, 236, 239, 242, 245, 251, 253, 256, 260, 266-74; iii. 112, 114; iv. 90, 102, 202
— of other houses, iii. 266, 267
Maniples, i. 78
Mantles, i. 84; iii. 150; iv. 69, 119, 167
Manure, ii. 152, 153, 181, 183, 186, 254, 260
Marbler, iv. 204
Mariners, ii. 140, 144, 145
Masons, ii. 130, 141, 142, 143, 144, 146, 148, 149, 157, 158, 178, 181, 184, 186, 196, 202, 205, 212, 220, 222, 227, 235, 237, 242, 245, 249, 253, 254, 260
Masses, *see* Liturgy

Masters, ii. 130, 146
— special, ii. 133, 135
Mats, i. 3, 8; ii. 148, 164; iv. 147, 152
Mattocks, i. 33; ii. 134, 168
Mattresses, i. 83, 87; iv. 118, 121
Mazers, i. 7, 8, 16, 17, 31, 32, 37, 38, 53, 54, 62-4, 68, 69, 75-7, 82, 90; ii. 168, 172, 186, 189, 211, 227; iv. 147, 148
Meals, iii. 99, 162, 163, 175, 176, 179; iv. 90, 147
Meat, i. 8, 33, 39; iii. 54, 64, 267; iv. 96
— licence to eat, iii. 80; iv. 49
Medecine, faculty of, iii. 261
Medecines, ii. 228, 255; iii. 175; iv. 169
Merchant, ii. 192
Messenger, ii. 181
Milk, iii. 55, 65
Mill, iii. 211
Mincer, i. 8; iv. 146
Miracle, iii. 116
Missal-stands, i. 3, 11, 30, 36, 52, 58, 67
Mittens, iv. 118
Mortmain, iii. 1; iv. 9, 15
Moss, ii. 127, 178, 191, 216, 235, 237, 258
Muniments, i. 7, 16, 32, 53; ii. 128, 130, 155, 156, 161, 164, 211, 227, 238, 243, 246, 252; iii. 194, 199, 200, 205; iv. 189, 191
Music, iv. 52, 152, 153
Mustard-pot, i. 33, 39, 70, 74; iv. 146

Nails, ii. 127, 141, 143, 146, 147, 152, 158, 161, 165, 166, 169, 181, 184, 186, 196, 203, 219
— bearing-, ii. 152
— board-, ii. 152
— brass, ii. 192
— clout-, ii. 216
— evestone-, ii. 158, 165, 169
— lath-, ii. 158, 202, 212, 225, 230, 242, 254
— slate-, ii. 131, 140, 189, 202, 249
— straw-, ii. 225
— twopenny, ii. 240
— threepenny, ii. 205, 222, 225, 240, 249, 254
— fourpenny, ii. 203, 205, 209, 217, 224, 230, 234, 240, 242, 248
— fivepenny, ii. 203, 219, 224, 230, 234, 242, 254

INDEX OF SUBJECTS

—sixpenny, ii. 203, 224, 230, 234, 254, 260
—tenpenny, ii. 203, 217, 234, 260
—*see also* Prigs
Napkins, i. 69, 84, 87, 90, 94; iv. 121, 147
—(manutergium) i. 7, 16, 32, 38, 58, 64, 67, 69, 74
Needles, ii. 250
Netherqueyvis, i. 84
Nobles, ii. 128, 153; iii. 177
Nuts (cups), i. 31, 37, 53, 63, 68, 75, 84, 87; ii. 246; iv. 148

Oaths, iii. 161, 165, 168, 169
Oats, ii. 137; iii. 55
Oblaciones, iv. 113
Oil, iv. 69, 168–71
Onions, ii. 156
Opposition, iii. 111, 169, 170, 174, 180, 246ff.; iv. 61, 81, 227
Oranges, iii. 133
Ordinaria, ii. 133, 138
Ordination, iv. 67, 186
Organ, i. 3, 11, 30, 36, 52, 58; ii. 230; iv. 152
Outhouses, ii. 256
Ovens, ii. 138, 175, 205; iii. 55; iv. 108
Oysters, iv. 188

Painting, i. 92; ii. 148, 151, 253; iii. 133; iv. 150–2
Paling, ii. 152, 156, 157, 189, 203, 205, 214, 243; iv. 98, 138, 143, 144
Pans (patella), i. 8, 17, 33, 39, 54, 65, 70, 74; ii. 156, 178, 211
—(patena), i. 37, 39; ii. 133, 138, 148
Pantry, ii. 134
Papal subsidy, ii. 170
Paper, i. 23, 25–7, 45, 46, 58, 68; ii. 126, 146; iii. 167
—painted, i. 90
Parchment, iii. 150; iv. 69, 71, 168–74, 176, 177, 183, 187, 193
Pargetting, ii. 144, 145; iv. 144
Paris work, i. 3, 7, 11, 16, 30
Parish clerk, ii. 131
Parliament, ii. 189
Parm', iv. 211
Partridges, iii. 134
Paryngyrys, ii. 172
Paten, i. 83
Paving, ii. 197, 258

Pawning, i. 84; iii. 181, 268; iv. 106, 155
Pax, i. 1, 9, 28, 30, 34, 36, 51, 52, 56, 58, 65, 67, 73, 75, 77; iv. 149, 151
Peacocks, iii. 132, 134
Pears, ii. 128
Peas, i. 70, 74; iv. 146
Peel, i. 39
—*see also* Shovels
Pepper-mills, i. 9; ii. 212; iv. 146
Pestles and mortars, i. 9, 17, 33, 39, 54, 64, 70, 74; ii. 135, 155; iv. 146
Peter's pence, ii. 131, 155, 162, 170; iv. 126
Pewter, ii. 168
Pheasants, iii. 133, 134
Philosophy, iii. 63, 123, 145, 174, 246ff.; iv. 55, 59, 60, 61, 99
Phthisis, ii. 244
Physicians, i. 93; iv. 74
Pick-axe, ii. 192
Picks, ii. 172
Pies, iii. 55
Pike, iii. 64, 133
Pilions, i. 84; iv. 119
Pillowcases, i. 84, 87, 90
Pillows, i. 84, 87, 94; iv. 118
Pincers, ii. 152; iv. 118
Pins, ii. 127, 254, 260
—lath-, ii. 225, 254
—*see also* Slate-pins, Tile-pins
Pipers, iii. 56
Pipes (barrels), i. 8; ii. 155; iii. 54, 64, 66; iv. 147
Pittances, ii. 135; iv. 115, 174, 212
Plague, ii. 206, 217, 228, 255, 258, 268–70, 274; iii. 118, 122, 159; iv. 75, 221
—*see also* Sweating sickness
Planks, ii. 148, 253; iv. 146
—*see also* Boards
Plate, iv. 5, 65, 148, 149, 151, 206
—iocalia, i. 7, 16, 54, 63, 77; ii. 217, 222; iii. 103, 167, 181; iv. 91, 120, 146, 211
—peciae, i. 7, 16, 77, 87; iii. 155; iv. 47
Platters, i. 54, 70, 74, 95
Plumbers, ii. 183, 211, 216, 219, 234
Points, iv. 118
Poor scholars, iv. 174, 180
Porches, ii. 203, 243; iv. 144
Porringers, i. 65, 70, 95; iv. 146
Porters, ii. 153, 189; iii. 66, 85; iv. 90

Posnets, i. 8, 17, 54
Post, ii. 166
Postern, *see* Gate
Pot-hooks, i. 9, 17, 33, 39, 70, 74; ii. 237
Pots, i. 8, 17, 32, 38, 39, 54, 64, 69, 70, 74; ii. 133, 138, 156, 186, 194, 222, 230; iii. 66; iv. 146
— for beer, i. 7, 16
— bell-pot, i. 32, 38
— for mustard, i. 39, 74
— for wine, i. 28, 36, 51, 56, 65, 72; ii. 148
Poulterer, iii. 55
Poultry, iii. 55; iv. 146
Preaching, ii. 135, 149; iii. 63, 96, 97, 119, 128, 129, 140, 144, 145, 151, 176, 247ff.; iv. 66, 115, 119, 193, 194, 196, 198, 201, 204–6, 218–20, 222, 224, 226
Precentor, iii. 182
— *see also* Chaplain
Presentation for degrees, iii. 86
Prigs, ii. 140, 142, 149, 152, 158, 196, 205, 214, 217, 222, 234, 240, 260
Primitive sciences, iii. 33, 63; iv. 54, 55, 59
Prior studentium, iii. 61, 144, 204; iv. 1, 30, 113, 116, 195
Privies, ii. 127, 131, 143, 149, 152, 153, 165, 175, 178, 189, 196, 205, 227, 230, 237, 240, 243, 252, 254; iv. 161, 185
Problems, iii. 170
Processions, iii. 63, 144, 251
Proctors, iii. 65, 85, 86, 144, 145, 259, 262, 266
— southern, ii. 161, 162; iii. 82
Promptuary, i. 7, 8, 17, 32, 38, 54, 64, 69, 74; ii. 148, 155, 161, 165, 178, 181, 189, 192, 193, 202, 209, 219, 223, 249; iii. 272; iv. 90, 108, 142, 144, 146, 147
Pueri collegii, i. 67, 73, 80, 88; ii. 184, 217; iii. 43, 44, 179, 180, 182; iv. 43, 44, 60, 85ff., 90, 100, 104, 144
— appointment, iii. 61, 63, 73, 100, 101, 129, 136, 150; iv. 85
— commons, ii. 129, 130, 133, 135–9, 147, 150, 151, 153, 154, 160, 163, 167, 171, 174, 177, 178, 180, 183, 185, 188, 191, 193, 195, 197–201, 204, 207, 208, 210, 211, 216, 218, 220, 221, 223, 224, 226, 229, 231–6, 238, 239, 241, 242, 244, 245, 247, 248, 250–3, 256, 258–60, 262–71; iii. 99, 179; iv. 86, 112, 115, 121, 152, 198, 201
— disputes with, ii. 153, 184; iii. 98, 99; iv. 88, 89
— *see also* Chambers
Pullets, ii. 137; iii. 55, 65, 132
Pump, iv. 207
Puncheons, ii. 235
Purses, i. 90; iv. 118
Pyxes, i. 1, 3, 9, 11, 28, 34, 51, 56, 65, 76, 76, 77; iv. 151
P^{ur}toins, ii. 143, 146

Quadrangle, ii. 135, 137–9, 141–4, 146, 152, 153, 181, 187, 191, 196, 205, 230, 236, 258; iv. 98
— *see also* Chambers
Quails, iii. 65, 132
Quarryman, ii. 157
Quarterage, ii. 138; iv. 116
Questions, iii. 170

Rabbits, iii. 55, 65, 66
Rakes, i. 17, 33, 39; ii. 134, 192
Ray (cloth), ii. 148
Refreshments, ii. 187
Regents, iii. 33, 65, 145, 160, 170, 174, 248, 251, 260; iv. 64, 67, 68
Registrar, i. 93; iii. 145, 262
Religious life, iii. 162, 179
Rent-collector, ii. 192
Repairs, ii. passim; iii. 171, 180; iv. 92, 112, 127, 185, 194, 198, 206, 207
Replication, iii. 145, 247, 260, 262
Reportatio, i. 22, 98, 106
Residence, iii. 164; iv. 62, 63, 66–8
— abroad, iii. 164; iv. 64, 78ff.
Responding, iii. 85, 170, 174, 247ff
Rhetoric, iv. 99
Ribbon, i. 90
Ring, i. 95
Roasting, ii. 178
— racks, ii. 178
Rods, ii. 156, 186
Romescot, *see* Peter's pence
Roofs, ii. 141, 158, 166, 169, 170, 178, 184, 194, 205, 216, 222, 225, 246, 248; iv. 138, 139, 140, 142, 143, 145, 162, 207
Rope, *see* Cords

INDEX OF SUBJECTS

Rosaries, i. 82, 83, 87, 90; iii. 268; iv. 121
Rushes, iii. 55; iv. 144, 147
Rydes, ii. 143, 196, 202

Sacristy, i. 29, 30, 36; ii. 175, 240, 253; iv. 150, 153
Salt, i. 32, 33, 38; ii. 155; iii. 55, 65
— cellars, i. 7, 8, 16, 31, 87; ii. 161, 183, 227; iv. 147, 148
— stoups, i. 33; iv. 146
Sanappys, i. 32, 38
Sand, i. 140–5, 147, 152, 157, 165, 169, 172, 181, 186, 194, 205, 212, 222, 225, 227, 230, 242, 243, 245, 248, 251, 260
Satin, i. 57, 58, 67, 73, 89; iv. 151
Sauce-boats, *see* Sawcers
Saw, i. 9; iv. 146
Sawcers, i. 33, 54, 70, 74, 95
— salsaria, i. 17, 37, 38, 53, 63, 64, 68, 69, 75, 77; ii. 148, 152, 175, 189, 192, 193, 209; iv. 146
— scultellule, i. 32, 33, 54, 65; ii. 227, 234
Sawyers, ii. 140–8, 152, 157, 158, 177, 196, 203, 205, 209, 219, 222, 225, 235, 246, 256, 260; iv. 207
Say, i. 68, 73, 74, 94; iii. 137; iv. 118, 147
Scaffolding, ii. 157, 168, 169, 242, 245
Scapular, iv. 119
Sconce, iv. 148
Screens, i. 7, 16, 38; ii. 165; iv. 108, 138, 144, 149, 150
Scribes, iii. 109; iv. 201, 202
Seals, i. 82; ii. 130, 164, 211; iii. 168, 169, 174, 178, 206, 266; iv. 30, 106, 148, 216
Secular scholars, iii. 11, 12; iv. 8, 23, 135, 137, 160
Sedilia, cloths for, i. 2, 29
Sequestration, ii. 128; iv. 184–6
Sermons, *see* Preaching
Servants, college, i. 63; ii. 133, 137, 139, 149, 153, 155, 164, 168, 169, 172, 181, 190, 194, 199, 204, 207, 211, 212, 217, 223, 226, 231, 233, 234, 236, 238, 239, 241, 242, 244–8, 250–3, 256, 257, 261; iii. 67, 109, 127, 128, 168, 169, 171, 177, 179, 263, 264, 272; iv. 65, 76, 89ff., 105, 112, 117, 126, 195–201, 227

— other, ii. 128; iii. 55, 66, 67, 134, 211, 271; iv. 69, 88, 90
Shanks (?stockings), i. 87
Sheets, i. 80, 82, 84, 94
Ship-coffer, i. 90
Ships, iii. 150
Shirts, i. 80, 94
Shovels, ii. 156, 209
— *see also* Peel
Shrouds, ii. 173
Shutters, ii. 209
Sickness, i. 93; ii. 255; iii. 114, 162, 245; iv. 5, 75, 76, 102, 148, 149, 202
Silk, i. 1–3, 9, 10, 28–30, 34, 51, 52, 56–8, 65–7, 72, 73, 78; ii. 196
Silver, i. 1, 4, 7–10, 16, 17, 28, 31, 32, 34, 36, 37, 50, 51, 53, 55, 56, 63–5, 68, 69, 75–7, 87, 90; ii. 172, 177, 183, 227, 228, 234, 240, 266; iv. 147–9, 151
Skimmers, i. 9, 17, 33, 39, 54, 64, 70, 74; ii. 152, 175, 183, 192, 209, 220, 230; iv. 146
Slate-pins, ii. 152, 165, 169, 202
Slaters, ii. 140, 143, 151, 165, 169, 172, 178, 187, 189, 191, 194, 196, 202, 212, 216, 222, 256, 260
Slates, ii. 127, 131, 140, 141, 143–7, 152, 158, 165, 169, 189, 191, 196, 202, 251, 258; iv. 143, 145, 207
— common large, ii. 202, 205
— eve, ii. 205, 212
— middle broad, ii. 169
— *see also* Stone
Sleygates, ii. 166
Socks, iii. 129
Sojourners, i. 93, 97, 99; ii. 127, 129, 151, 157, 165, 168, 169, 172, 173, 177, 179, 180, 187, 190, 193, 194, 199, 201, 204, 207, 213, 218, 221, 223, 224; ii. 69, 70, 81; iii. 96, 121, 134, 149, 177, 180, 243, 244, 263, 265; iv. 91ff., 102, 105, 114, 121, 139, 144, 160
Solar, ii. 219
Soldering, ii. 144, 151, 183
Sophisters, iii. 161, 163, 168, 170, 178, 180; iv. 87
Soup, i. 64, 70
Spades, i. 33, 39; ii. 134, 149, 156, 165, 172, 175, 181, 183, 186, 189, 194, 209
Spar, ii. 127, 166
Sparver, i. 68; iv. 147

Spere, *see* Screen
Spice allowance, iii. 88, 93; iv. 115, 167, 212
Spices, ii. 128; iii. 55, 65–7, 85, 132–4
Spits, i. 8, 17, 33, 38, 39, 54, 64, 70, 74; ii. 227, 237, 240; iv. 146
Spoons, i. 8, 16, 17, 32, 37, 38, 53, 54, 63, 64, 68, 69, 75, 77, 82, 87, 90; ii. 234; iv. 121, 147, 148
Stables, ii. 148; iii. 39; iv. 100, 133
Stained cloths, i. 2, 3, 7, 11, 29, 34, 36, 68, 76, 84, 85, 87, 90; iv. 145, 152
Stairs, ii. 168, 196, 203, 211, 217, 251; iii. 56; iv. 139
Stamins, i. 84, 87; iv. 119
Stanchions, ii. 237
Staple, ii. 251
Station (before services), i. 3; iv. 152
Stationers, i. 93, 94; ii. 196; iii. 85; iv. 162
Statutes, iii. 3, 45, 158ff.; iv. 11, 12, 13, 16, 19, 24, 41, 44, 45, 46, 106, 108, 190
Stills, iv. 207
Stock, ii. 152, 157, 219
Stole work, i. 30
Stoles, i. 77
Stone, i. 33; ii. 127, 130, 140, 142, 144–6, 166, 169, 173, 184, 186, 205, 222, 225, 227, 230, 231, 249, 251, 267; iii. 111; iv. 102, 108, 137, 144–6, 150, 161, 162, 204
— broad, ii. 165
— common, ii. 242, 243
— common large, ii. 242, 254, 260
— cotisfolde, ii. 245
— cuttable, ii. 157
— eve, ii. 158, 165, 169, 254, 260
— flag, ii. 172
— free, ii. 205; i. 28, 50
— large, ii. 141
— lesser, ii. 205, 242, 254, 260
— middle broad, ii. 165
— wall, ii. 157
—*see also* Cresting, Slates
Stools, i. 3, 30, 32, 37, 52, 54, 58, 63, 67, 68, 73, 75, 95 ii. 183, 211; iv. 148, 152
Storehouse,, ii. 251
Strails (stragula) i. 82, 84, 87, 92; iii. 66; iv. 118
Straining-basin, i. 33, 39, 54, 64, 70, 74; ii. 181, 183; iv. 146

Straw, ii. 127, 143, 149, 156, 186; iii. 56, 211; iv. 147, 152
Students, monastic, iv. 1–8, 167ff.
Studies (of books), i. 94; ii. 131, 142, 169, 175, 177, 179, 186, 202–4, 206, 207, 209–11, 213, 219, 223, 242, 243; iii. 180; iv. 4, 71, 92, 108, 140, 148
—*see also* Chambers
Studs, ii. 141, 143, 202, 235, 253
Sugar, iii. 65
Superaltars, i. 2, 10, 30
Supertunics, iii. 163
Supper, iii. 169, 180
Surgeon, i. 93; iv. 172
Surplices, i. 3, 11; ii. 171; iii. 99, 166
Swans, iii. 55, 65; iv. 212
Sweating sickness, iii. 244, 245; iv. 75
—*see also* Plague

Tabards, iii. 66, 163
Tabernacle, i. 55; iv. 150
Tablecloths, i. 85, 94; iv. 121, 147
— mappa etc., i. 7, 16, 32, 38, 64, 69, 75, 82, 90; iii. 66
— mantile, i. 38, 82
— naprona, iii. 55, 65
Tables, i. 7, 16, 32, 33, 37, 38, 53–5, 63, 64, 68, 69, 74, 75; ii. 169; iii. 150; iv. 121, 144, 148
Tables (images) i. 1, 3, 9, 11, 28, 30, 31, 34, 35, 36, 58, 67, 72, 73, 95; ii. 222; iii. 150; iv. 108, 121, 150
Tablets (writing), i. 86; iv. 118
Taffeta, iii. 66
Tailor, ii. 130
Tallies, ii. 141–4, 146
Tapestry, i. 7, 16, 37; iv. 145
Tartarin, iii. 85
Taverns, iii. 97, 98, 177
Tench, iii. 133
Tenements, iii. 51, 57, 102; iv. 180, 211–13
Tenth, clerical, ii. 130, 148, 149, 151, 154, 166, 170, 176; iii. 41, 49; iv. 190, 191
Testers, i. 16, 84, 87, 94; iv. 147
Theology, iii. 33, 63, 66, 80, 84, 89, 110, 130, 144, 145, 160, 169, 170, 174, 177, 179, 180, 246ff.; iv. 1, 3, 58–65, 67–73, 80–2, 91, 113, 191, 198, 222
— schools, iii. 247, 250
Thread, ii. 222, 227, 250

INDEX OF SUBJECTS

Thuribles, i. 1, 2, 9, 10, 28, 30, 34, 36, 52, 58, 67, 74, 75, 77; ii. 177, 194, 228; iv. 149, 151
Tick, i. 94
Tie-beams, ii. 158
Tile-pins, ii. 191, 194
Tilers, ii. 126, 127, 131, 143, 157, 158, 159, 203, 205, 225, 227, 234, 237, 242, 243, 245, 246, 248, 251, 254
Tiles, ii. 178, 231, 234, 258; iii. 210; iv. 162
— common width, ii. 248
— first width, ii. 248
Timber, ii. 128, 140, 145, 146, 149, 156–8, 161, 168, 173, 186, 196, 203, 205, 208, 209, 212, 216, 219, 222, 225, 234, 242, 248; iv. 133, 144
— elm, ii. 177, 208
— oak, ii. 166
Tin, i. 1, 3, 7, 8, 9, 11, 16, 17, 28, 31, 36, 37, 38, 51, 54, 55, 65, 70, 72, 73, 83; ii. 148, 155, 175, 178, 181, 183, 189, 202, 209, 220, 222; iv. 146, 147, 151
Tinker, ii. 220, 240; iv. 146
Tippet, i. 94
Tips, ii. 127, 128, 133, 139, 142, 144, 153, 155, 157, 161, 164, 168, 172, 177, 217; iii. 133; iv. 66, 91, 167, 170, 171, 178, 183, 184, 188, 194, 204, 205
Tissue, i. 78
Tithes, iii. 211–13
Tontynht, ii. 146
Torch, ii. 258
Towels, i. 52, 85
— for the lavatorium, i. 11, 30
— manutergium humerale, i. 32, 38
Travelling expenses, iii. 127, 164, 176; iv. 5, 66, 67, 109, 112, 126, 127, 167, 168, 173, 174, 178–80, 183, 184, 186–206, 215
Trestles, i. 7, 16, 33, 38, 55, 64, 69, 74; ii. 183, 211; iii. 150; iv. 121
Trivets, i. 8, 17, 33, 39, 54, 64, 70, 74; ii. 168, 192; iv. 146
Tub (labrum), i. 83
Tunicles, i. 1, 77, 78
Tunics, i. 80, 83, 90; iii. 123, 163; iv. 118, 119, 168, 170, 176

Undercook, ii. 128, 153, 189; iii. 168, 169; iv. 90

Urinal, i. 93
Usury, iv. 47

Vacation, iii. 161, 176, 254, 259, 260; iv. 5, 66, 86
Vegetables, i. 54
Velvet, i. 11, 29, 30, 35, 51, 52, 56, 58, 66, 72, 78, 89, 94
Venison, iv. 11
Verjuice, i. 8, 38; iv. 147
Vespers, academic, iii. 67, 84–6, 144, 255
— liturgical, iii. 99, 163, 182
Vessel, i. 8, 17, 32, 39, 54, 70; ii. 133, 138, 155, 168, 178, 181, 183, 189, 192, 202, 206, 209, 220, 222, 240; iii. 55, 66, 86
— see also Chargers, Dishes, Platters
Vestments, sets of, i. 1, 2, 10, 28, 29, 31, 32, 35, 51, 53, 56, 57, 63, 65, 66, 68, 72, 73, 78; iii. 167, 182; iv. 57, 148, 206
— making of, ii. 194
— ribbon for, i. 90
— washing and mending of, ii. 128, 131, 133, 135, 148, 151, 153, 164, 168, 171, 175, 177, 181, 183, 185, 188, 191, 193, 201, 204, 208, 216, 219, 222, 227, 234, 237, 240, 242, 245, 248, 250, 253, 256, 258
Vicechancellor, see Commissaries
Vice-wardens, ii. 190, 213, 267
Vinegar, iii. 65
Viols, ii. 245

Walking, iii. 163, 176
Walls, ii. 127, 130, 141, 143, 145, 149, 152, 155, 156, 165, 166, 168, 170, 173, 181, 186, 189, 202, 222, 227, 254, 258, 260, 267; iii. 56, 210, 211; iv. 126, 137, 144, 207
— sea-walls, ii. 172; iii. 210, 211; iv. 126
Wands, iii. 266
Warden, ii. 165, 190, 191; iii. 82, 83, 95, 99, 102, 103, 135, 161, 162, 164, 165, 167–70, 172–8, 181–3, 186–92, 198, 203–5, 222, 224, 263, 264; iv. 16, 17, 20, 23, 25, 40, 62–4, 76–8, 88, 90, 105, 107ff., 126, 127, 148, 151, 155, 156, 200
— accounts, ii. passim, iii. 113; iv. 92, 108ff.

Warden, *(cont.)*
— appointment, iii. 2, 3, 11, 14–16, 20, 36, 42–6, 48, 60, 68, 95, 102, 103, 106, 115, 138, 146, 160, 173; iv. 12–14, 19, 22, 35, 40–4, 48, 77
— commons, ii. 132
— cup, ii. 222
— inventories, iv. 107, 108
— payments from manors, ii. 262ff.
— removal, iii. 15, 16, 39, 59, 106, 138, 143, 165, 173, 203; iv. 19, 41, 77, 105
— seat in choir, i. 57, 66, 73; iv. 152
— — in hall, ii. 189
— servants, ii. 153
— stipend, ii. 129, 130, 133, 135, 138, 140, 147, 151, 154, 160, 163, 167, 171, 174, 180, 183, 185, 188, 193, 195, 204, 207, 211, 216, 218, 221, 224, 226, 229, 232, 233, 236, 239, 241, 245, 247, 250, 253, 256, 258, 259
— woodhouse, ii. 253
— *see also* Chambers
Washerwomen, ii. 133, 135, 139, 140, 155, 175, 211, 222, 224, 234, 245, 256, 258, 260; iii. 128; iv. 90, 114, 118
Water, ii. 141, 145; iii. 55, 99
Wattle, ii. 127
Wax, ii. 138, 148, 151, 164, 168, 171, 174, 181, 183, 186, 188, 191, 193, 195, 204, 208, 211, 216, 222, 224, 227, 230, 232, 234, 237, 240, 242, 245, 248, 250, 253, 256, 258, 260, 266; iv. 148
— *see also* Candles
Wedges, i. 9, 17; iv. 146
Weirs, iv. 126
Well, i. 9; ii. 149, 167, 172, 182, 184, 186, 192, 194, 223, 243, 254
Wharfage, ii. 140; iii. 54; iv. 204

Wheelbarrows, ii. 156, 157, 168, 172, 181, 186, 211, 237
Whisks, i. 9, 54, 64, 70, 74
Whitewashing, i. 141, 152, 165; ii. 249; iv. 146
Wind, ii. 246, 249
Windows, ii. 157, 258, 260; iv. 138–40, 143
— carpets for, i. 69, 76; iv. 148
— glass for, ii. 131, 164, 169, 170, 175, 181, 183, 187, 201, 202, 209, 212, 219, 223, 227, 228, 243, 246, 253; iii. 210, 253; iv. 144, 162
— ironwork of, ii. ?131, 140, 141, 143, 146, 147, 243
— shutters for, ii. 209
— small, ii. 172
— stonework of, ii. 184, 202, 203
— woodwork of, ii. 143
— *see also* Lattices
Wine, i. 28, 36, 51, 56, 65; ii. 128, 131, 135, 161, 162, 187, 189, 251, 274; iii. 64, 66, 84, 86, 97; iv. 115, 151, 200, 201
— white, iii. 54
— red, iii. 85
— sweet, iii. 85
Wire, ii. 164; iv. 150
Withes, ii. 166
Women, ii. 156, 237
Wooden objects, i. 3, 8, 11, 30, 33, 34, 38, 39, 52, 55, 77; iv. 108, 148, 151
Woodhouses, ii. 219; iv. 140, 207
Wool, i. 7, 16, 82, 83; iv. 145
Workmen, ii. 140, 156, 161, 165, 169, 172, 225, 230
— *see also* Labourers
Workshop, ii. 251
Worsted, i. 87; ii. 266

Yconomus, iv. 41–4

INDEX OF BOOKS AND AUTHORS

Abbas, i. 106; ii. 270
Albertus, i. 25, 26, 82, 88, 106, 110
Alcock, Reginald, i. 112
Alexander of Alexandria, i. 15, 25, 43, 49, 101
Alexander Nequam, i. 46, 105
Alexander versifice, i. 27, 103
Alexandri, Gesta, i. 6, 15, 26, 48; iv. 159
Alfonsus de Spina, i. 20, 42, 47, 101
Allegorie breves super biblia, see Richard of St. Victor
Altissiodorensis, i. 20, 62
Ambrose, i. 18, 19, 22, 40, 45, 60
Angelus de Camerino, i. 22, 102, 109
Angelus de Clavasio, i. 86
Anselm, i. 4, 13, 19, 40, 41, 45, 46, 47, 49, 76, 81, 83, 102, 104; iv. 158
Antiphoners, i. 4, 12, 30, 36, 52, 58, 67, 74; ii. 246; iv. 152, 153
Antonius (?Antoninus), i. 85, 108
Antonius Andreas, i. 15, 25, 26, 61, 101
Anwykyll, John, i. 110
Aristotle (including spurious works and commentaries etc.)
— de anima, i. 6, 14, 15, 25, 26, 43, 44, 50, 60, 61
— de animalibus, i, 15
— de celo et mundo, i. 6, 14, 15, 25, 43, 49, 60
— de generacione et corrupcione, i. 26
— Elenchi, i. 6, 15, 24, 25, 50, 60
— Ethics, i. 6–14, 26, 43, 48, 49, 60, 62, 86, 99, 105, 109
— libri naturales, i. 26, 60
— logical works, i. 60, 101
— Magna Moralia, i. 99
— Metaphysics, i. 6, 14, 15, 25, 26, 43, 44, 48, 49, 60, 62, 98
— Meteora, i. 6, 14, 25, 60
— opuscula, i. 81
— Perihermeneias, i. 24
— Physics, i. 6, 14, 15, 25, 26, 43, 49, 60, 61, 98, 101, 107
— Politics, i. 26, 43, 48; iii. 70
— Posteriora Analytica, i. 15, 24, 25, 61, 81, 107
— Predicamenta, i. 16, 24, 43, 60
— Priora Analytica, i. 6, 15, 24, 25
— Problemata, i. 6, 15, 25, 50, 62
— Rhetoric, i. 48
— Topica, i. 6, 15, 25, 88
— Questions on, i. 49
Armachanus, see FitzRalph
Arte alkumita, de, i. 26
Arte dictandi, liber de, see Francisci imperatoris
Athanasius, i. 85, 106, 108
Augustine, i. 4, 12, 13, 19, 22, 40, 41, 42, 45, 46, 47, 76, 83, 85, 100; iii. 80
Aurora, see Riga
Authentics, i. 24
Autoritates, i. 19, 101
Averroes (Expositor, Commentator) i. 6, 14, 15, 24, 25, 26, 43, 49, 60, 61
Avicenna, iii. 72

Bartholomeus abbas, i. 61, 106
Bartholomaeus Anglicus, i. 5, 13, 41; iii. 72
Bartholomew of Brescia, i. 5, 14, 43, 48, 99, 105, 106
Basil, i. 50, 102, 105
Bede, i. 44, 59, 62, 110
Bellum Troianorum, i. 88
Belyal, see James of Terano
Benedict, St., i. 42, 82, 86, 91, 105, 107; iii. 70
— exposicio regule, i. 49, 86, 91, 107, 109, 111
Benedictine Constitutions, i. 3, 11, 48, 76, 97, 105
Bernard of Breidenbach, i. 109
Bernard of Clairvaux, i. 4, 13, 19, 22, 41, 44, 46, 47, 50, 60, 81, 82, 85, 89, 98, 101; iii. 70
Bernard of Compostella, i. 5, 14, 48, 61, 99; iv. 159
Bernardinus de Busti, i. 85, 108

Beroaldus, Philippus, i. 62, 86, 106; iv. 83
Bestiarum, de naturis, i. 81
Bible, i. 3, 4, 11, 12, 18, 40, 43, 45, 60, 86, 87, 89, 94, 105; iv. 225
— Old Testament, i. 39, 45
— Pentateuch, i. 23, 45
— Genesis, i. 4, 12, 19, 22, 41, 42, 47, 50
— Exodus, i. 22, 42, 48
— Leviticus, i. 20, 23, 42, 43, 47, 50, 62
— Kings, i. 22, 40, 45
— Esdras, i. 21, 44, 59
— Tobias, i. 21, 59
— Judith, i. 21, 59
— Esther, i. 21, 59
— Job, i. 19, 21, 23, 41, 42, 46, 48
— Psalter, i. 3, 4, 5, 11, 12, 13, 18, 22, 30, 36, 40, 45, 53, 58, 62, 67, 74, 76, 85, 86, 88, 94; iv. 90, 153
— Proverbs, i. 21, 61
— Canticles, i. 20, 21, 59, 60; iv. 159
— Wisdom, i. 12, 18, 40, 41, 46, 85
— Prophets, i. 5, 13, 18, 22, 23, 40, 45, 60, ii. 206
— Isaiah, i. 21, 22
— Jeremiah, i. 22
— Lamentations, i. 12, 18, 23, 42, 46, 48, 76, 81, 82
— Ezechiel, i. 18, 20, 21, 40, 45, 59
— Gospels, i. 3, 11, 18, 19, 21, 23, 40, 41, 44, 45, 46, 50, 76, 82, 86
— Matthew, i. 4, 11, 12, 20, 22, 40, 45, 46, 59, 81, 83
— Mark, i. 4, 12, 20, 40, 44, 45, 50, 59
— Luke, i. 4, 12, 20, 40, 44, 45, 50, 59
— John, i. 4, 12, 20, 22, 40, 45, 59, 60, 62
— Acts, i. 4, 12, 21, 43, 50, 62, 83; iv. 159
— Epistles, i. 5, 13, 18, 21, 22, 39, 40, 41, 44, 45, 46, 49, 59, 60, 62, 81, 82, 83, 85, 106, 108; iv. 159
— Apocalypse, i. 21, 61, 62; iv. 159
— Glosses, commentaries etc., i. 3, 4, 11, 12, 18, 20, 21, 22, 23, 40, 42, 43, 44, 45, 46, 47, 48, 49, 50, 59, 60, 62, 81, 82, 85, 86, 89, 94; iv. 159
Bible versified, i. 21, 89; see also Riga
Biel, Gabriel, i.43, 48, 105
Billingham, Richard, i. 3, 11, 43, 97
Boccaccio, i. 59

Boethius, i. 18, 27, 41, 44, 47, 59, 60, 61, 76, 88
Bona fortuna, liber de, i. 99
Bonaventure, i. 5, 12, 20, 22, 41, 47, 85, 100, 104, 106
— Pseudo-, i. 105, 110, 111
Breviloquus, i. 62, 82, 87, 106, 107
Bridget, St., iii. 111
Britannie insula, de, i. 88, 110
Brito, William, i. 3, 11, 44, 49, 105
Bromyard, John, i. 86, 109
Brulefer, Stephen, i. 61, 62, 85, 106, 108
Bruni, Leonardo, i. 105
Bruto, i. 48, 103
Burley, Walter, i. 6, 15, 16, 24, 25, 26, 43, 49, 60, 87

Caesar, i. 81; iv. 83
Canon law texts, i. 61
Cantuariensis, see Langton, Stephen
Carmeliano, Pietro, i. 89, 110
Carpenter, Alexander, i. 82, 107
Carta de situ orbis, i. 86, 109
Casu et fortuna, de, i. 6, 14, 26; iv. 158
Catholicon, see Ianuensis
Cato moralisatus, i. 46
Cestrensis, see Higden
Chillynden, Thomas, i. 23, 103; ii. 206
Cicero, i. 15, 27, 60, 61, 62, 81, 82, 86, 87; iv. 83
Clement of Lanthony, i. 97
Clementines, i. 4, 13, 23, 43, 48; ii. 206
— repertorium super, i. 23, 43, 48
Code, i. 6, 24, 62
Colacionum, summa, see John Wallensis
Commemoracionum, liber, i. 86
Compendium artis dictatorie, i. 112
Compendium veritatis theologice (universitas), i. 21, 44, 50, 61, 86, 106, 109
— ?another work (alicui rei), i. 22, 102
Compostella, see Bernard
Concordanciae, i. 4, 5, 11, 12, 18, 19, 39, 45, 82, 89; iii. 128; iv. 121
Conflatus, see Franciscus de Maronis
Constituciones diversorum episcoporum Cant', i. 49, 105
Constituciones d. Gregorii etc., i. 5, 14, 24, 61, 99

INDEX OF BOOKS

Constituciones provinciales, i. 3, 11, 94, 97
Cornubiensis, see John of St Germans
Cornucopia, see Perotti
Corpore Christi, de, see Egidius
Corpus iuris canonici, i. 94
Chronicles in English, i. 91, 92, 111
— Cronica cronicarum, i. 89, 110
— Cronicarum, liber, i. 71
— Cronice Anglorum, i. 89
— Cronice breves, i. 27
— Cronykyllis, i. 92
— Supplementum chronicarum, see Iacobus Philippus

Dares, i. 27; iv. 158
David of Augsburg, i. 88, 89, 110
Decret', liber, i. 76
Decretals, i. 4, 5, 14, 23, 42, 44, 48, 61, 86, 99; ii. 270
— Casus decretalium, i. 23, 43
Decretum, i. 5, 14, 23, 62, 86
— Decreta minora, i. 24, 62
— Decreta nova, i. 4, 14, 23, 42, 48
— apparatus, i. 48 = Repertorium aureum by W. Durand, q.v.
— casus (distinccionis), i. 23, 43, 48
— casus (privilegia), i. 24
— excepciones, i. 24; iv. 159
— summa super casus, i. 24
— tabula, i. 48
Defensor of Ligugé (liber scintillarum), i. 12, 19, 41, 46, 100
Denis the Areopagite, i. 19, 41, 46, 85
Denis the Carthusian, i. 21, 102
Destructorium viciorum, see Carpenter
Diadema monachorum, see Smaragdus
Diccionarius pauperum, see Nicholas de Byard
Dictionarius, i. 18, 46
Didascalicon, see Hugh of St. Victor
Digest, i. 6, 14, 24, 61, 62
Dinus, i. 4, 13, 97
Discipulus, see Herolt
Distincciones evangeliorum, i. 19, 50, 61, 101
Diurnale, i. 30, 86; iv. 153
Donatus, i. 27, 62
Durand, William, i. 23, 43, 48, 61, 86, 100, 103, 106, 109
Duval, see Robertus de Valle

Egidius, i. 5, 13, 15, 22, 25, 26, 42, 43, 49, 62
Elegancie, i. 27
Elucidarium sacre scripture, i. 41, 46, 104
Epistola J. presbiteri, iii. 69
Eucharistia, tractatus de, iii. 94
Euclid, i. 15
Eusebius, i. 44, 86, 110
Excepciones, see Haymo
Exemplum continencie, i. 42, 105
Exequiae i. 86, 88
Exposicio hymnorum et sequenciarum, i. 89, 110
Exposicio vocabulorum super bibliam, see Brito
Exposiciones super evangelia et epistolas, i. 46
Expositor, see Averroes
Expositor (on Apoc.) i. 21

Faber Stapulensis, iii. 265
Fasciculus temporum, see Rolevinck
Felton, John, i. 19, 41, 46, 111
Fide, tractatus de, i. 41
Figuris crucis, liber de xxviij, i. 12, 21
Filelfo, i. vii, 86, 108; iv. 83
Fishacre, i. 22, 98, 105
FitzRalph, Richard, i. 22, 42, 47, 103, 105
Florarium poetarum, i. 60, 106
Florum, liber, i. 5, 13
Formula noviciorum, see David of Augsburg
Fortalicium fide, see Alfonsus
Francisci imperatoris, querimonia, (liber de arte dictandi), i. 27, 62, 104
Franciscus de Maronis (eodem modo), i. 20, 44, 62
— (cluditur), i. 42, 47
Franciscus Niger, i. 87
Fulgencius, i. 21, 22, 102

Gaius, iii. 70
Galen, i. 26, 49, 105
Garlandus, i. 6, 15, 99
Gatherings, i. 4, 7, 12, 16, 20, 21, 42, 50, 58, 62, 89, 103; iii. 94
— see also Lessons, Versicles
Geoffrey of Vinsauf (Anglicus), i. 26, 42, 49, 103, 104, 111, 112
Georgius Benignus, i. 86, 109
Geraldus, i. 61

Gerlandus of Besançon, i. 6, 15, 99
Gerson, John, i. 85
Gesta Romanorum, i. 89
Glanville, Ralph, i. 24, 50, 103; iv. 159
Gloria et requie animarum, de, i. 12, 22, 61
Goffredus of Trano, i. 5, 13, 19, 60, 70, 99, 100
Gorham, i. 5, 13, 22, 41, 46
Graduals, i. 4, 12, 30, 36, 52, 58, 67, 74; iv. 152, 153
Gramere, see John of Garland
Grammaticam, questiones antique super, i. 24
Gregory, i. 18, 20, 40, 45, 50, 70, 81, 85, 101
Grosseteste, Robert, i. 5, 12, 13, 15, 19, 20, 25, 40, 41, 47, 61, 70, 98; iii. 118; iv. 159

Haymo, i. 19, 23, 40, 46, 70; iv. 158
Henry of Ghent, i. 23, 42, 47, 60, 62
Henry of Hassia, i. 48, 105
Herolt, Jean, i. 86, 95, 109
Hervé de Nédellec (Natalis), i. 5, 13, 20, 42, 98, 106
Heytisbury, William, i. 99
Higden, Ranulph (Cestrensis), i. 88, 89, 110
Hilary, i. 12, 18, 42, 47
Hippocrates, iii. 71
Historia ecclesiastica, i. 71, 86, 89, 108, 110
Historia scolastica, see Petrus Comestor
Historiarum, magister, see Petrus Comestor
Holcot, Robert, i. 12, 18, 40, 41, 46, 85
Horace, i. 61
Hostiensis, i. 14, 23, 43, 48
Hucarius, i. 20, 40, 45, 101; iv. 156, 158
Hugh of Manchester, i. 102
Hugh of St. Cher, i. 85, 86, 109
Hugh of St. Victor, i. 19, 21, 22, 23, 41, 46, 47, 103; iv. 158
Hugh of Strassburg, i. 102, 106
Hugo de Prato Florido, i. 81, 107
Hugucius, i. 3, 6, 11, 15, 27, 28, 44, 49, 50, 60; iv. 60

Iacobus de Graytrode, i. 89, 110

Iacobus de Voragine, i. 86
Iacobus Philippus Bergomensis, i. 86, 109
Ianuensis, Iohannes, i. 3, 11, 19, 27, 40, 44, 46, 49, 94
Incendio amoris, liber de, i. 27, 104
Innocent IV, i. 14, 23, 24, 43, 100
Instituciones ecclesiastice, i. 22, 41, 46
Institutes, i. 6, 24, 43, 48
Interpretaciones hebraicorum nominum, see Langton, Stephen
Iohannes Andree, i. 23, 43, 48, 76, 102
Iohannes Canonicus, i. 82, 107
Iohannes de Valanc', i. 88, 110
Iohannicius, i. 26
Isagoge in moralem philosophiam, see William of Conches
Isidore, i. 23, 28, 41, 46, 61, 70, 76; iii. 72

James of Terano, i. 43, 48, 70, 105
Jerome, i. 18, 40, 45, 59, 85, 105, 108; ii. 206; iii. 150
— de laudibus et miraculis b. Ieronimi, i. 21, 102
John Chrysostom, i. 4, 11, 18, 19, 21, 40, 46, 50, 81, 85, 102, 105
John Damascene, i. 22, 42, 47
John of Fribourg, i. 4, 13, 23, 43, 48, 97
John of Garland, i. 27, 50, 62, 91, 92, 99, 101, 104, 111
John of La Rochelle, i. 60, 105; iv. 159
John de Ridevall, i. 102
John of St. Germans (Cornubiensis), i. 81, 107
John Wallensis, i. 21, 87, 101, 102, 108
John of Wallingford, i. 110
Josephus, i. 86
Justin (historian), i. 86, 109

Ketell, William, i. 102
Kilwardby, Robert, i. 15, 16, 101

Lactantius, i. 44, 50, 59, 85; iv. 83
Langton, Stephen (Cantuariensis), i. 5, 13, 21, 22, 23, 40 ('Symon'), 45, 60, 61, 104; iii. 88
Lathbury, John, i. 12, 18, 23, 40, 42, 46, 48, 76, 82, 107

INDEX OF BOOKS

Lavacrum consciencie, *see* Iacobus de Graytrode
Legenda, i. 4, 12, 30, 36, 52, 58, 67, 74; iv. 153
Legenda sanctorum, i. 12, 19, 41, 46, 89; iv. 217
Legibus et constitucionibus Anglie, liber de, *see* Glanville
Lessons, sheets for, i. 7, 16
Letters, model, i. 112
Lincolniensis, *see* Grosseteste
Littere apostolice de publicacione anni iubilei, i. 21, 44, 102, 105
Livy, iii. 109
Logic texts, i. 6, 15, 24, 25, 43, 44, 49
— antiquus liber super logicam, i. 25
— exposicio antiqua, i. 24, 25
— liber diversorum tractatuum, i. 27
— liber logice, i. 43
— notule super logicam, i. 98
— questiones antique, i. 24
— sentencie super logicam veterem, i. 60
Lombard History, i. 42, iv. 159
Lucan, i. 27, 61, 81; iv. 158
Ludolph of Saxony, i. 85, 105, 108
Lumen anime, *see* Matthias
Lyndwood, William, i. 136
Lyra, Nicholas of, i. 18, 39, 45, 89, 94; iii. 128; iv. 121, 164

Macer, *see* Odo Magdunensis
Mandeville, John, i. 91, 92
Manipulus florum, i. 19, 50
Marbers, John (Canonicus), i. 107
Martianus Capella, i. 26, 49; iv. 158
Martinus Polonus, i. 82, 107
Matthias Farinator, i. 86, 108
Maximus, i. 19; iv. 158
Medicinalis, liber, i. 61
Merke, Thomas, i. 112
Mertonis, tractatus clerici collegii, iii. 98
Michael de Hungaria (de Carcano), i. 82, 107
Milverley, William, i. 25, 103
Miraculis, de, i. 21, 41, 47, 101, 104
Missals, i. 4, 12, 30, 36, 52, 58, 67, 73, 86, 88; ii. 131, 175, 181, 246; iv. 92, 153
Missarum mysteriis, de, *see* Albertus

Naturis rerum, libri de, i. 15, 100
Nennius, i. 110
Nicholas, i. 42
Nicholas de Blony, i. 85, 108
Nicholas de Byard, i. 86, 109
Nicholas de Orbellis, i. 61, 85
Nova preregrinacio, i. 86, 109
Nuremberg Chronicle, i. 110
Nyder, John, i. 82, 106

Ockham, William of, i. 6, 15, 25, 26, 43, 49, 86, 109
Odo of Cheriton, i. 19, 46, 50, 61, 101
Odo Magdunensis, i. 61, 105, 106
Officium B.M.V., i. 88
Optatian, i. 100
Opus regale, i. 85, 108
Opusculum exiguum, i. 81
Orationum, liber, i. 61
Ordinale, i. 4, 12, 28, 30, 36, 53, 58, 68, 74, 86, ii. 181; iv. 153
Originalia, *see* Manipulus florum
Orosius, i. 4, 13, 26
Ortus vocabulorum, i. 89
Ottobonus, i. 5, 13, 23, 43, 48, 103
Ovid, i. 27

Pantheon, *see* Goffredus
Papa stupor mundi, *see* Geoffrey
Parisiensis, i. 18, 19, 40, 41, 46
— Iohannes (Quidort), i. 106
Partibus beatitudinis, liber de, i. 22, 102
Passio sancte Katerine et Elphegi, i. 88
Patronis ecclesie, de, i. 89, 110
Paulus Attavanti, i. 86, 108
Penitencia, tractatus de, i. 44, 61
Penitenciale, i. 61, 70
Penitencie, summa, *see* Thomas de Chobham
Perez de Valencia, Iacobus, i. 85, 108
Perotti, Nicholas, i. 86, 109; iv. 201
Peter of Auvergne, i. 5, 20, 47
Peter of Blois, i. 19, 26, 41, 42, 46, 103
Peter Lombard (texts and commentaries etc.), i. 3, 4, 5, 11, 12, 13, 20, 21, 22, 41, 42, 44, 47, 48, 49, 50, 59, 60, 61, 62, 81, 82, 85, 86, 105, 108; iii. 174; iv. 160, 217
Peter of Poitiers, i. 5, 13, 98
Peter of Tarentaise, i. 5, 13, 20, 42, 44, 47, 62

Petrus de Aquila, i. 85
Petrus de Aureolis, i. 19, 42
Petrus Comestor (magister historiarum), i. 3, 4, 11, 13, 18, 23, 40, 41, 45, 50, 62, 104
Petrus Crinitus, i. 86, 109; iv. 83
Petrus Hispanus, i. 25
Petrus de Palude, i. 86, 106, 108
Petrus de Vinea, i. 104
Philip de Monte Calerio, i. 21, 102
Philobiblon, see Richard of Bury
Philosophie textus, i. 14, 25, 43, 81, 100
— philosophie naturalis textus, i. 6, 43, 49, 99
— questiones super diversos libros philosophie, i. 26
— tractatus de philosophia, i. 48, 81, 105
Picus de Mirandola, i. vii, 86; iv. 83
Plato, i. 27
Pliny, i. 106; iii. 72
Plutarch, i. vii, 21, 71, 102, 105; iv. 83
Poetrie, liber diversorum operum, i. 27
Pomponius, i. 62, 109
Porphyry, i. 6, 15, 16, 24, 25, 43, 49, 60, 62, 99, 101; iii. 265
Prepositinus, i. 21, 60, 102
Pricksong, book of, i. 53, 58, 67; iv. 152, 153
Priscian, i. 6, 15, 27, 44, 49, 61, 81, 104; iv. 60, 158
Processione sancti Spiritus, de, see Anselm
Profectuum religiosorum, see David of Augsburg
Propagacione humane nature, de, i. 26, 48
Prudentius, i. 27,
Ptolemy, i. 86
Pupilla oculi, i. 61, 88

Quadragesimale Gemma Fidei, i. 85, 108
Quatuordecem partibus beatitudinis, liber de, i. 44
Quentin, John, i. 82, 107
Questiones de generato, i. 76
— de quanto, i. 60, 104
— de incarnacione Verbi, i. 62
— theologie (vel causis), i. 5, 13, 22
— — (naturale), i. 41, 43, 49, 105
— universales, i. 60

Quidort, Jean (Parisiensis), i. 106

Rabanus Maurus, i. 100
Racionale divinorum officiorum, i. 4, 12, 23, 41, 46
Raymond of Pennaforte, i. 5, 14, 20, 99
Re militari, de, see Vegetius
Regimen egritudinis, i. 49
Regimine principum, de, (cum) see Egidius
— (possumus) i. 49, 50
Registrum, see Gregory
Regule grammaticales, i. 89
Remigius of Auxerre, i. 27, 40, 62, 102, 104
Repertorium aureum, see Durand
Repertorium iuris, i. 14, 23; iv. 159
Repyngdon, Philip, i. 19, 40, 46
Resolucio theologorum, i. 86, 108
Reuchlin, Iohannes, i. 106, 107
Richard of Bury, i. 22, 102
Richard of Middleton (de Media Villa), i. 5, 13, 20, 60; iv. 217
Richard of St. Victor, i. 21, 102
Riga, Petrus, i. 18, 40, 45, 101; perhaps also i. 21, 89 (Bible versified)
Ringstead, Thomas, i. 21, 61, 101
Robertus de Licio (Caracciolo), i. 81, 107
Robertus de Valle Rothomagensi (Duval), i. 62, 86, 106, 109
Rolevinck, Werner, i. 82, 107
Rolle, Richard, i. 104
Rosarii, sermones, see Bernardinus
Rubrica, i. 7, 16, 28, 53, 58; iv. 153

Scintillarum, liber, i. 12
Scot, Michael, i. 25
Scotus (doctor subtilis), i. 4, 11, 12, 20, 25, 26, 42, 47, 48, 49, 50, 61, 81, 82; iii. 121
Seneca, i. 27, 49; iv. 158
Sententiarum, magister, see Peter Lombard
Septimus, liber, i. 14, 23
Sequenciarum, liber, i. 68, 88; iv. 153
Sermones de tempore et de sanctis, i. 60
— diversi, i. 46
— dominicales (est rex), see Felton
— sermonum liber (dat et orat), i. 22

INDEX OF BOOKS

—— (triplex), i. 22, 44, 60 (sermones dominicales)
—— liber parvus, Latin and French, i. 22; iv. 159
Service-book, i. 87; ii. 246
Sex principiorum, liber, i. 16
Sext, i. 4, 13, 14, 23, 48, 99; ii. 206
— repertorium super, i. 48
Sharp, John, i. 15, 25, 101
Smaragdus, i. 22, 44, 102
Solinus, i. 86, 88
Sophismata, i. 15, 16, 25
Sophistrie liber (duo), i. 44
—— (equipollencia), i. 15, 27, 43
—— (necessarium), i. 27
— liber diversorum tractatuum, i. 27, 104
— tractatus communis, i. 6, 15
Sophistrie et logice, liber diversorum tractatuum, i. 27
Speculum exemplorum, i. 89
Speculum iudiciale, i. 14
Spirituali veneno, de, *see* Grosseteste
Statius, i. 27
Stephanus Cantuariensis, *see* Langton
Stoneham, Robert, i. 6, 15, 99
Summa angelica, *see* Angelus de Clavasio
Summa aurea, i. 60
Summa colacionum, *see* John Wallensis
Summa confessorum, *see* John of Fribourg
Summa iuris canonici, i. 61
Summa penitencie, *see* Thomas de Chobham
Summa predicancium, *see* Bromyard
Summa summarum, i. 23, 48, 76
Summa super titulis iuris, i. 48
Sutton, Thomas, i. 24, 43, 49, 76, 103
Swineshead, Roger, i. 6, 25, 99
Symon, i. 40, *see* Langton, Stephen

Tabula philosophiae, *see* Billingham
Tabula prime distinccionis, i. 42, 105
Tegni, *see* Galen
Templum Domini, *see* Grosseteste
Terence, i. 87; iii. 125
Theodulph, i. 20, 101
Thomas Aquinas, i. 4, 5, 11, 13, 14, 18, 19, 20, 21, 22, 25, 26, 40, 41, 42, 43, 45, 46, 47, 48, 49, 60, 76, 81, 85, 105
— doctor defendens, i. 20, 47

Thomas de Chobham, i. 21, 42
Thomas de Hibernia, i. 101
Thomas de sancto Nicholao, i. 6
Traversari, Ambrogio, i. 105
Trendlye, i. 68, 74; iv. 153
Tria sunt, i. 26, 27, 104, 112
Trivet, Nicholas, i. 22, 42, 44, 48
Trogus Pompeius, i. 109
Turrecremata, Iohannes de, i. 91, 105, 111

Unum ex 4^{or}, i. 4, 12, 20

Validos mendicantes, liber contra, i. 89
Valla, Lorenzo, i. 62, 82, 105, 107; iv. 83
Vallensis, *see* John Wallensis
Vegetius, i. 27, 42, 48
Veni mecum, *see* Bernard of Clairvaux
Veritate contricionis, de, *see* Vivaldus
Veritates theologiae, *see* Thomas Aquinas
Versicles, sheets of, i. 4, 12, 30
— book of, i. 36; iv. 153
Viciis et virtutibus, de (multum), i. 41, 46
— summa de, *see* John of La Rochelle
— tractatus de (stipendia), i. 5, 13, 22, 41, 46
—— (-tas mentis), i. 22, 44, 50
Virgil, i. 60, 81; iv. 83
Vita etc. Christi, i. 41, 45, 91, 92, 105, 111
— philosophorum, i. 49, 105
— sancte Siburge, i. 88, 110
— sancti Thome (various), i. 19, 42, 48, 49, 50, 81, 89, 91, 110, 111
Vitae patrum, i. 41, 46, 89, 92
— sanctorum, iv. 223
Vivaldus, Iohannes Ludovicus, i. 85, 86, 108, 109

W. de Rupella, *see* John of La Rochelle
Wallencia, *see* Perez
Walter of Châtillon, i. 99, 103
Willelmus de Bosco, i. 60, 106
William of Auxerre, i. 86, 108
William of Conches, i. 60, 105
Wyclyffe, J., i. 12; iv. 159

Zacharias Chrysopolitanus, i. 97